Learn Python Game Development with ChatGPT

Techniques for creating engaging games with generative AI

Micheal Lanham

www.bpbonline.com

First Edition 2024

Copyright © BPB Publications, India

ISBN: 978-93-55516-435

All Rights Reserved. No part of this publication may be reproduced, distributed or transmitted in any form or by any means or stored in a database or retrieval system, without the prior written permission of the publisher with the exception to the program listings which may be entered, stored and executed in a computer system, but they can not be reproduced by the means of publication, photocopy, recording, or by any electronic and mechanical means.

LIMITS OF LIABILITY AND DISCLAIMER OF WARRANTY

The information contained in this book is true to correct and the best of author's and publisher's knowledge. The author has made every effort to ensure the accuracy of these publications, but publisher cannot be held responsible for any loss or damage arising from any information in this book.

All trademarks referred to in the book are acknowledged as properties of their respective owners but BPB Publications cannot guarantee the accuracy of this information.

To View Complete
BPB Publications Catalogue
Scan the QR Code:

www.bpbonline.com

Dedicated to

For those who dream of a future with AI, may your imagination be boundless, your innovations endless, and your journey as remarkable as mine has been. I dedicate this book to all us dreamers

About the Author

Micheal Lanham is a recognized software and technology innovator with over 25 years of experience. He has significantly contributed to game development, graphics, web and desktop applications, engineering, AI, GIS, and ML. Micheal is mainly known for pioneering the integration of evolutionary computation with deep learning models. Starting his career at the turn of the millennium, he focused on neural networks and evolutionary algorithms in game development. His expertise has established him as a developer, consultant, and author of numerous projects. Currently, Micheal resides in Calgary, Alberta, with his large family, who enjoys cooking for him.

Acknowledgement

I always thank my family, friends, and coworkers for supporting and acknowledging my writing. Their support drives me to write more innovative and exciting titles like this one. But my genuine support comes from my wife, Rhonda, for always being by my side. Also, a special acknowledgment to my kids, Ava and Aaron Thiessen, who assisted me in reviewing, playing games and just fun to pester.

I especially want to thank BPB Publications for their assistance and nudging to complete this book. Building a book driven by AI was a unique journey for everyone, and the editors, reviewers, and technical experts all successfully took to the challenge.

Of course, I also need to acknowledge the tireless work of those in the field of AI. Even being as close as I was to the AI field just a few years ago, I would have never thought I could collaborate with AI to write a book. Thanks, ChatGPT and the AI revolution.

Preface

I have worked full-time as a game and graphics developer several times throughout my career and even tried my hand at founding a studio. The game studio fell flat, not because I couldn't write games but because I couldn't find the artists and coders who could help me. But that has all changed with the advent of AI.

A big part of what I wanted to showcase in this book is how a game developer can create games independently or with a small team. I still genuinely believe that gaming needs to return to the small, lean, agile development team—teams that can push the edge of game development and how we think of games.

I also wanted to encourage people developing games to be adventurous. AI now gives us the ability to push ourselves beyond our capabilities. If you don't know how to make a game, or build a feature, or create an animation, ask ChatGPT or another AI service.

To me, AI can empower all of us to be the best we can be. I learned this through my journey writing this book. AI is a tool. In competent hands, it is powerful, but it is still a tool. That may change, but for now, be better with AI.

General introduction to the book followed by,

Chapter 1: ChatGPT and the Magic of Prompt Engineering – This chapter introduces readers to ChatGPT and the concept of prompt engineering. It explains how to use ChatGPT effectively to generate Python code, particularly in game development. The chapter covers constructing effective prompts, understanding ChatGPT's decision-making process, and leveraging system prompting. Readers will engage in practical exercises to create simple Python games, gaining hands-on experience using ChatGPT to automate coding tasks.

Chapter 2: Text Adventure: Entering the Enchanted Realm – In this chapter, readers dive into the world of text-based games by creating a game like the classic Zork. The focus is on fundamental game development concepts such as managing player input, building game worlds, and handling items and non-player characters (NPCs). By the end of the chapter, readers will have created a functional text adventure game and learned about game loops, data management, and narrative design.

Chapter 3: The AI Chronicles: Text Game Evolution – Building on the previous chapter, this chapter introduces visual elements and more complex game mechanics to the text adventure game. Readers will learn to use tools like Streamlit for creating web-based interfaces and Stable Diffusion for generating images. Additionally, the chapter covers integrating SQLite databases to manage game state and progress. By the end of the chapter, readers will have enhanced their text game with visuals and a persistent game world.

Chapter 4: 2D Platformer: Leap into Pixelated Fun! – This chapter transitions readers from text-based games to 2D platformers. It covers the basics of building a platformer, including player controls, movement mechanics, and level design. Readers will also learn about sprites and animation to bring their game characters and environments to life. The chapter introduces AI tools for generating game assets, helping readers create visually appealing games. By the end, readers will have a functional 2D platformer game.

Chapter 5: Bot Brawls: AI Opponents Enter the Arena – This chapter teaches readers how to create a fighting game with AI-controlled opponents. It covers the development of a Street Fighter clone, focusing on integrating behavioral AI for dynamic and challenging gameplay. Topics include behavior-driven AI, managing AI difficulty levels, and restyling the game with AI-generated assets. By the end of the chapter, readers will have created a game where players can battle against intelligent AI opponents.

Chapter 6: Revving up: Cars, Ramps, and Pymunk – This chapter explores game physics through the creation of a car jump challenge game. Readers will learn to use the Pymunk physics library to simulate realistic motion and rotation. The chapter covers building a game engine that incorporates physics-based interactions, including adding particle systems for enhanced visual effects. By the end, readers will have a deeper understanding of game physics and a completed car physics game.

Chapter 7: Building Isometric Worlds – In this chapter, readers explore creating 2.5D isometric games. They also explain the complexities of isometric perspectives, including world-to-screen space conversion and designing isometric tile maps. Readers will learn to add detail and variation to their maps with overlays and integrate user interfaces and menus within the isometric world. By the end of the chapter, readers will be able to create intricate and visually engaging isometric game worlds.

Chapter 8: Leveling up with GPT Agents and AutoGen – This chapter focuses on integrating intelligent GPT powered agents into games using AutoGen. Readers will learn how to set up an OpenAI account and configure AutoGen for game development. The chapter covers the fundamentals of GPT agents and demonstrates how to use them to enhance game functionality, such as creating assistant agents for various game tasks. By the end, readers will have a deeper understanding of AI integration in games and practical experience with AutoGen.

Chapter 9: Building a 3D First-Person Shooter – This chapter introduces readers to the development of 3D first-person shooter (FPS) games. It covers implementing 3D player controls, camera movement, and understanding 3D coordinate systems. The chapter also discusses using materials and textures to create realistic environments to enhance gameplay. By the end, readers will have a foundational understanding of 3D game development and a basic FPS game.

Chapter 10: Games That Respond to Your Voice – This chapter explores the creation of voice-controlled games. Readers will learn to implement speech recognition systems and text-to-speech functionalities using tools like ElevenLabs and ChatGPT. The chapter covers building a voice-driven game where players interact with the game world through spoken commands. By the end, readers will have created a unique game that leverages voice input for an immersive experience.

Chapter 11: The Future Beckons: Developing GPT Games – The final chapter looks to the future of AI in game development. It covers creating games with OpenAI GPT assistants, focusing on designing engaging and fun GPT-based games. The chapter discusses the potential future trends in AI-driven game development, including generative AI for creating game content. By the end, readers will understand the cutting-edge possibilities in game development and ideas for future projects.

Code Bundle and Coloured Images

Please follow the link to download the
Code Bundle and the *Coloured Images* of the book:

https://rebrand.ly/88ts118

The code bundle for the book is also hosted on GitHub at
https://github.com/bpbpublications/Learn-Python-Game-Development-with-ChatGPT.
In case there's an update to the code, it will be updated on the existing GitHub repository.

We have code bundles from our rich catalogue of books and videos available at **https://github.com/bpbpublications**. Check them out!

Errata

We take immense pride in our work at BPB Publications and follow best practices to ensure the accuracy of our content to provide with an indulging reading experience to our subscribers. Our readers are our mirrors, and we use their inputs to reflect and improve upon human errors, if any, that may have occurred during the publishing processes involved. To let us maintain the quality and help us reach out to any readers who might be having difficulties due to any unforeseen errors, please write to us at :

errata@bpbonline.com

Your support, suggestions and feedbacks are highly appreciated by the BPB Publications' Family.

Did you know that BPB offers eBook versions of every book published, with PDF and ePub files available? You can upgrade to the eBook version at www.bpbonline.com and as a print book customer, you are entitled to a discount on the eBook copy. Get in touch with us at :

business@bpbonline.com for more details.

At **www.bpbonline.com**, you can also read a collection of free technical articles, sign up for a range of free newsletters, and receive exclusive discounts and offers on BPB books and eBooks.

Piracy

If you come across any illegal copies of our works in any form on the internet, we would be grateful if you would provide us with the location address or website name. Please contact us at **business@bpbonline.com** with a link to the material.

If you are interested in becoming an author

If there is a topic that you have expertise in, and you are interested in either writing or contributing to a book, please visit **www.bpbonline.com**. We have worked with thousands of developers and tech professionals, just like you, to help them share their insights with the global tech community. You can make a general application, apply for a specific hot topic that we are recruiting an author for, or submit your own idea.

Reviews

Please leave a review. Once you have read and used this book, why not leave a review on the site that you purchased it from? Potential readers can then see and use your unbiased opinion to make purchase decisions. We at BPB can understand what you think about our products, and our authors can see your feedback on their book. Thank you!

For more information about BPB, please visit **www.bpbonline.com**.

Join our book's Discord space

Join the book's Discord Workspace for Latest updates, Offers, Tech happenings around the world, New Release and Sessions with the Authors:

https://discord.bpbonline.com

Table of Contents

1. ChatGPT and the Magic of Prompt Engineering 1
    Introduction 1
    Structure 1
    Objectives 2
    Entering the realm of ChatGPT 2
    Exploring ideas to interactions 6
    Unlocking potential with system prompting 8
    Engaging retrieval augmented generation with EasyCode 14
    Conclusion 20
    What we learned 20
    Exercises 20

2. Text Adventure: Entering the Enchanted Realm 21
    Introduction 21
    Structure 21
    Objectives 22
    Venturing into the world of text-based games 22
    Prompting your first game: PyZork 26
    Parsing the player: Managing player input 32
    Crafting your own game world: Building the map 38
    Unleashing unexpected game challenges: Items and NPCs 43
    Conclusion 55
    What we learned 55
    Exercises 56

3. The AI Chronicles: Text Game Evolution 57
    Introduction 57
    Structure 57
    Objectives 58

Unleashing PyZork with Streamlit.. 58
Picturing the story using stable diffusion... 67
Crafting the story with the command interface 76
Remembering the world, adding a game database with SQLite 83
Completing the MUSH.. 89
Conclusion 92
What we learned 92
Exercises 93

4. 2D Platformer: Leap into Pixelated Fun!...95
Introduction 95
Structure 95
Objectives 96
Building a platformer 96
Mastering controls and movement by introducing difficulty 102
Levelling up your obstacles with level design 108
Unleashing your creativity with sprites and animation.. 112
Generating assets with AI: Stable Diffusion and control nets 120
Conclusion 127
What we learned 127
Exercises 127

5. Bot Brawls: AI Opponents Enter the Arena 129
Introduction 129
Structure 129
Objectives 130
Loading the game: The Street Fighter Clone.. 130
Introducing AI-controlled enemies: Battle Royale edition....................................... 133
Ruling the AI: Introducing behavior-driven AI... 141
Challenging players again: AI dynamic difficulty levels 150
Revisiting the assets: Restyling the game with SDXL... 154
Conclusion 158
What we learned 158
Exercises 158

6. Revving up: Cars, Ramps, and Pymunk 161

Introduction 161

Structure 161

Objectives 162

Starting your engine: Introduction to game physics............................... 162

Driving forces: Understanding motion and rotation 165

First iteration... 167

Second iteration 168

Revving the engine: Adding physics to a car... 170

First iteration... 172

Second iteration 173

Third iteration 174

Jumpstarting your game: Building the ultimate car jump challenge 174

Fourth iteration 175

Fifth iteration.. 177

Sixth iteration... 179

Effecting the atmosphere: Adding particle systems with physics 180

Seventh iteration 180

Colliding clouds: Finishing the game with a goal................................... 185

Eighth iteration 185

Ninth iteration.. 188

Conclusion 190

What we learned 191

Exercises 191

7. Building Isometric Worlds.. 193

Introduction 193

Structure 193

Objectives 194

Into the depth: Understanding 2.5D isometric perspectives 194

The art of transformation: World to screen space conversion 201

Grids in the third dimension: Designing isometric tile maps 206

Adding detail and variation: Map overlays 213
Beyond the game field: Layering UI and menus in an isometric world 218
Conclusion 225
    What we learned 225
Exercises 225

8. Leveling up with GPT Agents and AutoGen 227

Introduction 227
Structure 227
Objectives 228
Unlocking the achievement: Setting up your OpenAI account 228
Power boost: Configuring AutoGen with ease 231
Grasping the GPT agent fundamentals 236
Asteroids ascending: Revamping a classic with assistant agents 241
The game shop: Building a reusable agent workshop 244
Conclusion 252
    What we learned 252
Exercises 252

9. Building a 3D First-Person Shooter 255

Introduction 255
Structure 255
Objectives 256
Implementing 3D player controls and camera movement 256
Enter the action-packed world of 3D FPS games 261
Understanding the 3D world, 3D coordinate systems 271
Covering up with materials and textures 275
Unleashing game AI agent support.. 280
Conclusion 284
What we learned 284
Exercises 285

10. Games That Respond to Your Voice 287

- Introduction 287
- Structure 287
- Objectives 288
- Speak and be heard: Building speech recognition systems 288
- Listening to text: Implementing text to speech 290
- Meeting an AI Pirate: Using ElevenLabs for speech 292
- Meeting an AI Pirate: Using ElevenLabs for speech 294
- Secret words: Powering games with ChatGPT 300
- The detective: Creating a murder mystery vocal game 302
- Dialogue with destiny: Understanding voice-driven game mechanics 307
- Conclusion 309
- What we learned 309
- Exercises 309

11. The Future Beckons: Developing GPT Games 311

- Introduction 311
- Structure 311
- Objectives 311
- Building an OpenAI GPT Assistants game 312
- Designing a fun GPT game 316
- Adding assets to a GPT game 321
- The future of AI in game development 323
  - *The AI generative game engine* 325
  - *The future of game development* 326
- Conclusion 326
  - *What we learned* 327
- Exercises 327

Index 329-333

CHAPTER 1
ChatGPT and the Magic of Prompt Engineering

Introduction

This book will take you on a journey to learn game programming-starting, from text games to 2D platformers, 3D games, and even the future of speech-based games. There will be a lot of information to cover, but thankfully we will employ an AI tool called **ChatGPT**.

In this chapter, we will explore how ChatGPT can help us learn to build games or anything beyond the horizon. We will explore how to effectively use ChatGPT, from constructing effective prompts with prompt engineering to exploring the reasoning behind the AI's decisions.

Structure

This chapter explores the following topics:

- Entering the realm of ChatGPT
- Exploring ideas to interactions
- Unlocking potential with system prompting
- Engaging retrieval augmented generation with EasyCode

Objectives

Our objective for this chapter is to learn how to use ChatGPT effectively. While our book focuses on learning to make games, the skills you will learn may be applied to numerous problems. Once you start using ChatGPT, you most likely will want to keep using it.

Entering the realm of ChatGPT

In late 2022, the world was changed forever with the release of **ChatGPT 3.5**, a chat-based AI tool that allowed users to ask questions and receive some insightful answers. Since these answers were shockingly high in quality, OpenAI, the industry that made ChatGPT, reflected upon its capabilities of what it could build.

> **Trivia time: ChatGPT was the first application to break 100 million users in a week. Do you know what the next app to break that record was?**

Before we get into using ChatGPT let us go over some technical specifications. ChatGPT is a deep learning model comprised of billions of parameters using a transformer architecture. It is trained using an updated loss mechanism called **Reinforcement Learning from Human Feedback (RLHF)**. Initially, the GPT model was trained on billions of documents, then fine-tuned on millions, and finally optimized with RLHF on thousands.

The core GPT model ChatGPT is built on is a chat completion model. That means it only tries to complete the content/text it is given. A GPT model is designed to consume text as tokens. It uses an internal probability engine to reply with the next most likely token. This type of GPT model, designed to respond with text, is called a completion model.

ChatGPT, however, is trained a few steps above a base GPT model. *Figure 1.1* shows the progression of GPT model training and what makes ChatGPT special:

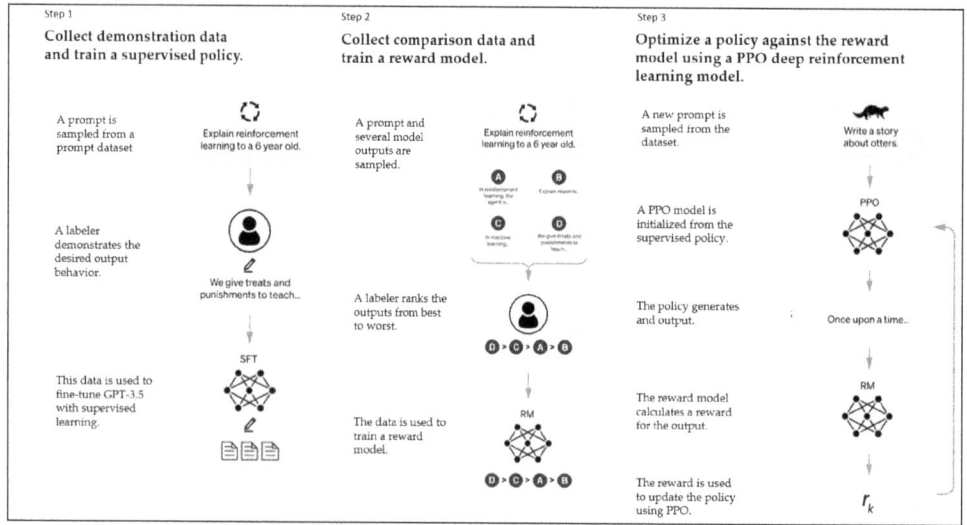

Figure 1.1: Training ChatGPT

Figure 1.1 illustrates how ChatGPT is trained from the initial supervision of human feedback for building a reward model. It finally uses reinforcement learning to optimize the model. We only need to fully understand the process to identify how this form of training makes ChatGPT so unique and powerful. The power of ChatGPT comes from fine-tuned labeling provided by human feedback augmented with a reward model.

This extra training transforms the GPT model from a generalist to a model that can fine-tune its responses through continued prompting or chatting. But what makes this transformation interesting and so special is that it can extend this ability to identify the steps or process of a conversation chain. And, if we extend this further, ChatGPT can follow a chain of thoughts or reasoning processes.

We will take advantage of ChatGPT's ability to reason throughout this book. For now, let us get some hands-on experience using ChatGPT, partaking in a couple of quick experiments in the exercise below:

Exercise 1.1: Conversing with ChatGPT

1. Open your web browser to: **https://chat.openai.com/**

2. Go ahead and either log in or sign up and log in. *Figure 1.2* shows the ChatGPT login screen:

Figure 1.2: *ChatGPT login screen*

3. Our first prompt will be the basic *write me a game* and assess its response.

4. In the prompt input, enter the following text and hit enter, as shown in *Figure 1.3*.
   Prompt: `Please write me a snake game in Python using PyGame.`

4   *Learn Python Game Development with ChatGPT*

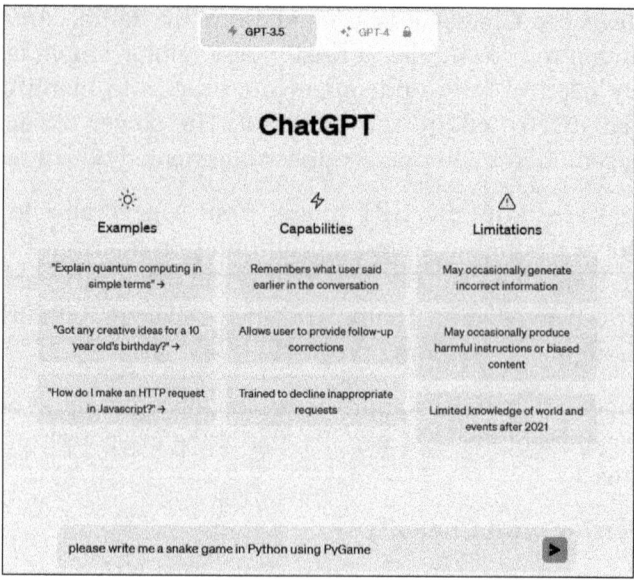

Figure 1.3: *ChatGPT interface*

5. After some time, depending on your version, ChatGPT will respond with some Python code explaining how to use it, as shown in *Figure 1.4*:

```
                            Default (GPT-3.5)
GRID_SIZE =
GRID_WIDTH, GRID_HEIGHT = WIDTH // GRID_SIZE, HEIGHT // GRID_SIZE
FPS =
WHITE = (     ,    ,    )
RED = (    ,  ,  )
GREEN = (  ,   ,  )

# Initialize pygame
pygame.init()
win = pygame.display.set_mode((WIDTH, HEIGHT))
pygame.display.set_caption("Snake Game")

# Snake class
class Snake:
    def __init__(self):
        self.body = [(GRID_WIDTH //  , GRID_HEIGHT //  )]
        self.direction = ( ,  )

    def move(self):
        head = self.body[ ]
        x, y = head[ ] + self.direction[ ], head[ ] + self.direction[ ]
        self.body.insert( , (x, y))
```

Figure 1.4: *ChatGPT outputs a snake game*

6. Next, we will take the produced code and run it on your desktop. This book assumes you have some experience writing Python code, so if you are unsure how to set up your environment, consult *Appendix A*.

7. First, install the dependencies into your virtual Python environment:

   1. `pip install pygame`

8. Then, copy the code from ChatGPT using the **copy code** button on the top right and paste it into a new file called **snake_game.py**. Make sure to save the file after pasting.

9. Run the file from the console using Python:

   1. `python snake_game.py`

10. You should see a PyGame window open, as shown in *Figure 1.5* and the snake game running. Try and use the *up/down/left/right arrows* to control the snake.

Figure 1.5: *Snake game running*

What makes ChatGPT great is that this exercise likely worked for most readers but not all. If your code does not work the first time, go back and try again by opening a new chat prompt and entering the prompt we used earlier.

Not all the responses you receive will match what you see in the book. This is because, by its nature, ChatGPT produces variable output. As this book uses ChatGPT for most exercises, you may see wildly different results if you use a different version or a completely different LLM.

Indeed, you can go back and perform this same exercise multiple times and it will likely produce very different versions of that snake game. Is this something we need to worry about? How will we fix or address this concern?

Well, it all comes down to the prompt and what we ask and want from ChatGPT. As we will see in the next section, it is important to plan how and what we ask of ChatGPT.

Exploring ideas to interactions

As we discovered in the last section, ChatGPT can be unpredictable. It tends to fabricate. In ChatGPT prompt engineering parlance, we call this hallucinating. Hallucinations can be a big problem when you are working in any area that is new or was created after the model was trained.

ChatGPT 3.5 was trained on content up to September 2021. This means that anything developed after this date will be unknown. Depending on how you ask ChatGPT the question, it may explicitly say it does not know, or it may hallucinate.

Hallucinations can be a big issue when using ChatGPT to code. However, it can be easily rectified using well-established prompts, now called **prompt engineering**, and being more thoughtful in planning our tasks.

For the exercise in this section, we will revisit making a snake game. This time though, we are going to be more thoughtful as well as use some prompt engineering techniques.

Exercise 1.2: Improving the snake game with prompt engineering.

1. Open up ChatGPT and start a new chat and enter the following prompt:

    Prompt: `You are a Python game developer who needs to write a snake game in Python using Pygame. The game should use the up, down, left, and right arrows to control movement. As well the player should be able to pause the game using the space bar. When the game is paused be sure to write Paused on the screen.`

2. After a few moments, ChatGPT should respond with the code for your game. Copy and paste that code into a new file called **snake_game_prompted.py**.

3. Run the game using Python by running the following command from your Python environment console:

    1. `python snake_game_prompted.py`

This will run the game, and now when you press the space bar, the game should pause.

Figure 1.6: *Paused snake game*

Be sure the pause key works. If it does not open a new ChatGPT window, re-enter the prompt to generate a new code file.

However, you may notice several new changes or tweaks to the previously generated snake game, like the *background color, snake color, food color*, etc. We can fix these nuances in one of two ways, by adding to our initial prompt or suggesting changes to ChatGPT.

For this exercise, we are going to make suggestions to improve and/or standardize the snake game interface. Keeping your ChatGPT session open with your last working code, including the pause button, add the following prompt to the chat:

Prompt: `The game looks spectacular but requires a few changes. Please make the game background color black, the snake green, and the food blue in color. We also want to display the player's score, and the number of food pieces the snake has eaten. Display the score by writing the score label in the top right corner of the window.`

Copy the generated code to a new file called **snake_game_score.py**, and be sure to save the file. Run the file using the following command:

1. `python snake_game_score.py`

Now, the game output should have a black background, green snake, and blue food and show the score in the top right. If it does not, you can start from a new conversation or ask ChatGPT to fix the code. Refer to *Figure 1.7*:

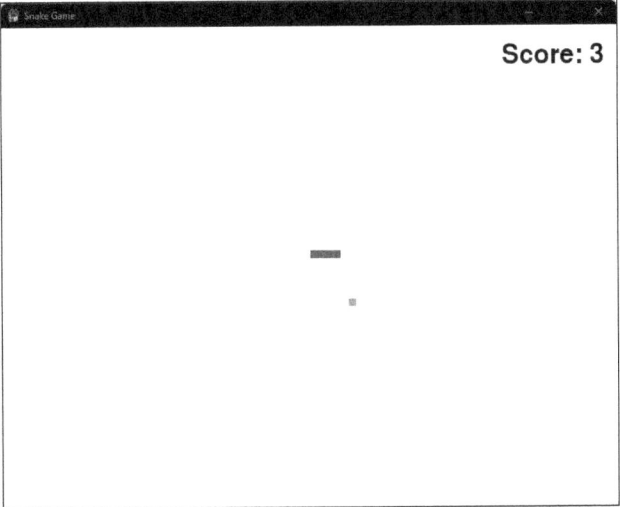

Figure 1.7: Improved snake game

As you can see, by being more specific in our request to ChatGPT, we were able to improve and standardize the interface. We did this all without understanding any game programming and minimal Python. Moreover, we improved on the generated game by simply asking ChatGPT.

This is great, but it will only take us so far. For a simple and classic concept like the snake game, it can produce good results. Additionally, you could continue to add more features, but at some point, you would hit the limits of use prompting.

Fortunately, we are not limited to simply conversing with ChatGPT. There are multiple ways to interact with the model, from retrieval augmentation to system prompts. We will explore both methods later with system prompting in the next section.

Unlocking potential with system prompting

User prompting, or conversational prompting, is the typical usage for ChatGPT. This form of the tool responds to the users' requests or prompts. As we saw in the last section, you can even get quite detailed with your requests.

However, you can start encountering hallucinations, mixed-up responses, confusion, and complaining if you give highly complex prompts to ChatGPT. Let us see how this happens in the following exercise, where we test ChatGPT's ability to handle overly detailed requests.

Exercise 1.3: Exercising ChatGPT

Open ChatGPT and start a new conversation by entering the following prompt:

Prompt: `Please write me a lunar lander game in Python. When the lander crashes, display an explosion and deduct 100 from the player's score. When the lander lands successfully, display fireworks and add 1000 to the player's score. Display the player's score in the top right corner of the window.`

Make the lander white in color and the background black with stars. The surface of the planet is represented with a line. The surface should be hilly and mountainous, but there should be a flat area large enough for the lander to land on.

Note: All prompts for the book will be in the chapter's source code in a file called chapter_prompts.txt. Feel free to copy the prompts from there and paste them into ChatGPT.

After you enter this prompt, there is a high chance that ChatGPT will respond with a complaint that a full lunar lander game would require physics, graphics, sound, and so on. However, it will likely output some code. Go ahead and copy/paste the code into a new file in VS Code, then run it. Is it what you expected?

Chances are the code is not even close to the game you were hoping to play. Of course, ChatGPT likely did warn you not to get your hopes up. So how can we fix this?

As it turns out, there are numerous ways to fix this, from better planning strategies to prompt decomposition. Before we get to those tools, let us look at how we can improve some of the last prompt's output using system prompts.

We will use the same prompt as last time, but this time introduce a system prompt before the full request. Enter all of the following text into a new chat window, be sure to enter all of the text as is:

Prompt: `[SYSTEM] You are a Python game developer. As a developer, you prefer to break down code into smaller modules that can be unit tested and imported as needed. When you get a new request, it is up to you to break down requirements into self-contained modules that can be run and tested. If you are unsure of which modules to develop first, please ask the user.`

`[USER] Please write me a lunar lander game in Python. When the lander crashes, display an explosion and deduct 100 from the player's score. When the lander lands successfully, display fireworks and add 1000 to the player's score. Display the player's score in the top right corner of the window.`

`Make the lander white in color and the background black with stars. The surface of the planet is represented with a line. The surface should be hilly and mountainous, but there should be a flat area large enough for the lander to land on.`

This time, the response is completely different. The following is a direct excerpt from ChatGPT detailing the development of the lunar lander game:

ChatGPT: Sure, let us break down the requirements into smaller modules that we can develop step-by-step. Here is how I would structure the development of the lunar lander game:

- Setting up the game window:
    - Create a game window with a black background and stars.
    - Display the player's score in the top right corner.
    - Use a rendering library like Pygame for the graphical interface.
- Drawing the planet surface:
    - Generate a random hilly and mountainous surface.
    - Ensure there is a flat area for the lander to land on.
    - Draw the surface line on the game window.
- Creating the lander:
    - Design a white-colored lunar lander.
    - Implement physics for the lander's movement, thrust, and gravity.
    - Update the lander's position and velocity accordingly.

- Collision detection and scoring:
  - Implement collision detection for the lander and the planet's surface.
  - When the lander crashes, display an explosion animation and deduct 100 from the player's score.
  - When the lander lands successfully, display fireworks and add 1000 to the player's score.
- Game loop and user input:
  - Create a game loop that updates the lander's position, checks for collisions, and handles user input.
  - Allow the player to control the lander's thrust using keyboard inputs.
- Unit testing:
  - Write unit tests for each module to ensure they function correctly in isolation.
- Integration and final testing:
  - Integrate all modules into the main game loop and test their interactions.
  - Perform final testing to ensure the game works as expected.

The response also likely contained code for the starting window, shown as follows:

```
1.  import pygame
2.  import random
3.
4.  # Initialize Pygame
5.  pygame.init()
6.
7.  # Game window dimensions
8.  WINDOW_WIDTH = 800
9.  WINDOW_HEIGHT = 600
10.
11. # Colors
12. BLACK = (0, 0, 0)
13. WHITE = (255, 255, 255)
14.
15. # Create the game window
16. window = pygame.display.set_mode((WINDOW_WIDTH, WINDOW_HEIGHT))
```

```
17.    pygame.display.set_caption("Lunar Lander Game")
18.
19.    # Font for displaying the score
20.    font = pygame.font.Font(None, 36)
21.
22.    # Initialize player score
23.    player_score = 0
24.
25.    # Game Loop
26.    running = True
27.    while running:
28.        for event in pygame.event.get():
29.            if event.type == pygame.QUIT:
30.                running = False
31.
32.        # Clear the screen
33.        window.fill(BLACK)
34.
35.        # Display player's score in the top right corner
36.        score_text = font.render(f"Score: {player_score}", True, WHITE)
37.        score_rect = score_text.get_rect(topright=(WINDOW_WIDTH - 10, 10))
38.        window.blit(score_text, score_rect)
39.
40.        pygame.display.flip()
41.
42.    # Quit Pygame
43.    pygame.quit()
```

We will get into more details about how this basic window runs later, but what we have here is a proper start to a full game with the help of ChatGPT. The code is also well documented and thus far modular.

Keep the same chat window open, and now let us complete the next step of the plan that ChatGPT provided for us, building the planet's landscape. Enter the following prompt into the same chat window:

Prompt: [USER] That is an excellent plan. Now that we have the window, add a new module that creates the moon's landscape in a file called landscape. Inside the module, make two functions, one to generate the landscape and another to render it to the window. Then import the module into the main game.

ChatGPT will respond with code for the **landscape.py** file and the needed updates to the main game file. Follow the directions to create the new **landscape.py** file and update the main game window code. This will require some copy/pasting into the right areas.

When you have everything copied, go ahead and run the game. If you cannot get your version to work, use the version provided in the chapter's code by running:

1. `python lunar_lander_landscape.py`

Figure 1.8 shows the results of running the code provided, you will likely see similar results:

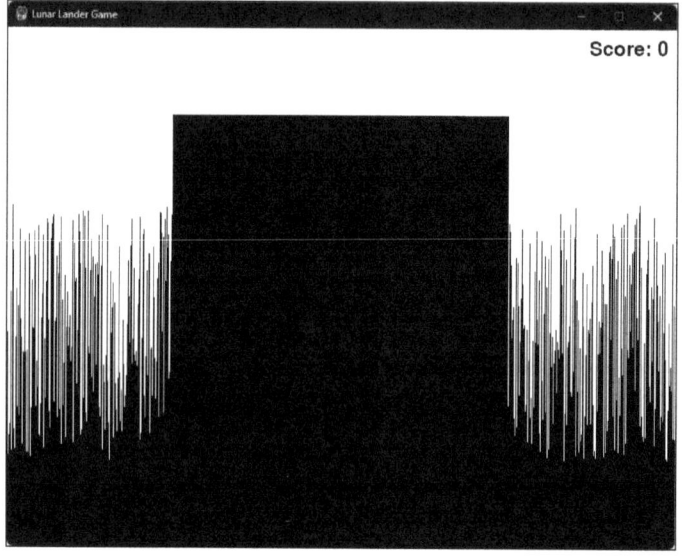

Figure 1.8: Running the lunar lander game

There are a few things wrong with the output, this is because the request was vague and lacked detail. For instance, we did not describe what a good landing zone should look like or how random the landscape should look.

Previously, if we wanted to alter our landscape, we would have to get ChatGPT to rebuild the entire code, much like what we did in the earlier exercise. However, now that we have asked GPT to break the code into modules, our ability to alter the code has become much easier.

For the final prompt in this exercise, we will ask ChatGPT to update the landscape module with a better landing zone and a more natural-looking landscape. Using the same chat, enter the following prompt:

Prompt: [USER] The landscape looks okay, but let us update the generate_landscape function so that the flat landing area is lower to the ground at 100 and only 75 pixels wide and placed randomly. Also, fill the landscape with a random number of mountain peaks. Each peak is drawn as a triangle with a random base width from 50 to 250 pixels.

ChatGPT should respond with the updated code for the **generate_landscape** function. Copy/paste the code into the old or a new file called **landscape2.py**. Be sure to update the import in your old code to import **landscape2**.

Figure 1.9 shows the results of running the updated code. It is a little better, but we still have some obvious issues:

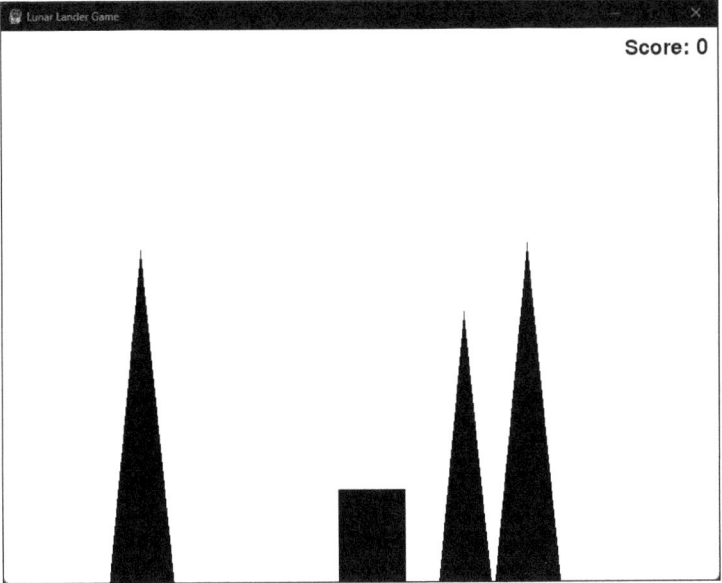

Figure 1.9: Updating the generate_landscape function

At this point, we have two options: continue pestering ChatGPT until it produces better results, or work through and update the code on your own. This is a key decision that we will face throughout this book, so let us highlight some considerations for each option:

- **Increment on ChatGPT**: Chances are your first inclination will be to continue asking ChatGPT to improve its code. However, this can lead to diminishing returns as you iterate further and further. The reason for this is that the conversation will become poisoned with all the previous poor requests.

- **Update the code yourself**: In most cases, updating the code yourself will get the best results, but coding takes time and effort. Our goal throughout this book is to use AI tools, like ChatGPT, to make us more efficient. Except, it is important for you, at a minimum, to understand what the code is doing and how it can be fixed or enhanced.

Ultimately, the best strategy, of course, is to use both. Utilizing ChatGPT to write the general code and then our skills to make it unique and your own. While we could accomplish this with the OpenAI ChatGPT interface, there are better ways which we will explore in the next section.

Engaging retrieval augmented generation with EasyCode

As we started to see at the end of the last section, conversing with ChatGPT has limits. It can be easy for your chat dialog to get confused or repetitive. This can be especially true if you are trying to fix a bug or improve code through iteration. Fortunately, there exists a more powerful mechanism to integrate ChatGPT with your text or code, be it a game, book, or PDF.

Retrieval augmented generation (**RAG**) is a technique that uses information from your documents as text embeddings. In RAG, documents are indexed by converting text into embeddings and then saving the resultant vector arrays into a vector database.

Text embeddings can be generated by chunking document text into smaller chunks fed into an embedding model. This model converts the text into an array of numbers called a vector. This vector represents the context, semantics, and similarity of the text and can be used for quick lookups when placed in a vector database.

Figure 1.10 shows the basic components of a RAG system. In this system, documents are indexed into a vector database that the retriever uses to augment the questions. In essence, the retriever is adding more relevant context to the queries without the need for the user to do this on their own. Please refer to the following figure:

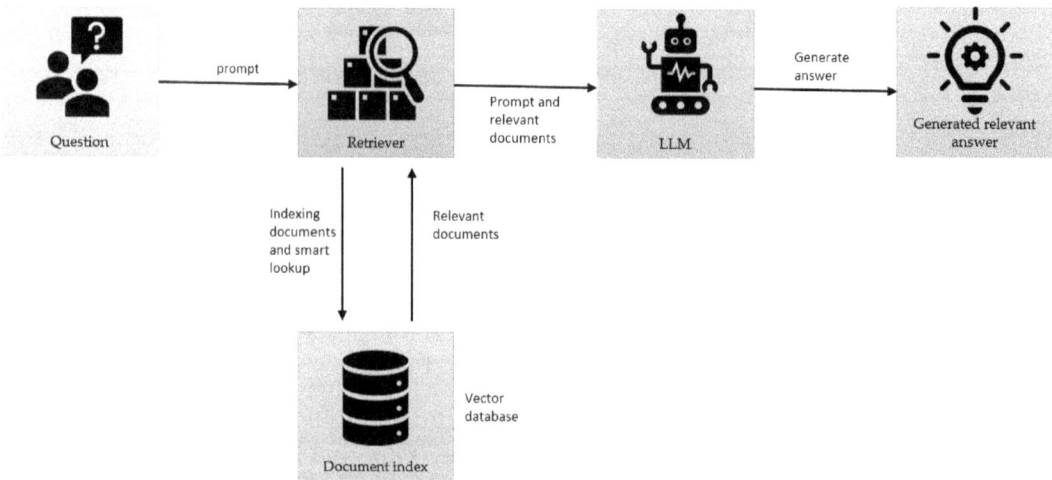

Figure 1.10: The basic components and workflow of RAG

There are plenty of RAG tools out there, from lower-level code your own tools to more encapsulated and easier-to-use systems. For our purposes, we are going to stick to a higher-level tool that is both free, powerful, and easy to use in the next exercise.

Exercise 1.4: Employing retrieval augmented generation with EasyCode

1. Open the extensions panel in VS Code and search for **ChatGPT EasyCode** as shown in *Figure 11.1*:

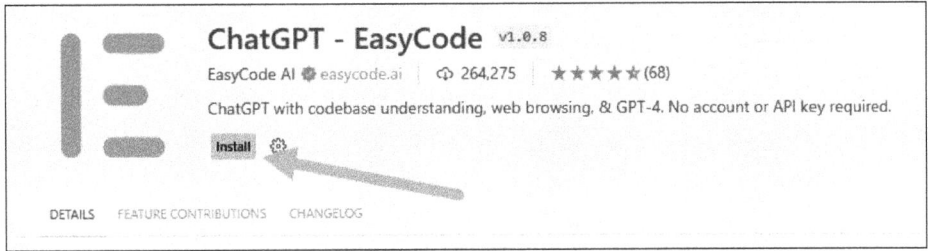

Figure 1.11: Installing EasyCode

2. Click the Install button to install the extension into VS Code.

3. EasyCode does not require an OpenAI key like many of the other tools do, but it does require you to sign up to use it for free. An alternative is adding your OpenAI key in the settings panel, but for now, we will stick with the free version.

4. Click the **EasyCode** extension icon, on the left side panel, and then enter your email and password. Click the **Sign Up** button to complete the registration as shown in *Figure 1.12*:

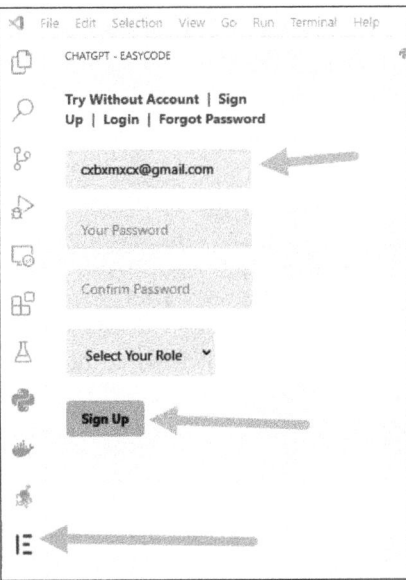

Figure 1.12: Signing up for EasyCode

5. After registering and logging in, you must select the options for use. Since we want to use **RAG** to add context to our code, select the **Ask Codebase** option, as seen in *Figure 1.13*:

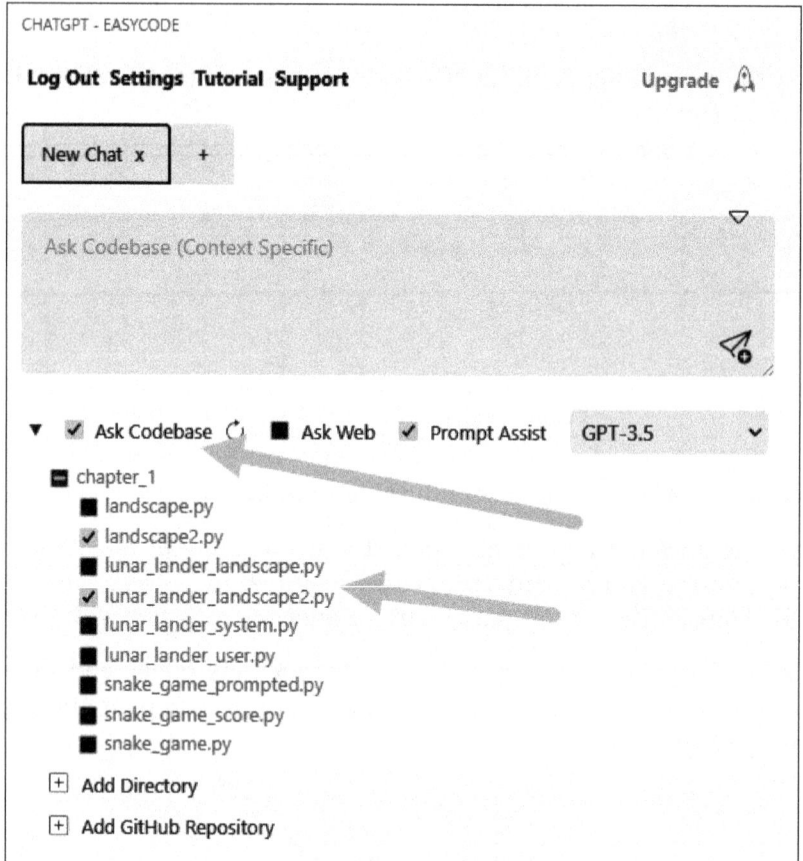

Figure 1.13: Selecting the files you want to index

6. Next, select the files you want to index. Let us use the last example we worked on in the last section, the lunar lander game. Select the lunar lander files you want to ask questions about, and then click the refresh button beside the **Ask Codebase** option.

Now that we have the extension installed and the code indexed, let us ask a question. In the question dialog, write the following question and click the **submit** button as shown in *Figure 1.14*:

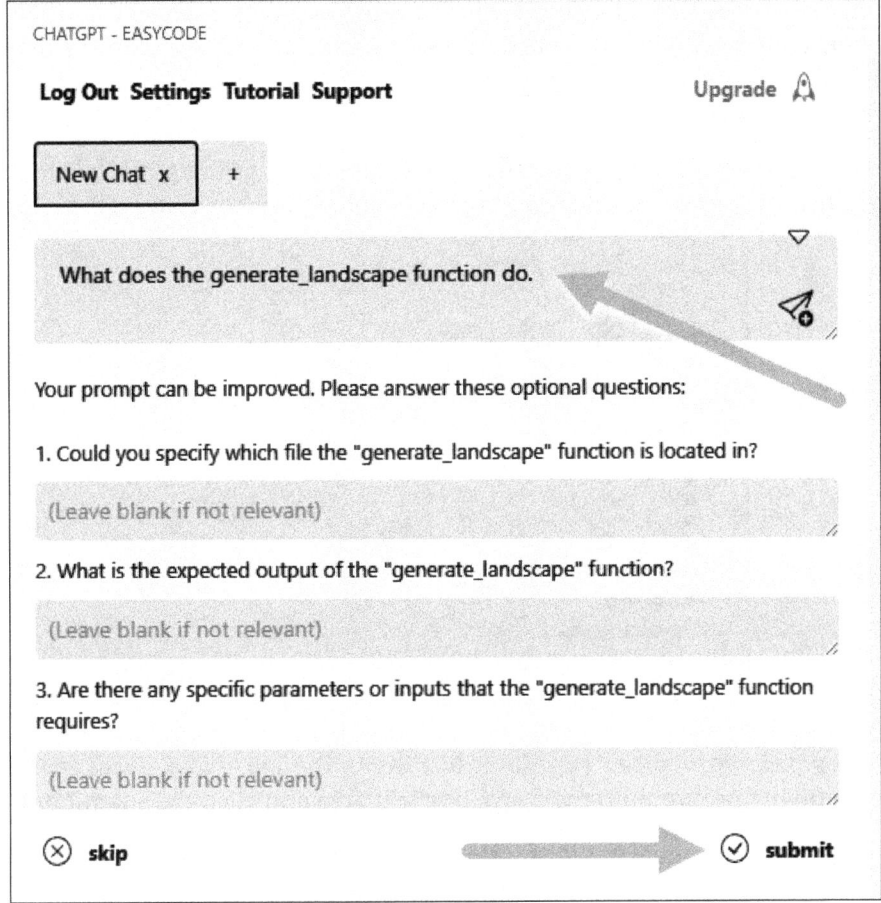

Figure 1.14: Asking a question of the code base

Question: What does the generate_landscape function do?

If everything is working, you will now see a comprehensive and verbose description of what the function does. This can be an excellent way to learn how a piece works and aid in extending it. What is more powerful is we no longer need to maintain a chat history or consult previous sessions. Everything is at our fingertips, provided we index all the relevant code.

Now that we have a tool that can help us iterate cleaner, let us revisit our landscaping problem from the lunar lander game. For our final exercise of the chapter, we are going to use EasyCode to help us fix the `generate_landscape` function.

Exercise 1.4: Fixing the lunar landscape

We start off by copying the main game file `lunar_lander_landscape2.py` to `lunar_lander_landscape3.py` and likewise the landscape module from `landscape2.py` to `landscape3.py`.

In the future, we will look at using local Git repositories to manage iterative changes instead of file copying. Managing code changes is essential when working with an AI tool like *ChatGPT*. Unlike classic coding, you are more likely to make large and widespread changes when using AI.

Open the EasyCode extension, select the newly copied files, and remove the old ones from the index. Click the refresh button to index the new files, as shown in *Figure 1.15*:

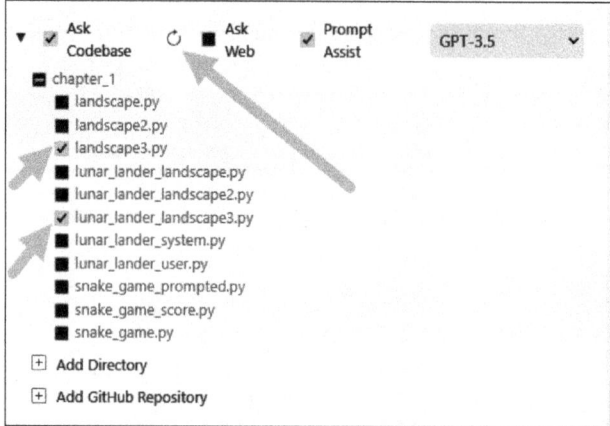

Figure 1.15: Refreshing the vector index

With the files indexed, we can now look to rewrite the **generate_landscape** function. Enter the following prompt into the EasyCode text area and click the submit button:

Prompt: `Completely rewrite the generate_landscape and render_landscape functions. First, the generate_landscape function should return a list of points, (x, y coordinate pairs) that represent the surface of the landscape.`

Generate the landscape points using the following algorithm:

start at $x = 0$, $y = random$ value from 250 to window height: 50

increment x by some random value, take random value of y from 250 to window height: 50

add the point x, y to the set and check that x is not greater than the window width if it is finished.

Create the landing area by altering the set of points.

As you enter this prompt, notice a couple of things. We switched tactics, and instead of visually explaining what we wanted to see, we provided an algorithm to define a set of points. Hopefully, this will better align with what we are looking for.

After ChatGPT responds, copy, and paste the updated code to generate and draw landscape functions into the new landscape module. Likewise, you may need to update the call to generate the landscape in the main file.

Open the main file (**lunar_lander_landscape3.py**) in VS Code and make the following changes:

Alter the import to the new module file:

```
1. import landscape3 as ls
```

Then alter the generate and draw landscape function calls like so:

```
1. #before the game loop
2. landscape = ls.generate_landscape(WINDOW_WIDTH, WINDOW_HEIGHT)
3.
4. # within the game loop
5. ls.render_landscape(window, landscape)
```

We could, of course, ask ChatGPT to suggest what changes we needed to make in the main game file, but it is often better to refactor some code yourself. Not only will this force you to learn how the code works, but if things break, you will be more aware of what needs fixing.

After you make the changes save the file and launch the game from the console using:

```
1. python lunar_lander_landscape3.py
```

This will run the game and you should now see a screenshot resembling *Figure 1.16*. You may likely see a different landscape but expect to see a white line mimicking mountains and a flat area for landing. Please refer to the following figure:

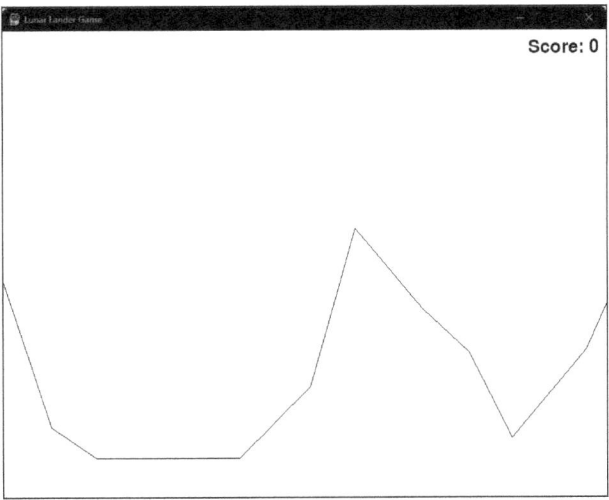

Figure 1.16: *The updated lunar landscape*

We will revisit this project again in *chapter 6* where we will look to complete this game. For now, though, let us conclude the chapter with what we learned in the next section.

Conclusion

In this chapter, we started learning game development with ChatGPT. We explored how to use ChatGPT and looked at building a couple of little games.

In the next chapter, we delve into game development foundations by building a text-based game. Text games will provide us with a foundation in understanding game data, game loops and game design workflows.

What we learned

- How ChatGPT works and was trained. A key element to using AI tools effectively is understanding how they work and what their limitations are.
- How to ask ChatGPT to write code using a variety of techniques from prompt engineering, system/user prompting, and using retrieval augmented generation tools like EasyCode.
- How to structure and break down what you ask of ChatGPT using system prompts. From using ChatGPT to designing the list of high-level tasks to implementing low level drawing functions.
- At a high level, how retrieval augmented generation works and how it can be used to better iterate in designing code.
- How to install, set up, and use EasyCode, a ChatGPT extension that provides RAG document indexing.

Exercises

Use the following exercises to improve your knowledge and understanding of the material.

1. Test ChatGPT by asking it to write another classic and well-known game like *tic-tac-toe* or *checkers*. Copy and run the code; how did it do? How can it be improved?
2. Ask ChatGPT to add a second player to the snake game. Construct the prompts to get the features you want for a second player, like *movement controls* and *scoring*. Then, decide what needs to happen if 2 players collide. How do you detect collisions?
3. Write a new system prompt that describes the role of a game designer. Then add a user prompt to ask ChatGPT system to design a cool and fun snake game. How well does it do?
4. Improve the lunar lander game landscape by making the window larger, say *1200x900*, and adding additional landing zones. You may even want to highlight the landing zones. What do you need to ask ChatGPT?
5. Explore the **Prompt Assist** option in EasyCode. Get the extension to provide some prompts by selecting the option. How well do the prompts work?

CHAPTER 2
Text Adventure: Entering the Enchanted Realm

Introduction

Game development is complicated. There are many things a developer must be aware of when developing a game. Indeed, many a new game developers focus on graphics and the look of a game when that is only a tiny component of a good game. Experienced game developers realize that good games are not always about what you see.

Therefore, in this chapter, we start building games without graphics, focusing on text-based games. We will look at how to prompt a full text-based game in ChatGPT and then fill in the details to make a fun playable game.

Structure

This chapter explores the following topics:

- Venturing into the world of text-based games
- Prompting your first game: PyZork
- Parsing the player: Managing player input
- Crafting your own game world: Building the map
- Unleashing unexpected game challenges: Items and NPCs

Objectives

This chapter's objective is to understand a game's core objects using classic text-based games. Games are developed using a common pattern and share many components at their core.

Venturing into the world of text-based games

Text-based computer games have been around as long as we have interfaced with computers using a console (1969). In fact, one of the first text games for computers was the lunar lander game. The game we revisited in the last chapter, working hard to get ChatGPT to write a proper landing pad, was initially a text-based game.

Our goal in this chapter will be to write a version of the classic text-based adventure game *Zork*. We will use Zork as it is a well-known game that became the basis for many features, we see in most of the games today. These are the same features that we will want to replicate using ChatGPT and our own coding skills.

Before we do that though, let us jump into an exercise and see what ChatGPT knows about games like *Zork*:

Exercise 2.1: Asking ChatGPT to write PyZork

1. Open your web browser to OpenAI ChatGPT: **https://chat.openai.com/**

2. In the prompt input, enter the following text and hit enter:

   Prompt: `Write me a classic game like Zork in Python and call it PyZork.`

3. More than likely, ChatGPT will respond that a full game would take much more code, but here is a quick example, and then it will provide some basic code. Do not worry about using the system prompt just yet, for now we are interested in what the basic game looks like.

4. Open VS Code and copy the code produced by ChatGPT into a new file called **pyzork.py** and save it. If there was no code generated, just ask ChatGPT to regenerate. Also, if you think the code that was produced could be better, ask it to regenerate.

5. Run the code in debug mode. From the menu, select **Run | Start Debugging**, as shown in *Figure 2.1*:

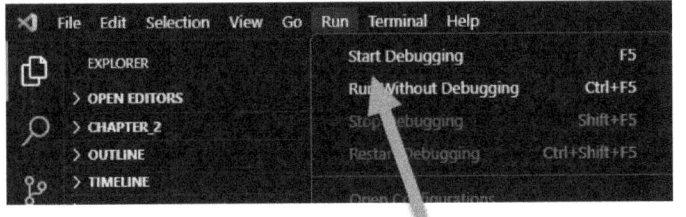

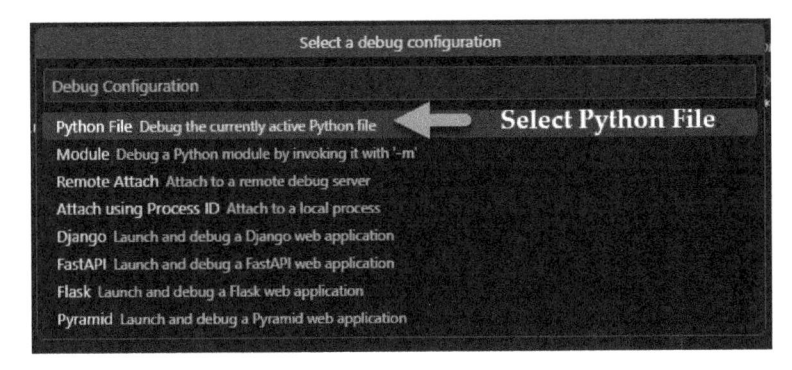

Figure 2.1: Starting in debug mode

If this is your first time, the command panel will open and ask what is to be debugged. Select the file and in a few seconds the terminal will open (as shown in *Figure* 2.2). Hopefully, it show a running game. If the code does not run or has an error, open the source code of *Chapter 2* and use the **pyzork.py** file.

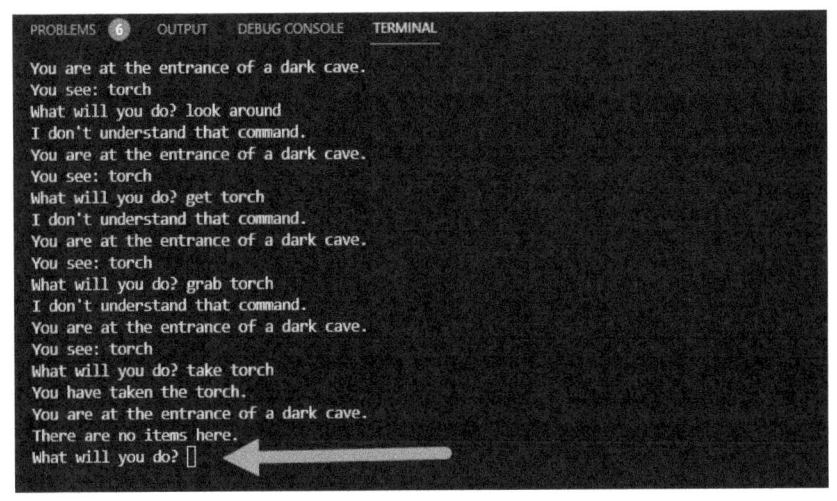

Figure 2.2: Playing the PyZork game

Go ahead and play the game. Your version of the game may be different but hopefully, you are allowed to pick up objects and move around. If your version of the ChatGPT written game does not do this, run the **pyzork.py** file from the chapter source code.

Here are a few things you may have noticed while playing the game:

- **Parsing**: The commands need to be exact. For example, to get the torch or other items, you need to type **take torch**. No other commands will work. This was kind of the fun of the old classic games. However, the technology today will help us achieve much better.
- **Inventory**: The player could pick up and drop items.
- **Items**: Items were available to pick up and use.
- **Rooms**: The player could move from room to room. Rooms had a description.
- **World**: Rooms were connected by doors or paths.
- **Player**: The player was an entity in the game and had an inventory of items.
- **Game engine**: The player played the game by getting descriptions and entering commands. This process of entering commands and getting feedback is a simple game loop.
- **Monsters {opponents/Non-player characters (NPCs)}**: You likely did not see a troll in this simple version. However, to make the game fun and engaging, we will want to introduce monster challenges later.
- **NPCs**: NPCs were not included in the original Zork, but our updated version will include a couple.

Figure 2.3 shows a pictorial version of the elements we want to include in PyZork. It is useful to draw out the main elements of your game to better plan your design and features, at least at a high level:

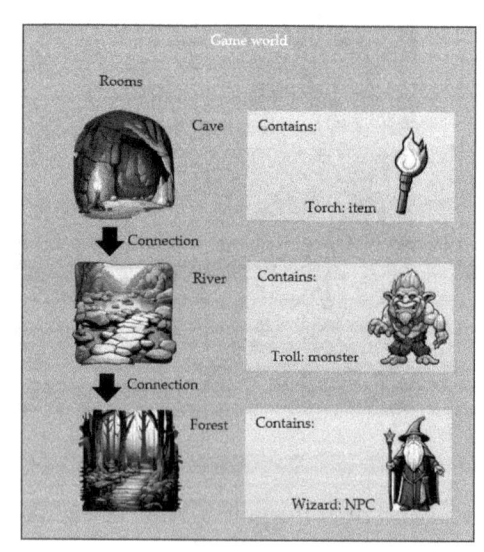

Figure 2.3: The elements of the PyZork game

Note: All the artwork generated for this chapter is done using Stable Diffusion XL. The latest open-source version at the time of writing and a great image generation tool.

We have divided the game components into two sections: The player and the game world. Separated between these sections are the game interface and game loop. The game interface is how the player interacts with the game world. Here are some key elements to remember about the game interface/loop:

- **Game loop**: Games continuously run in a loop, called the game loop. The game loop is responsible for updating what the player sees. It also updates the world, and this may include NPCs moving or other activities.

- **Game interface**: This is how the player visualizes and interacts with the game world. The form of the game interface is described by the genre of game we may be building. Below is a short list of game genres and their interface:

    o **Text-based**: Player interaction with the game is entirely through free-form text input. Players will typically view the world through text descriptions but 2D or 3D graphics may also be an option.

    o **2D platform**: It is reminiscent of the classic arcade games like *Snake* and *Lunar Lander*. Players typically interact with the game using a joystick or simple keyboard commands. We will look to explore this type of game interface in *Chapter 5*.

    o **3D first-person**: The more modern first-person perspective is a common game interface that shows the game world through the perceived player's eyes. Players typically interact with these games using a game controller or mouse and keyboard. This is an interface we will explore in *Chapter 7*.

    o **Human brain interface**: There exist commercially available game controllers that function through thought. While the technology is still in its infancy, this may yield whole new ways to play games in the future. Game development for this type of interface requires special equipment, and for that reason, we will omit it from learning in this book.

    o **Vocal/audio**: Another new and emerging way to play games is using just audio. Here, the player or players speak commands, answers, or questions and the game world is presented through audio and/or physical game pieces. With the advent of advancing AI, this interface may augment or replace entire ways we play classic games like *board games*, *party games*, and role-playing games like *Dungeons* and *Dragons*. In *chapters 9* and *10*, we will spend time building a couple of vocal/audio game examples.

Now that we understand all the elements of the game we want to build, we can go back to ChatGPT and ask it to start building us some code.

Prompting your first game: PyZork

Based on our previous quick research, we have understood all the elements/features we want for our text-based adventure game. The hard part now is crafting the prompt so ChatGPT can produce some modular code we can build off. Let us jump into the next exercise and start crafting that prompt.

Exercise 2.2: Prompt engineering ChatGPT to write PyZork

1. Open your web browser to OpenAI ChatGPT: **https://chat.openai.com/**

2. In the prompt input, enter the following text and hit enter.

Prompt: `[SYSTEM] You are a Python game developer. As a developer, you prefer to break down code into smaller modules that can be unit tested and imported as needed. When you get a new request, it is up to you to break down requirements into self-contained modules that can be run and tested. If you are unsure of which modules to develop first please ask the user.`

`Begin by writing the main game modules and interfaces for all the key elements of the game. Instruct the user on how to build the game using the game modules and provide examples.`

`[USER] Write me a classic game like Zork in Python and call it PyZork.`

Note: You do not need to type all the text. All prompts can be found in the book's source code for the relevant chapter.

This time we are using a system prompt like the one we used in the previous chapter. The addition of this prompt will engage ChatGPT to describe the code in modules and even code some foundational classes. Go ahead and hit the **Regenerate** button, as shown in *Figure 2.4*, a few times to see the different variations ChatGPT responds with:

Figure 2.4: The ChatGPT regenerate button

As you can see, even with a good system prompt, ChatGPT can provide a skeleton of a game. However, that game may miss important features that need to be core to our game design or features that may be difficult to add later. Therefore, we are going to alter our prompting strategy a little and use our previous research to guide us.

Start a new ChatGPT conversation and enter the following prompt:

Prompt: `[SYSTEM] You are a Python game developer. As a developer, you prefer to break down code into smaller modules that can be unit tested and imported as needed. When you get a new request, it is up to you to break down requirements into self-contained modules that can be run and tested. If you are unsure of which modules to develop first please ask the user.`

`Begin by writing the main game modules and interfaces for all the key elements of the game. The user will help define key modules of the game by making the text all caps. For example, PLAYER would represent the player module. Be sure to write Python code for each module the user identifies.`

`Instruct the user on how to build the game using the game modules and provide examples.`

`[USER] I want to write a classic text-based adventure game in Python and call it PyZork after the classic game Zork.`

`In this game, the player will interact with the game world using free-from-text input. The game will respond with text descriptions of rooms, items and NPCs.`

`Here are the important features of my game:`

`The PLAYER has an inventory of ITEMs they can carry and use.`

`The WORLD is composed of ROOMs that are connected through LINKs, a PLAYER may use a LINK to move to another ROOM by using the right ACTION`

`The WORLD is inhabited by ITEMs and NPCs. ITEMs may be picked up and used by the PLAYER. NPCs may be spoken to, traded with or attacked.`

`Can you help me by starting to write this game please. Be sure to include the main game module that will host the game engine and game interface loop.`

It is a lengthy prompt but the extra details will help define exactly what we need to build our game. In most cases, the results of the above prompt will be similar. Although by its nature, it may vary significantly. Therefore, if you to follow along exactly with the example, use the link to the author's shared chat and our first checkpoint:

https://chat.openai.com/share/0783ea85-884c-44d4-aa67-2494b39096dc

The above link is also available in the book's source code for *Chapter 2* in the **Chapter_prompts.txt** file. You can also use the above link as a checkpoint and visit it again if you get lost and need to start a new session.

Output from the above prompt should direct you to create several modules and copy the code to each module. Go ahead and copy the code from the chat into each of the following modules/files:

- **main.py**: The main game loop code is as follows:

```
1.  # main.py
2.  from player import Player
3.  from world import World
4.  
5.  def main():
6.      # Initialize the game world, create rooms, items, NPCs, and Links.
7.  
8.      player = Player()
9.      world = World()
10. 
11.     # Game Loop
12.     while True:
13.         # Display current room description, inventory, and available actions.
14.         # Get player input.
15.         # Parse and process player input.
16.         # Update game state and respond to player actions.
17.         # Check for game over conditions or win conditions.
18.         pass
19. 
20. if __name__ == "__main__":
21.     main()
```

- **player.py**: It defines the **Player** class:

```
1.  # player.py
2.  class Player:
3.      def __init__(self):
4.          self.inventory = []
5.  
6.      def add_item(self, item):
7.          # Add an item to the player's inventory.
8.          pass
```

```
 9.
10.    def remove_item(self, item):
11.        # Remove an item from the player's inventory.
12.        pass
13.
14.    def use_item(self, item):
15.        # Use an item from the player's inventory.
16.        pass
17.
18.    def take_action(self, action):
19.        # Handle player actions.
20.        pass
```

- **world.py**: It defines `World` class that holds details about the whole game world:

```
 1. # world.py
 2. class World:
 3.     def __init__(self):
 4.         self.rooms = {}
 5.         self.items = {}
 6.         self.links = {}
 7.         self.npcs = {}
 8.
 9.     def add_room(self, room):
10.         # Add a room to the game world.
11.         pass
12.
13.     def add_item(self, item):
14.         # Add an item to the game world.
15.         pass
16.
17.     def add_link(self, link):
18.         # Add a link connecting two rooms.
19.         pass
20.
```

```
21.     def add_npc(self, npc):
22.         # Add an NPC to the game world.
23.         pass
```

- **room.py**: It defines the **Room** class and represents an area in the game world:

```
1.  # room.py
2.  class Room:
3.      def __init__(self, description):
4.          self.description = description
5.          self.items = []
6.          self.npcs = []
7.
8.      def add_item(self, item):
9.          # Add an item to the room.
10.         pass
11.
12.     def remove_item(self, item):
13.         # Remove an item from the room.
14.         pass
15.
16.     def add_npc(self, npc):
17.         # Add an NPC to the room.
18.         pass
19.
20.     def remove_npc(self, npc):
21.         # Remove an NPC from the room.
22.         pass
```

- **item.py**: It defines the **Item** class and represents objects the player can interact with within the game world:

```
1.  # item.py
2.  class Item:
3.      def __init__(self, name, description):
4.          self.name = name
5.          self.description = description
```

```
6.
7.     def use(self, player):
8.         # Define how the item is used.
9.         pass
```

- **link.py**: It defines the **Link** class which represents a connection between 2 rooms in the world:

```
1. # link.py
2. class Link:
3.     def __init__(self, source_room, target_room, action):
4.         self.source_room = source_room
5.         self.target_room = target_room
6.         self.action = action
7.
8.     def use(self, player):
9.         # Define how the link is used to move between rooms.
10.        pass
```

- **action.py**: It defines the **Action** class and represents what actions a user may take:

```
1. # action.py
2. class Action:
3.     def __init__(self, name, description):
4.         self.name = name
5.         self.description = description
6.
7.     def execute(self, player):
8.         # Define what happens when the player takes this action.
9.         pass
```

- **npc.py**: It defines the **NPC** class and represents non-player characters the user may interact with:

```
1. # npc.py
2. class NPC:
3.     def __init__(self, name, description):
4.         self.name = name
5.         self.description = description
```

```
6.
7.     def talk(self, player):
8.         # Define how the player can interact with the NPC.
9.         pass
10.
11.    def trade(self, player):
12.        # Define trading logic with the NPC.
13.        pass
14.
15.    def attack(self, player):
16.        # Define combat logic with the NPC.
17.        pass
```

Create all the module files in a new folder called **pyzork_v0** and save all the code. You can then run the game by selecting the **main.py** in VS Code and typing **F5** or using the menu **Run | Start Debugging**.

The current version of the game when run is likely to not produce anything and give an error. It may feel like a step back from our previous attempts, however, we now have a well-developed shell to cleanly build upon.

Another reason for going through this exercise is to help you identify the main code that will comprise our game engine. Since this code is modular, we can also get a good idea of how things will bind together. At this point, it is more important than a working game.

With the main elements of the game now in hand, we can move on to build the text interface our player will interact with within the next section.

Parsing the player: Managing player input

In many games, player input is very easy to manage; it may just be certain keys or reading a game controller. For others, like our text-based game, player input can get incredibly complex. For now, we are going to keep things simple and in the spirit of the old classic games.

In the classic text-based adventure games, player input was broken down into two parts: the action and object, where an action represented the interaction between a game world object. Actions would often be specific to a particular object context. The following are some examples of action–object pairs in the form of player input:

Action - object

- **Throw torch**: The action is throwing or attacking, and the object is a torch.
- **Talk wizard**: The action is talking, and the object is the wizard **non-player character (NPC)**.
- **Attack troll**: The action is attacking, and the object is the troll NPC.
- **Move north**: The action is moving, and the object is a room link.

These action-object phrases will allow the player to interact with the game world. However, we cannot allow the player to just type **attack troll** from anywhere within the game to kill the troll. We need to also associate a context or multiple contexts with an action.

This means, if a player types **throw torch**, we need to first verify they have the correct context. In this example, that context is to verify the player is carrying the torch. Likewise, a player typing **move north** requires the room to have a link that represents the object context. *Figure 2.5* shows the context for each of the example commands:

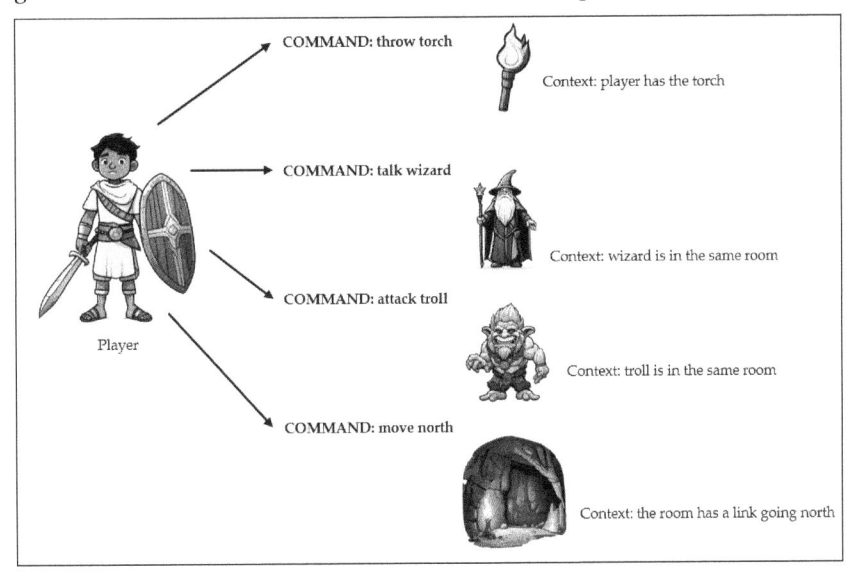

Figure 2.5: Understanding command context

Now that we understand how the basic text interface will work as well as identify context, we can ask ChatGPT to update our code in the next exercise.

Exercise 2.3: Prompting the game input parser

We are going to continue where we left off. You can continue with the last prompt or use the following link to reset to the book's last checkpoint: **https://chat.openai.com/share/0783ea85-884c-44d4-aa67-2494b39096dc**

Prompt: Now please write the text input command parser. Text commands will come in the form of action on an object, where an action is defined by the Action class and an object could be one of Room, Item or NPC.

The Action class should define a list of verbs that activate the action as well as the context of the action. Context of an action may require the player to carry a specific object in inventory, or for the object to be in the same area as the player.

Here are some examples of action-object commands.

move north - the action is moving using a ROOM LINK to another ROOM, the context of the action is the ROOM has a LINK

throw torch - the action is throwing and the context is the PLAYER is carrying the torch ITEM

talk wizard - the action is talking and the context is the wizard NPC is in the same ROOM as the PLAYER

attach troll - the action is attacking and the context is the troll NPC is in the same ROOM as the PLAYER

pickup torch - the action is getting and the context is the torch ITEM is in the same ROOM as the PLAYER

There is a lot going on here. Therefore, ChatGPT can still provide several variations on how to accomplish this task. Some, of course, may be better than others and some may fit our immediate needs but work long-term. Being able to read and understand the code will be essential for deciding which generated output will work best.

Go ahead and click the **Regenerate** button several times to see the various ways in which the parsing task can be solved. This new ability for AI to quickly generate variations on code can significantly help improve your learning. Not only is it a great way to view different interpretations, but it also gives suggestions you may have missed in your design.

Fortunately for us, the code is still relatively simple. Since your code may be different, we are going to look at an example selected in the link to the chat output and our next checkpoint: **https://chat.openai.com/share/3012e85e-acd3-44ed-b373-d2e6eb6776b4**

To keep things clean, create a copy of the **pyzork_v0** folder and name **pyzork_v.1** and copy the suggested code changes ChatGPT suggested into the appropriate files.

Below is the updated code for the action module defining the **Action** class. The important element added to the class is a function to check if an action can execute.

```
1.  class Action:
2.      def __init__(self, name, description, verbs, context=None):
3.          self.name = name
```

```
4.        self.description = description
5.        self.verbs = verbs
6.        self.context = context
7.
8.    def can_execute(self, player, obj):
9.        # Check if the action can be executed based on the context.
10.       if self.context is None:
11.           return True
12.       if self.context == "inventory":
13.           return obj in player.inventory
14.       # Add more context checks as needed.
15.
16.    def execute(self, player, obj):
17.        # Execute the action.
18.        pass
```

In the example chosen, the only other change was to the **main** module. The changes to the **main** module are the addition of a parser to read, verify and execute the player commands right within the main game loop. The entire **main.py** file is shown below:

```
1.  from player import Player
2.  from world import World
3.  from action import Action
4.
5.  def main():
6.      # Initialize the game world, create rooms, items, NPCs, and links.
7.
8.      player = Player()
9.      world = World()
10.
11.     # Define actions
12.     actions = [
13.         Action("Move", "Move to another room", ["move"], context="link"),
```

```
14.            Action("Throw", "Throw an object", ["throw"],
       context="inventory"),
15.            Action("Talk", "Talk to an NPC", ["talk"],
       context="npc"),
16.            Action("Attack", "Attack an NPC", ["attack"],
       context="npc"),
17.            Action("Pickup", "Pick up an item", ["pickup"],
       context="room")
18.       ]
19.
20.       # Game loop
21.       while True:
22.            # Display current room description, inventory, and
       available actions.
23.            # Get player input.
24.            command = input("Enter your command: ")
25.            parts = command.split()
26.
27.            if len(parts) >= 2:
28.                 verb = parts[0].lower()
29.                 obj_name = " ".join(parts[1:]).lower()
30.
31.                 # Find matching action based on verb
32.                 matching_actions = [action for action in actions if
       verb in action.verbs]
33.
34.                 if matching_actions:
35.                      action = matching_actions[0]
36.                      obj = None
37.
38.                      if action.context == "link":
39.                           # Check if the room has a link in the
       specified direction
40.                           pass
41.                      elif action.context == "inventory":
```

```
42.                    # Check if the player has the object in inventory
43.                    pass
44.                elif action.context == "npc":
45.                    # Check if the NPC is in the same room
46.                    pass
47.                elif action.context == "room":
48.                    # Check if the object is in the same room
49.                    pass
50.
51.                if obj:
52.                    if action.can_execute(player, obj):
53.                        action.execute(player, obj)
54.                    else:
55.                        print("You can't do that.")
56.                else:
57.                    print("Object not found.")
58.            else:
59.                print("Invalid action.")
60.
61.        # Update game state and respond to player actions.
62.        # Check for game over conditions or win conditions.
63.
64. if __name__ == "__main__":
65.     main()
```

Not only has ChatGPT written the code, but it has also placed comments and hints for the remaining code that needs to be written. Of course, you may well have found a more elegant solution in your generation or regenerations. If you do find something interesting, feel free to pursue it.

Go ahead and run the code from the console or in debug mode with VS Code. As much as there are a few actions defined we have yet to define the context or target of those actions. Therefore, in the next section, we will target our first context, rooms, and links to those rooms.

Crafting your own game world: Building the map

So far, we have the basic modules for the game and a way to parse command input. Now, we need to start creating the game world, and typically, the best place to start is the foundation or world map. This means we need to start constructing rooms and links to those rooms.

Of course, ChatGPT is going to help us by continuing the same conversation but taking a little bit different approach in the next exercise.

Exercise 2.4: Building the world

We are going to continue exactly where we left off. You can continue with the last prompt or use the following link to reset to the book's last exercise checkpoint: **https://chat.openai.com/share/3012e85e-acd3-44ed-b373-d2e6eb6776b4**

Prompt: `Create 5 adventure fantasy-style rooms and add the links to connect those rooms.`

`Then update the following section of code in the main loop, so that a player can move from room to room using actions, context and links.`

`if action.context == "link":`

`    # Check if the room has a link in the specified direction`

`    pass`

ChatGPT checkpoint: https://chat.openai.com/share/5d89a7bc-1218-4c36-a395-2348d3e28a67

This time, in our prompt, we reference lines of code to make sure ChatGPT understands our specific context and boundary. If we did not include this example code, we may get new code that does not align well with our existing code. Therefore, when building on new code, it is often helpful to refer to previous code sections. Tools like the *VS Code extension EasyCode* can do this for us automatically.

Before adding to and modifying the code, make a new copy of our game project from folder **pytorch_v.1** to **pytorch_v.2**. Then, update the code given by output starting with the world module:

1. `# world.py`
2. `class World:`
3. `    def __init__(self):`
4. `        self.rooms = {}`
5. `        self.items = {}`

```
 6.        self.links = {}
 7.        self.npcs = {}
 8.
 9.    def add_room(self, room):
10.        self.rooms[room.name] = room
11.
12.    def add_link(self, source_room, target_room, direction):
13.        self.links[(source_room, target_room)] = direction
14.        self.links[(target_room, source_room)] = opposite_direction(direction)
15.
16. def opposite_direction(direction):
17.    if direction == "north":
18.        return "south"
19.    elif direction == "south":
20.        return "north"
21.    elif direction == "east":
22.        return "west"
23.    elif direction == "west":
24.        return "east"
```

The updated world module now implements the **add_room** and **add_link** functions. This will allow rooms and room connections (links) to be added. Notice that ChatGPT added an automatic backlink in the opposite direction for us when adding a new link.

Next, the room module has also been updated with implementations for adding items and NPCs to rooms. The code changes should be self-explanatory:

```
1. class Room:
2.    def __init__(self, name, description):
3.        self.name = name
4.        self.description = description
5.        self.items = []
6.        self.npcs = []
7.
8.    def add_item(self, item):
9.        self.items.append(item)
```

```
10.
11.     def remove_item(self, item):
12.         self.items.remove(item)
13.
14.     def add_npc(self, npc):
15.         self.npcs.append(npc)
```

Then, within the **main** module, we have several changes starting with building the world in a new function, **create_world**. This new function creates the 5 rooms we asked for, and adds connecting links with corresponding directions.

```
1.  def create_world():
2.      world = World()
3.
4.      # Create rooms
5.      room1 = Room("Forest Clearing", "You are in a tranquil forest clearing.")
6.      room2 = Room("Cave Entrance", "A dark cave entrance looms ahead.")
7.      room3 = Room("Cave Interior", "The cave is dimly lit with mysterious symbols on the walls.")
8.      room4 = Room("Riddle Chamber", "You stand in a chamber filled with riddles.")
9.      room5 = Room("Treasure Room", "You have found a room filled with glittering treasures!")
10.
11.     # Add rooms to the world
12.     world.add_room(room1)
13.     world.add_room(room2)
14.     world.add_room(room3)
15.     world.add_room(room4)
16.     world.add_room(room5)
17.
18.     # Create links between rooms
19.     world.add_link(room1, room2, "north")
20.     world.add_link(room2, room3, "east")
```

```
21.     world.add_link(room3, room4, "south")
22.     world.add_link(room4, room5, "west")
23.
24.     return world
```

Then, farther down in the **main** module, we can see the updates to parsing and how link context is now handled:

```
1.  if action.context == "link":
2.      # Check if the room has a link in the specified direction
3.      direction = obj_name
4.      target_room = world.links.get((current_room, direction),
    None)
5.
6.      if target_room:
7.          current_room = target_room
8.          print("You move to the", direction)
9.      else:
10.         print("You can't go that way.")
```

Quite simply if the context is a link, then the code searches for all links from the current room which match the direction the player wants to travel. If no link exists, **target_room** is **None** and the player will be informed that they cannot travel in that direction.

Go ahead and run the code using debug mode or from the console. Try moving from one room to another. If you need hints, refer to the **create_world** function code.

What you will find is that the code has a bug, and the player would not be able to use the move action at all. Now we could try and solve this issue by asking ChatGPT to resolve the bug or rolling up our sleeves and doing it the old-fashioned way. Depending on the issue, ChatGPT may be able to resolve the issue quickly or you may get stuck in a bug loop.

ChatGPT bug loops can be exhausting to iterate over and as we have seen before more iterations are typically not better. For this example, we are going to resolve the issue by just debugging the code.

Before launching the code in debug mode, set a breakpoint as shown in *Figure 2.6*. Then launch the code in debug mode and at the command type **'move north'**.

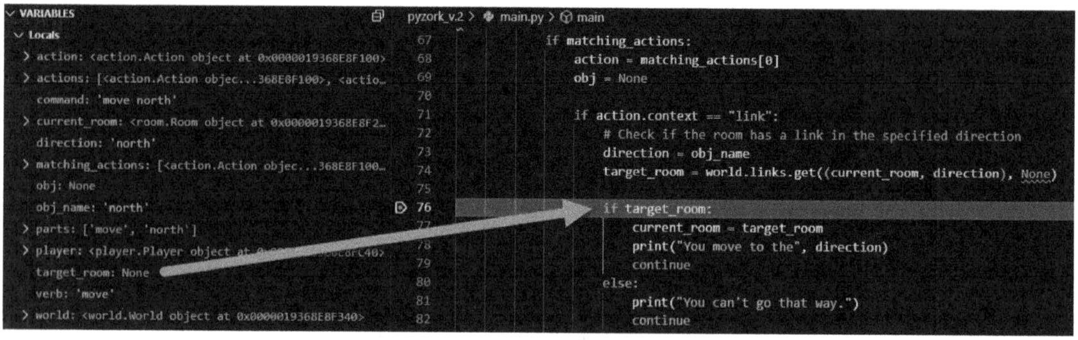

Figure 2.6: Debugging the parsing code

We can see from the variables that the **target_room** is getting returned as **None** when we call **world.links.get** on the previous line. This means the search for the tuple (**current_room, direction**) is not returning anything, when it should.

Let us go back and check the world module code that adds the links:

1. def add_link(self, source_room, target_room, direction):
2.   self.links[(source_room, target_room)] = direction
3.   self.links[(target_room, source_room)] = opposite_direction(direction)

Did you catch the error? The bug is that when we add the link to the links collection, we are adding them as a tuple in the form (**source_room, target_room**). However, recall that the get search is looking for the tuple in the form of (**source_room, direction**).

We can easily fix this by updating the **add_link** function to the following:

1. def add_link(self, source_room, target_room, direction):
2.   self.links[(source_room, direction)] = target_room
3.   self.links[(target_room, opposite_direction(direction))] = source_room

The fix here is simply making sure that we include the **direction** in the tuple and return the **target_room**. After you update the code, go ahead and run it again, as shown in *Figure 2.7*. Use the move action to move around the various rooms and see if you can move around to all the rooms:

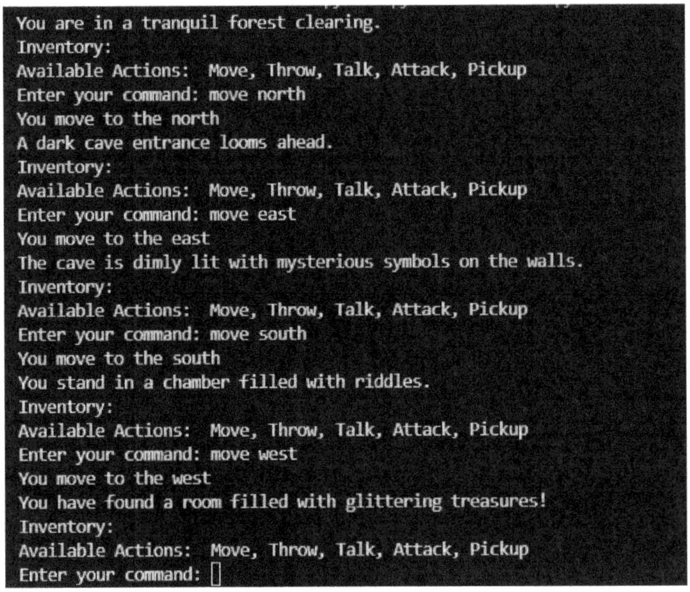

```
You are in a tranquil forest clearing.
Inventory:
Available Actions:  Move, Throw, Talk, Attack, Pickup
Enter your command: move north
You move to the north
A dark cave entrance looms ahead.
Inventory:
Available Actions:  Move, Throw, Talk, Attack, Pickup
Enter your command: move east
You move to the east
The cave is dimly lit with mysterious symbols on the walls.
Inventory:
Available Actions:  Move, Throw, Talk, Attack, Pickup
Enter your command: move south
You move to the south
You stand in a chamber filled with riddles.
Inventory:
Available Actions:  Move, Throw, Talk, Attack, Pickup
Enter your command: move west
You move to the west
You have found a room filled with glittering treasures!
Inventory:
Available Actions:  Move, Throw, Talk, Attack, Pickup
Enter your command:
```

Figure 2.7: Moving around the game world

Our text-based game now allows the player to move around the world from room to room. In our final section of this chapter, we are going to add some of the NPCs that may populate the world as well as the various items that may help or challenge the player.

Unleashing unexpected game challenges: Items and NPCs

The next step in developing our game will be adding elements to both challenge and help the player. Non-player characters are one such element that can provide both assistance and despair. Items, the things players can interact with, are another such element. Not only can both elements provide a challenge, but they can also add richness and depth to the game world.

Modern game worlds can be populated by thousands of unique items and NPCs. For our simple game, we are going to add just a couple of NPCs, one helpful and one to challenge. In the next exercise, we are going to start by adding a helpful Gandalf-like wizard for the players to interact with.

Exercise 2.5: Adding the wizard

Open the last checkpoint link to continue where we left off from the last exercise: **https://chat.openai.com/share/5d89a7bc-1218-4c36-a395-2348d3e28a67**

Enter the following prompt:

Okay I now want to add a friendly wizard the player can talk to and get advice/suggestions.

Put the wizard in one of the rooms and add the code to chat. Please use the following context in order to update the code:

```
if matching_actions:
    action = matching_actions[0]
    obj = None
    if action.context == "link":
        # Check if the room has a link in the specified direction
        pass
    elif action.context == "inventory":
        # Check if the player has the object in inventory
        pass
    elif action.context == "npc":
```

ChatGPT checkpoint: https://chat.openai.com/share/56a6ae3b-6d1d-4f8a-a710-65be9d50c9a8

Before adding new code, clone your existing game folder, **pyzork_v.3**, to a new folder called **pyzork_v.4**. If you prefer to start fresh, use the **pyzork_v.3** folder from the book's source code.

The response from the ChatGPT checkpoint is concise and provides the code modifications for adding in the wizard NPC. We will go through this response and make the required code changes, step by step.

We will start by adding a couple of new lines of code to the **create_world** function in the **main.py** file:

```
1. def create_world():
2.     world = World()
3.
4.     # ... (previous code)
5.
6.     # Create NPCs
7.     wizard = NPC("Wizard", "A wise and friendly wizard greets you.")
8.
9.     # Add NPCs to rooms
10.    room3.add_npc(wizard)   # Add the wizard to the cave interior
```

```
11.
12.         return world
```

The code to add the wizard is quite simple but ChatGPT omits adding the required import at the top of the file for the NPC class. Go ahead and do this by adding a line to the top of the **main.py** file – **from npc import NPC**.

Next, we will add to the parser the ability to talk to an NPC. ChatGPT creates the code for us we just need to inject it in the proper place. Add the code to the **action.context == "npc"**, if statement as shown in the listing as follows:

```
1.  # Game Loop
2.  while True:
3.      # ... (previous code)
4.
5.      if action.context == "npc":
6.          # Check if the NPC is in the same room
7.          npc = next((npc for npc in current_room.npcs if obj_name == npc.name.lower()), None)
8.
9.          if npc:
10.             if action.name == "Talk":
11.                 npc.talk(player)  # Call talk method of the NPC
12.             else:
13.                 print("You can't do that with the", npc.name)
14.         else:
15.             print("NPC not found.")
16.
17.     # ... (rest of the code)
```

Now, we need to modify the talk function of the **NPC** class as shown in the listing below:

```
1.  class NPC:
2.      def __init__(self, name, description):
3.          self.name = name
4.          self.description = description
5.
6.      def talk(self, player):
7.          if self.name == "Wizard":
```

```
8.          print("Wizard:", "Greetings, young adventurer! I
   can offer you advice on your journey.")
9.          print("Wizard:", "If you're stuck, try asking for
   hints or suggestions.")
10.        else:
11.            print(f"{self.name}:", "There's nothing much I have
   to say right now.")
```

Let us run the game and see what talking to the wizard looks like. We will assume we are using the ChatGPT checkpoints and expect the wizard to be in room 3. The easiest way to get there is to go north and then east.

If you run the game and move into the correct room, you will not see the wizard, but you can talk to him. Unfortunately, ChatGPT has again given us the 90% solution and missed an important detail, of seeing where the wizard is.

Fortunately, the fix, assuming you are comfortable with Python, is simple and only requires a single line of code. Just inside the game loop, add the new line of code shown at *line 5* in the following code listing:

```
1.  # Game Loop
2.  while True:
3.      # Display current room description, inventory, and
        available actions.
4.      print(current_room.description)
5.      print("NPCs: ", ", ".join([npc.description for npc in
        current_room.npcs]))
6.      print("Inventory: ", ", ".join([item.name for item in
        player.inventory]))
7.      print("Available Actions: ", ", ".join([action.name for
        action in actions]))
```

Go ahead and run the game again. Move to room 3, see the wizard, and talk to him as shown in *Figure 2.8*:

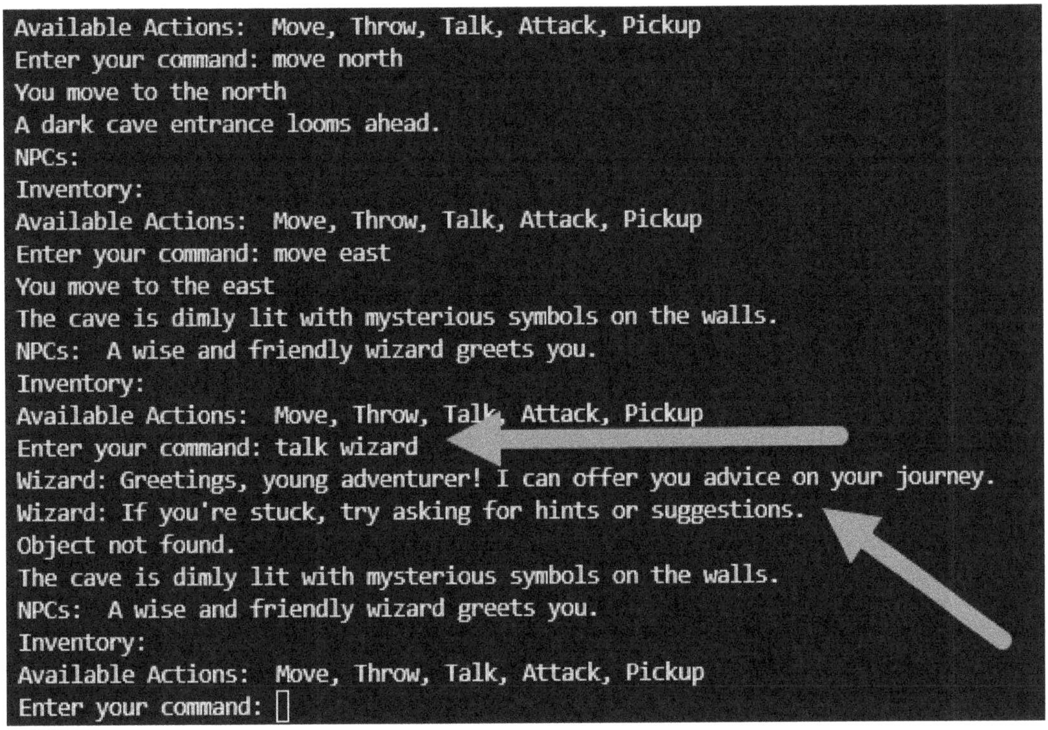

```
Available Actions:  Move, Throw, Talk, Attack, Pickup
Enter your command: move north
You move to the north
A dark cave entrance looms ahead.
NPCs:
Inventory:
Available Actions:  Move, Throw, Talk, Attack, Pickup
Enter your command: move east
You move to the east
The cave is dimly lit with mysterious symbols on the walls.
NPCs:  A wise and friendly wizard greets you.
Inventory:
Available Actions:  Move, Throw, Talk, Attack, Pickup
Enter your command: talk wizard
Wizard: Greetings, young adventurer! I can offer you advice on your journey.
Wizard: If you're stuck, try asking for hints or suggestions.
Object not found.
The cave is dimly lit with mysterious symbols on the walls.
NPCs:  A wise and friendly wizard greets you.
Inventory:
Available Actions:  Move, Throw, Talk, Attack, Pickup
Enter your command:
```

Figure 2.8: *Talking to the wizard*

You will notice that the wizard NPC provides hints and suggestions for further points of conversation. At this point, asking the wizard for hints or suggestions could be implemented in numerous different ways. We could extend the action parser or add a dialog system, both of which would require significant work, albeit not difficult work.

Another solution to adding conversational capabilities to an NPC is using **large language models** (**LLMs**) like ChatGPT. LLMs are an option which will help to improve our NPC interactions and the way the player interacts with the game. We will explore this in the next chapter.

For now, though, let us look to add our final element to the game, items. We would not employ a lot of functionality to the items, for now, other than to allow the player to pick up and drop items from their inventory in the next exercise:

Exercise 2.6: Adding items and inventory

Open the last checkpoint link to continue where we left off from the last exercise: checkpoint: **https://chat.openai.com/share/56a6ae3b-6d1d-4f8a-a710-65be9d50c9a8**

Enter the following prompt:

`Next, we want to add the ability for the player to pickup and drop or throw items.`

```
Please add the functionality to allow for the player to pickup and throw an
axe.
Be sure to also modify the parser action context code:
if len(parts) >= 2:
          verb = parts[0].lower()
          obj_name = " ".join(parts[1:]).lower()
```

Note: Additional code was removed for brevity, please refer to the chapter's GitHub repository for the full prompt.

ChatGPT checkpoint: https://chat.openai.com/share/21bfb160-c03c-42a5-8bcd-21054e6460cd

As always, the results you get from ChatGPT will likely differ, so go ahead and open the last ChatGPT checkpoint in your browser to follow along with the code changes.

We will again go step by step and implement the changes ChatGPT suggests, starting with updating the **create_world** function to add a new item:

```
1.  def create_world():
2.      world = World()
3.
4.      # ... (previous code)
5.
6.      # Create items
7.      axe = Item("Axe", "A sharp and sturdy axe for chopping wood.")
8.
9.      # Add items to rooms
10.     room1.add_item(axe)   # Add the axe to the forest clearing
11.
12.     return world
```

The code is very similar to how we added the wizard NPC to the game world. Also, just like before, be sure to add the import statement for the Item at the top of the file. (**from item import Item**).

Next, you will notice that ChatGPT suggests updating the action creation to a new function along with some other minor updates. Go ahead and delete the old actions creation and add a new function called after/before the **create_world** function:

```
1.  def create_actions():
2.      actions = [
```

```
3.        Action("Move", "Move to another room", ["move"],
   context="link"),
4.        Action("Throw", "Throw an object", ["throw"],
   context="inventory"),
5.        Action("Talk", "Talk to an NPC", ["talk"],
   context="npc"),
6.        Action("Attack", "Attack an NPC", ["attack"],
   context="npc"),
7.        Action("Pickup", "Pick up an item", ["pickup"],
   context="room")
8.    ]
9.    return actions
```

Then add the new **create_actions** function to the main game initialization code:

```
1. def main():
2.    # Initialize the game world, create rooms, items, NPCs, and
   Links.
3.
4.    player = Player()
5.    world = create_world()
6.
7.    actions = create_actions()
```

Next, we will move on to update the action/context parsing code as suggested by ChatGPT:

```
1. # Game Loop
2.    while True:
3.        # ... (previous code)
4.
5.        if action.context == "inventory":
6.            # Check if the player has the object in inventory
7.            item = next((item for item in player.inventory if
   obj_name == item.name.lower()), None)
8.
9.            if item:
10.               if action.name == "Throw":
11.                   item.use(player)  # Call the use method of
   the item
```

```
12.              else:
13.                  print(f"You can't do that with the {item.name}.")
14.          else:
15.              print("Item not found.")
16.
17.      elif action.context == "room":
18.          # Check if the object is in the same room
19.          item = next((item for item in current_room.items if obj_name == item.name.lower()), None)
20.
21.          if item:
22.              if action.name == "Pickup":
23.                  player.add_item(item)  # Add the item to player's inventory
24.                  current_room.remove_item(item)   # Remove the item from the room
25.                  print(f"You picked up the {item.name}.")
26.              else:
27.                  print("You can't do that with the", item.name)
28.          else:
29.              print("Item not found.")
30.
31.      # ... (rest of the code)
```

Go ahead and run the code. The first thing you will notice is we cannot see the items. Therefore, we need to add the code to visualize the items in a room.

```
1. # Display current room description, inventory, and available actions.
2. print(current_room.description)
3. print("Items: ", ", ".join([item.name for item in current_room.items]))
4. print("NPCs: ", ", ".join([npc.description for npc in current_room.npcs]))
5. print("Inventory: ", ", ".join([item.name for item in player.inventory]))
```

```
6.  print("Available Actions: ", ", ".join([action.name for action
    in actions]))
```

Simple enough, add the code and run the game again. Pick up the axe and then throw it. Refer to *Figure 2.9*:

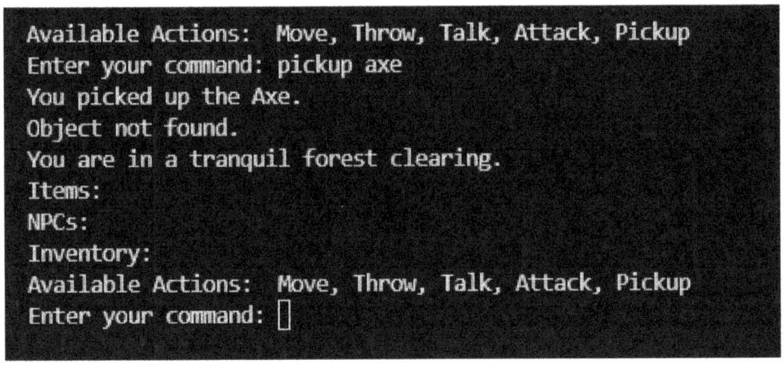

```
Available Actions: Move, Throw, Talk, Attack, Pickup
Enter your command: pickup axe
You picked up the Axe.
Object not found.
You are in a tranquil forest clearing.
Items:
NPCs:
Inventory:
Available Actions: Move, Throw, Talk, Attack, Pickup
Enter your command: []
```

Figure 2.9: *Picking up the axe*

Unfortunately, ChatGPT forgot to add some critical code again, that is, the code to update the player's inventory. Fortunately, adding that can be as simple as asking ChatGPT or doing it ourselves. Since we want to be better game developers, let us add the code manually by just updating the **Player** class:

```
1.  class Player:
2.      def __init__(self):
3.          self.inventory = []
4.
5.      def add_item(self, item):
6.          # Add an item to the player's inventory.
7.          self.inventory.append(item)
8.
9.      def remove_item(self, item):
10.         self.inventory.remove(item)
```

We just add (append) or remove the item from the inventory list. However, look back to the parsing code when the player uses the throw action. You will notice that the code does not drop the axe but instead uses it. This is not the behavior we want, for now anyway, so let us update the code.

We will modify the throw action parser to drop the item instead of using the item, as it does now. The player will now be able to pick up items and throw them to add and conversely remove it from inventory.

```
1.  if action.context == "inventory":
2.      # Check if the player has the object in inventory
```

```
3.      item = next((item for item in player.inventory if obj_name
    == item.name.lower()), None)
4.
5.      if item:
6.          if action.name == "Throw":
7.              # item.use(player)  # remove line
8.              player.remove_item(item)
9.              current_room.add_item(item)
10.         else:
11.             print(f"You can't do that with the {item.name}.")
12.     else:
13.         print("Item not found.")
```

Throw may not be the best term to use for removing an item from the inventory, so let us also extend the verbs a player can use to drop an item from the inventory.

Go to the **create_actions** function and modify the Throw action to add new verbs like the listing below shows:

```
1.  def create_actions():
2.      actions = [
3.          Action("Move",
4.              "Move to another room",
5.              ["move"],
6.              context="link"),
7.          Action("Throw",
8.              "Remove an object from inventory",
9.              ["throw", "drop", "remove", "place"]
10.             context="inventory"),
```

Now, we may also want to rename the action from **Throw** to perhaps **Drop** to make it more explainable, but we will leave that for a later exercise. See if you can see other areas where this code may need improvement.

Finally, for the last exercise of the chapter, we are going to look at adding the Troll NPC into the game as our primary player nemesis, at least to start.

Exercise 2.7: Adding the troll

At this stage, we have a significant chat history, and as we discussed before, this may make generating good content from ChatGPT problematic. However, if we provide the right

Text Adventure: Entering the Enchanted Realm 53

context (code) to ChatGPT, we can overcome some of these issues. Therefore, for this last exercise, we are going to employ EasyCode to provide that context.

Open up VS Code and clone the **pytorch_v.4** folder to a new folder called **pytorch_v.5**. Then open the **EasyCode** extension and refresh the codebase index with the contents of the new folder, as shown in *Figure 2.10*:

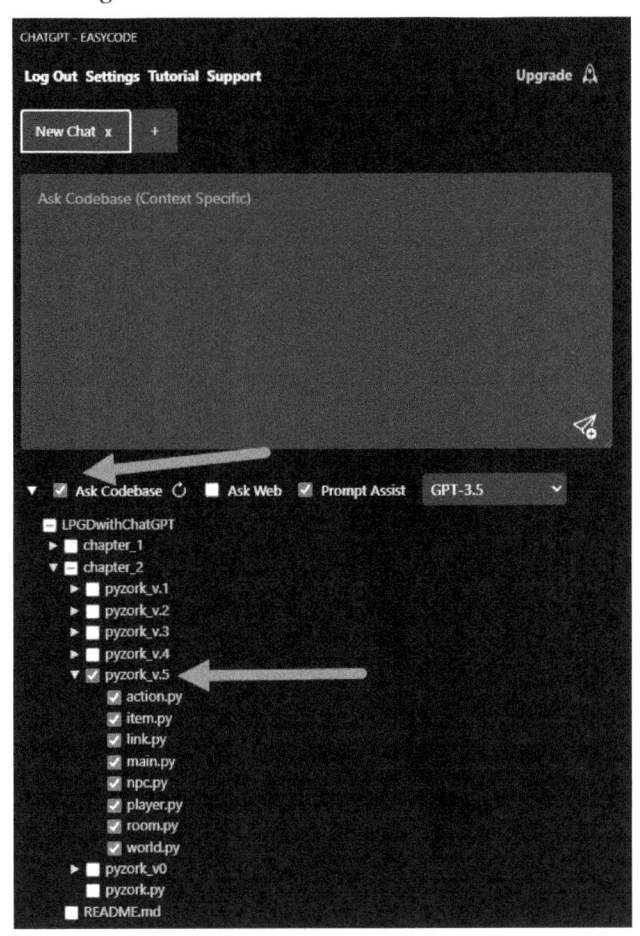

Figure 2.10: *Reseting the codebase index*

Enter the following prompt into the EasyCode chat area:

```
Add a troll NPC to the game into a new ROOM that describes a bridge.
The bridge room should connect to 2 ROOMs in the existing WORLD.
The troll NPC will block the player from moving across the bridge until it is given the axe.
```

EasyCode (ChatGPT) will respond with several suggested changes, as shown in *Figure 2.11*. It will also provide a play button, allowing you to automatically make those changes. Unfortunately, this option is only available for paid subscribers.

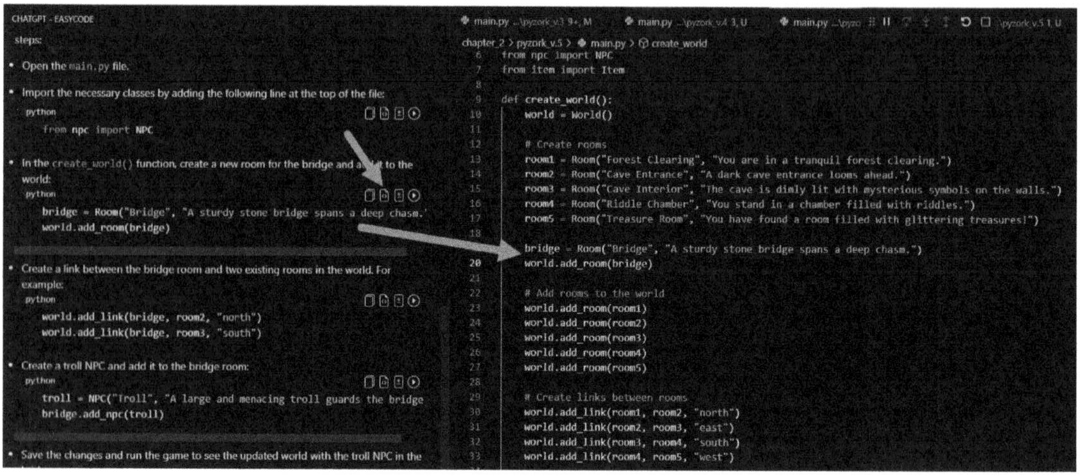

Figure 2.11: Adding the code changes

You can still use EasyCode to make the code changes, you just have to find the area of code you want to make the change, place your cursor, and use the insert code button, as shown in *Figure 2.11*.

Go ahead and place the cursor in the **create_world** function and then insert the code to add the links and troll NPC to the game world. The completed code looks like the following:

1. `# Create links between rooms`
2. `world.add_link(room1, room2, "north")`
3. `world.add_link(room2, room3, "east")`
4. `world.add_link(room3, room4, "south")`
5. `world.add_link(room4, room5, "west")`
6. `world.add_link(bridge, room2, "north")`
7. `world.add_link(bridge, room3, "south")`
8.
9. `    # Create NPCs`
10. `wizard = NPC("Wizard", "A wise and friendly wizard greets you.")`
11. `troll = NPC("Troll", "A large and menacing troll guards the bridge.")`
12.
13. `# Add NPCs to rooms`
14. `room3.add_npc(wizard)   # Add the wizard to the cave interior`
15. `bridge.add_npc(troll)`

Look over the code, did you notice anything problematic? It is hard to spot but we now have duplicated links to a couple of rooms. See if you can think about how to resolve the problem.

You will also notice that EasyCode (ChatGPT) did not even attempt to provide the other functionality with the troll NPC. If you recall, we wanted the troll to block the bridge until the player gave it the axe.

Go ahead and run this version of the game, as mentioned, you will still encounter a few bugs but overall, we have the start of a working and extensible game. We will look to improve on this game in the next chapter.

Conclusion

In this chapter, we constructed the foundations of a classic text-based adventure game with the help of ChatGPT. We learned that games, regardless of their genre or platform, share common elements like the *game loop*, *input*, and *game world*. Modular development of these elements simplifies future enhancements and extensions. The game loop is crucial, acting as the primary control and feedback mechanism for player interaction. Planning a game's development, possibly by asking ChatGPT to draft a basic game example, is beneficial for identifying key components and potential areas for improvement. While ChatGPT excels at coding, its adherence to consistent coding styles may vary, making it advisable to provide specific code examples for enhancement or troubleshooting.

For the next chapter, we will continue working with the text-based *PyZork* game but look to enhance using various AI tools. From employing LLMs for command parsing to using AI generators to provide visual backdrops to the game.

What we learned

- All games regardless of genre and platform have some common elements, such as the *game loop*, *game input*, and the *game world* or *playing area*.

- Decomposing game elements into modules will make the job of enhancing and extending a game much easier in the future. Asking ChatGPT to think in terms of modular development will help in how it generates code.

- Game input is managed through a game loop. The game loop is core to any game and provides the main control mechanism the player uses to interact with a game. As well it is also the primary point of feedback back to the player.

- It is often helpful to do some planning before developing a game. A good option for planning is to ask ChatGPT to write a basic example of a game. This can often help identify the main elements your game requires as well as identify key areas you may want to extend or enhance.

- ChatGPT is excellent at writing code, but it may not always follow or keep consistent coding styles, even within the same conversation. Therefore, it is often best to provide ChatGPT with examples of code you want to be enhanced, extended, or fixed.

Exercises

To help you continue your learning on this material, please challenge yourself to a couple of exercises. As we progress through the book, the content and exercises will get progressively harder.

1. Make a map of your game world with the rooms and room connections (links) you want to populate. Then, update the code in the **create_world** function to add the rooms and room links.

2. Add some more NPCs to the game. Provide them with a description, perhaps a backstory, and plan how they will interact with the player. Update the game code to add in your new NPCs to the rooms they inhabit.

3. Update the current set of actions by adding new verbs to each action. This will give the player some flexibility on what commands they can perform. As before, update the code that creates the action with your added list of verbs for each action.

4. In the classic *Zork* game, players could type **n**, **w**, **s**, or **e** to move in that direction. How could we support this form of using a single character for movement in the game?

5. Add more items to the game. Think of five or more items you can add to the game, their description and what they do. You could even use ChatGPT to help you describe the new items. As always, then update the game code to add the new items to the various rooms on the map.

6. [BONUS] *Zork* spawned numerous text-based adventure games in all genres and styles. From the *Leisure Suit Larry* series to more wholesome adventure titles, numerous different genres were explored. For this exercise, think about a genre you may like to create an adventure game for. You can ask ChatGPT for help.

CHAPTER 3
The AI Chronicles: Text Game Evolution

Introduction

Text-based games evolved into the adventure, role-playing, and survival games we play today. In the later 1980s, before the internet, **multiple user dungeons** (**MUDs**) and **multiple shared hallucinations** (**MUSHes**) were played via **bulletin board systems** (**BBS**). These games continued to be popular after the foundation of **massively multiplayer online role playing games** (**MMORPGs**) and other **massively multiplayer online** (**MMO**) games because they provided the player with a richer experience.

MUDs and MUSHes were so popular because they allowed the user to alter the game environment. Today, this in-game transformation ability is called **crafting**. But MUDs and MUSHes went a step further in allowing the game itself to be changed from within the game itself. While some games today provide for in-game modifications, most can only be modified with the right tools and experience.

Structure

This chapter explores the following topics:
- Unleashing PyZork with Streamlit
- Picturing the story using stable diffusion

- Crafting the story with the command interface
- Remembering the world, adding a game database with SQLite
- Completing the MUSH

Objectives

In this chapter, we will entirely transform PyZork into an extensible platform that can be added to and enhanced while playing. Further, we will create a new interface using Streamlit and add to it the ability to display visual cues (images) using generative AI models like *Stable Diffusion SDXL* from ComfyUI.

Unleashing PyZork with Streamlit

We will start the chapter by upgrading the console version of PyZork to a web interface using *Streamlit*. Streamlit is a lightweight framework that allows you to build web applications using just Python. While it is designed for more forms-based sites and is not well suited to making games, it will fit our purposes for PyZork.

Unlike previous chapters, this chapter begins by focusing more on the code than the process of using *ChatGPT*. While ChatGPT is a great companion, its current knowledge is limited to 2021. This means it will have limited knowledge of new emerging frameworks like Streamlit and GPT4All, resulting in it making stuff up and/or hallucinating.

Exercise 3.1: Creating a Streamlit interface

1. Open the book's source code folder **chapter_3** in VS Code and then the file **streamlit.py**.

    Prompt used: `Create a basic Streamlit app allowing a user to upload and display images.`

The source code for the file is shown below:

```
1. import streamlit as st
2. from PIL import Image
3.
4. # Title of the app
5. st.title("Image Upload Example")
6.
7. # Upload image through streamlit
8. uploaded_image = st.file_uploader("Choose an image"…",
   typ"=[""pg", "j"eg", ""ng"])
```

```
9.
10.    # Display the uploaded image
11.    if uploaded_image is not None:
12.        image = Image.open(uploaded_image)
13.        st.image(image, capti"n="Uploaded Im"ge", use_column_
       width=True)
14.        st.wri"e("Image successfully uploaded and displayed
       abo"e.")
```

This code creates the entire app. After the imports, we use the **st.title** to set the page title. Next, we add a file uploader with **st.file_uploader** which returns the uploaded file. After checking a file has been uploaded with the **if** statement, we display the image using **st.image**.

To run this code, be sure you have a Python virtual environment setup and then open a terminal window from VS Code, *Ctrl+,* or *Cmd+*.

1. Install the Streamlit package using the command:

   1. `pip install streamlit`

2. Next, run the Streamlit app using the module from the command line by entering:

   1. `streamlit run streamlit.py`

3. This will start a web server and show the hosted URL as given in *Figure 3.1*:

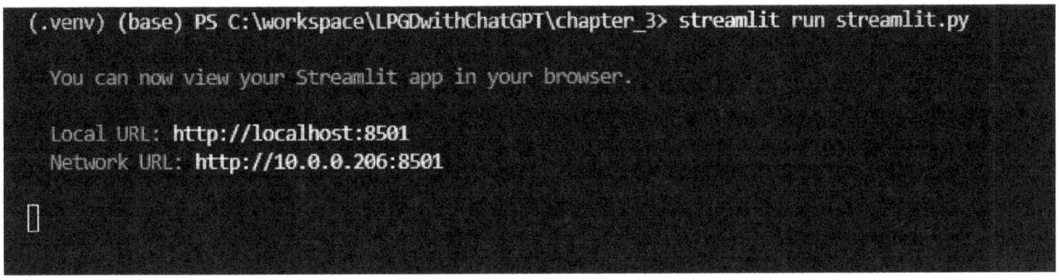

Figure 3.1: Terminal window showing web app starting

4. Your default browser will open to the hosted URL **localhost:8501**, the default for Streamlit. *Figure 3.2* shows the app running after an image has been uploaded and displayed in the app. Go ahead and upload your images.

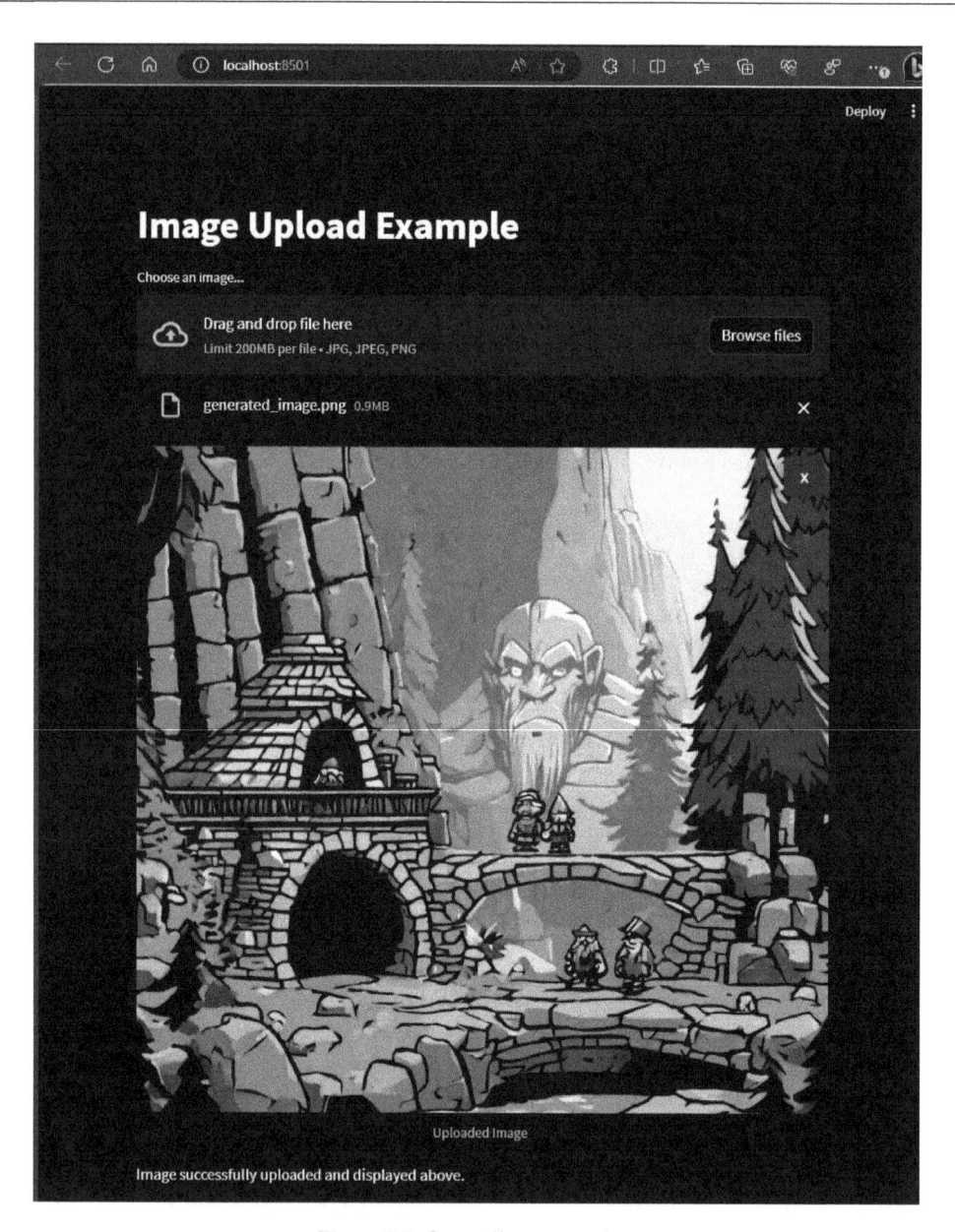

Figure 3.2: Streamlit app running

Note: All background images were generated using Stable Diffusion SDXL and ComfyUI.

Review the code again and notice how the `st.image` is not called until the `uploaded_image` variable is not `None`. When an image is uploaded the entire page reruns again. This time, the value of `uploaded_image` is not `None`, and the image is loaded and displayed. It might take time to adapt to this behavior, especially if you have used other frameworks.

Streamlit is an excellent platform for creating simple applications quickly. It is heavily used in the AI and ML communities to demonstrate model performance. Look at the functionality that is contained in the simple example application. In other frameworks/languages, the same code could take dozens of lines to reproduce the same functionality.

There are a few pointers with Streamlit which are important to be aware of, and we will make note of them here:

- **Reruns**: Every action in Streamlit, a button click, for example, causes the entire file to be re-run. As a result, this requires a different approach from the way typical web UIs are developed.
- **Caching**: Streamlit has effective caching strategies to overcome the rerun problems. Caching can also be used to hold the state of any object, including games.
- **Fixed layout**: The layout in a Streamlit app is fixed to a main panel and sidebar with the option to layout columns. Customizing layouts and other components are available, but if you need a specific look, this app framework may not be for you.
- **Customization**: While it is possible to add custom HTML and JavaScript to an app, it can be problematic. There are several community components available, but your mileage may vary based on your needs.

Now that we have covered some basics of Streamlit, let us look at upgrading PyZork to use a web interface in the next exercise.

Exercise 3.2: Creating a chat web interface

Open the book's source code folder **chapter_3** in VS Code, and then the file **pyzork_streamlit.py**.

Prompt used: `Write a Streamlit chat app with the following specifications:`
`1) The chat history is displayed in the sidebar.`
`2) The user message prompt is on the main page with a button displayed next to the text input. The button should have the label Send. Use a Streamlit form so that if the user types enter, the form is submitted.`
`3) Allow for an image to be displayed at the top of the main page`

Getting the code right, given the above specifications, took several iterations and regenerations with ChatGPT. We will not go through those iterations here other than to say not all code ChatGPT produces may work the first time as we have seen. Sometimes, it takes patience to regenerate code until you get something that does what you want. And, in the end, you will likely need to manually tweak the code to get it perfect.

Before we look at the code, let us go ahead and run the app. Be sure to stop any other Streamlit apps from running and run the app from the terminal using:

```
1. streamlit run pytorch_streamlit.py
```

Figure 3.3 shows the app running after the user has entered a few messages. Notice how we have the image already set and a place to enter a message. Enter a few messages and click **Send** or hit *Enter* and you will see the message added to the **Chat History** sidebar. We will want to tweak this interface later but for now, it is a good start. Please refer to the following figure:

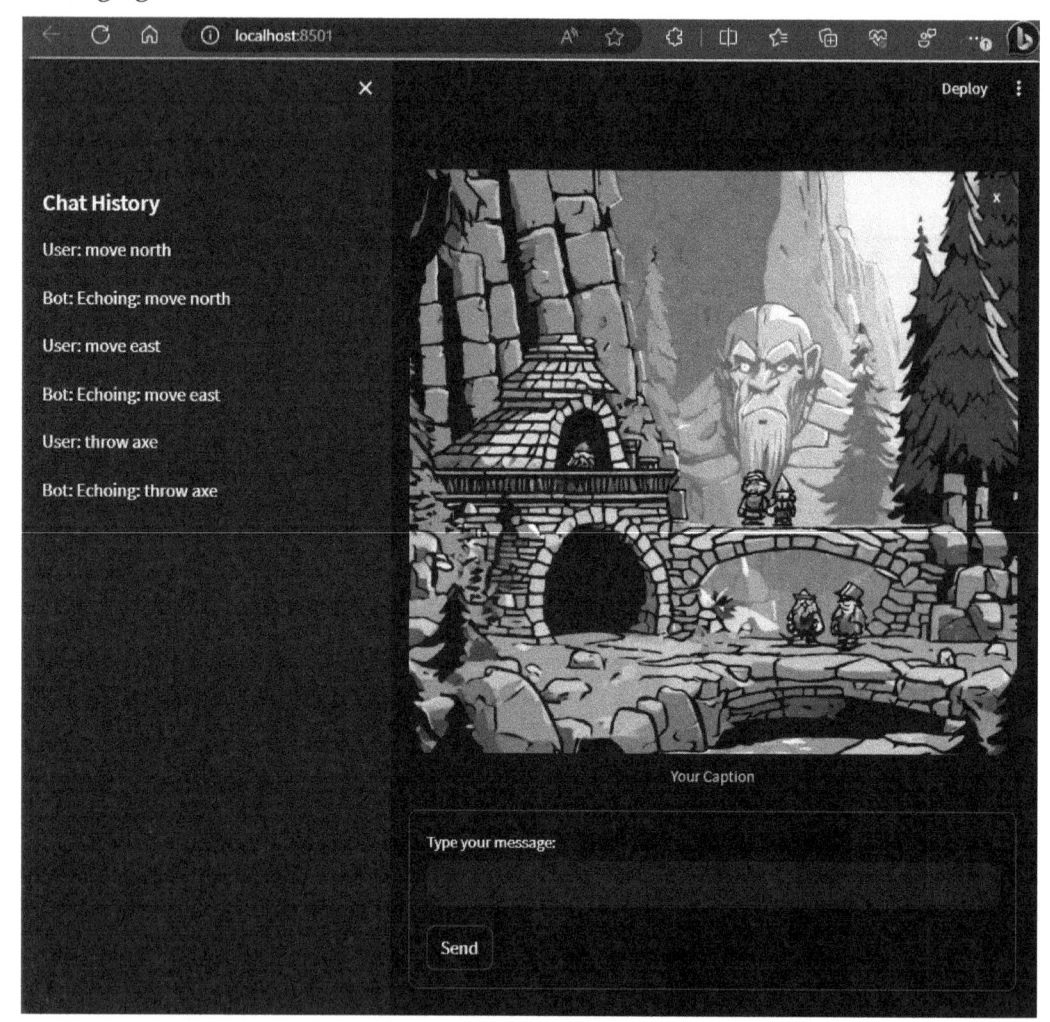

Figure 3.3: The chat interface Streamlit app

The full code listing for the app is shown below:

```
1. import streamlit as st
2. 
3. # Function to manage chat history
4. def manage_chat_history(state, user_input):
```

```python
5.      state.chat_history.append({"user": user_input})
6.      bot_reply = f"Echoing: {user_input}"
7.      state.chat_history.append({"bot": bot_reply})
8.
9.  # Initialize state
10. if 'chat_history' not in st.session_state:
11.     st.session_state.chat_history = []
12.
13. # Initialize a "version" counter
14. if 'input_version' not in st.session_state:
15.     st.session_state.input_version = 0
16.
17. # Display an image at the top of the main page
18. st.image("generated_image.png", caption="Your Caption",
19.         use_column_width=True)
20.
21. # User message prompt in the main page
22. with st.form(key='chat_form'):
23.     user_input = st.text_input("Type your message:",
24.                         key=f'input_key_{st.session_state.input_version}')
25.     send_button = st.form_submit_button(label='Send')
26.
27.     if send_button and user_input:
28.         manage_chat_history(st.session_state, user_input)
29.
30.         # Increment the version counter to trigger a rerender of the text input
31.         st.session_state.input_version += 1
32.         st.experimental_rerun()
33.
34. # Display chat history in sidebar
35. st.sidebar.header("Chat History")
36. for chat in st.session_state.chat_history:
```

```
37.        for role, message in chat.items():
38.            st.sidebar.write(f"{role.capitalize()}: {message}")
```

This interface simply reads a message from the user and adds it to the chat history where an echo bot echoes the input. The user input and bot echoes are added to the list in the sidebar labeled **Chat History**.

Look through the code and try to understand at a high level what it is doing. To keep the message history and clear the form message window after sending, a few Streamlit state tricks are used. Do not worry too much about understanding the state transition code. Our main objective is just to get a clean web interface for *PyZork*.

With a clean new interface ready we can now move on to adding the game code developed in the last chapter. This will allow us to play PyZork from a web interface and perhaps even deploy it to friends.

Exercise 3.3: Upgrading PyZork to a web interface

Open the book's source code folder **chapter_3/pytorch_v.6** in VS Code and then the file **game.py**. This is an updated version of the PyZork game, if you want to refer to the previous version check the folder **pytorch_v.5**.

Prompt used: None, all code was manually edited.

The code in this file used to be in the **main.py** file and was responsible for creating the game world and running the game loop. The code in this file was refactored into some primary functions (**create_world** and **create_actions**) as well as introduced a new class to encapsulate our game logic. The **GameEngine** class is partially shown below:

```
1.  class GameEngine:
2.      def __init__(self) -> None:
3.          self.player = Player()
4.          self.world = create_world()
5.          self.actions = create_actions()
6.
7.          self.current_room = self.world.rooms["Forest Clearing"]
8.
9.      def observe(self):
10.         items = ", ".join([item.name for item in self.current_room.items])
11.         npcs = ", ".join([npc.description for npc in self.current_room.npcs])
12.         inventory = ", ".join([item.name for item in self.player.inventory])
```

```
13.         actions = ", ".join([action.name for action in self.
   actions])
14.         return dict(room=self.current_room.description,
15.                     items=items,
16.                     npcs=npcs,
17.                     inventory=inventory,
18.                     actions=actions,
19.                     )
20.
21.     def parse_command(self, command):
22.         # parse player input.
23.         parts = command.split()
24.
25.         #same parsing code as before
26.
```

The new **GameEngine** class encapsulates all the functionality we previously put into the **main.py** that was our previous game engine. When the class is initiated, a new player is created along with the world and available actions. Parsing commands is done in the **parse_command** function, which is the same code we developed previously to parse player actions.

With the game code refactored, we can move on to including it in the Streamlit interface. Open **pyzork.py**, which is the main game file now.

We only need to focus on a couple of updates as seen in the code below:

```
1.  import streamlit as st
2.  from game import GameEngine
3.
4.  #new function to load GameEngine as a cached resource
5.  @st.cache_resource       ←A
6.  def get_game_engine():
7.      return GameEngine()
8.
9.  # Function to manage chat history, extended with response
10. def manage_chat_history(state, user_input, response):     ←D
11.     state.chat_history.append({"Player": user_input})
```

```
12.        response = f"PyZork: {response}"
13.        state.chat_history.append({"bot": response})
14.
15. # ... code omitted (no changes)
16.
17. ge = get_game_engine()          ←B
18. st.write(ge.observe())
19.
20. # User message prompt in the main page
21. with st.form(key='chat_form'):
22.     user_input = st.text_input("Type your message:",
23.                                 key=f'input_key_
       {st.session_state.input_version}')
24.     send_button = st.form_submit_button(label='Send')
25.
26.     if send_button and user_input:
27.         response = ge.parse_command(user_input)    ←C
28.         manage_chat_history(st.session_state, user_input,
       response)
29.
30.  # ... remaining code (no changes)
31.
```

Highlighted in the code are the four primary changes and explained below:

a. We added a new function to load the **GameEngine** class as a cached resource. This means when the page is rerun after every input or update, the game engine maintains state. If we did not do this, the player would be continually restarting the game.

b. We created an instance of the **GameEngine** using the cached function. We will then use the cached instance as needed through the code.

c. We called the game engine **parse** function to parse player input and send the log of the response to the command history sidebar using the **manage_chat_history** function.

d. We updated the **manage_chat_history** function to also include the parsed response and output of the player action.

Go ahead and run the updated game by opening a terminal window into the **pyzork_v.6** folder and running the **pyzork.py** file as shown below:

1. `cd chapter_3/pyzork_v.6`
2. `streamlit run pyzork.py`

This will start the web server. Open a browser and run the game. Go ahead and try some commands, move around as you did before. *Figure 3.4* shows a sample of these interactions:

Figure 3.4: *PyZork running in Streamlit*

Now, we have the basic text-based game we developed in the last chapter completely running in a Streamlit web interface. You may have noticed that some parts of the UI are still rudimentary, and we will look to fix that later. Now that we can display images within the game interface, let us see how we can create our own images in the next section.

Picturing the story using stable diffusion

Text-based games evolved into displaying images as a way of further immersing players. While those images were very rudimentary, this opened the popularity of the genre, and many classics were borne. The artists that created the images in these games also became extremely popular and the whole industry around game art was also born.

Game art and game assets are critical elements of any game. The look and feel of a game can attract or detract users. If the art is done poorly, the game will typically suffer. However, constructing game art and assets in the past was not trivial and often required great expense, that is, until recently.

Now, AI can create amazing game art using various tools for cheap or, in some cases, free. The ability to economically create high-quality game art will surely change the game industry. New and independent game developers are most likely to benefit from using these tools.

In this section, we are going to explore the popular open-source and extraordinary image generation model *Stable Diffusion SDXL* using a UI tool called **ComfyUI**. The ability to generate custom images for our game using room descriptions will be a huge benefit. Furthermore, in the later chapters, we will use this tool to continue building other artistic assets.

The first exercise we will undertake is downloading the model and UI to perform image generation on your machine. This typically requires a more performant machine, and if this is not available several online tools are also an option. However, art generation can be a highly iterative process, and online tools can become expensive.

Exercise 3.4: Installing and setting up ComfyUI

ComfyUI can be downloaded for your operating system or run from *Google Colab* using the following link: **https://github.com/comfyanonymous/ComfyUI#installing**. Follow the instructions for your OS.

> **Tip: There are plenty of YouTube videos that demonstrate the installation of ComfyUI and model checkpoints, if you get stuck with these generic instructions.**

If you have a lower-end computer, you may want to use the *Google Colab* notebook. Google Colab is free and provides **graphic processing units** (**GPUs**) for machine learning use. While the free version of **Colab** can be useful, an upgraded license can provide better computing horsepower.

After the software is installed, open the folder where you placed it. On Windows, you will have the option to run the GPU or **computer processing unit** (**CPU**) versions. The GPU version is recommended but only supported for *Nvidia* graphics cards with 8 GB RAM.

Figure 3.5 shows the Windows batch files that will start the ComfyUI server. Double-click on the file that best matches your machine or use one another option given the OS/configuration. Please refer to the following figure:

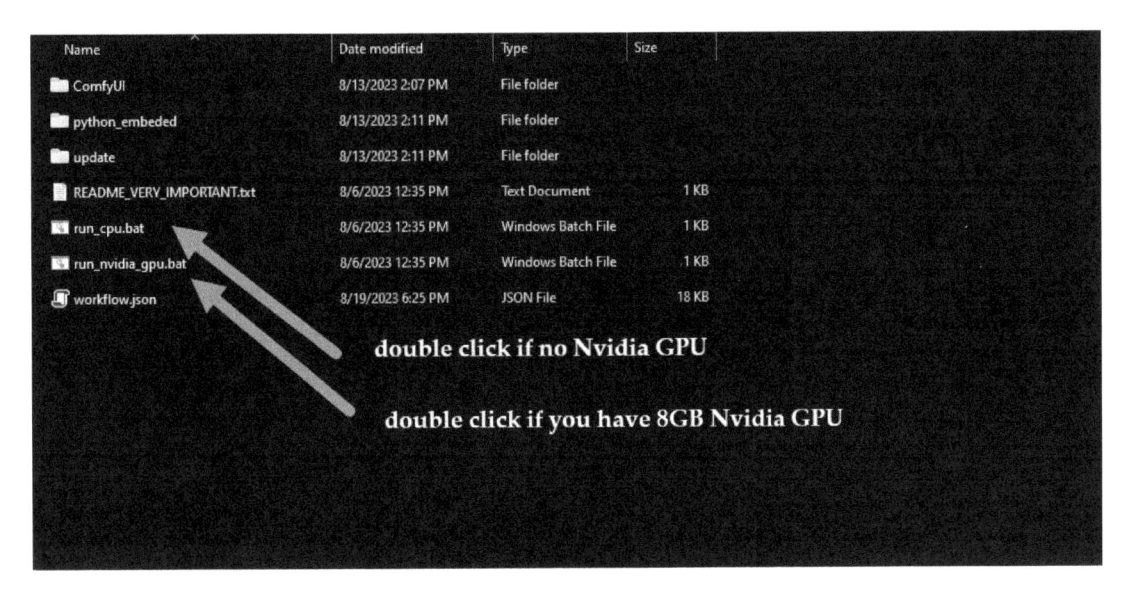

Figure 3.5: Starting ComfyUI on Windows

You will notice the ComfyUI server starts in a new terminal window, and after a few seconds, a new browser tab will open showing the default UI, as shown in *Figure 3.6*:

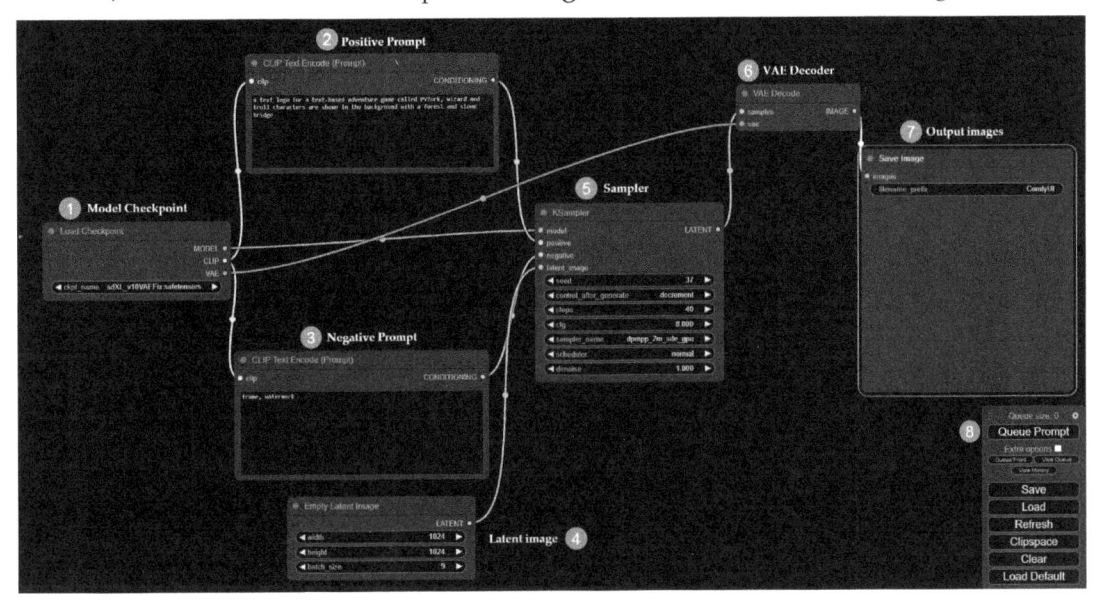

Figure 3.6: ComfyUI interface

The UI may be overwhelming at first but will start to make more sense as we go through each component in more detail given as follows:

- **Model checkpoint**: This is the saved model being used to generate the image. We will need to download and set a model to run the tool.

- **Positive prompt**: Think of this as ChatGPT but for images. This is where you describe what you want the image to look like. We will dig more into image prompting later.

- **Negative prompt**: Image generation will often include items you may not necessarily want. The negative prompt allows you to exclude content you want to avoid.

- **Latent image**: This is the starter image, and, in this case, it is just random noise. However, in many cases, you may want to modify an existing image, and this is where you can inject an existing image. This is an advanced workflow we will explore later.

- **Sampler**: The sampler is the component that brings the model, prompts and latent image together to generate a sampling. This sampling is later decoded into an image. This item is the workhorse of the process and the options you adjust here can significantly alter your results. Leave the defaults, for now.

- **VAE decoder**: This component takes the sample from the Sampler and decodes it into images.

- **Output images**: This is where the results are displayed depending on the number of images and aspect ratio you selected to generate your images.

- **Queue prompt**: Clicking this button will start the process. If a model has not been loaded, it will do so and then run through the steps as shown in the *Figure 3.6*.

    With the UI open, let us go through and make sure each component is configured correctly starting with the checkpoints.

- **Checkpoints**: Download a model checkpoint to the ComfyUI/models/checkpoints folder as shown in *Figure 3.7*:

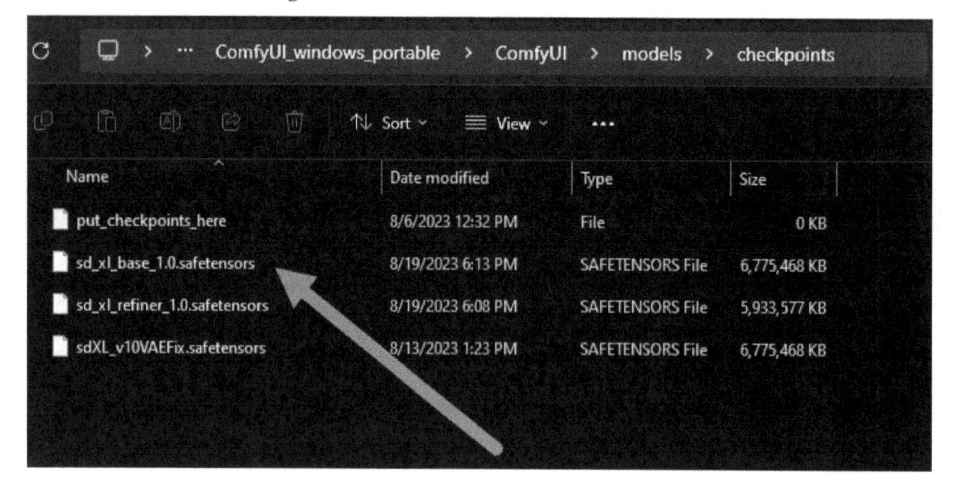

Figure 3.7: Installing the model checkpoints

o You can download the model checkpoints from **Hugging Face** at **https://huggingface.co/stabilityai/stable-diffusion-xl-base-1.0/tree/main.**

o If you want more recent model checkpoints either search *Hugging Face* or *Google*. These models improve substantially over time, so you likely want to grab the most recent checkpoint.

o After you install a new checkpoint, be sure to refresh the browser page and then select the model from the list, shown in *Figure 3.8*:

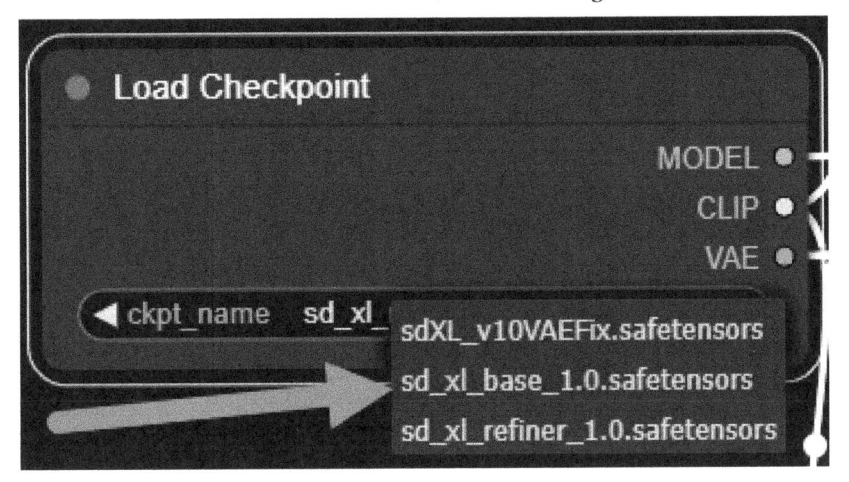

Figure 3.8: Loading the checkpoint

- **Positive prompt**: Keep this as the default or add your own.
- **Negative prompt**: Use the default or leave it blank.
- **Latent image**: Set the image size to *1024x1024* and the number of images you want to generate at a time. If you do not have a GPU, you may just want to stick with a single image.
- **Sampler**: Switch the sampler's name to **dpmpp_2m_sde_gpu** if you have a GPU or **dpmpp_2m_sde** for CPU. This sampler can significantly improve image quality.
- **VAE decoder**: Use the default.
- **Output images**: Keep the default name or update it to your own.
- **Queue prompt**: Click the button when you are done and watch the images get generated.

The results of a sample image generation are shown in *Figure 3.9*. As much as we tried to generate readable text, you can see this model and settings struggle. However, for most of our work, we will want to create images without text. Overall, though, the images look impressive but can certainly be improved upon.

Figure 3.9: Results of image generation

Before we jump into creating images for the game, let us revisit some of our previous descriptions and get some ChatGPT help to update them in the next exercise.

Exercise 3.5: Creating better room descriptions with ChatGPT

1. Open your browser to ChatGPT and enter the following prompt.

    Prompt: I am writing an adventure game and want to produce several room descriptions for a fantasy game.

    Here is a brief synopsis of the game: The player needs to get across a stone bridge guarded by a troll. A powerful wizard who lives in the forest holds the secret to defeating the troll. The player starts in a small village next to the forest and needs to find their way to the troll bridge and beyond.

    I want to create room descriptions for the following:

    - The village

- Entrance to the forest
- The forest path
- A fork in the road
- The wizards abode
- The troll bridge
- The tower beyond the bridge
- Please provide descriptions for each of the room that are detailed enough for an artist to recreate an image of.

Prompt checkpoint: https://chat.openai.com/share/74cb198f-1ce4-4aeb-bab8-4e82871ea1e4

2. After all the descriptions are generated, copy-paste the description into ComfyUI or another image generator to see the results.

   The results will likely be not so impressive. This is because AI image generators are trained on keywords and get confused when presented with full descriptions. Therefore, to get better images we need to convert our descriptions to prompts. Fortunately, ChatGPT can help us easily do that.

3. Enter the following continue prompt in the same conversation.

   Prompt: You are now an AI image prompt generator. Convert all the previous room descriptions into prompts that can be used to generate the image.

   Prompt checkpoint: https://chat.openai.com/share/74cb198f-1ce4-4aeb-bab8-4e82871ea1e4

   Below is an example of the description of the village, beside the converted prompt:

The Village (description)

A quaint little hamlet bathed in the golden light of a setting sun. Cobblestone streets weave through a smattering of wooden cottages with thatched roofs. Lush gardens brimming with vibrant flowers and neatly trimmed hedges line the front of each home. A modest inn with a swinging wooden sign reading *The Cozy Hearth* stands at the village center. Villagers are seen going about their business—children playing with wooden swords, women haggling over fruit prices, and an old blacksmith hammering away at his anvil. At the far end of the village square, a grand old oak tree serves as the communal gathering spot, its large branches shading the stone benches beneath it.

The village (this is the generated prompt):

- A quaint village during sunset with cobblestone streets and wooden cottages with thatched roofs.

- Lush gardens with vibrant flowers and neatly trimmed hedges in front of homes.
- An inn at the center with a swinging wooden sign reading "The Cozy Hearth."
- Villagers going about their business: children playing, women haggling, a blacksmith at an anvil.
- A large old oak tree with stone benches beneath it at the far end of the village square.

This will create better images but with the same style. Fortunately, AI image generators allow us to easily swap styles by just adding to the prompt. Previous image generators allowed for the mention of a particular artist to mimic their style. However, this has been seen as obvious copyright infringement, so the latest public models are trained in more generic styles.

Now, there are entire YouTube channels and content creators to document tips and tricks for style generation. As of writing, this link takes you to a page featuring 106 styles you can apply: **106 styles for Stable Diffusion XL model - Stable Diffusion Art (stable-diffusion-art.com)**

You can use any of those styles by copying the positive and negative style keywords to the positive and negative in *ComfyUI*. For example, if we were using the *3D Model* style the positive and negative keywords are listed as:

- **Positive**: Professional 3d model {prompt}. octane render, highly detailed, volumetric, dramatic lighting
- **Negative**: ugly, deformed, noisy, low poly, blurry, painting

For the positive portion, you need to place your prompt in between the **curly braces** {}. Then for the negative, just replace it with the keywords.

Figure 3.10 shows the results of generating the village prompt nine times, first with no style and then eight variations using the described style keywords in the above article:

Figure 3.10: Style comparison on village prompt

You can spend hours swapping styles and trying to find the best look, the possibilities can be endless. You can even mix and match style keywords to create your styles. Creating a look you like may take a few minutes or hours depending on your needs. This is why you will want to avoid paying for image generation by running these models yourself.

We will continue to use ComfyUI to generate all forms of art assets in the later games we create. Here are the ten rules, summarized by ChatGPT to remember when creating art assets for games:

- **Be specific**: Clearly define the details you want in the image, such as *objects*, *actions*, and *settings*.

- **Consider composition**: Specify the visual layout, like *angles* or *closeness*, to get the desired composition.

- **Factor in style**: Include the artistic style you want, such as *impressionism* or *pixel art*.

- **Keep it concise**: Use clear and short prompts to avoid confusing the AI model.

- **Include examples**: Use example images alongside text prompts, if the platform allows it, to guide the AI.

- **Test and iterate**: Make multiple attempts, tweaking the prompt to improve the generated image.

- **Account for ethics**: Avoid creating images that may be socially or ethically problematic.

- **Be cognizant of copyright**: Beware of generating images that could violate copyright laws.

- **Experiment and be creative**: Try abstract or unusual prompts for novel image outputs.

- **Understand the tool's limitations**: Familiarize yourself with the AI tool's constraints to tailor your prompts effectively.

Remember that the art assets you use for your game can set the whole tone of your game world. While being able to generate art quickly and cheaply is great, it still requires an artistic eye and a sense of style. Your game may not go over very well, if you use a *Cyberpunk* art style for your fantasy game.

However, the more detailed and professional your game assets look, the more likely your players will appreciate it and understand your vision. It is still the early days of AI-generated art assets being used in games, but this is a trend that will surely upend the industry.

Now that we have a way of generating images for *PyZork*, let us move to the next section and begin adding them to the game.

Crafting the story with the command interface

MUSHes and **MUDs** allowed players to extend the game by using the same text interface. We are going to implement the same feature in PyZork to not only allow players to extend the game later but also to help us build the base game. Today, many game developers often implement in-game modding tools to support their artists and designers. Perhaps, even later releasing those tools to the public.

For the exercise in this section, we are going to add the ability to add new objects to the game. Objects will consist of three types, **rooms**, **items**, and **NPCs**. We will start by adding the room type with our new images and descriptions. We will leave it up to you to implement adding the other objects to the game.

Exercise 3.6: Adding an admin interface to PyZork

1. Make a copy of **pyzork_v.6** to **pyzork_v.7** or refer to the folder in the book's source code.

2. Open your browser to ChatGPT and enter the following prompt:

   Prompt: I want to write a tool for a game written in Python that allows players to add new rooms, items and npcs to a game.

   Please write a Streamlit app that allows a player to add the following to a game:
   - Object type: choose from ROOM, ITEM, NPC
   - Object name: string
   - Object description: string
   - Object image: image file
   - Object special:
     o When an object is of type ROOM, allow the player to add exits to other rooms.
     o When an object is of type ITEM, allow the player to add item context.
     o When an object is of type NPC, allow the player to add background.

   Prompt checkpoint: https://chat.openai.com/share/84f2c022-0703-42e3-82a8-cd42288caed4

   This will create the following basic code that sets up an **Admin** interface for PyZork. Make a folder called pages in the **pyzork_v.7** folder. Then, create a new file called **admin.py** and copy the code to this file:

   1. import streamlit as st
   2.
   3. # Define the main function for adding game objects
   4. def add_game_object():

```
5.      object_type = st.selectbox("Object Type",
6.                                  ["ROOM", "ITEM", "NPC"])
7.      object_name = st.text_input("Object Name")
8.      object_description = st.text_area("Object Description")
9.      object_image = st.file_uploader("Object Image",
10.                                      type=["jpg", "jpeg", "png"])
11.     object_special = None
12.
13.     if object_type == "ROOM":
14.         object_special = st.multiselect("Exits to Other Rooms",
15.                                          ["Room 1", "Room 2", "Room 3"])
16.     elif object_type == "ITEM":
17.         object_special = st.text_input("Item Context")
18.     elif object_type == "NPC":
19.         object_special = st.text_area("NPC Background")
20.
21.     if st.button("Add Object"):
22.         # Here you would write code to add the object to your game logic or database
23.         # You can use the gathered information like object_type, object_name, etc.
24.         st.success("Object added successfully!")
25.
26. # Streamlit UI
27. st.title("Game Object Editor")
28. add_game_object()
29.
```

3. Now go ahead and run the **pyzork.py** file with the Streamlit module using the same command as previously, like so:

```
1. streamlit run pyzork.py
```

This will run the *PyZork* game but now you will see a menu with the pages. Select the admin page and you should see something like *Figure 3.11*:

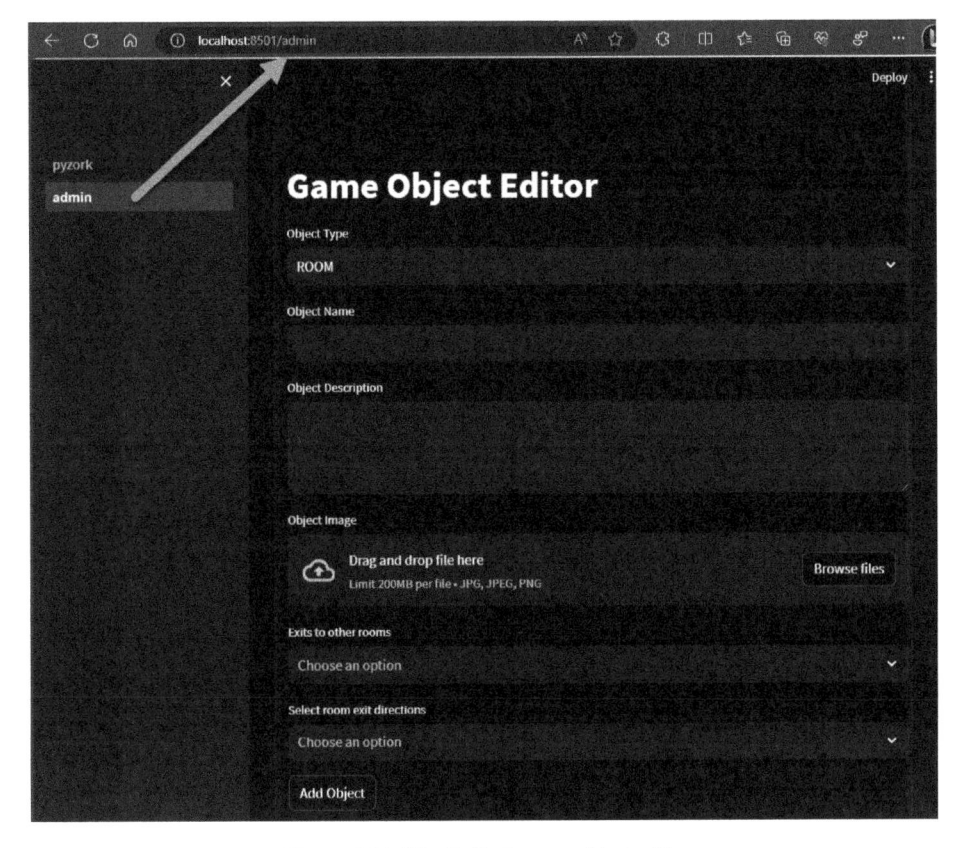

Figure 3.11: The PyZork game object editor

Nothing will work until we connect the game engine code and add a new function to add objects to the game world. Also, the initial admin page did not quite solve all the features so some manual coding was done to connect elements and fix missing features.

You can see the full completed results in the book's **chapter_3/pytorch_v.7** folder. We will also go through the major updates, here so you can see how things are assembled starting with the **admin.py** file.

Updates to **admin.py**:

```
1.  import streamlit as st
2.  from game import GameEngine
3.
4.  @st.cache_resource          ← A
5.  def get_game_engine():
6.      return GameEngine()
7.
```

```
8.  ge = get_game_engine()
9.  # Define the main function for adding game objects
10. def add_game_object():
11.     # code omitted
12.
13.     room_list = [room for room in ge.world.rooms.keys()]     ←B
14.     if object_type == "ROOM":
15.         object_rooms = st.multiselect("Exits to other rooms",
16.                                       room_list)
17.         object_special = st.multiselect("Select room exit …ions",
18.                                         ["North", "South", "East", "West"])
19.     # code omitted
20.
21.     if st.button("Add Object"):
22.         try:
23.             ge.add_object(object_type,     ←C
24.                           object_name,
25.                           object_description,
26.                           object_image,
27.                           object_rooms,
28.                           object_special
29.                           )
30.             st.success("Object added successfully!")
31.         except Exception as ex:     ←D
32.             st.error(ex)
33.
34.     # code omitted
```

a. The **get_game_engine** function provides access to the cached game engine resource.

b. Extract the list of all rooms in the world. This will be used the **st.multiselect** to select room links and directions. Also added was the ability to select the direction the exit is in. For now, just the cardinal directions are used but you could add other direction options.

c. Added a new function of the **GameEngine** class called **add_object**, which takes several parameters used to describe an object, even an image. This function will be responsible for adding the objects to the game world.

d. Added exception handling in case any errors occur.

Next, we will look at updates to the **game.py** file:

```
1.  def create_world():        ←A
2.      world = World()    #create just an empty world
3.      return world
4.
5.  class GameEngine:
6.      def __init__(self) -> None:
7.          self.player = Player()
8.          self.world = create_world()
9.          self.actions = create_actions()
10.         self.current_room = None    ←B
11.
12.     def observe(self):    ←C
13.         if self.current_room:
14.             returns dictionary contents of current room
15.         else:
16.             return dict(description="You are in a void.",
17.                         image=None,
18.                         items=None,
19.                         npcs=None,
20.                         inventory=None,
21.                         actions=None,
22.                         )
23.
24.     def add_object(self,    ←D
25.                    object_type,
26.                    object_name,
27.                    object_description,
28.                    object_image,
```

```
29.                      object_rooms,
30.                      object_special
31.                  ):
32.          if object_type == "ROOM":
33.              new_room = Room(object_name, object_description,
     object_image)   ←5
34.              self.world.add_room(new_room)
35.              if self.current_room is None:
36.                  self.current_room = new_room
37.              if object_rooms and object_special:
38.                  rooms = zip(object_rooms, object_special)
39.                  #add links to room
40.                  for room, dir in rooms:
41.                      link_room = self.world.rooms.get(room, None)
42.                      if link_room:
43.                          self.world.add_link(new_room,
44.                                              link_room,
45.                                              dir.lower())
46.
47.          elif object_type == "ITEM":
48.              pass
49.          elif object_type == "NPC":
50.              pass
```

a. The **create_world** function now just returns an empty world. This means when the game starts the player is in a void of nothingness. The player would not see anything until the first room is created.

b. The **current_room** is set to nothing to start.

c. The observe function was updated to replace an image as well as detect when a player is not in a room.

d. Added a new function called **add_object** was added to the **GameEngine** class. This function is responsible for adding an object to the game world. The room object is currently the only object implemented.

e. The **Room**, **Item** and **NPC** classes, not shown, have been updated to include an image parameter.

Go ahead and run the game from the command line. After the game has started, create a new room with a description and image. The first room will never start with connections/links, but those can be added later. *Figure 3.12* shows adding the first room **The Village**, with the description and image we selected from the admin panel and in the game:

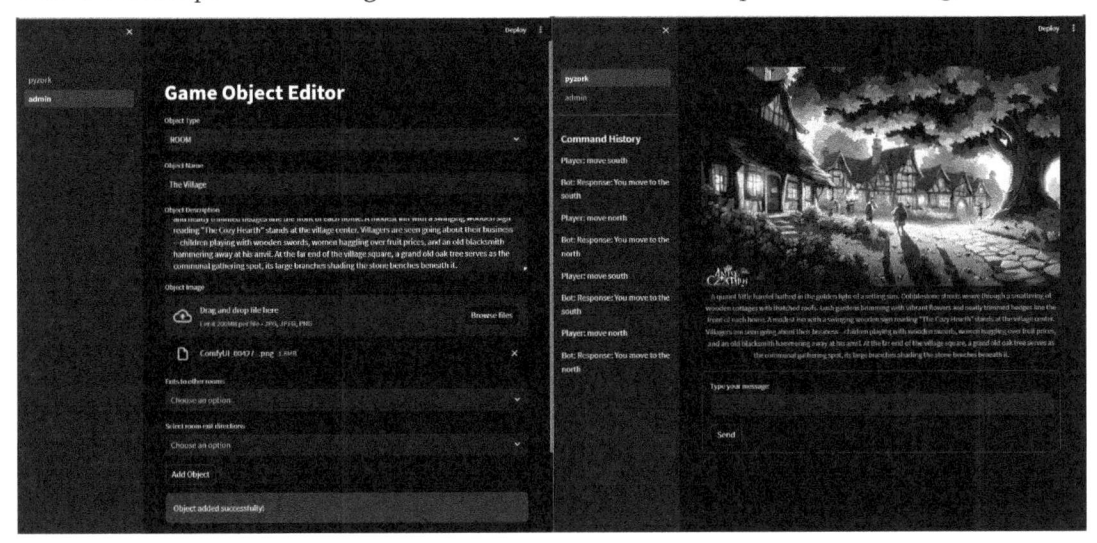

Figure 3.12: Adding a room to the game

Now, add another room, perhaps the forest entrance and link them with an exit from the new room. After you add a new room, you can now use the action move and the appropriate direction to move to the next room and back.

Do not add a bunch of rooms at this stage. Any rooms you add will vanish from memory when you stop the Streamlit server. Our game now needs a way of persisting game objects and player states between game sessions. This means adding a data persistence layer to our game and is something we will cover in the next section.

Remembering the world, adding a game database with SQLite

We can add game content but now we need a way to store it. The simple way to use ChatGPT is to ask it to create a relational database such as SQLite. As a Python developer, you may have already worked with SQLite databases. If you have not, this will be a good opportunity to see how they work.

SQLite has been embedded into Python for over a decade and there is a massive amount of code written with it. This makes it an ideal candidate for ChatGPT to generate detailed and specific code we know will work. Generally, if there is a lot of *public domain* code, ChatGPT will excel in generating variations of it.

In the next exercise, we are going to add an SQLite database to the game. We are also going to use the **EasyCode** plugin so that we can reference our existing code. This will allow us to easily refactor in changes or ask questions when things break, which happens.

Exercise 3.7: Adding data persistence to PyZork

Make a copy of **pyzork_v.7 to pyzork_v.8** or refer to the folder in the book's source code.

Open your **VS Code** and the **EasyCode** extension. If you need to install **EasyCode**, refer to *Chapter 1*.

Within EasyCode select the **Ask Codebase** option and then select the **pyzork_v.8 folder**. Click the *refresh* button to update the RAG and then enter the prompt. *Figure 3.13* shows the steps in the interface.

EasyCode prompt: `I want to add a SQLite database to the game to store game objects.`

```
The objects that need to be stored are:
```
- ROOM
- ITEM
- NPC
- LINK

`Please put all the code to load and save the game objects into the World class.`

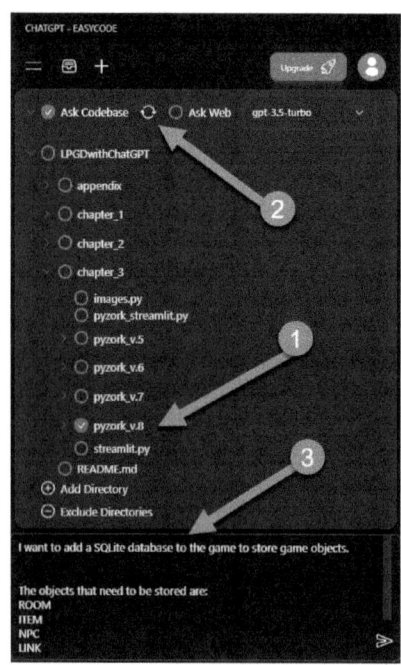

Figure 3.13: Asking the Codebase in EasyCode

ChatGPT/EasyCode will respond with the changes as they need to be applied to the code. There are several changes, but the code is generally repeated for the base game objects **Room**, Item, and NPC with a few changes for **Links**. We will review the major modifications to the code here, but it is recommended you read through the code yourself.

Open the **world.py** file and let us review the top of the file below:

```
1.  class World:
2.      def __init__(self, db_file):
3.          self.db_file = db_file        ←A
4.          self.conn = sqlite3.connect(db_file)
5.          self.cursor = self.conn.cursor()
6.          self.create_tables()          ←B
7.          self.load_world()             ←C
8.
9.      def create_tables(self):          ←D
10.         self.cursor.execute('''CREATE TABLE IF NOT EXISTS rooms
11.             (name TEXT PRIMARY KEY, description TEXT, image BLOB)''')
12.         #omitted items and npcs as similar code
13.
14.         self.cursor.execute('''CREATE TABLE IF NOT EXISTS links
15.             (source_room TEXT, target_room TEXT, direction TEXT,
16.              FOREIGN KEY(source_room) REFERENCES rooms(name),
17.              FOREIGN KEY(target_room) REFERENCES rooms(name),
18.              PRIMARY KEY (source_room, target_room, direction))''')
19.         self.conn.commit()
```

Updates to **world.py**:

a. Added initialization parameter for database name and path. SQLite database files end with the **suffix .db**. The game currently defaults to creating a **game.db** file. You can use a tool like DB Browser to look at the tables and the data they contain.

b. Tables are created from the world initialization.

c. The **create_tables** function is where the database tables are created. Since we only ever want these tables created once, we append the SQL **"IF NOT EXISTS"**. This tells the SQL creation statement to only run if the table does not exist.

d. The **load_world** function is responsible for loading all the game objects.

Scroll down in **world.py** and you will see the add and get object code:

```
1.  def add_room(self, room):          ←A
2.      self.connect_database()
3.      self.cursor.execute("INSERT INTO rooms VALUES (?, ?, ?)",
4.                          (room.name,
5.                              room.description,
6.                              img_to_blob(room.image)))
7.      self.conn.commit()
8.
9.  # omitted item/npc code
10.
11. def add_link(self, source_room, target_room, direction):   ←B
12.     self.connect_database()
13.     self.cursor.execute("INSERT INTO links VALUES (?, ?, ?)",
14.                         (source_room.name, target_room.name, direction))
15.     #create the back link
16.     self.cursor.execute("INSERT INTO links VALUES (?, ?, ?)",
17.                         (target_room.name,
18.                          source_room.name,
19.                          opposite_direction(direction)))
20.     self.conn.commit()
21.
22. def get_rooms(self):          ←C
23.     self.connect_database()
24.     self.cursor.execute("SELECT * FROM rooms")
25.     rows = self.cursor.fetchall()
26.     rooms = {}
27.     for row in rows:
28.         room = Room(*row)
29.         rooms[room.name] = room
30.     return rooms
31.
```

```
32.    #omitted item/npc code
33.
34.    def get_links(self):        ←D
35.        self.connect_database()
36.        self.cursor.execute("SELECT * FROM links")
37.        rows = self.cursor.fetchall()
38.        links = {}
39.        for row in rows:
40.            link = Link(*row)
41.            links[(link.source_room, link.action)] = link.target_room
42.        return links
```

The code highlights are as follows:

a. When a room or other object is added to the game, it is now added to the database first.

b. Likewise, for link objects, we also add the back links, so players do not get trapped in a room.

c. The get functions load the object data from the database and instantiate a new object of the type. Then, the dictionary of objects is returned.

d. Links again are special and require the link dictionary items to be set as a tuple using the source room and action to reference the target room.

Lastly, we want to look at the image saving and retrieval code. Image handling is typically problematic in databases. ChatGPT can write the code, but it becomes problematic because we are using Streamlit.

Therefore, to understand the right image handling code ChatGPT was asked to create a Streamlit example that was saved to an SQLite database. The generated code example, **streamlit_sqlite_images.py** in the **chapter_3** folder shows the proper technique to load and save images to SQLite with Streamlit.

From that code example, the following functions were extracted into **world.py** and shown below:

```
1.    def img_to_blob(image):
2.        image = Image.open(image)
3.        buffered = io.BytesIO()
4.        image.save(buffered, format="PNG")
```

```
5.      img_byte = buffered.getvalue()
6.      blob = sqlite3.Binary(img_byte)
7.      return blob
8.
9.  def blob_to_img(blob):
10.     image = Image.open(io.BytesIO(blob))
11.     return image
```

These two functions were manually extracted from the ChatGPT example and helped to facilitate saving and loading images from an SQLite database.

The only other changes required setting the **current_room** to the first world room when the game loads or the void if no rooms and fixing the link reference in action parsing, shown below:

```
1.  if action.context == "link":
2.      # Check if the room has a link in the specified direction
3.      direction = obj_name
4.      target_room_name = self.world.links.get(
5.          (self.current_room.name, direction), None)
6.
7.      if target_room_name:
8.          self.current_room = self.world.rooms[target_room_name]
9.          return f"You move to the {direction}»
10.
11.     else:
12.         return "You can't go that way."
```

Instead of referring directly to the target room object, links now refer to the room name. This just requires a simple mapping.

When you are done or want to see what the code looks like run **pyzork.py** with the **streamlit** module. You will need to add a few rooms and links to rooms. After you do that, you will be able to explore across a couple rooms, as shown in *Figure 3.14*:

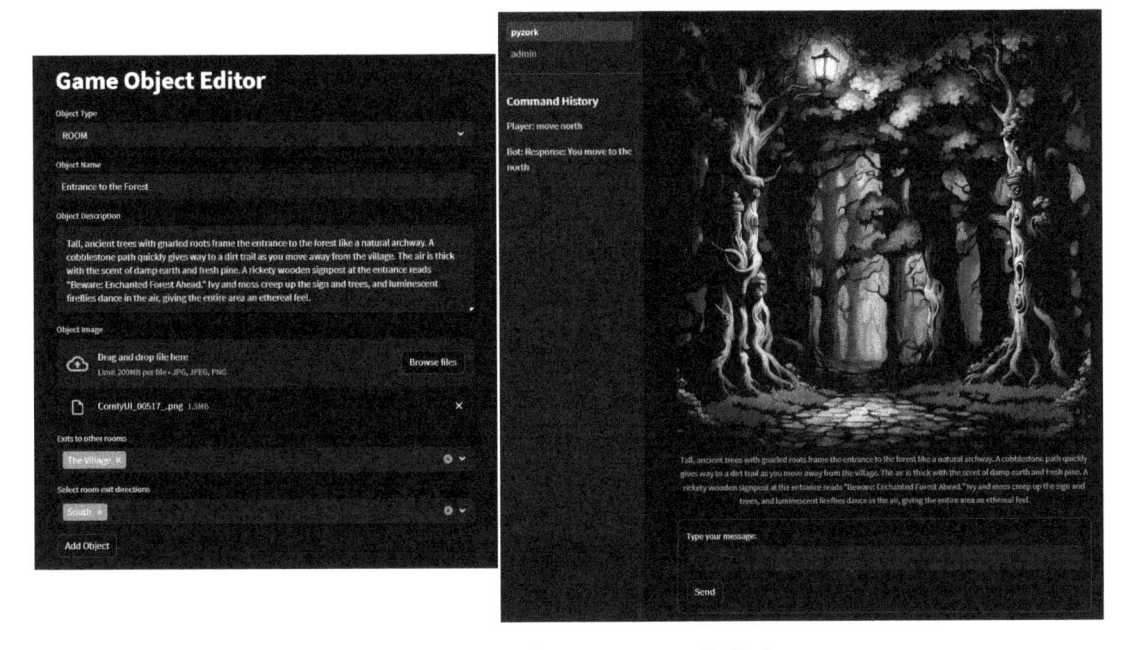

Figure 3.14: Adding new rooms to PyZork

At this point, we could add items and NPCs but we will leave that for later. The next big hurdle we want to achieve is making the game multiplayer. We want to create our *MUD* or *MUSH*, and we see how to do that in the next section.

Completing the MUSH

Creating a multiuser game can be a major undertaking, from networking, player management, player interactions and more. Whole books have been written about creating multiplayer games. Fortunately, for use, we have ChatGPT, Streamlit and a section to get PyZork running for multiple players.

In the next exercise, we are going to add multiple players to PyZork. The implementation will be simple, but it will allow for multiple people to play at a time from the same server.

Exercise 3.8: Adding multiple players to PyZork

Make a copy of **pyzork_v.8** to **pyzork_v.9** or refer to the folder in the book's source code. Open your *VS Code* and the *EasyCode* extension. If you need to install EasyCode, refer to *Chapter 1*.

Within EasyCode select the **Ask Codebase** option and then select the **pyzork_v.9** folder. Click the *refresh* button to update the RAG and then enter the prompt. *Figure 3.13* can help you refresh your memory at to the specific steps.

EasyCode prompt: `I want to add multiple players to the game. Add the code to the world class that saves and loads players from the SQLite database.`

`Players will have the following properties:`

- `name, string`
- `current_room, string`
- `online, Boolean`

After entering this prompt ChatGPT will generate the code for the new **World** class. You can either select everything or copy and paste the new elements into the existing code. Check the books **chapter_3/pyzork_v.9/world.py** file for the completed code. Since we have covered these changes before, we would not review them any further here.

The next couple of changes are just updates to the existing code and can be done with the assistance of EasyCode/ChatGPT or manually. Let us look at the changes required in the **game.py** file first:

```
1.  def observe(self, player_name):
2.      self.world.load_world()   # update the world view of any changes
3.      player = self.world.players.get(player_name, None)
4.      if player is None:
5.          # player needs to be added to the game
6.          starting_room_name = next(iter(self.world.rooms))
7.          player = Player(player_name, starting_room_name, True)
8.          self.world.add_player(player)
```

The first big change is to the **observe** function which now takes the **player_name** as input. Then, it checks if the player is in the game and if not, it adds the player to the first room. Then the remainder of the code, not shown, outputs the updated observation including any other players in the same room.

The second change is the parse function, which also now requires the **player_name** to make the command, as shown below:

```
1.  def parse_command(self, command, player_name):
2.      player = self.world.players[player_name]
3.      if player is None:
4.          return "Player not in world"
```

There are also further changes to parsing the link/movement context but those will be familiar now and can be reviewed by yourself.

Go ahead and run the game from the terminal and open a second alternate browser to the same server URL. Enter a name for your player in each browser and watch as you can now see the other player. *Figure 3.15* shows an example of two players playing the game:

Figure 3.15: Multiple players playing PyZork

There are additional changes to the Streamlit interface file **pyzork.py** in the listing below which shows how the **player_name** is tracked in the Streamlit **state_session**:

```
1.  if 'player_name' not in st.session_state:
2.      player_name = st.text_input("Enter your player name:")
3.      if player_name:
4.          st.session_state.player_name = player_name
5.  else:
6.      player_name = st.session_state.player_name
7.
8.  if player_name is None or player_name == <>:
9.      exit()
10.
11. ge = get_game_engine()
12. observation = ge.observe(player_name)
```

Of course, several key features are missing from the game but those with the help of ChatGPT should be relatively straightforward to complete. What is impressive is we have the foundation for a multiplayer text-based game that also supports custom images. Images that are designed specifically for the content descriptions and styled however we desire.

Text-based games laid the foundations for multiple genres of games. From roleplaying, open world, survival, and adventure as well as laying the grounds for many game worlds that still have not been completely replicated.

The concept of multiple-user shared hallucinations has been replicated on platforms like *Second Life*. However, these games still require substantial work by the player/admin to create those experiences. Hopefully, the power of generative AI brought to games will bring about more rich game worlds players can experience.

Conclusion

In the 1980s, making a game like *PyZork* would have been a considerable achievement. We managed to build a significant amount of the game in just two chapters with the help of AI. In the future, this will be even more impressive but for now it is not bad.

In the next chapter, we dive into creating 2D graphic games. Where we will look to create a classic platform arcade game using *Pygame* and the assistance of ChatGPT.

What we learned

We learned the following in the chapter:

- How to build a Streamlit app as a text-based game. Including making this game multiple players.

- How to use ComfyUI to run the latest Stable Diffusion models locally on your own machine. We also learned how to prompt AI image generation models like *SDXL* to produce beautiful and unique artwork assets for the games we build.

- How to create an interface in Streamlit that can allow players to add their own content as they played. Including allowing the player to add images for any game object.

- How to use ChatGPT/EasyCode to add an SQLite database backend to the PyZork game. As well we learned how to overcome image handling in the database and Streamlit interface.

- How to easily convert the PyZork game into a multiplayer shared experience.

Exercises

The exercises at the end of this section will certainly help you further learn the material but also can help you complete the features of the game.

1. Think of other themes and styles you could use for a text-driven adventure game. Perhaps an illustrated novel that lets you pick your story or a roleplaying game that takes place in some fantastic world you imagine. The possibilities are endless with generative AI tools at your fingertips.

2. When we added the ability to create objects and added multiple players, we broke items and NPCs. Write or assist in writing the code to allow the player to pick up items, drop items, and maybe even give other players items.

   Hint: You will need to remember where items are, be it in a room or within a player's inventory.

3. Add a new player action called teleport and allow the player to teleport to any room. This can be a great tool to help level design or just give players more freedom of movement. Obviously this is not a feature you would give an adventure-style game, but for a MUSH, it can work well.

4. Same as above, but this time add the code for NPCs.

   Hint: you will also need to remember what room an NPC is in.

5. Allow players to talk with each other in the game. Perhaps add an action called shout, that broadcasts a message to all player's chat history. Or another action called say, that only sends messages to players in the same room.

6. Implement a system of money. Allow players to give/get money from other players and NPCs. This could even allow NPCs or players to be shop owners for instance.

7. **BONUS:** MUSHes allowed players to create NPC bots. These bots would execute scripts that allowed them to be interacted with by other players or allow them to explore on their own. Implement an NPC bot system in your game. This may even be a way to implement all NPCs.

8. **BONUS:** Use a network proxy tool like *ngrok* to make PyZork running on your local computer available for outside users. Another option is to deploy your game as a free site on Streamlit itself.

Join our book's Discord space

Join the book's Discord Workspace for Latest updates, Offers, Tech happenings around the world, New Release and Sessions with the Authors:

https://discord.bpbonline.com

CHAPTER 4
2D Platformer: Leap into Pixelated Fun!

Introduction

Arcade games have been around almost as long as text-based games. Unlike text games, the 2D arcade-style game has continued to remain wildly popular. It is a genre that has spawned multiple variations, styles and formats including the 2D platformer and runner, which we will explore in this chapter.

Structure

This chapter explores the following topics:

- Building a platformer
- Mastering controls and movement by introducing difficulty
- Levelling up your obstacles with level design
- Unleashing your creativity with sprites and animation
- Generating assets with AI: Stable diffusion and control nets

Objectives

In this chapter, we are going to create a clone of the popular 2D platformer/runner game *Flappy Bird*. We will start by getting ChatGPT to create the base game. From there, we will move on to review that code in depth. Then, we will add enhancements to the game, starting with level difficulty, level design and adding sprites and animations using generative AI assets.

Building a platformer

Flappy Bird (**FB**) was a sleeper hit released in 2013 by a *lone Vietnamese game developer*. The game was a 2D platformer/runner called a **side-scroller**, where the player controlled a bird flying between vertical sections of pipes. *Dong Nguyen*, the developer, had developed the game in just a few days and never expected the phenomenon for such a simple game.

FB is also an excellent way to introduce 2D game development, especially with ChatGPT. The game itself is simple and has been replicated countless times by developers looking to capitalize on the same success as FB. It has also spawned numerous clones and other game styles making FB a great foundation for developing other games.

In the next exercise, we are going to start as we typically have, asking ChatGPT to build us an FB clone. We will use just a user prompt to build the base game as the style of this game is simple and popular.

Exercise 4.1: Creating a Flappy Bird Clone

1. Open up ChatGPT and enter the following prompt:

    Prompt: `I want to write a clone of the Flappy Bird game in Python with Pygame. Please follow the below specifications to make the game:`

    `In the game, the player can jump by typing the space key.`

    `Please draw the game background using light blue.`

    `Draw the obstacles as dark grey vertical blocks.`

    `Draw reward blocks away from the obstacle blocks. When the player collides with a reward, they get 5 game points.`

    `Continue running the main game loop until the player collides with an obstacle. Stop the game loop when a player collides with an obstacle and display the player's score in the game points. Let the player start a new game by typing the G key.`

    `Please help me by starting to write this game. Be sure to include the main game module that will host the game engine. As well as the classes for the player, game obstacles and game rewards in the same file.`

Prompt checkpoint: https://chat.openai.com/share/41f95a32-4241-4591-bd1f-ea99866acfae

This prompt should push ChatGPT to put all code into a single file. Copy the contents of that file into a new folder and file called **flappy_bird_v.1/flappy_bird.py**.

At this point, you can follow along exactly to the book using the prompt checkpoint or go your own way and just follow along with the main elements we will focus on. Most generated code will likely be very similar owing to the specificity of the prompt and the popularity of the *FB game*. As we have learned, ChatGPT can usually get us 90% of the way, but we can expect to add or fix things.

2. When everything is copied, run the code from the command line using the VS Code debugger. If you are using the checkpoint of the books source code, this is what you should see:

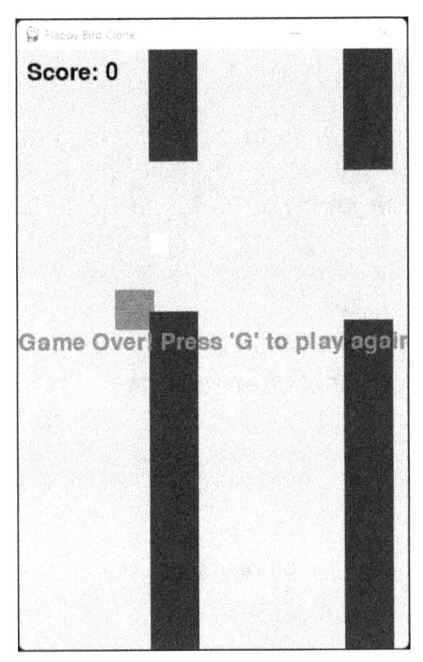

Figure 4.1: Playing the Flappy Bird clone

3. If you are using the code in the prompt checkpoint then as soon as you run the game, the player will collide, and the game will be over. This is because the game loop is missing a timing or delay mechanism. We can quickly fix this by returning to our ChatGPT chat and adding the following to the previous conversation:

Prompt: `This is quite good, but the game runs very fast, how can I slow the game loop down?`

Prompt checkpoint: https://chat.openai.com/share/41f95a32-4241-4591-bd1f-ea99866acfae

4. In this case, ChatGPT will respond with the following code snippet and how to fix the game loop:

```
1.  # ...
2.
3.  # Create a Clock object to control the frame rate
4.  clock = pygame.time.Clock()        ←A
5.
6.  # Game Loop
7.  running = True
8.  game_over = False
9.
10. while running:       ←C
11.     for event in pygame.event.get():
12.         # ...
13.
14.     if not game_over:
15.         # ...
16.
17.     # Clear the screen
18.     screen.fill(BACKGROUND_COLOR)
19.
20.     # Draw player, obstacles, rewards, and score
21.     player.draw()
22.     for obstacle in obstacles:
23.         obstacle.draw()
24.     for reward in rewards:
25.         reward.draw()
26.
27.     score_text = font.render(f"Score: {score}", True, (0, 0, 0))
28.     screen.blit(score_text, (10, 10))
29.
30.     if game_over:
31.         # ...
```

```
32.
33.      pygame.display.update()
34.
35.      # Control the frame rate (e.g., limit to 30 frames per
         second)
36.      clock.tick(30)    ←B
```

The code callouts are described below:

   a. Introduce the Pygame clock. Clock is a tool for getting/setting the frame rate of the game loop.

   b. Set the number of frames we want the game to run in. 30, represents 30 frames per second. Most games run from 30 to 60 frames per second.

   c. Start of the game loop: The running variable controls if the game is running or stopped.

Unlike the game loop for text-based games, the game loop in a graphic game is always running without a pause. The game loop may end but we generally never pause a game loop.

In a graphic game, 2D or 3D the game loop is typically in control of and responsible for the frame rate. The Pygame clock component is a simple abstraction for controlling the number of frames a game runs in. In lower-level game frameworks, you typically need to monitor the system clock and create your own delay mechanism. With Pygame, this is built right in.

Remember the game loop is responsible for everything in a game, from player input to game output. In a graphics game, it means we need to upgrade the screen every run through the game loop or game frame. This is how our game loop is rendered currently and the code that performs each step:

   1. All events in the event quee are looped over and acted on accordingly. The event queue keeps track of the keys typed or game controller movements.

```
1.  for event in pygame.event.get():
2.      if event.type == pygame.QUIT:
3.          running = False
4.      elif event.type == pygame.KEYDOWN:
5.          if event.key == pygame.K_SPACE:
6.              if not game_over:
7.                  player.jump()
8.          elif event.key == pygame.K_g and game_over:
```

9.   # Reset the game
10.   player = Player()
11.   obstacles = []
12.   rewards = []
13.   score = 0
14.   game_over = False

2. New obstacles and/or rewards are generated. As the game is a side-scroller, the game keeps track of what obstacles and rewards are currently on screen. If this number drops below some threshold, the code creates new obstacles and rewards.

1. # Generate obstacles and rewards
2. if len(obstacles) == 0 or SCREEN_WIDTH - obstacles[-1].x >= 200:
3.   obstacles.append(Obstacle(SCREEN_WIDTH))
4.
5. if len(rewards) == 0 or SCREEN_WIDTH - rewards[-1].x >= 300:
6.   rewards.append(Reward(SCREEN_WIDTH))

3. Update the player position and other game objects. Obstacles and rewards are always on the move.

1. player.move()
2. for obstacle in obstacles:
3.   obstacle.move()
4. for reward in rewards:
5.   reward.move()

4. Check for collisions with the player and other game objects.

1. for obstacle in obstacles:
2.   if player.x + 40 > obstacle.x and player.x < obstacle.x + 50:
3.   if player.y < obstacle.height or player.y + 40 > obstacle.height + 150:
4.   game_over = True
5.
6. for reward in rewards:
7.   if player.x + 40 > reward.x and player.x < reward.x + 20:
8.   if player.y < reward.y + 20 and player.y + 40 > reward.y:
9.   rewards.remove(reward)
10.   score += 5

5. Begin rendering the frame by clearing the background to light blue color.
   1. `screen.fill(BACKGROUND_COLOR)`
6. Render/draw the player and other game objects.
   1. `# Draw player, obstacles, rewards, and score`
   2. `player.draw()`
   3. `for obstacle in obstacles:`
   4. `    obstacle.draw()`
   5. `for reward in rewards:`
   6. `    reward.draw()`
   7.
   8. `score_text = font.render(f"Score: {score}", True, (0, 0, 0))`
   9. `screen.blit(score_text, (10, 10))`
7. Check if the game has ended and if it has, then display the player's score and game reset instructions.
   1. `if game_over:`
   2. `    game_over_text = font.render("Game Over! Press 'G' to play again.", True, (255, 0, 0))`
   3. `    screen.blit(game_over_text, (SCREEN_WIDTH // 2 - 200, SCREEN_HEIGHT // 2 - 20))`

Now with the game clock added, the game will control rendering to 30 FPS. This will allow the player more time to make decisions. Go ahead and play the game again and see what high score you can achieve.

Figure 4.2: *Playing the game*

If you played the game for any amount of time, you would realize this version is incredibly hard. Of course, the original FB game was also extremely hard, and this was a contributing factor to the game's success. However, for most games you develop, you will want to control the difficulty, and this is what we will cover in the next section.

Mastering controls and movement by introducing difficulty

Addressing the difficulty of a game is often the first thing you will want to focus on as part of game design and development. A game's difficulty can be set in many ways, but for 2D action games the most common methods are shown in the summarized list below:

- **Game levels**: As you progress in difficulty through levels in many games, a game level will often be the design of the game scene itself. Harder levels may be designed through the environment's construction or the NPCs a player encounters. A player can progress through levels by completing previous levels.

- **Game settings**: They allow the player to select the level of game difficulty from the start. This may allow them to jump levels or just give them advantages in game mechanics including world physics.

- **Game physics**: Altering the physics of the game can be an easy way to increase or decrease difficulty. This could be subtle changes like the speed of a jump or how fast something falls. However, these are changes that may not make sense to change across difficulty levels as it could be jarring to players.

- **Dynamicity**: It refers to smart games that learn to adjust to the player's ability. This is not a new concept but one being reconsidered by many new game developers because of the explosion in AI. The basic idea is the game adapts to the player's ability and adjusts itself to increase/decrease difficulty as the player plays. Dynamic game difficulty provides an individual experience for every player.

We will consider all the above methods for making a game more or less difficult in this and in later chapters. Understanding the difficulty of our *FB clone* will also reveal much about how the game works and how we can alter various settings.

In the next exercise, we are going to explore what settings we can alter in the game to make the game less or more difficult. This will later allow us to create game difficulty levels a player may pick before playing.

Exercise 4.2: Adding game difficulty levels

a. Open up VS Code to the books **chapter_4** source code folder or continue to use your own version. We will start by copying the current code in **flappy_bird_v.1** to a new folder called **flappy_bird_v.2**.

b. There are numerous settings we can adjust but for purposes of game difficulty, we will just focus on player mobility for now. Open the **flappy_bird.py** file in VS Code and let us review the player settings in the **Player** class that control movement as shown in the listing below:

```
1.  class Player:
2.      def __init__(self):
3.          self.x = 100
4.          self.y = SCREEN_HEIGHT // 2
5.          self.velocity = 0
6.          self.gravity = 0.5        ←A
7.
8.      def jump(self):
9.          self.velocity = -10       ←B
10.
11.     def move(self):
12.         self.velocity += self.gravity
13.         self.y += self.velocity   ←C
14.
15.     def draw(self):
16.         pygame.draw.rect(screen, PLAYER_COLOR, (self.x, self.y, 40, 40))
```

The code callouts are described below:

a. Gravity is a constant of **.5**. This means every frame the player's velocity will increase in a positive direction. Something to mention is that our world coordinates on the vertical or y-axis are flipped. It means a positive velocity is falling and a negative velocity is upward movement.

b. When a player jumps, their velocity is set to a constant of **-10**. Remember negative means moving up.

c. In every frame, the player's velocity is altered by the addition of gravity. The player's velocity is then added to the player's previous position to create a new position. This means when thinking of velocity, it is the movement during a single frame.

If you go back and play the game, you may now realize two things: One, the player moves up too fast and falls too slowly. Indeed, a single jump or flap could be reduced in strength. Also, we could alter the gravity from a constant to be more realistic and include acceleration.

a. Go back to the same conversation as before or use the previous prompt checkpoint and enter the following prompt:

Prompt: `Again, this is great, and you are fantastic. I want to add a couple of new features/changes and I hope you can help me:`

o `Add acceleration to the player's gravity.`

o `When a player jumps the increase to the velocity should be additive and not constant as it is now.`

Prompt checkpoint: https://chat.openai.com/share/41f95a32-4241-4591-bd1f-ea99866acfae

This generates the following code which as per usual is 90% complete:

```
1.  # ...
2.
3.  # Constants
4.  GRAVITY_ACCELERATION = 0.6        ←A
5.  JUMP_STRENGTH = -5        ←1
6.
7.  # Classes
8.  class Player:
9.      def __init__(self):
10.         self.x = 100
11.         self.y = SCREEN_HEIGHT // 2
12.         self.velocity = 0
13.         self.gravity = 0  # Initialize gravity to zero
14.
15.     def jump(self):
16.         self.velocity += JUMP_STRENGTH
17.         self.gravity = 0        ←B
18.
19.     def move(self):
20.         self.velocity += self.gravity
21.         self.y += self.velocity
22.
23.     def apply_gravity(self):        ←C
24.         self.gravity += GRAVITY_ACCELERATION
```

```
25.
26.     def draw(self):
27.         pygame.draw.rect(screen, PLAYER_COLOR, (self.x, self.y,
    40, 40))
28.
29. # ...
30.
31. # Inside the game loop
32. while running:
33.     for event in pygame.event.get():
34.         # ...
35.
36.     if not game_over:
37.         # ...
38.
39.         # Apply gravity acceleration to the player
40.         player.apply_gravity()          ←C
41.
42.     # ...
```

There are a couple of things we want to update or change to make this code complete:

1. We adjusted the velocity from **-10** to **-5**. Since the velocity is additive, we may even want to reduce this further. Leave gravity as it is for now, but this is a value you may want to adjust.

2. The original version kept adding gravity to the velocity or constantly accelerating the object. However, when an object is stationary or exerts a force upwards, gravity needs to be reset back to zero. A new line resetting gravity to zero was added to the jump function.

3. A separate function has been added to the player as a means of accelerating gravity from frame to frame.

4. Make the changes in code to the **flappy_bird_v.2** version and run the game again. The game may feel a little better, or maybe even worse, but overall, it remains inconsistent and that has to do with boundaries.

This is because the player's velocity has no boundaries or limits, and the controls could allow the player to quickly get out of control. We can fix this manually or ask ChatGPT directly or through EasyCode. Controlling gameplay is typically a finicky process, requiring multiple iterations. Therefore, in most cases, it just makes sense to do it manually from the start.

Here are the manual updates to the code with the details of each code change outlined below:

1. GRAVITY_ACCELERATION = 0.2
2. MAX_GRAVITY = .6   ←A
3. JUMP_STRENGTH = -10
4. MAX_VELOCITY = -10   ←A
5.
6. # Create the screen
7. screen = pygame.display.set_mode((SCREEN_WIDTH, SCREEN_HEIGHT))
8. pygame.display.set_caption("Flappy Bird Clone")
9.
10. # Classes
11. class Player:
12.   def __init__(self):
13.   self.x = 100
14.   self.y = SCREEN_HEIGHT // 2
15.   self.velocity = 0
16.   self.gravity = 0
17.
18.   def jump(self):
19.   self.velocity = max(MAX_VELOCITY, self.velocity+JUMP_STRENGTH)   ←B
20.   self.gravity = 0
21.
22.   def apply_gravity(self):
23.   self.gravity = min(MAX_GRAVITY, self.gravity + GRAVITY_ACCELERATION)   ←C
24.
25.   def move(self):
26.   self.velocity += self.gravity
27.   self.y += self.velocity

The code callouts are described below:

a. We add new constants to define the maximum gravity and the maximum velocity of an object. This in effect mimics the real world where a falling object will have a maximum velocity when falling. Likewise, we want to make sure the object has a maximum velocity. In this case, as velocity is negative it becomes a minimum, but we call it a maximum.

b. To apply this limit, we wrap everything in the max function. This function takes the maximum value of the player's adjusted velocity and the maximum velocity. Since velocity is a negative number, if the player's velocity is less than the max negative velocity, then the **MAX_VELOCITY** is used.

c. We use the same principle for gravity, but since gravity is a positive number, the **min** function is instead used. Where the minimum value between the maximum gravity and current plus the acceleration is returned. This means if the gravity exceeds the max gravity, then the **MAX_GRAVITY** is returned.

5. To make sure these values are in the ranges we expect, we can also add a useful debugging output to the game screen by adding the following output code:

   1. `debug_text = font.render(f"velocity={round(player.velocity, 2)}, gravity={round(player.gravity, 2)}", True, (0, 1, 0))`
   2. `screen.blit(debug_text, (10, 30))`

6. Now, as we play the game, we can see the actual values of velocity and gravity, as shown in *Figure 4.3*:

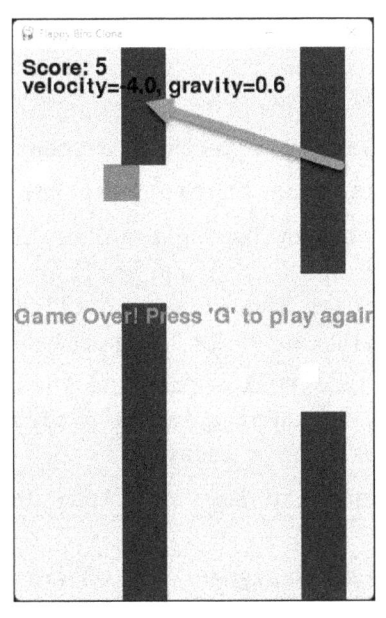

Figure 4.3: Playing the less difficult game

We were able to adjust the game's difficulty and make it more playable and hopefully fun. The question of whether you would modify the velocity/gravity to create different levels of game difficulty is open to discussion. Generally, you want to keep the physics of the game world as consistent as possible and introduce other ways to increase/decrease the level of difficulty.

In the next section, we will look at a more general approach to adding difficulty to a game, the design of a game level.

Levelling up your obstacles with level design

Game-level difficulty in the form of game design is as old as arcade games themselves. What we typically call game-level design is the practice of making a game more difficult by introducing more difficult environments and challenges. Not only does this add a sense of accomplishment to the player when they complete a particularly hard level but also adds continued playability.

In our next exercise, we are going to explore the creation of game levels and game-level design by developing a game-level editor. Before ChatGPT, you likely would have just done the level design by hand or with pen and paper. Now with advanced AI, we can quickly build a game-level editor exactly for our needs.

Exercise 4.3: Creating a game level designer with ChatGPT

1. Open a new ChatGPT conversation. We recommend using ChatGPT-4 (which will hopefully be freely available when this book is published) because of the complexity and length of this prompt.

    Prompt: Please help me create a game level editor for my Flappy Bird clone game.

    I want to add the two game objects to a scene, the REWARD and OBSTACLE.

    The Player object is shown in the center of the scene.

    Obstacles can be placed by typing the O key and then clicking the mouse button to denote the height (y) and position (x) of the object. Rewards can be placed by typing the R key and clicking the left mouse button to denote the objects center (x, y) position.

    Allow the designer to scroll across the level using the left and right arrow keys. A level is infinite in the x direction so allow objects to be placed at any positive x location.

    Allow for the designer to save and load level designs from files in JSON format.

    Please place the level designer into an entirely new file that can run on its own.

> Below is the Flappy Bird game code, please reuse the REWARD, PLAYER and OBSTACLE classes:
>
> [copy the entire contents of the flappy_bird.py file here]

Prompt checkpoint: https://chat.openai.com/share/b10b24b7-179b-421e-a7ce-4a956557b0c4

This is a big and complicated request, but ChatGPT-4 can accomplish it in one prompt. If you are limited to using ChatGPT-3.5, it may take you a few iterations to get the code working quite right. As always, you can use the checkpoint or the book's source code as a fallback.

2. Copy the generated code to a new file in the **flappy_bird_v.2** folder called **flappy_bird_level.py**. Then run the code using the VS Code debugger or run the file from the terminal.

    You will now be able to create a game level by placing obstacles and rewards. Move across the level using the left/right arrow keys and save/load game-level files by typing s and l respectively. *Figure 4.4* shows the level editor running:

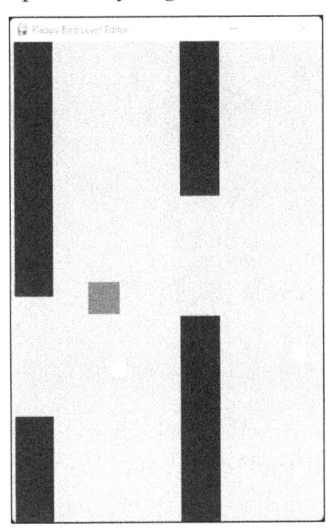

    Figure 4.4: Running the Flappy Bird level editor

3. Go ahead and run the level editor. Create a new level and then save it by typing s. Then, restart the game and type l to load the saved file. Make sure the game level is as you designed it and then we can continue. If the code is not performing as you like, go back to ChatGPT or EasyCode to fix it.

    The code is like the game code, so we would not go through it any further here. However, it is recommended you take some time to review the code, especially the game loading code as we will be incorporating that back into the game next.

    With the ability to make levels, we will jump into a new exercise that will add the code to load the levels into the game.

Exercise 4.4: Importing game levels

For now, we are going to support a single level saved to a file called **level.json**. This is the default file the level editor we designed earlier will save/load from. Before we start making modifications, let us keep our history by making a copy of the **flappy_bird_v.2** folder to a new folder called **flappy_bird_v.3**.

Open VS Code and make the following code changes to the **flappy_bird_v.3/flappy_bird.py** file as shown in the steps below:

1. Add a new import for **json** at the top of the file:

   ```
   import json
   ```

2. Update the **Reward** and **Obstacle** class **__init__** functions to take the **y** and height of the object respectively:

   ```
   class Obstacle:
       def __init__(self, x, h):
           self.x = x
           self.height = h
   
   # ...
   
   class Reward:
       def __init__(self, x, y):
           self.x = x
           self.y = y
   ```

3. Add a new **load_level** function which loads the obstacles and rewards from the **level.json** file. Call the **load_level** function to populate the rewards and obstacles.

   ```
   def load_level():
       with open("level.json", "r") as f:
           data = json.load(f)
           obstacles = [Obstacle(x, h) for x, h in data[«obstacles»]]
           rewards = [Reward(x, y) for x, y in data["rewards"]]
           return obstacles, rewards
   
   obstacles, rewards = load_level()
   ```

4. Load the **obstacles** and **rewards** when the game is reset:

    1. `elif event.key == pygame.K_g and game_over:`
    2. `    # Reset the game`
    3. `    player = Player()`
    4. `    obstacles, rewards = load_level()`
    5. `    score = 0`
    6. `    game_over = False`

5. Remove the old obstacles and reward creation code:

    1. `# # Remove obstacles and rewards generation code`
    2. `# if len(obstacles) == 0 or SCREEN_WIDTH - obstacles[-1].x >= 200:`
    3. `#     obstacles.append(Obstacle(SCREEN_WIDTH))`
    4.
    5. `# if len(rewards) == 0 or SCREEN_WIDTH - rewards[-1].x >= 300:`
    6. `#     rewards.append(Reward(SCREEN_WIDTH))`

After you make the changes save the file and run the game. Now, the level you created in the editor will be shown and you can play through that. Since the file is loaded, on every reload you can now run the game editor and game beside each other. That way as you play the game, you can add new rewards and obstacles, save the file, and automatically see the new level in the game.

Figure 4.5 shows the *Flappy Bird* game and editor running beside each other, editing, and playing the same game level at the same time:

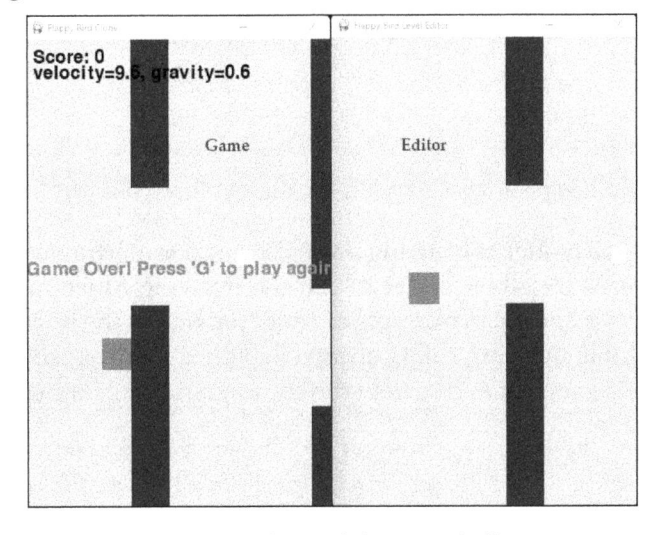

Figure 4.5: *Flappy Bird game and editor*

We now have the foundations for a fun game we can easily extend. There are, of course, numerous improvements we can add at this point, but we will start with the most obvious and look at improving the graphics in the next section.

Unleashing your creativity with sprites and animation

Our FB clone is working well. Now, it is time to enhance the game with characters and animations. Adding animation to the game will bring the characters to life and endear players to our game, providing they like the characters. For now, we will address just the animation and character style and looks in the next section.

Before we get into animation, let us review how 2D game graphics work for a library like *Pygame*. Generally, any 2D game system will follow the same concepts, but what typically differs is the definition of the y-axis. In Pygame, for instance, the axis center of the window is the top left corner, as shown in *Figure 4.6*. x and y values grow across the window. Please refer to the following figure:

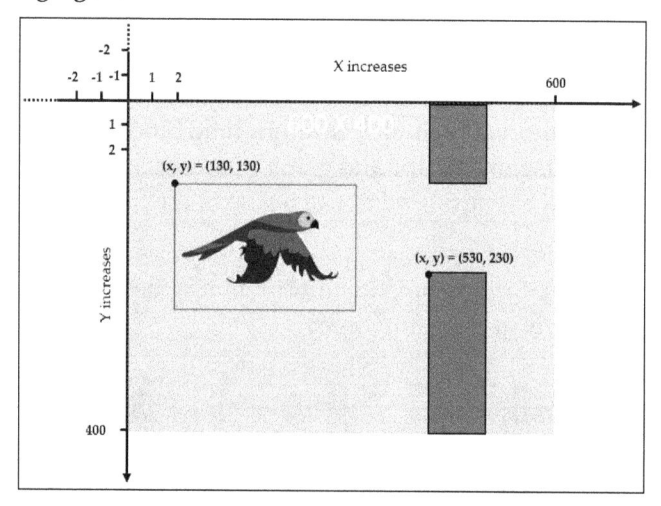

Figure 4.6: Understanding Pygame drawing coordinates

Drawing in Pygame is a matter of drawing an object to screen or drawing surface. Typically, drawing an object uses the draw object to call the drawing function, depending on the type of object. *Figure 4.7* shows an example of code that draws the reward rectangle on the screen. If you recall this drawing call is encapsulated in the **draw** function of the **Reward** class in the FB game. Go ahead and review the code again for the other classes as well, the **Player** and **Obstacles**.

```
pygame draw           REWARD_COLOR
```
draw object of type — reference to screen - drawing surface — RGB color to draw — drawing coordinates (top left corner x, top left corner y, width, height)
rectangle (rect)

Figure 4.7: Example code to draw the reward rectangle

Our current game works well just by rendering basic drawing shapes (rectangles). We want to add the ability to render images for the character and even do animations. Fortunately, ChatGPT can easily generate some demo code for us to visualize and understand the code. In the next exercise, we will let ChatGPT generate a demo of a flying bird.

Exercise 4.5: Creating a flying bird animation demo

1. Open a new ChatGPT conversation and enter the following prompt.

    Prompt: `Create a simple demo in Python and Pygame that shows an animated bird character flying across the screen.`

    `Please load the character animation from a 2D sprite map.`

    `Please create a class to encapsulate the animated bird character.`

    `After the character exists the right side of the screen start the animation again from the left.`

    Prompt checkpoint: https://chat.openai.com/share/b10b24b7-179b-421e-a7ce-4a956557b0c4

2. Copy the code from the chat conversation into a new file called **animated_bird_demo.py**. You can also use the version in the book's source code or from the prompt checkpoint.

3. Go ahead and run the code in the VS Code debugger or directly from the terminal. What you will see is an error because we now need to provide a 2D sprite animation sheet. A sprite is a 2D drawing image or fame and an example of a sprite animation sheet is shown in *Figure 4.8*:

Figure 4.8: 2D sprite animation sheet of a bird flying

2D sprite sheets can be defined for a single game character/object and/or animation or be inclusive of all game characters, objects, and animations. For the code ChatGPT generated for us, we just need a single character animation defined over multiple rows and columns, as shown in *Figure 4.8*.

You can use the sprite animation sheet provided in the **chapter_4/images** folder or do a Google Image search for the *flying bird 2D sprite animation sheet* to see other options. Update the generated (**animated_bird_demo.py**) code to point to your image file as shown below:

    A. `sprite_sheet = pygame.image.load("./images/bird_sprite_sheet.png")`

4. Now, when you the demo again, you should see a bird flying across the screen. If you would like to see a better visualization open the **chapter_4/animated_bird_demo_frames.py** in VS Code and run the demo in the debugger by selecting **Run | Start Debugging** from the menu.

Figure 4.9 shows a screen capture of the demo running. What this demo shows is the bird animation of 9 birds flying in a single animation frame behind each other. Since there are nine frames in the animation, each bird is shown in a distinct frame in the animation cycle. Please refer to the following figure:

Figure 4.9: Animation demo of bird flying by animation frame

Creating demos like this with ChatGPT can be a quick way to pull apart and understand the code needed to perform something. You can then either go back and add the code manually to your project or try and use ChatGPT or EasyCode to make the suggestions. Since we want to learn more about how this all works, we will do the code update manually in the next exercise.

Exercise 4.5: Adding the flying bird animation to FB

1. Open VS Code and make a clone of the current game version **flappy_bird_v.3** to **flappy_bird_v.4**. Then open the **flappy_bird_v.4/flappy_bird.py** game file and make the following additions or you can also just review the books source.

2. Merge the **Player** class and new **Bird** class together. Notice how the new class extends from the **Sprite** class, this will be important later. We want to keep aspects of the **Player** class like physics/movement (velocity and gravity) but also add the sprite loading and drawing code.

```
1.   class Bird(pygame.sprite.Sprite):
2.
3.       def __init__(self, x, y, sprite_sheet, cols, rows):
4.           super().__init__()
5.           self.velocity = 0      ←A
6.           self.gravity = 0
7.           self.frames = []
8.           sprite_width = sprite_sheet.get_width() // cols
9.           sprite_height = sprite_sheet.get_height() // rows
10.
11.          for i in range(rows):
12.              for j in range(cols):
13.                  frame = sprite_sheet.subsurface(pygame.Rect(
14.                      j * sprite_width,
15.                      i * sprite_height,
16.                      sprite_width,
17.                      sprite_height,
18.                  ))
19.                  self.frames.append(frame)
20.
21.          self.current_frame = 0
22.          self.image = self.frames[self.current_frame]
```

```
23.            self.rect = self.image.get_rect()
24.            self.rect.x = x        ←B
25.            self.rect.y = y
26.
27.        def update(self):
28.            self.current_frame = (self.current_frame + 1) %
       len(self.frames)
29.            self.image = self.frames[self.current_frame]
30.            self.move()        ←C
31.            self.apply_gravity()
32.            if self.rect.x > SCREEN_WIDTH:
33.                self.rect.x = -self.rect.width
34.
35.        def flap(self):        ←D
36.            self.velocity = max(MAX_VELOCITY, self.velocity+JUMP_
       STRENGTH)
37.            self.gravity = 0
38.
39.        def apply_gravity(self):        ←F
40.            self.gravity = min(MAX_GRAVITY, self.gravity + GRAVITY_
       ACCELERATION)
41.
42.        def debug_draw(self):        ←E
43.            pygame.draw.rect(screen, PLAYER_COLOR, self.rect)
44.
45.        def move(self):        ←F
46.            self.velocity += self.gravity
47.            self.rect.y += self.velocity
```

The code callouts are described below:

a. Merge velocity and gravity into the class to keep the same physics system.

b. The player object is now internally represented by a rectangle object. This means any reference to *x* or *y* needs to reference the object's internal rectangle.

c. The update function now abstracts any code needed to update the object. That means the code to move the player and apply gravity is called within this function now.

d. We changed the name of the jump function to flap to be more consistent with the bird theme.

e. Add a helper function that draws the old player rectangle underneath the sprite. This will allow us to see if the object is rendering correctly and if the collision system still works as expected.

f. The move and **apply_gravity** functions have a slight modification to reference the internal rectangle.

3. Load the sprite sheet and initialize the player. Notice how we use a sprite **Group** class called **all_sprites** which contains a reference to all sprite objects. On *line 6*, the newly instantiated player is added to this group. This group collection of sprites allows us to work with all the sprites at the same time:

   ```
   1. sprite_sheet = pygame.image.load("./images/bird_sprite_sheet.png")
   2.
   3. # Game initialization
   4. all_sprites = pygame.sprite.Group()
   5. player = Bird(100, SCREEN_HEIGHT // 2, sprite_sheet, 3, 3)
   6. all_sprites.add(player)
   ```

4. Next, we will look at the event handling code. We update the **player.jump** function call to **player.flap** and instead of creating a new player when the game resets, we just reset the player's position back to the starting y value.

   ```
   1. player.flap()
   2. elif event.key == pygame.K_g and game_over:
   3.     # Reset the game
   4.     player.y = SCREEN_HEIGHT // 2
   5.     obstacles, rewards = load_level()
   6.     score = 0
   7.     game_over = False
   ```

5. Remove the call to **player.update** with the **all_sprites.update** call. This allows for all the sprites to call their respective update function. It is a cleaner method than iterating over all the objects such as rewards and obstacles.

   ```
   1. all_sprites.update()
   2. for obstacle in obstacles:
   3.     obstacle.move()
   ```

4. for reward in rewards:
5.   reward.move()

6. Then we likewise modify the code to draw the game objects and sprites. We currently have the manual call to **player.debug_draw** just for debugging purposes but this function will be removed later. The actual code to draw the player sprite is **all_sprites.draw**. Again, this code is designed to draw all the game sprites but for now only the player is a sprite.

1. player.debug_draw()
2. all_sprites.draw(screen)
3. for obstacle in obstacles:
4.   obstacle.draw()
5. for reward in rewards:
6.   reward.draw()

When you have reviewed and/or made all the changes, run the **flappy_bird_v.4/flappy_bird.py** file in the VS Code debugger. *Figure 4.10* shows the results of the sprite in the game:

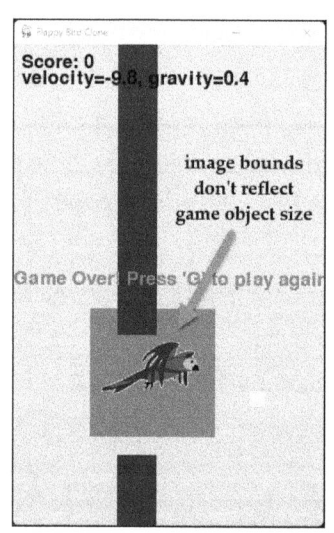

Figure 4.10: Sprite not working as expected

So, as it turns out, we have a couple of problems here. Let us review the issues in the list below:

- The image size is larger than player collision detection bounds. If you look at the old code, the player was a rectangle of size *40,40*. It means that the object is drawn as a rectangle *40x40*. However, that also means that the games collision detection code is detecting a player object of size *40x40* as seen in the code below. Where a collision is detected by adding the player size of *40* to the **player.x** and **player.y** when testing for collisions. What this means is we either need to make the sprite much smaller or update the collision detection code.

1. `for obstacle in obstacles:`
2. `    if `**`player.x + 40`**` > obstacle.x and player.x < obstacle.x + 50:`
3. `        if player.y < obstacle.height or `**`player.y + 40`**` > obstacle.height + 150:`
4. `            game_over = True`

- The sprite itself is much smaller than its bounding rectangle shown in red, *Figure 4.10*. This means two things: one, the object will appear much smaller, and two, the objects collision boundary would not match. There will, in effect, be a space that could still collide with objects.

To fix these issues, we can simply update the sprite sheet we are using for the game. Go ahead and update the sprite sheet loading code to the code shown in the listing below. Notice that we also changed the columns X rows to *2x2*.

1. `sprite_sheet = pygame.image.load("./images/bird_sprite_sheet_fixed.png")`
2.
3. `# Game initialization`
4. `all_sprites = pygame.sprite.Group()`
5. `player = Bird(100, SCREEN_HEIGHT // 2, sprite_sheet, 2, 2)`

Figure 4.11 shows how the bird now looks with an updated sprite map shown on the side of the figure:

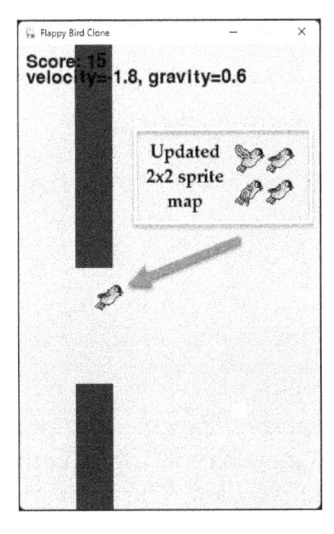

Figure 4.11: Update game with animated bird

The updated sprite map we used was from a quick Google Image search. There are image sites that can provide 2D sprite animation sheets for a wide variety of characters. However, they are not free, may be difficult to align with your needs and costly. Instead, we will look at creating your animation assets using generative AI in the next section.

Generating assets with AI: Stable Diffusion and control nets

As we have already seen in *Chapter 3*, creating game assets can be quickly done using tools like *Stable Diffusion* and *ComfyUI*. By using prompts and prompt styles, we found that we could easily create scenes that gave our game more depth and style. We can continue to use generative AI to create game assets and animations with some help.

Out of the box, **Stable Diffusion** creates amazing images and can certainly be used to generate multiple versions of a single character. However, using the default configuration it can be difficult to create well-aligned animations that could be used for games. Fortunately, ComfyUI supports various helpers called control nets that can help us better structure what we ask *Stable Diffusion* to generate.

In the next exercises, we are going to jump back into **ComfyUI** and look at how we can generate 2D animation sprite sheets using control nets. Before doing that though, we need to install control nets into ComfyUI.

Exercise 4.6: Installing control nets into ComfyUI

Note: This exercise moves quickly over some complex material. There are plenty of YouTube videos that describe this same process, just search for ComfyUI Controlnets and/or check out the following links:

Scott Detweiler: https://www.youtube.com/@sedetweiler has a great series on ComfyUI and several episodes on learning the ins and outs of the tool.

Installing and using control nets: **https://youtu.be/DMxnf4WXMsY?si=8b4huTCqUOpJjxB0**

Installing ComfyUI and the basics: **https://youtu.be/AbB33AxrcZo?si=Sh-QzcqvjxUARSbS**

Below is a step-by-step instruction list for installing and using *ControlNets*, refer to the above video links if you need more assistance. Before starting, make sure your ComfyUI, install is not running.

1. **Install the ComfyUI manager**: Execute the following command from the path specified to clone the manager repo into ComfyUI. The path starts from your ComfyUI root installation folder. The above videos also have all the links mentioned here. The manager makes the remaining installation steps much easier.

1. `_comfyUI_installation_folder\comfyui\custom_nodes> git clone https://github.com/ltdrdata/ComfyUI-Manager.git`

2. **Install the ControlNet custom nodes**: Start ComfyUI, open the **Manager,** and click the **Install Custom Nodes** button from the **Manager** menu. Search for and then select **Install** on the ControlNet package as shown in *Figure 4.12*:

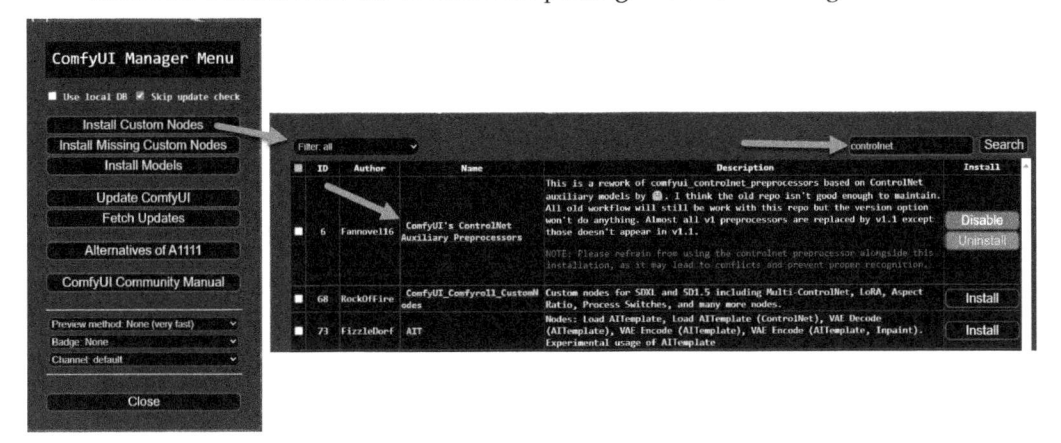

Figure 4.12: Installing the ControlNet custom nodes

3. **Shut down ComfyUI**: After installing, close the ComfyUI terminal window.

4. **Install the ControlNet models**: From a terminal, navigate to your ComfyUI installation folder and then to the **comfyui/models** folder. This is like what you did in *Step 1*. Then execute the following commands in the terminal to install the ControlNet models from *Hugging Face*. The first command installs the large file service extension in Git so that large models can be downloaded.

    1. `git lfs install`
    2. `git clone https://huggingface.co/stabilityai/stable-diffusion-xl-base-1.0`

5. **Update ComfyUI**: Run the update script for your installation. On Windows, this is a batch script called **update_comfyui.bat** found in the **update** folder from the ComfyUI root installation folder. It is generally a good idea to shut down and rerun this script every time you install new custom nodes.

6. **Startup ComfyUI**: Your installation should be complete, and you can start using ControlNets. Import the ComfyUI workflow file by clicking the **Load** button from ComfyUI UI and select the **chapter_4_workflow_controlnets.json** from this chapter's source code folder and as shown in *Figure 4.13*:

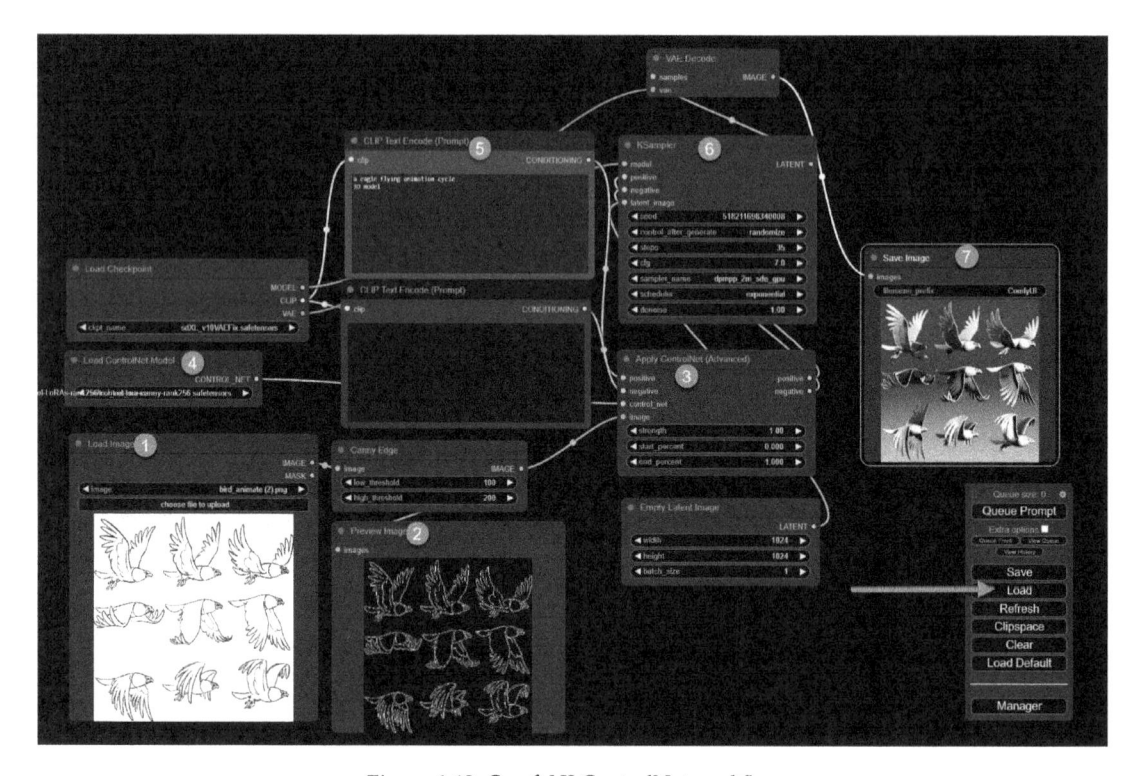

Figure 4.13: ComfyUI ControlNet workflow

Figure 4.13 shows the workflow for using a canny edge detection control net to guide **Stable Diffusion** to create filled-in characters. In the lower-left corner, you can see the guiding image, which is a rough hand-drawn animation of a bird.

The process for using a ComfyUI ControlNet is shown in *Figure 4.13* and outlined in the following steps:

1. **Loading guiding image**: Load an image you want to use to guide the generated output. In this case, we are using a hand-drawn animation of a bird.

2. **Applying the ControlNet**: There are numerous ControlNet filters that can be applied alone or as a chain. In *Figure 4.13*, a canny edge detection filter is applied to the guiding image. The effect of this is to extract lines we want the AI generator to follow. Stable Diffusion will use those lines like a coloring book and fill in those areas using the appropriate prompt.

3. **Setting the ControlNet settings**: In most cases, keep the defaults and notice how the various inputs and outputs map. As you get more experienced, you may want to play with the settings.

4. **Loading the ControlNet model**: You need to make sure and load the correct control net model you want to use as a guide. There are several variations and sizes, so you may want to experiment with this option.

5. **Updating positive/negative prompts**: Update the prompts to match your desired output. Keep things simple to begin with and then provide more details and styles as you experiment with generating output.

6. **Setting the KSampler denoise**: The denoise setting on the KSampler controls how much to use the guide, a value of 1.0 equals 100% or follows the guide strictly. A value of .2 or 20% would follow the guide roughly 20% of the time. This will vary by the type of ControlNet you are using. For the lines (canny edge detection) example it effectively means how strict the generator follows the lines. Lower values of denoise will essentially allow the AI to draw outside the lines.

7. **Examining the output**: Check the output-generated image and if it works save it where you can use it later. Of course, if the image is not what you expected, go back to your prompt or other settings and tweak things. Be mindful of how many options you change in a single iteration until you get more experience in using the tool.

Scott Detweiler's previously mentioned YouTube series can also help by showing tips and tricks beyond what we cover here. In the next exercise, we will explore the basic workflow for creating your own sprite 2D animation assets.

Exercise 4.7: Generating 2D animation Sprite sheets – a workflow

This exercise covers a general workflow you can use to generate 2D animation assets for your games. Creating animation assets, yourself not only frees you from expensive asset generation but can help you learn more about the use and design of animation. As a game developer, understanding animation can help with programming animations.

Here is the general workflow for creating 2D sprite animation assets. Hopefully, in the future, someone may make some of these steps into a ComfyUI plugin or workflow.

1. Search for or create the basic character animation cycle laid out in animation frames. *Figure 4.14* shows an example that has already been converted from a base image. What you want is the frames of animation to be in sequence and numbered. Numbering the sequences will help you track the frames as we go through the process. It is also very helpful to create and overlay a grid representing the cells of your animation. Do not worry about the spacing of the character in the frame just yet. Keeping extra space in an image helps SDXL, fill in the details better without getting confused.

2. The frames in your animation can be very rough or more polished like the example in *Figure 4.14*. Remember, we are only extracting the lines from this base image to be used to guide the AI image generation process.

    Below is a set of guidelines for the base animation image:

    - Base image size should be *1024x1024* (base input for SDXL).
    - Number the cells and overlay a grid.

- Keep the character objects center of mass in the center of the frame, make sure and be consistent with the spacing around the figure:

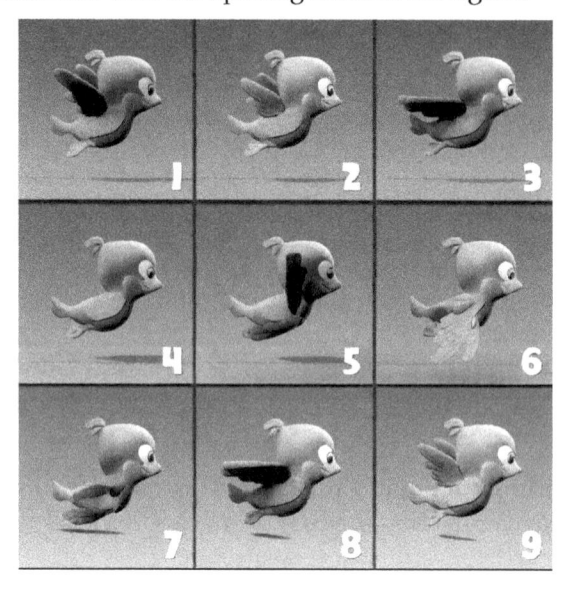

Figure 4.14: Base animation cycle

3. Convert the base image into a new asset. Now, import the base image into ComfyUI and enter your prompts to style the character how you like. *Figure 4.13* shows an example base image imported and run through ComfyUI. *Figure 4.14* shows the output of using a different base image that showed the grid and numbering.

4. This technique can be very useful for creating character skins in multiple different forms. Depending on the level of detail of your character, it may also help you create new characters. Remember you can also easily change the style of any image by just appending to the positive and negative prompts.

5. Next is the tedious step of cleaning up each animation cell and making them game ready. Depending on your image editing experience, you may have tools you already prefer to use. One great online tool to help align characters into animation cells is called **Piskel**, **https://www.piskelapp.com/**. Here are the steps you take in an app like *Piskel* to create game-ready 2D sprite animations:

    a. Use a graphics image editor like *Paint*, *Photoshop*, or *Gimp* to load the generated image.

    b. Make a square selection of one of the characters and copy it into a new sprite in *Piskel*. You will also want to make sure your selection area is big enough to capture all your characters. This means you may want to measure the size of each animation before deciding on your selection size. *Figure 4.15* shows you what this may look like:

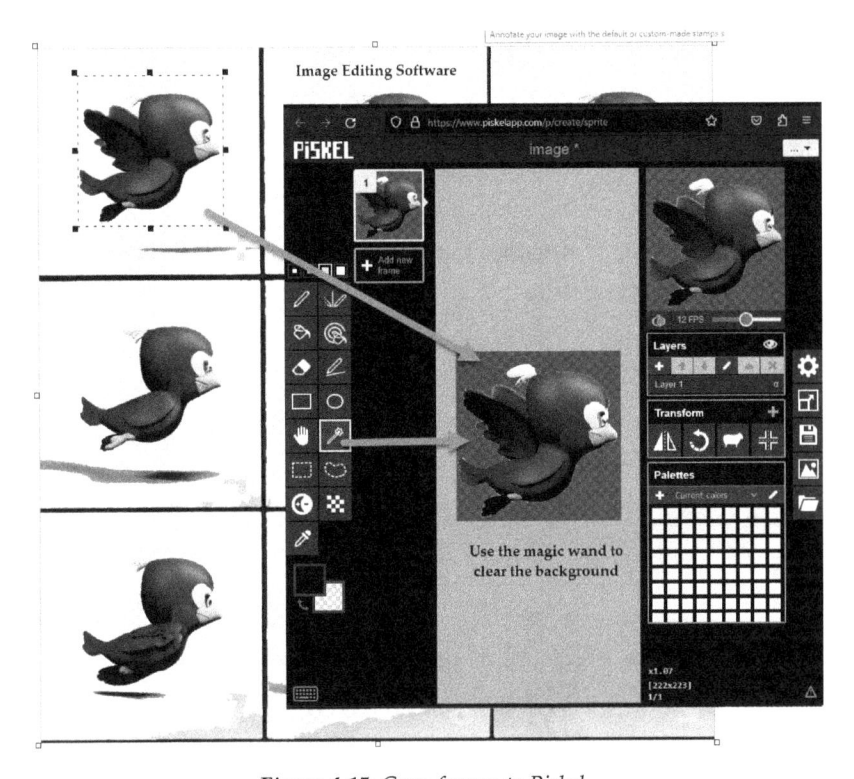

Figure 4.15: Copy frames to Piskel

  c. Click **Add new frame** to add new frames and copy the remaining character animation cells. Be sure that each selection you make is square and the same size as the first image cell. Also, try to keep the center of the character in the center of the selection.

  d. As you add frames to your animation sheet, **Piskel** will show your animation running in the top right corner. This is perfect for making edits or modifications to animation frames.

  e. When you are done adding all the image selections and are happy with the animation, preview click the **Export** button on the lower right toolbar. Then, select **png** as the output with 3 rows and 3 columns.

6. Load the exported image from *Piskel* into your image editing software again. Make sure the transparency is preserved and then resize the image to your required sprite sheet size. For example, if your generated sprite sheet is *720x720* pixels and is 3 frames x 3 frames, then we divide 720 by 3 on each side to get 120 pixels x 120 pixels.

So, that means each frame of the exported animation would be *120x120* pixels in size. If you recall, our game used a sprite size of 40x40. That means, we must resize our sprite sheet by 1/3 or *120x120* pixels.

7. Name and copy the file into the images folder where your game looks to load assets from.

8. Modify the code to load the new image and adjust any frame settings as well. See the example code below, recall that the previous sprite had *2x2* cells and the sprite had *3x3* cells.

```
1. sprite_sheet = pygame.image.load("./images/ai_gen_sprite_sheet.
   png")
2.
3. # Game initialization
4. all_sprites = pygame.sprite.Group()
5. player = Bird(100, SCREEN_HEIGHT // 2, sprite_sheet, 3, 3)
```

9. Run the game and see the sprite in action. *Figure 4.16* shows the result of the new game asset running in the *Flappy Bird Clone* game:

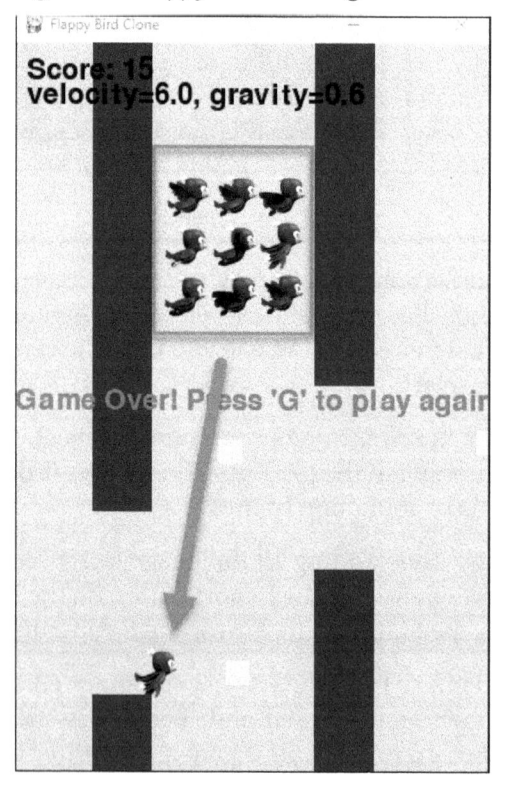

Figure 4.16: New assets added to the game

With the previous workflow, you can go back and any animations or objects you may like just by having a basic shape and idea. This technique of controlling where the AI image generator paints can be used to create numerous other assets as we will see later.

Conclusion

2D games, and specifically platformer games have been a popular gaming genre for many years. In this chapter, we looked at creating a simple platformer/side-scroller game clone of the popular *Flappy Bird* franchise.

In the next chapter, we will explore more about animation and collision detection in 2D games by building an action fighting game. Fighting games are deceptively complex and tricky to get right, and therefore make an excellent platform to learn more about animation and collisons.

What we learned

Here is a summary of what we learned in this chapter, exercises, and some further exercises to help you continue learning:

- How to build the basic structure of a 2D game in Pygame using ChatGPT prompting.
- How to control the framerate of a game using the Pygame clock.
- How to control the physics and movement of a character and adjust the difficulty of the game.
- How to create a game-level designer that could be used to edit and add new levels to the game.
- How things are drawn in a 2D game using simple primitives like rectangles to be drawing images with sprites.
- How to animate a sprite in a game and draw it on the screen.
- Understand what collision detection is and the basics for determining when an object collides.
- Understand how to use AI image generators to create consistent game animation assets for a character or game object.
- How to use *ComfyUI* and *ControlNets* to create unique custom-styled game assets in any shape and form you desire.

Exercises

The exercises at the end of this section will certainly help you further learn the material but also can help complete features of the game. Be sure to go ahead and tackle at least a couple of these exercises:

1. Altering the scoring of the game so that a player scores a point when they pass an obstacle. As it is right now, the player could complete the entire level without any score at all.

2. Add the ability for a game level to be finished or complete. This could be accomplished by tracking how far the player has gone. Say after traveling 2000 pixels in the X direction the level ends. Perhaps add some ending screen when the character completes a level.

3. Assuming you completed the above step now go ahead and more levels to the game. Levels could be a progression or perhaps just random, the decision is up to you.

4. Add sprite images for the obstacles and reward objects. Use *ComfyUI* and *ControlNets* to generate objects of the desired shape and import them into the game.

5. Refactor the game code that handles the rewards and obstacles to extend from the *Pygame Sprite* object. Implement the update function as we did for the player object and likewise add the sprites to the main sprite manager object.

Join our book's Discord space

Join the book's Discord Workspace for Latest updates, Offers, Tech happenings around the world, New Release and Sessions with the Authors:

https://discord.bpbonline.com

Chapter 5
Bot Brawls: AI Opponents Enter the Arena

Introduction

The 2D action fighting game stands out as a true classic out of all genres that have continued popularity. It is a game style that has spawned countless variations and spinoffs including upgrades to 3D. However, this style is not overly shared in books or online tutorials and therefore needs to be the focus of the next chapter.

Structure

This chapter explores the following topics:

- Loading the game: The Street Fighter Clone
- Introducing AI-controlled enemies: Battle Royale edition
- Ruling the AI: Introducing behavior-driven AI
- Challenging players again: AI dynamic difficulty levels
- Revisiting the assets: Restyling the game with SDXL

Objectives

We begin the chapter by exploring a fully developed 2D action game clone of the popular Street Fighter series. Then, we will quickly move on to extending this game by adding AI-controlled combatants - first by introducing a general AI and then increasing difficulty again through game levels and second, by giving each of the combatants a slightly individual personality. We will conclude the chapter by using generative AI to restyle the game assets into our behavioral-driven AI.

Loading the game: The Street Fighter Clone

As with the previous chapters, we could start by asking ChatGPT to write us a basic game and go from there. However, the fighting game genre has not been popular for demos and tutorials. This implies that ChatGPT would struggle to create a game. Go ahead and try it yourself. While you may get a game, it would be quite basic and require a lot of work.

Instead, in this chapter, we are going to look at a fully completed fighting game written in Pygame by *Adrian Adewunmi*, with the help of *Coding from Ross* YouTube series: **https://www.youtube.com/watch?v=s5bd9KMSSW4**. This is an excellent starting point and one we are sure ChatGPT would learn well from in the future.

For the first exercise of the chapter, we are going to clone the source code from GitHub. If you have downloaded the book's source code, you will already be familiar with GitHub but if you require a refresher consult *Appendix B*.

Exercise 5.1: Cloning the Street Fighter Clone

Open a terminal window, navigate to your preferred working folder and type the following command:

1. `git clone https://github.com/AAdewunmi/Street_Fighter_Game`

The **chapter_5** folder in the book's source code contains all the code as well if you prefer to start there.

You can run the game by changing to the source folder (**Street_Fighting_Game**) and running the **main.py** file as shown below:

1. `LPGDwithChatGPT\chapter_5>cd Street_Fighter_Game`
2. `LPGDwithChatGPT\chapter_5\Street_Fighter_Game> python main.py`

Figure 5.1 shows an example of the game running and the wizard and warrior fighters pairing off. Go ahead and play the game, the keyboard instructions to play the game are shown below:

- Warrior
  - Movement
    - a ←→ d

- o Jumping
  - w
- o Attacking
  - z or x
- Wizard
  - o Movement
    - h ← → k
  - o Jumping
    - u
  - o Attacking
    - n or m

Figure 5.1: *2D action game running*

Not only is this a full game in Pygame but is also concisely contained in two files: **main.py** and **fighter.py**. The best way to describe this example is textbook Pygame and game development in general.

You can now review and read through the code in the **main.py** and **fighter.py** files. But, to help us get familiar with the code base quicker, we are going to use ChatGPT with EasyCode to summarize.

Open VS Code and make sure your workspace includes the **Street_Fighter_Game** folder. Click the **EasyCode** extension button on the left toolbar to open it. We now want to index the code using the extension so we can perform some retrieval augmented generation **retrieval augmented generation** (**RAG**) with ChatGPT.

Locate your code folder in the extension as seen in *Figure 5.2*. Next, click the Ask Codebase radio button and then the refresh button to index the code:

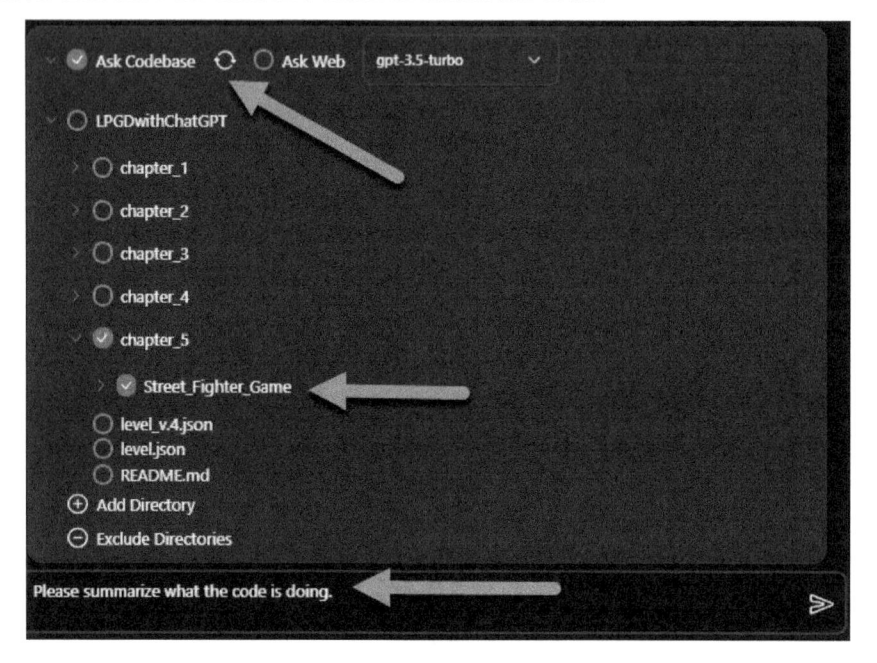

Figure 5.2: Using EasyCode to RAG with ChatGPT

We can then use the following prompt to ask a question of the codebase:

EasyCode prompt: `Please summarize what the code is doing.`

ChatGPT/EasyCodes response will be something like the below, remember you may get something a little different:

```
The code is for a Street Fighter style fighting game implemented in Python
using the Pygame library. It consists of multiple files:
```

- `fighter.py`: Defines the Fighter class, which represents a player/fighter in the game. It contains methods for loading sprite sheet images, handling movement, updating animations, attacking, and drawing the fighter on the screen.
- `main.py`: The main file of the game. It initializes Pygame, sets up the game window, loads assets like images and sounds, defines functions for drawing elements on the screen, creates instances of the Fighter class

for the two players, and contains the main game loop that updates and draws the game elements.

- `README.md`: A documentation file that provides an overview of the project, lists the tech stack used, explains how to install and play the game, and gives credit to the original creator.

The code handles player movement, animation, attacking, collision detection, health tracking, scoring, and game over conditions. It also includes features like background music, sound effects, and victory screens.

This is a great summary of what the code does, and which parts do what. You can do further queries on your own of the files or sections of the file. This is especially helpful if you are unfamiliar with any parts of the code.

Here are some other prompts you may want to try to get help understanding the code, be sure to try the last couple on your own:

- `Please summarize how the Fighter class handles animations.`
- `Please summarize how the Fighter class handles collisions.`
- `Please summarize how I can change the game background.`
- `Please tell me how I can modify the Fighter lass so that keyboard keys for movement can be generalized.`
- `Please show me how I can make one of the fighters controlled by AI.`

ChatGPT (EasyCode) will be quite helpful and provide the summarization for the code we ask for. Moreover, it will try to give us helpful suggestions to modify the code for our last 2 queries. However, it is quite likely the suggestion will not be ideal and there is likely a better way.

As we know, ChatGPT can respond extremely well to knowledge it has learned and even provide insights into new code. Except, it does not always do a very good job of understanding the big picture, at least for now. While that may change in the future right now, we must sometimes nudge ChatGPT in a direction we deem better as we will see in the next section.

Introducing AI-controlled enemies: Battle Royale edition

Having a full Street Fighter game clone is great but playing such a game on a single keyboard may not be the best experience. It was not a good experience when the early fighting games were first launched on a **personal computer** (**PC**). This means we could fix the problem in one of two ways: Add a better game controller, or add AI-controlled non-player combatants.

It is clear from the title of this section, we are going to add the ability of AI to control the second player. We will do this by first breaking out the game input into a new controller class. Separating the game input into a new class will allow us to add a new AI controller for one or both players.

In the next exercise, we are going to lay the foundations of adding AI by creating a **Controller** class to manage game input. This time instead of using *EasyCode*, we are going to use ChatGPT-4 (Plus) with a plugin called **AskTheCode**. If you do not have ChatGPT Plus you can use EasyCode but you may need to iterate a few times. As always though, the example code is always available in the book's source code.

Exercise 5.2: Adding the AIController

As always, we start by cloning the **Street_Fighter_Game** folder to a folder named **Street_Fighter_Game_v.1**. This will allow us to make changes to the new code and go back in case we break anything. You, of course, can also use git to manage your changes, as per your discretion.

Open **ChatGPT** and switch to **ChatGPT-4**. Enable plugins and search for and enable the **AskTheCode** plugin as shown in *Figure 5.3*:

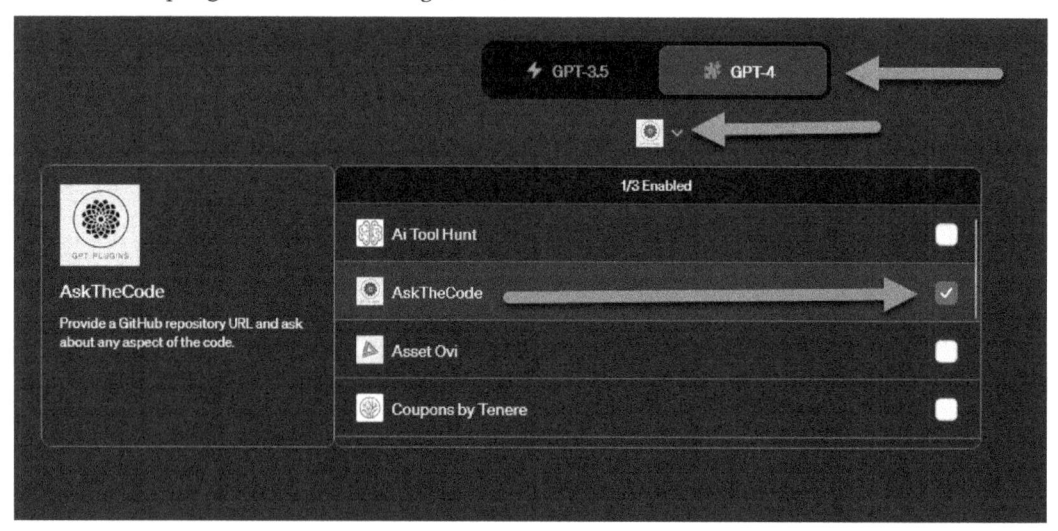

Figure 5.3: Enabling the ChatGPT plugin

We first want to attach to the **Street_Fighter_Game** GitHub repository. Enter the following prompt:

Prompt: `Please summarize the code at this GitHub url: https://github.com/AAdewunmi/Street_Fighter_Game`

ChatGPT using *AskTheCode* will provide a summary of the code like what we have already seen in the last section. Doing this can now provide context through RAG from the indexed code/content of the game repository.

Next, enter the second prompt in the same chat to generate the code changes we need to add the AI controller.

Prompt: `I want to add AI controlled opponents to the game. In order to do that I want to break out the control code in the Fighter class to a new Controller class.`

`The Controller class should be called by the main game loop and take the current state of the game and the get_action function will return a state changes dictionary that can update the Fighter class.`

`The basic state changes dictionary will look something like:`
```
{
    "action" : "movement | attacking | jumping | none"
}
```

`Additional parameters will be added to the dictionary based on the type of change:`
`Movement: return velocity dx`
`Attacking: return attack_type 1 or 2`
`Jumping: no extra data`
`No action: no extra data`
`Here is the format of the game_state dictionary that is passed to the Controller class get_action function.`

```
game_state = {
    "fighter_1": {
        "position": fighter_1.rect,
        "alive": fighter_1.alive,
        "health": fighter_1.health
    },
    "fighter_2": {
        "position": fighter_2.rect,
        "alive": fighter_2.alive,
        "health": fighter_2.health
    },
    "round_over": round_over
}
```

Prompt checkpoint: https://chat.openai.com/share/6e42dc61-da5b-4a3e-b0f2-1f96cc5a104f

This time we are providing the AI a specific prompt with guidelines to define what we need. The better we can define the requirements, the better the code will fit and require fewer changes to integrate. ChatGPT-4 will generally work better for these more specific requests but may not be perfect.

Now, unsurprisingly the code returned is not perfect, but it gets close. We will go through the first two generated sections of code additions/changes next.

The first generated section is a new **AIController** class shown below. Copy this code to a new **controller.py** file in the **Street_Fighter_Game_v.1** folder:

```
1.  import pygame
2.
3.  class AIController:
4.      def __init__(self, player):
5.          self.player = player
6.
7.      def get_action(self, game_state):
8.          state_changes = {}
9.
10.         # Extract relevant game state information
11.         fighter = game_state[f"fighter_{self.player}"]
12.         opponent = game_state[f"fighter_{3 - self.player}"]
13.         round_over = game_state["round_over"]
14.
15.         # Implement your AI logic here
16.         if not round_over:
17.             if fighter["alive"]:
18.                 # Example: Simple logic to move towards the opponent
19.                 if fighter["position"].x < opponent["position"].x:
20.                     state_changes = {
21.                         "action": "movement",
22.                         "dx": 1
23.                     }
24.                 elif fighter["position"].x > opponent["position"].x:
25.                     state_changes = {
26.                         "action": "movement",
27.                         "dx": -1
```

```
28.                    }
29.                    # Add more logic for attacking, jumping, etc.
30.
31.        return state_changes
```

This code is basic and only moves the AI-controlled player to the opponent player. It does this by checking the distance in the reported positions passed in from the **game_state** input. For the AI to make informed decisions, we pass the current state of the game.

Next, we will look at the updates to **main.py** file. Here, we add a new AI controller for both players, 1 and 2. Then, inside the game loop, we create the new **game_state** dictionary and populate it with the current game state. After that, we call the controller **get_action** function to return the next action by the AI.

```
1.  # Create controller instances
2.  controller_1 = AIController(1)
3.  controller_2 = AIController(2)
4.
5.  # Inside the game loop
6.  while run:
7.      # ... (existing code)
8.
9.      # Create the game_state dictionary
10.     game_state = {
11.         "fighter_1": {
12.             "position": fighter_1.rect,
13.             "alive": fighter_1.alive,
14.             "health": fighter_1.health
15.         },
16.         "fighter_2": {
17.             "position": fighter_2.rect,
18.             "alive": fighter_2.alive,
19.             "health": fighter_2.health
20.         },
21.         "round_over": round_over
22.     }
23.
```

```
24.     # Get state changes from controllers
25.     state_changes_1 = controller_1.get_action(game_state)
26.     state_changes_2 = controller_2.get_action(game_state)
```

The last thing we need to update is the **Fighter** class. It is done by removing the control logic from the move function and instead using the controller's **action** dictionary. Below are the changes to the **move** function of the **Fighter** class:

```
1.  def move(self, screen_width, screen_height,
2.          target, round_over, state_change):
3.      SPEED = 10
4.      GRAVITY = 2
5.      dx = 0
6.      dy = 0
7.      self.running = False
8.      self.attack_type = 0
9.
10.     # Can only perform other actions if not currently attacking
11.     if not self.attacking and self.alive and not round_over:
12.         action = state_change.get("action", "none")
13.         if action == "movement":
14.             dx = SPEED * state_change["dx"]
15.             self.running = True
16.         elif action == "attacking":
17.             self.attack_type = state_change["attack_type"]
18.             self.attack(target)   # Assuming attack is a method in Fighter class
19.         elif action == "jumping" and not self.jump:
20.             self.vel_y = -30
21.             self.jump = True
22.     # …
```

What we did here is to remove all the keyboard input handling code and track all updates to the fighter through the **action/state_change** input. This means that a human player can no longer play the game. Not to worry, we will rectify that shortly.

Go ahead and run the game and look at what happens. Sure enough, both players now quickly rush to each other and then just stand there. This may not look like much, but we have the beginning of an AI-controlled player or players.

Before we close out this section, let us add a new **PlayerController** that handles the same human player keyboard input. This is quite simple and merely requires some copying/pasting of the old control code to a new class as shown below. The code works by capturing the actions of each keyboard event into a new **state_changes** (action) dictionary:

```
1.  class PlayerController:
2.      def __init__(self, player):
3.          self.player = player
4.
5.      def get_action(self, game_state):
6.          state_changes = {}
7.
8.          # # Get Key-presses
9.          key = pygame.key.get_pressed()
10.
11.         # Check Warrior player controls the game
12.         if self.player == 1:
13.             # Player movement coordinates
14.             if key[pygame.K_a]:
15.                 state_changes = {
16.                     "action": "movement",
17.                     "dx": -1
18.                 }
19.             if key[pygame.K_d]:
20.                 state_changes = {
21.                     "action": "movement",
22.                     "dx": 1
23.                 }
24.             # Player Jumping
25.             if key[pygame.K_w]:
26.                 state_changes = {
27.                     "action": "jumping"
28.                 }
29.
30.             # Player Attacking
```

```
31.            if key[pygame.K_z] or key[pygame.K_x]:
32.                # Determine which attack type was used
33.                if key[pygame.K_z]:
34.                    state_changes = {
35.                        "action": "attacking",
36.                        "attack_type": 1
37.                    }
38.                if key[pygame.K_x]:
39.                    state_changes = {
40.                        "action": "attacking",
41.                        "attack_type": 2
42.                    }
43.        # code for the Wizard is very similar
```

We then need to go back to **main.py** and change one of the controllers to be a **PlayerController** as shown in the code snippet below:

```
1. # Create controller instances
2. controller_1 = PlayerController(1)
3. controller_2 = AIController(2)
```

You can switch the order of the controller, remember that player 1 is the Warrior and player 2 is the Wizard.

Go ahead and run the game again. This time, you can control the first player, but the second player is AI-controlled and will continually just move to your player, as shown in *Figure 5.4*:

Figure 5.4: *The AI-controlled shadow*

Now that we have the basis for a working AI controller, we can move on to adding the AI in the next section.

Ruling the AI: Introducing behavior-driven AI

Game AI has gone through many evolutions over the years from simple rule-based systems to advanced deep reinforcement learning and now **ChatGPT**. Of course, ChatGPT is not applicable to real-time systems control or a fighting game, at least not yet. Instead, we will use a tried-and-true game AI method called behavior trees to power the fighting bot.

Behavior trees are a popular game AI and robotics method for real-time systems or systems, like games, that need to respond in less than milliseconds. They are based in part on rule and state-based systems and are often referred to as hierarchal rules-based systems. The concept itself has been around for years and many games and robotics system use them.

Before we dive into an exercise to generate the code, let us look at how we want the AI fighting bot to behave. *Figure 5.5* shows a simple behavior tree we may use to control a fighting bot. In the tree, you can think of the root node as the beginning state of the agent. Please refer to the following figure:

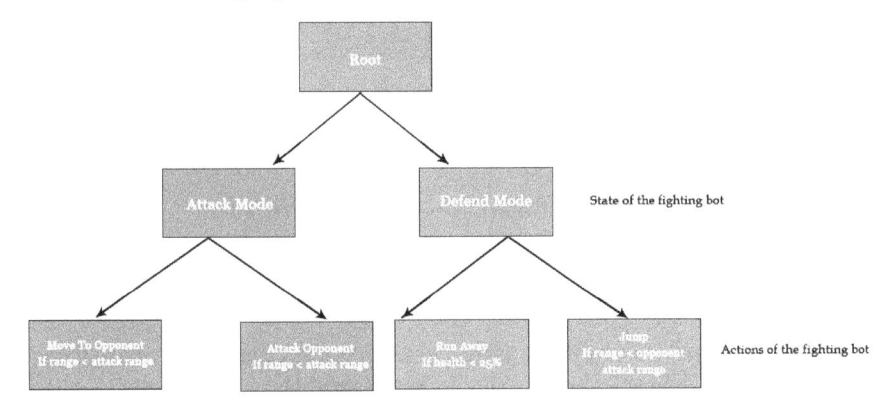

Figure 5.5: AI fighting bot behavior tree

In a behavior tree, the branches represent decision points and/or state transitions. For the AI tree in *Figure 5.5*, the first decision or state transition has been broken down into two paths, **Attack Mode**, and **Defend Mode**. Then, each of the decisions below the mode is an action, like *move*, *retreat*, *attack*, and *jump*.

Behavior trees can become very complex and represent numerous states, state transitions and actions. What makes a behavior tree especially useful is the ability to transition from state to state, state to action, action to state and so on. The possibilities are endless and powerful when constructed correctly.

For our next exercise, we are going to build an AI that implements the behavior tree in *Figure 5.5*. It is important to keep in mind this is complex stuff and while behavior trees are well established they can be both bad and good for code generation. There are so many varied implementations of behavior trees that it becomes difficult for ChatGPT to not hallucinate.

Exercise 5.3: Creating a py_trees behavior demo

We will again use the **AskTheCode ChatGPT** plugin to provide context to the correct **py_trees** implementation. This is one of those cases where there are numerous similar variations and forks of **py_trees**. It only makes sense to augment the generation using the code base. If you do not want to use the plugin with ChatGPT-4, the other option is clone the **py_trees** repository and use EasyCode.

Open ChatGPT and switch to ChatGPT-4. Enable plugins and make sure the **AskTheCode** plugin is activate as shown in *Figure 5.3*.

Prompt: `Please review and summarize the code at this GitHub url: https://github.com/splintered-reality/py_trees`

The **AskTheCode** plugin will now index the repository which ChatGPT will consume and then summarize a brief description of the high-level elements. This step makes sure that ChatGPT has the context of the right code base. Again, you generally only need to do this step if you find multiple conflicting variations.

Another indication over saturation can be a problem is if ChatGPT completely alters the generated output, when using the regenerate function. If you find ChatGPT is not at all consistent with the regenerated code, you need to narrow the context using *RAG*.

Continue the same chat conversation using the following prompt:

Prompt: `Please create a demo of behavior trees using the py_trees package and Python.`

```
Demonstrate    an    AI    that    uses    the    following    behavior    tree:
The  AI  will  be  in  attack  mode  when  its  health  is  greater  than  50%  of
its  starting  health,  or  if  the  AI  has  greater  health  than  its  opponent.
When    the    AI    is    not    in    attack    mode,    it    is    in    defend    mode.
When    in    attack    mode,    the    AI    moves    toward    the    opponent,
that    is,    when    the    range    is    greater    than    the    attack    range.
When in attack mode, the AI attacks when the range is less than the attack range.
When in defend mode, the AI moves away from the opponent when its health is below 25%.
When in defend mode, the AI jumps when the opponent is within attack range.

Use an AIController class to control the AI. Be sure this class is injected
into each behavior so that the update function can query the controller for
state changes like range, attack range and health.
```

Make sure the code for the demo will run in a single Python file and there are no errors. Also, log messages when decisions are made in the behavior tree and please use the py_trees visualization tools to output the final tree.

Prompt checkpoint: https://chat.openai.com/share/a1d5b213-5609-4dcb-acaa-b4df1e104e2c

Go ahead and copy the output to a file called **pytrees_demo.py** and run it in the terminal or debug the code with VS Code. You will likely get an error when you run the code. Go ahead and copy the error and continue the conversation by pasting the error and asking ChatGPT to fix it.

You will likely need to do a few iterations of pasting errors and asking for fixes before you get a working version. If you want to see a complete conversation, refer to the prompt checkpoint above and the **chapter_5/pytrees_demo.py** code to see a working version.

Figure 5.6 shows the output of a fully working version of the AI using the behavior tree running over 10 ticks. The output is simple because the actions run from the behavior currently do nothing. So, if the bot moves towards the opponent, it will remain the same distance.

In the next exercise, we are going to manually refactor the complex code that makes up the pytrees demo into the fighting game. The idea here is to give our AI opponent the ability to fight back.

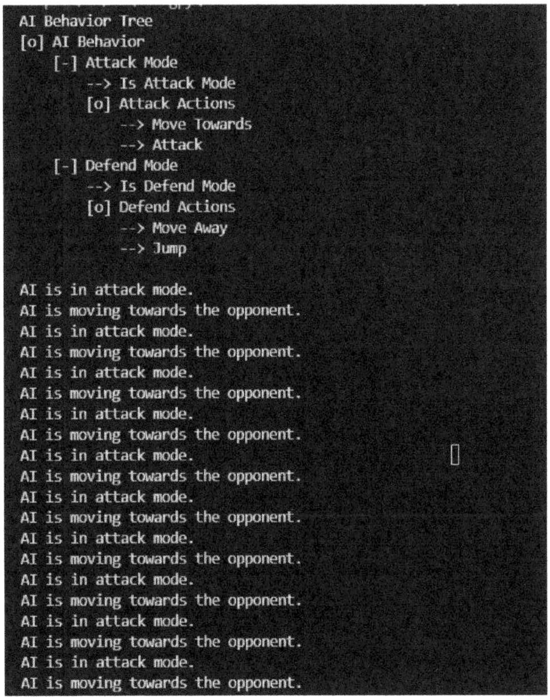

Figure 5.6: Output of the pytrees_demo.py

Now, the heavy lifting part comes in. This means we must merge the AI behavior code with the fighting game.

Exercise 5.4: Adding behavior trees to the fighting bot

As usual, open VS Code and make a copy of our working project folder **chapter_5/Street_Fighter_Game_v.1** to **chapter_5/Street_Fighter_Game_v.2**.

Copy and remove the **AIController** class from **controller.py** into a new file called **ai.py**. This new file will host all the functionality of the AI controller and behavior trees.

Now for the heavy lifting, copy all the functions and **CustomBehavior** class code from the **pytrees_demo.py** file to before the **AIController** class in the file. For each of the action functions, be sure to set the state changes on the AI for the respective action, below is the updated code:

```
1.  def is_attack_mode(ai_controller):
2.      if ai_controller.health > 50 or ai_controller.health > ai_controller.opponent_health:
3.          print("AI is in attack mode.")
4.          return pt.common.Status.SUCCESS
5.      else:
6.          return pt.common.Status.FAILURE
7.
8.  def is_defend_mode(ai_controller):
9.      if ai_controller.health <= 50 and ai_controller.health <= ai_controller.opponent_health:
10.         print("AI is in defend mode.")
11.         return pt.common.Status.SUCCESS
12.     else:
13.         return pt.common.Status.FAILURE
14.
15. def move_towards(ai_controller):
16.     if ai_controller.range_to_opponent > ai_controller.attack_range:
17.         print("AI is moving towards the opponent.")
18.         ai_controller.state_changes = {
19.             "action": "movement",
20.             "dx": -ai_controller.direction_to_opponent
21.         }
```

```
22.         return pt.common.Status.SUCCESS
23.     else:
24.         return pt.common.Status.FAILURE
25.
26. def attack(ai_controller):
27.     if ai_controller.range_to_opponent <= ai_controller.attack_
    range:
28.         print("AI is attacking the opponent.")
29.         ai_controller.state_changes = {
30.                     "action": "attacking",
31.                     "attack_type": 1
32.                     }
33.         return pt.common.Status.SUCCESS
34.     else:
35.         return pt.common.Status.FAILURE
36.
37. def move_away(ai_controller):
38.     if ai_controller.health < 25:
39.         print("AI is moving away from the opponent.")
40.         ai_controller.state_changes = {
41.                     "action": "movement",
42.                     "dx": ai_controller.direction_to_opponent
43.                 }
44.         return pt.common.Status.SUCCESS
45.     else:
46.         return pt.common.Status.FAILURE
47.
48. def jump(ai_controller):
49.     if ai_controller.range_to_opponent <= ai_controller.attack_
    range:
50.         print("AI is jumping.")
51.         ai_controller.state_changes = {
52.             "action": "jumping"
53.             }
```

```
54.            return pt.common.Status.SUCCESS
55.        else:
56.            return pt.common.Status.FAILURE
57.
58.  class CustomBehaviour(pt.behaviour.Behaviour):
59.      def __init__(self, name, fn, ai_controller):
60.          super().__init__(name)
61.          self.fn = fn
62.          self.ai_controller = ai_controller
63.
64.      def update(self):
65.          return self.fn(self.ai_controller)
```

Each of the actions and states of the behavior tree is defined by a function. These functions either define the state of the AI or an action it will take. Inside the action functions, the code to return the action state changes has been added. Remember, this is like the code in the **PlayerController** class found in the **controller.py** file.

Now, we will look at the updates to the **AIController** class in the **ai.py** file:

```
1.   class AIController:
2.       def __init__(self, player):
3.           self.player = player
4.           self.state_changes = {}
5.           self.create_btree()
6.
7.       def get_action(self, game_state):
8.           self.state_changes = {}
9.
10.          # Extract relevant game state information
11.          fighter = game_state[f"fighter_{self.player}"]
12.          opponent = game_state[f"fighter_{3 - self.player}"]
13.          round_over = game_state["round_over"]
14.
15.          self.health = fighter["health"]
16.          self.opponent_health = opponent["health"]
17.          range = fighter["position"].x - opponent["position"].x
```

```
18.         self.range_to_opponent = abs(range)
19.         self.direction_to_opponent = math.copysign(1, range)
20.         self.attack_range = 150
21.
22.         print(f"AI State H{self.health}, O{self.opponent_
    health}, R{self.range_to_opponent}, A{self.attack_range}")
23.
24.         # Implement your AI logic here
25.         if not round_over:
26.             if fighter["alive"]:
27.                 self.tree.tick()
28.
29.         return self.state_changes
```

In the PyTrees demo, the health and ranges were all hard coded. The updated code expects the **game_state** to contain all the information needed. This code extracts all the relevant state information that will be used by the behavior tree. At the bottom of the above listing, you can see where the controller checks if the round is not over, and the fighter is alive. If these checks pass then the behavior tree ticks, makes one step of the tree.

One step of the behavior tree is one complete pass through all the decision points. Put another way, one step or tick is the complete execution of the tree for the relevant nodes. This means when the AI/tree is in attack mode, only the attack tree nodes will be executed. Likewise, the opposite is true. This efficient way of processing decisions and state transitions is what makes btrees ideal for fast execution.

Finally, for the last block of code. The construction of the btree can be added to a new function within the AIController class, as shown below:

```
1.  class AIController:
2.      # ...
3.
4.      def create_btree(self):
5.          ai_controller = self
6.
7.          root = pt.composites.Selector(
8.              name="AI Behavior",
9.              memory=False,
10.             children=[
```

```
11.             pt.composites.Sequence(
12.                 name="Attack Mode",
13.                 memory=False,
14.                 children=[
15.                     CustomBehaviour("Is Attack Mode", is_
    attack_mode, ai_controller),
16.                     pt.composites.Selector(
17.                         name="Attack Actions",
18.                         memory=False,
19.                         children=[
20.                             CustomBehaviour("Move Towards",
    move_towards, ai_controller),
21.                             CustomBehaviour("Attack",
    attack, ai_controller)
22.                         ]
23.                     )
24.                 ]
25.             ),
26.             pt.composites.Sequence(
27.                 name="Defend Mode",
28.                 memory=False,
29.                 children=[
30.                     CustomBehaviour("Is Defend Mode", is_
    defend_mode, ai_controller),
31.                     pt.composites.Selector(
32.                         name="Defend Actions",
33.                         memory=False,
34.                         children=[
35.                             CustomBehaviour("Move Away",
    move_away, ai_controller),
36.                             CustomBehaviour("Jump", jump,
    ai_controller)
37.                         ]
38.                     )
39.                 ]
```

```
40.                    )
41.                ]
42.            )
43.
44.            self.tree = pt.trees.BehaviourTree(root)
45.            print(console.green + "AI Behavior Tree" + console.
        reset)
46.            print(pt.display.ascii_tree(self.tree.root))
```

The last line of code outputs the btree as seen in *Figure 5.6*. Look at the remaining code, it comprises some complex nesting focus on the high-level elements. Notice the use of the **Selector** and **Sequence** nodes. A Selector node is a state decision, and a **Sequence** node is a list of actions to be checked and executed.

Notice, how we only had to modify a couple of files and the bulk of our changes were in a single file, this is good. Go ahead and run the code and see how well the AI opponent can fight, *Figure 5.7*:

Figure 5.7: The AI Wizard wins again, can you beat the AI?

Well, we now have a working AI that we can play against. Fortunately, or unfortunately, this AI may be easy to beat. As we discussed in the previous chapter, we want to give the player some form of difficulty ascension. Understanding how we can make the game difficult will be the focus of our next section.

Challenging players again: AI dynamic difficulty levels

In this section, we are going to do two things, make the AI less predictable and add some difficulty levels to the game. Right now, the AI is predictable and somewhat easy to beat. By making the AI more unpredictable, this will make the AI harder, much harder. Then, we can tune the level of difficulty.

For the next exercise, we are going to add manual updates to the code to introduce an element of arbitrariness to the AI. These changes will be simple but effective at making the AI much harder.

Exercise 5.5: Making the AI less predictable

As usual, open VS Code and make a copy of our working project folder **chapter_5/Street_Fighter_Game_v.2 to chapter_5/Street_Fighter_Game_v.3**.

Open the **ai.py** file in VS Code and make the following set of changes to the top of the file:

```
1.  import random          ←A
2.
3.
4.  def is_attack_mode(ai_controller):
5.      if ai_controller.health > random.randint(0, 50)     ←B
6.      or ai_controller.health > ai_controller.opponent_health:
7.          print("AI is in attack mode.")
8.          return pt.common.Status.SUCCESS
9.      else:
10.         return pt.common.Status.FAILURE
11.
12. def is_defend_mode(ai_controller):
13.     if ai_controller.health <= random.randint(0, 50)    ←C
14.     and ai_controller.health <= ai_controller.opponent_health:
15.         print("AI is in defend mode.")
16.         return pt.common.Status.SUCCESS
17.     else:
18.         return pt.common.Status.FAILURE
```

The code callouts are described below:

a. Import the random package. Random will be used to create arbitrariness over certain decision points in the btree.

b. Change the health check in the **is_attack_mode** function on the static value of 50 to a random check with 50 as the max value. This will have the effect of making the AI more aggressive, since the average value is around 25. The AI will be more likely to move to attack mode now.

c. Likewise, we change the static health check in the **is_defend_mode** function to a random value between 0 and 50. This has the effect of making the AI even more aggressive and less likely to enter the defend mode.

Before we go ahead and run this, let us make one more change to the fighter's health. Right now, the health only decreases, and this can quickly lead to imbalance. We can fix this by adding a minor bit of healing after every time step. Open the **fighter.py** file and enter the following code into the update or move functions:

1. `#add a minor amount of healing`
2. `self.health = min(self.health*1.001, 100)`

This simple bit of code will have the effect of giving the fighter a .1% boost in health every time step. Adding the **min** function to check against the value of 100 assures us the value will never go above 100. It works just like a bounds check.

We are done and now we can go ahead and run the game again from the terminal or through VS Code debugger, as shown in *Figure 5.7*. Indeed, this time the AI will be significantly more difficult to beat. Go ahead and play a few rounds to see if you can beat the AI.

We can also make both controllers AI again and see what effect this has. Go ahead and make both controllers into AI controllers from the **main.py** file:

1. `# Create controller instances`
2. `controller_1 = AIController(1)`
3. `controller_2 = AIController(2)`

Run the game and sit back and watch a few bouts, at least 5 but the more the better. *Figure 5.8* shows the results of running the game for 10 bouts (1 currently running) with the AI fighting itself:

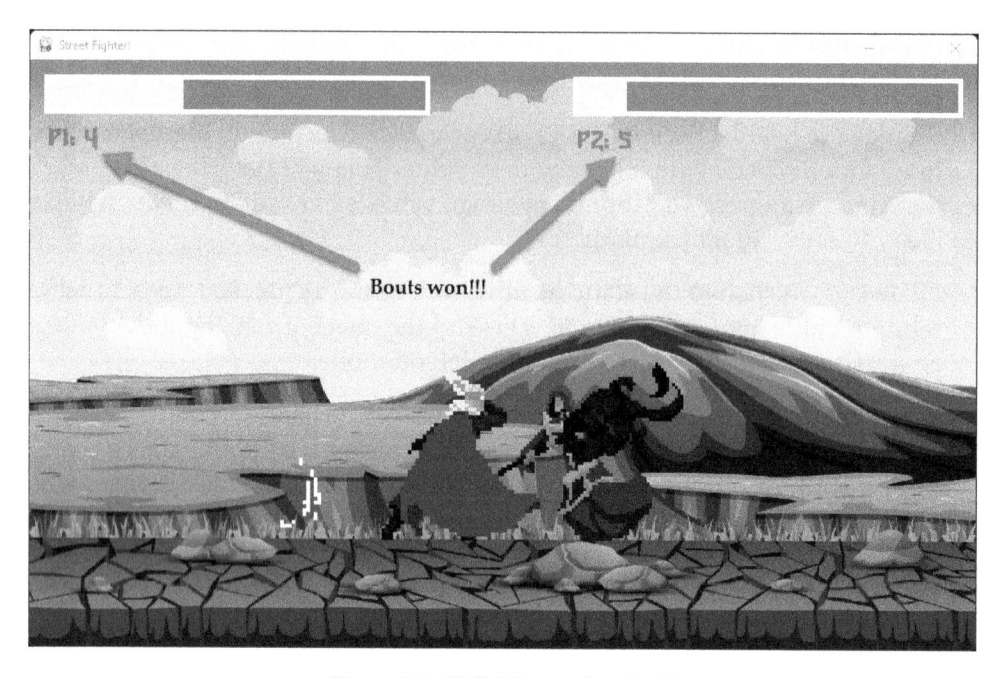

Figure 5.8: AI fighting against itself

All things considered, the AI should beat itself an equal number of times given both fighters are exact copies.

We are going to use the ability of the AI to fight itself to create a baseline of AI difficulty in the next exercise. Surprisingly, adding difficulty to the AI is relatively easy and can be done by adding a new parameter to the AI-Controller.

Exercise 5.6: Adding dynamic difficulty levels to the AI

This time we do not need to make another clone of the project and we can make the changes in **chapter_5/Street_Fighter_Game_v.3** directly. Open the AI-Controller class in VS Code. We are going to add a new parameter called difficulty which will determine how likely the AI decides during a step. Below is the code:

1. # Implement your AI logic here
2. if not round_over:
3.   if fighter["alive"]:
4.   if random.random() < self.difficulty*.1:
5.   self.tree.tick()

On *line 4*, in the code above, we add a new check that determines the likelihood the AI will make a decision (**tree.tick**). At a difficulty level of 1, the AI will decide every game step 10% of the time. This in turn will cause the AI to pause in indecision and allow the player to react and attack. As a side note, we also added the difficulty parameter to **PlayerController** class, so they can be treated consistently.

Bot Brawls: AI Opponents Enter the Arena 153

Next, we are going to adjust the difficulty level of the controller after the end of every round. If one player beats the other, we increase the difficulty of the other. This means, as the difficulty increases the AI will make faster and faster decisions.

Open the **main.py** file and note the changes to code that handles either fighter dying in battle:

```
1.  # Check for player defeat
2.  if not round_over:
3.      if not fighter_1.alive:
4.          score[1] += 1
5.          round_over = True
6.          controller_1.difficulty += 1        ←A
7.          round_over_time = pygame.time.get_ticks()
8.      elif not fighter_2.alive:
9.          score[0] += 1
10.         round_over = True
11.         controller_2.difficulty += 1        ←B
12.         round_over_time = pygame.time.get_ticks()
```

The code callouts are described below:

a. Increase the difficulty of player 1 when player 2 dies.

b. Likewise, increase the difficulty of player 2 when player 1 dies.

Of course, we also want to show the player what difficulty they are currently challenging. So, we will also update the countdown text with the following code:

```
1.  #display level difficulty
2.  draw_text(f"Level {controller_2.difficulty}",
3.      count_font,
4.      WHITE,
5.      SCREEN_WIDTH / 2-100,
6.      SCREEN_HEIGHT / 3-100)
```

Be sure to also make player 1 the player controller again by changing the controller setup code to the following:

```
1.  # Create controller instances
2.  controller_1 = PlayerController(1)
3.  controller_2 = AIController(2)
```

When that is done, go ahead and run the game again and play several rounds. What is the level you can attain is shown in *Figure 5.9*:

Figure 5.9: Adding levels to the game

At this point, you can go ahead and tweak and update the code as you see fit. You may even want to change the behavior tree and add some new states and/or actions. That is as far as we will take updating the game play. In the next section, we will focus on adding new backgrounds via *Stable Diffusion SDXL*.

Revisiting the assets: Restyling the game with SDXL

In this last section of the chapter, we are going to look at adding new assets using *Stable Diffusion SDXL* and *ComfyUI*. This time we are going to focus on adding new backgrounds for the various game levels by using *ControlNets*.

If you missed the end of the last chapter, where we setup control nets in ComfyUI, you will need to complete that before proceeding. For the next exercise, we will use a different control net to help us create new background images.

Exercise 5.7: Adding new game backgrounds

Go ahead and make a copy of the project folder **chapter_5/Street_Fighter_Game_v.3** to **chapter_5/Street_Fighter_Game_v.4**. We would not make a lot of changes to the new version but for consistency and ease of tracking changes making a copy works well. Again, if you are familiar with Git that is also another option for tracking changes.

Locate the **background.jpg** file located in the **assets/images/background** folder. This image is currently at a size of *1920x1484* but we need to resize the image to 1024 pixels on the longest edge for SDXL to consume it. Use an image editor to resize the image to *1024x792* and save it to a new location.

Startup ComfyUI and load the workflow from the **chapter_5** source folder called **workflow_depth_map_background.json**. Click the **Load (1)** button on the ComfyUI control panel as shown in *Figure 5.10*:

Figure 5.10: The ComfyUI command panel

After you load the workflow, you will see the layout resembling that shown in *Figure 5.11*:

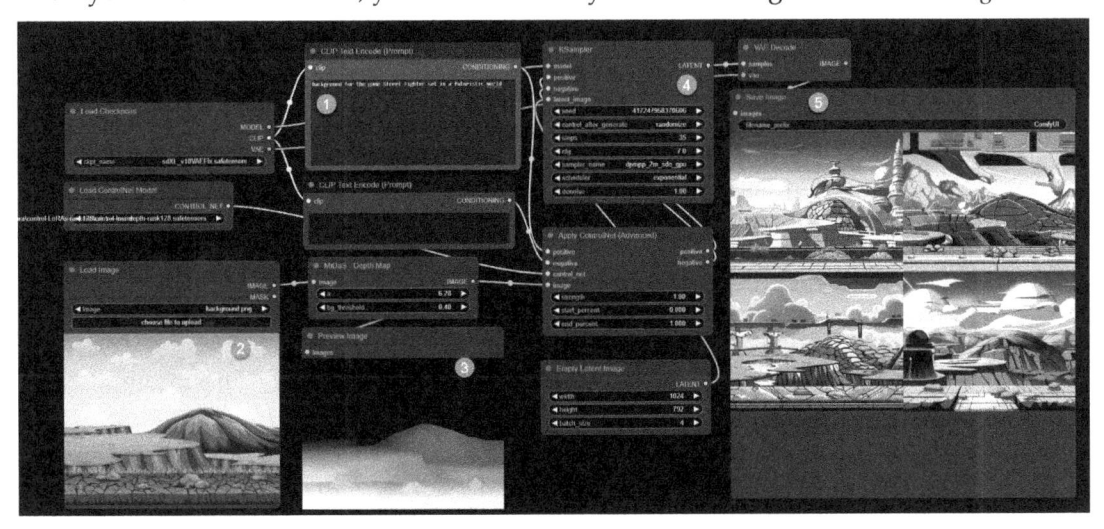

Figure 5.11: ComfyUI with depth map workflow loaded

This time we are going to use a different control net to extract the depth map of the background image. Then use that to guide the image generation to match our current background image. The steps below are identified in the figure and show what you need to undertake:

1. Enter your prompt, a good place to start is something like what is shown in the figure. Background for the game *Street Fighter* set in a futuristic world.

2. Load the resized background image, remember the image needs to be 1024 on the long side for SDXL. There are ways to resize the image in the workflow, but we will do the resizing using an external editor for now.

3. When the control net runs, the depth map will extract the depth of the objects as they appear from the camera. Notice how the depth map of the background has extracted all the main features. *Figure 5.12* shows how the depth map is used to align the features just like the canny edges were used previously:

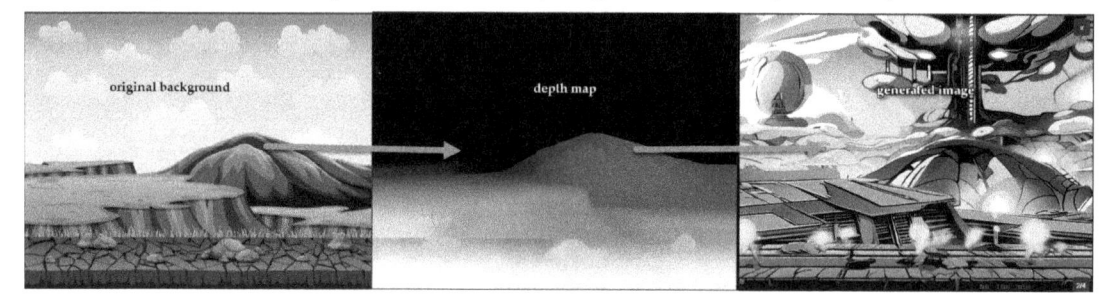

Figure 5.12: Depth map extraction and generation

4. Leave the noise in the KSampler at 1.0 for now. This means the depth map will 100% guide the output. You can always alter this parameter for variation to the output.

5. After you *Queue* the prompt (2 in *Figure 5.10*) in the UI, you will get 4 images all matching your background features. You can right-click any of the generated images and save them to a working image folder. Perhaps, the same one you used for the **background.jpg.**

Now you need to finish up the remaining steps not seen in the figure.

1. Open the saved image in an image editor program and use the image resize feature to set the image size to *1920x1484*, the original for the background.

2. Save the resized image as **background_1.jpg** in the assets/images/background folder.

3. Go ahead and repeat the process enough times to produce 10 new background images labelled **background1.jpg, background2.jpg, ..., background10.jpg.**

We updated the assets, now it is time to update the code. Open **main.py** in VS Code and make the following modifications:

```
1.  # Update Countdown
2.  if intro_count <= 0:
3.      # Move Fighters
4.      fighter_1.move(SCREEN_WIDTH, SCREEN_HEIGHT, fighter_2, round_
    over, state_changes_1)
5.      fighter_2.move(SCREEN_WIDTH, SCREEN_HEIGHT, fighter_1, round_
    over, state_changes_2)
6.  else:
7.      if intro_count == 3:          ←A
8.          # Load Background Image
9.          next_level = controller_2.difficulty
10.         bg_image = pygame.image.load(f"assets/images/
    background/background{next_level}.jpg").convert_alpha()      ←B
```

- We add a new if statement to check when the **intro_count** is just starting. When it is, we load the background image.

- Next the image is loaded according to the **controller_2.difficulty**. For difficulty of 1 then **background1.jpg**, we be used as the background image.

When you are done making the edits and/or reviewing the code, save the file and run the game from the terminal or debugger. *Figure 5.13* shows the results of the new image be loaded for level 2 of the fighting game:

Figure 5.13: New background image for the level

The new background images look great but now it is apparent we should upscale and alter the animation sprites for the fighters. Since we have already covered that in *Chapter 4*, we leave that expedition in your capable hands. Otherwise, this completes this chapter of adding AI bots to a fighting game.

Conclusion

In this chapter, we took a complete barebones implementation of the fighting game and added several new features including the addition of AI-controlled fighters, game difficulty levels and new backgrounds to match those levels. For the AI controls, we looked at a game AI and robotics technology called **Behavior Trees** to control the fighters. Then, we added player difficulty levels using decision timing. We concluded the chapter using *ComfyUI* and *ControlNets* to restyle the games background by level.

In the next chapter, we will continue with 2D and Pygame but move on to the more advanced topic of physics by developing a physics game. Good physics gameplay can set your game apart from other games and is a well-learned skill for game developers.

What we learned

- How to load GitHub code repository into ChatGPT and question the code base using *RAG*.
- How to add an AI controller to a 2D fighting game using *ChatGPT* to suggest code refactoring.
- What are behavior trees and how they fundamentally worked.
- How to construct a behavior tree using *ChatGPT* assisted by *AskTheCode* a GitHub RAG plugin.
- How to add randomness and decrease the predictability of a game AI using behavior trees.
- How to adjust and create player difficulty levels by altering how frequently an AI can make decisions. We learned that the slower the AI took to respond it was generally easier to defeat.
- How to use *ComfyUI* and *Stable Diffusion SDXL* with ControlNets to extract the depth map from an image for use in generating new depth-guided images.

Exercises

The exercises at the end of this section will certainly help you further learn the material but also can help complete features of the game. Be sure to go ahead and tackle at least a couple of these exercises.

1. Update the amount of damage different attacks do. You will likely also want to extend the animation time for those bigger attacks to highlight the extra effort.

2. Update the wizard and warrior animation sprite sheets using the canny edge detection and guided generation workflow we used in *Chapter 4*.

3. Add extra behaviors to the current tree the AI is using. New behaviors could include things like moving back when in attack mode or jump in attack mode.

4. Add a new state to the behavior tree. A new state could be something like *planning* or *resting*. Perhaps when resting the fighter continually moves away from the opponent.

5. Add a new behavior tree to control the fighting AI. This could include new states and actions. Be sure to put this new tree in the same `ai.py` file and just make it a setting or configuration. You may even want to create different behaviors for different levels of fighters, just like a proper fighting game.

6. Add new moves to the warrior or wizard. This will require adding new animations for the move or reusing others and modifying the timing.

7. **BONUS:** Add new characters to the game. This is a big one because it will require creating whole new animation sprite sheets for the new character.

Join our book's Discord space

Join the book's Discord Workspace for Latest updates, Offers, Tech happenings around the world, New Release and Sessions with the Authors:

https://discord.bpbonline.com

CHAPTER 6
Revving up: Cars, Ramps, and Pymunk

Introduction

Game physics can be the most complex element to add to any game. Yet, good game physics can make an incredible difference in the playability and immersion of the game. Games with poor physics will generally annoy players especially if physics is an important element of game play. In some cases, physics may not be a primary element of the game but may play a role in game effects like particle systems.

Structure

This chapter explores the following topics:

- Starting your engine: Introduction to game physics
- Driving forces: Understanding motion and rotation
- Revving the engine: Adding physics to a car
- Jumpstarting your game: Building the ultimate car jump challenge
- Effecting the atmosphere: Adding particle systems with physics
- Colliding clouds: Finishing the game with a goal

Objectives

In this chapter, we dive into the realm of physics and physics systems or engines. We start by looking at what are the basic elements of physics. Then we explore how game objects can use physics to interact with the game world. From there we introduce a car, a complex multiple-part system that employs physics. We will then enhance the car demo into a game that challenges the player to drive over terrain. Finally, the chapter is complete with an introduction to particle systems that use physics.

Starting your engine: Introduction to game physics

Game physics covers a wide range of complex simulations from rigid body dynamics, water, cloth, materials, and even hair. For this basic introduction, we are going to look closely at rigid body dynamics. This area of game physics is well established and the most common form you will use in games.

Rigid body dynamics is an area of physics that describes the interactions between solid and partially elastic objects. Objects like a *box*, *ball*, or *car* can all be described using rigid body dynamics. Yet, this does not include elastic and deformable materials like *water*, *cloth*, and *hair*, typically handled by much more sophisticated engines.

Figure 6.1 shows a car object represented in terms of rigid body dynamics/physics. This system has been simplified just to highlight the element forces in the system. It is also important to consider where these forces act. In general, all forces acting on a body will typically focus on the center of mass (center of gravity). For simple systems, we often use the object's physical center to keep things easy, but this may not always be the case. If we were modeling a real car, for example, we would typically shift the center of mass closer to the engine or front of the car. Please refer to the following figure:

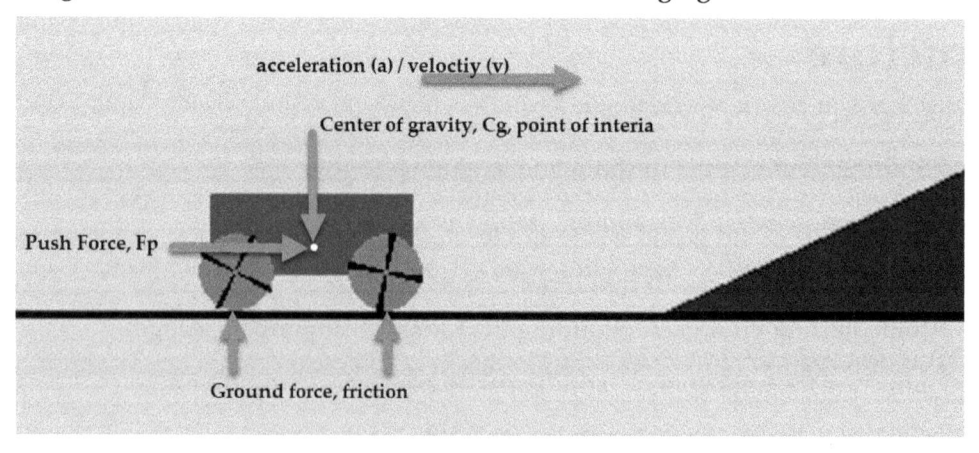

Figure 6.1: Rigid body physics of a car

Physics engines for games were once sold as a stand-alone component and were very pricey. Now, most game engines or game systems employ some form of rigid body physics engine built in. While Pygame is built as a graphics engine, it does not embed a physics engine directly but there is an option, we can use called **Pymunk**.

Pymunk is a Python implementation of a 2D rigid body physics engine, **http://www.pymunk.org/en/latest/**. It is fast, well documented, connects well to Pygame, and has been around for a while. This makes it an excellent option for us to use with Pygame and for Python game development.

In the next exercise, we will employ ChatGPT to build a Pygame/Pymunk physics demo using a basic ball. This will help set the stage and introduce the concepts of embedding Pymunk into a Pygame game.

Exercise 6.1: Building a Physics Demo

1. Open a new conversation with ChatGPT and enter the following prompt:

   Prompt: `Please write a game demo of a dropping ball. Write the demo using Python, Pygame and pymunk for physics. In the demo, the player drops a ball from any height controlled by the mouse. When the player clicks the left mouse button puts a new ball into the scene at the x,y coordinates of the mouse.`

   `After the ball drops, it will hit the ground plane at the bottom of the screen and bounce according to the object's elasticity.`

   `Remember that in Pygame the y axis is inverted and the positive y direction is down.`

   Checkpoint: https://chat.openai.com/share/550431dd-1eae-48bb-be93-51a58d019542

2. Copy the generated code into a new **chapter_6** folder and call it **ball_drop.py**. As always, refer to the book's source code, if you need to see the full baseline or the conversation checkpoint.

3. We would not review all the code here since you should be familiar with the general Pygame code now. Instead, we will focus just on the new physics code starting with the base game object setup shown below:

   1. `# Create a Pymunk space`
   2. `space = pymunk.Space()`
   3. `space.gravity = (0, -900)  # Set gravity (positive y direction is down)`
   4.
   5. `# Create a ground plane`

6. `ground = pymunk.Segment(space.static_body, (0, 0), (SCREEN_WIDTH, 0), 5)`
7. `ground.elasticity = 0.8`
8. `space.add(ground)`

This code creates the **pymunk** scene called space, sets the gravity, and then adds a ground line or segment. The ground elasticity of .8 means the ground is not entirely rigid and has some forgiveness to it. This means that the ground can deform and bounce back. For example, an elastic ball will bounce back when it hits a rigid body with little or no elasticity.

4. Next, we will look at the code that places the ball when the user clicks the left mouse button. When they do, a ball is added to **x, y** position of the mouse as shown below:

1. `elif event.type == pygame.MOUSEBUTTONDOWN and event.button == 1:`
2. `    # Get the mouse position`
3. `    x, y = pygame.mouse.get_pos()`
4.
5. `    # Create a Pymunk circle body and shape`
6. `    mass = 10`   ←A
7. `    radius = 20`
8. `    inertia = pymunk.moment_for_circle(mass, 0, radius)`   ←B
9. `    body = pymunk.Body(mass, inertia)`   ←C
10. `    body.position = x, SCREEN_HEIGHT - y  # Invert y-axis`
11.
12. `    shape = pymunk.Circle(body, radius)`   ←D
13. `    shape.elasticity = 0.7  # Set elasticity`   ←E
14. `    space.add(body, shape)`
15. `    balls.append(shape)`

Let us get into this code in some detail, as shown by the following points:

a. All rigid body objects have a mass.

b. Inertia or the inertial reference point of an object represents the point all forces will act on an object. *Figure 6.1* represents the center where all forces will act on the object. In a ball, that point is often the center of the ball/circle.

c. All physical objects need a body, short for a rigid body and a point of inertia.

d. The shape of an object may often be different. We do this to represent physics objects in some lower form and more efficient form of geometry. For example, the shape of a ball is a whole collection of points and connecting segments. But we would not want to test every point on a circle/ball for physical interactions, which could be expensive. Instead, the body of the ball is represented by a point and radius, which makes calculating physical interactions much easier.

e. The elasticity of a shape again represents how malleable an object is and how well it bounces back.

5. Save the file, **ball_drop.py**, and run it from the terminal or debug it with VS Code. *Figure 6.2* shows an example of the balls dropping and bouncing around the screen:

Figure 6.2: Running the ball drop demo

This last demo showcased a very simple example of game physics using Pymunk. In the next section, we are going to upscale this demo to include more objects and different shapes.

Driving forces: Understanding motion and rotation

We are going to jump right into the next demo and look at how multiple objects interact with each other in real time. This includes understanding the effects of object rotation, elasticity, and rotation. Let us jump right into the next exercise and see what we can build with *ChatGPT*.

Exercise 6.2: Adding more scene objects

1. Open a new conversation with ChatGPT and enter the following prompt:

    Prompt: `Create a scene demonstrating game physics using Python, Pygame and Pymunk.`

    `The scene should have objects: 10 balls, 10 boxes and a ground plane.`

    `Make sure the ball and box can both rotate on the z axis.`

    `The ground plane at the bottom of the screen will stop all objects.`

    `Please be sure to account for the positive y axis in the downward direction.`

    Checkpoint: https://chat.openai.com/share/c32b5f0e-b025-4928-a428-0d10a6ae85cf

2. Copy the generated code into a new file called **box_ball.py**. Then, run the code from the terminal or with the VS Code debugger. *Figure 6.3* shows the output of running the demo. Notice how the boxes collide with the balls and other boxes but remain fixed and do not rotate. Please refer to the following figure:

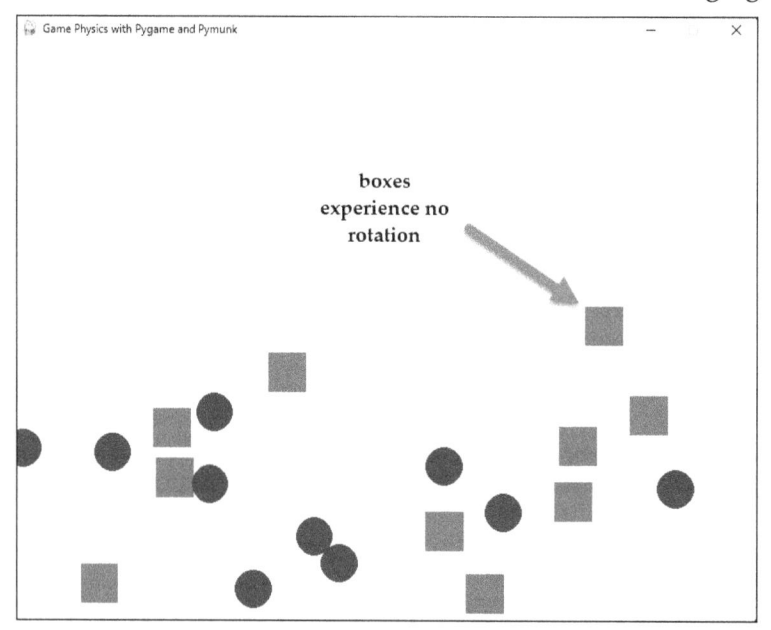

Figure 6.3: Running the box and ball demo

We can go back and ask ChatGPT what is wrong and try to fix it through iteration. Below is a summary of the conversation. The complete version can be found at the checkpoint link mentioned above.

First iteration

Prompt: `The boxes do not rotate when they collide, what is missing?`

ChatGPT will respond that the code it initially provided was missing the angular velocity term when it initially created the objects. Below is the corrected code included in the function that creates the boxes:

```
1.  def create_box(space, x, y):
2.      mass = 1
3.      size = 40
4.      moment = pymunk.moment_for_box(mass, (size, size))        ←A
5.      body = pymunk.Body(mass, moment)        ←A
6.      body.position = x, y
7.      body.angular_velocity = random.uniform(-1, 1)        ←B
8.      shape = pymunk.Poly.create_box(body, (size, size))        ←C
9.      shape.elasticity = 0.95
10.     space.add(body, shape)
11.     return shape
```

The above code callouts are described below:

a. These lines construct the rigid body. To begin with, a moment of inertia is created for an object of a given mass and dimensions, defined by (size, size) a square box. Then, the body is created with the mass and the inertial reference point.

b. We set the object's angular velocity randomly from **-1** to **1**. This line is actually not needed, as we will see.

c. This line creates the shape of the object. In this case, the boxes' physical body and visual shape are the same. As mentioned above, this may not always be the case, especially if the visual shape is more complex such as a 3D mesh.

If you go ahead and copy/paste the updated code and run it, you will be disappointed. The boxes still do not rotate. So, let us look at the code and see what ChatGPT may be missing, below is the drawing/rendering code for the boxes/balls:

```
1.  for shape in space.shapes:
2.      if isinstance(shape, pymunk.Circle):
3.          x, y = shape.body.position
4.          pygame.draw.circle(screen, (0, 0, 255), (int(x), int(y)), int(shape.radius), 0)
```

```
5.     elif isinstance(shape, pymunk.Poly):
6.         points = shape.get_vertices()
7.         points = [(int(shape.body.position.x + x), int(shape.body.position.y + y)) for x, y in points]
8.         pygame.draw.polygon(screen, (255, 0, 0), points)
```

Looking at the code again, you can see both the box and circle are just getting drawn from the objects' center point of reference. This code does not look to be accounting for any of the object's rotation, let us ask ChatGPT.

Second iteration

Prompt: `I do not think you are accounting for the box's rotation vector when drawing the box, can you add the code to render the box with the rotation vector, please?`

Indeed, ChatGPT comes back quickly with an updated listing. Go ahead copy/paste the code into the same file and run it using your preference. *Figure 6.4* now shows the boxes rotating when they collide:

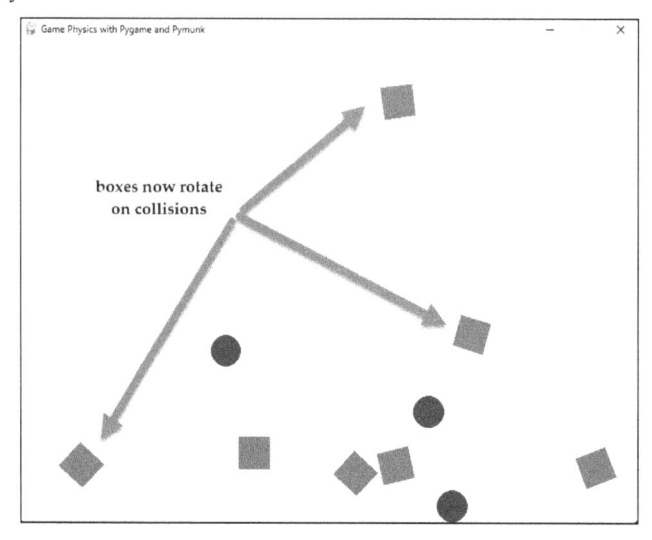

Figure 6.4: Updated demo showing rotating boxes

This appears to have fixed the problem. Let us open the code and check out what the fix was by looking at the updated rendering code for the boxes:

```
1. elif isinstance(shape, pymunk.Poly):
2.     body = shape.body
3.     vertices = [p.rotated(body.angle) + body.position for p in shape.get_vertices()]    ←A
```

```
4.      vertices = [(int(x), int(y)) for x, y in vertices]      ←B
5.      pygame.draw.polygon(screen, (255, 0, 0), vertices)       ←C
```

The code callouts are described below:

a. The code now extracts the vertices or points that comprise the box's shape outline and rotates them according to the angle of the rigid body.

b. The vertices or shape points are now converted into a list of **x, y** tuples called **vertices**. The box will have four vertices that define the coordinates of the box's corners.

c. Finally, the vertices are drawn to the screen using the **draw.polygon** function.

We have now seen how to rotate the box given the underlying rigid body. Although there is a function that can do this automatically; here, for some reason, in this version, ChatGPT avoided using it. However, there are also other reasons why you often want to draw the shape entirely yourself.

Calculating all the interactions in a rigid body physics environment is computationally expensive. For this reason, you generally want to keep the description of your rigid body objects to be expressed using simple geometries like a box, sphere, and cylinder. This helps simplify the calculations, but it sometimes comes with a penalty.

Figure 6.5 shows what this may look like for a full character in 2D or 3D. The character is constructed of simple rigid bodies, like *circles/spheres* and *cylinders*. The shape or how the character is drawn is controlled by the rigid body. This same concept is applied to 2D and 3D games alike. It is often more important for 3D games since the extra dimension can make physics calculations even more expensive. Please refer to the following figure:

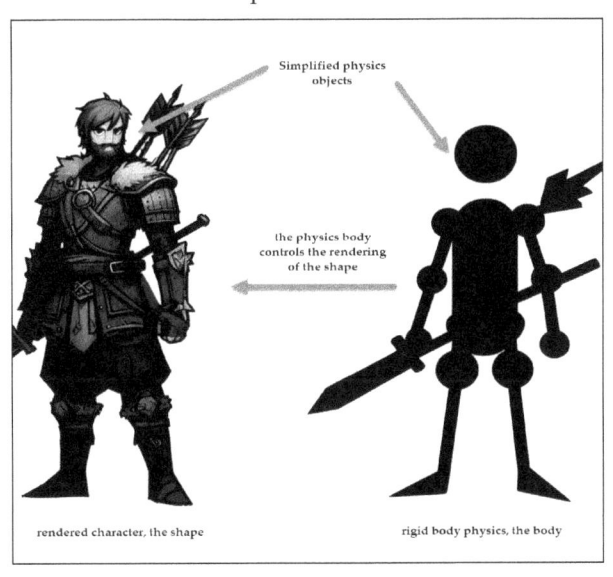

Figure 6.5: Showing differences between shapes and bodies in physics systems

For complex physical objects like *game characters* and *cars*, we need to connect multiple simpler rigid body geometries to comprise the entire object. We will see how this works in the next section where we start our car game.

Revving the engine: Adding physics to a car

The racing game and other games with cars provide an excellent introduction to physics in games. Car physics development in games was a precursor to many of the fantastic physics systems we see today. From a car's springing suspension to the acceleration raise of the hood or declination when breaking, physics in cars can be quite simple or highly complex.

In the next exercise, we are going to start the project we will continue to the end of the chapter. It will take us several iterations and tweaks to get this right. At the same time, this will also be a great learning experience in using ChatGPT to tackle complex coding problems.

Exercise 6.3: Creating the base car game

1. Open a new conversation with ChatGPT and enter the following prompt:

    Prompt: `Please create a game demo with Python, Pygame and pymunk for physics.`

    `In the demo, create a basic 2D car in profile with a body and 2 wheels.`

    `The car sits on a static ground plane at the bottom of the screen (x=0, y=SCREEN_HEIGHT). The ground plane should be infinite in both directions (10000).`

    `The player can push the car (mass=1000) with a positive force (2000) in the x direction by typing the key. The player can also apply a negative force (-2000) in x direction by typing the D key.`

    `Be sure to make the wheels on the car rotate as the car moves. To demonstrate this, draw a simple spoke pattern on the car's wheels. Make sure the wheels are attached to the car and don't fall off when the car moves.`

    `When the car moves off the screen, move the screen/camera to focus on the car, making the ground plane infinite in both directions so the car never falls off.`

    `Please add grey cloud shapes to the background placed at random locations across the entire limits of the ground plane. This will allow the player to see the car move across the screen.`

    `Please only show the code and nothing else.`

2. Go ahead and enter this prompt into ChatGPT, a saved text version is also available in the *Chapter 6* source code folder under `Chapter_Prompts.txt`. Copy/paste the code into a new file called `car_force.py` and run it, using your preference.

3. What you will likely find, regardless of whether you use ChatGPT 3.5 or 4 and even later versions, is that we are asking for too much. This will result in a demo that does not work and probably just seems way off. We can of course rectify this by being more methodical.

   Open a new chat conversation and enter the following prompt:

   Prompt: `Please create a game demo with Python, Pygame and pymunk for physics.`

   `In the demo, create a basic 2D car in profile with a body and 2 wheels.`

   `The car (mass=1000) sits on a static ground plane at the bottom of the screen. The ground plane should be infinite in both directions (10000).`

   `The player can push the car with a positive force (2000) in the x direction by typing A key. The player can also apply a negative force (-2000) in x direction by typing the D key.`

   `Make sure the wheels are attached to the car and do not fall off when the car moves. Also, please show the wheels rotate as the car moves.`

   `Remember that in Pygame the y axis is inverted, y positive is down.`

   `SYSTEM: ONLY RETURN THE CODE AND NOTHING ELSE, NO COMMENTS ONLY CODE.`

   Checkpoint: https://chat.openai.com/share/b7d85277-a736-4381-a91d-b8da150bbe16

This time we limited our request to three or so main features we wanted from the car demo/game. There is also the addition of a System prompt to make sure ChatGPT only returns the code and no commentary. Remember that ChatGPT has a token limit, and it often makes sense to trim any unnecessary conversation. This will help ChatGPT be more focused on the code.

Since this is going to take numerous iterations, create a new file called `car_push_a.py` and copy the generated code. *Figure 6.6* shows the result of running the code. It looks like something is wrong, go ahead and ask ChatGPT:

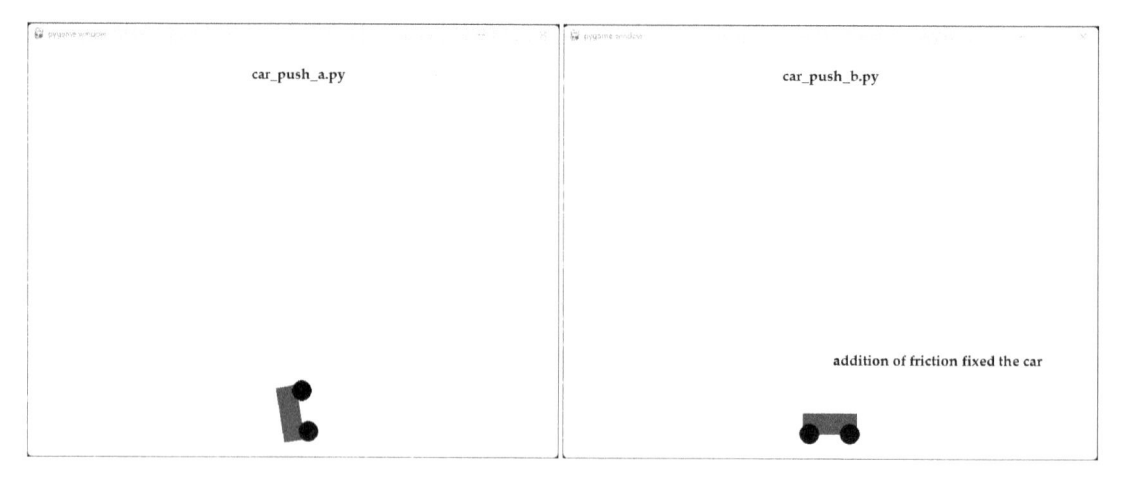

Figure 6.6: Running the car demo before and after the addition of friction

First iteration

Prompt: That is almost there. When the car lands on the ground, it bounces and flips over. Can you make the car more stable?

Copy the generated code into a new file called **car_push_b.py** and run it. You will see the results of the car now landing upright. ChatGPT will also inform us that it omitted to add friction into the system but has since added it. Below is the code showing the rigid body car construction in more detail:

```
1. space = pymunk.Space()
2. space.gravity = (0, 900)
3. space.damping = 0.9  # Apply damping to reduce bouncing effect
4.
5. car_body = pymunk.Body(1000, pymunk.moment_for_box(1000, (80, 30)))
6. car_body.position = 400, 300
7. car_poly = pymunk.Poly.create_box(car_body, (80, 30))
8. car_poly.friction = 0.7  # Increase friction          ←A
9. space.add(car_body, car_poly)
10.
11. wheels = []
12. for offset in [-30, 30]:
13.     wheel_body = pymunk.Body(50, pymunk.moment_for_circle(50, 0, 15))
```

```
14.        wheel_body.position = car_body.position.x + offset, car_
       body.position.y + 15
15.        wheel_shape = pymunk.Circle(wheel_body, 15)
16.        wheel_shape.friction = 1.0        ←B
17.        space.add(wheel_body, wheel_shape)
18.        wheels.append(wheel_body)
19.        slide_joint = pymunk.SlideJoint(car_body, wheel_body,
       (offset, 15), (0, 0), 0, 25)        ←C
20.        space.add(slide_joint)
21.        pin_joint = pymunk.PivotJoint(car_body, wheel_body, (car_
       body.position.x + offset, car_body.position.y + 15))        ←C
22.        pin_joint.collide_bodies = False
23.        space.add(pin_joint)
```

The above code callouts are described below:

a. Add friction to the car body. Keep in mind that this will only affect objects moving directly against the car body.

b. For each of the wheels, we add a very high coefficient of friction. This is the friction between the wheel and what it touches but not the car body. The connection to the car body is different.

c. Each of the wheels also needs to be connected to the car's rigid body but in a manner that still allows them to rotate. This is done using a pin and slide joints. The pin joint acts as the car axle and the slide joint is like the suspension or spring. You can find more info about joints in Pymunk here: **https://www.pymunk.org/en/latest/tutorials/SlideAndPinJoint.html**

So now, we have a car on the screen. We can push it using the *A* or *D* keys. What you will find though is that you can quickly push the car off-screen. So now, we can add a couple of features to fix this behavior and add some other elements.

Second iteration

Open the same chat conversation and enter the following prompt:

Prompt: Please update the code with these features:

Be sure to fix the camera to the car and move the camera with the car. To show the car is moving, create a background of random clouds from x=0 to x = 10000.

Please return the entire listing and only the listing

Copy the generated code listing into a new file called **car_push_c.py**. Then, run the file using your preferred method. *Figure 6.7* shows the results of running this new version. Evidently, we have a bit more work to do:

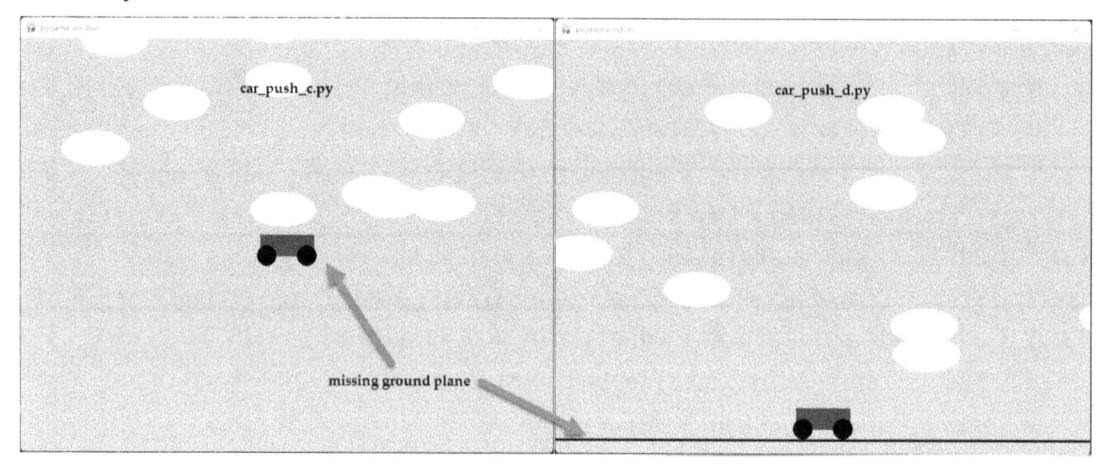

Figure 6.7: Making sure the ground plane is drawn

Fortunately, the fix is not so difficult, keep the same conversation open and enter the next prompt, in the *third iteration*.

Third iteration

Prompt: `Please draw the ground plane at the bottom of the screen.`

`SYSTEM: always return the full listing and nothing else.`

Again, we remind ChatGPT with a System prompt to return just the generated code and nothing else. Take the generated output, copy it to another new file, **car_push_d.py**, save it, and run it. The fix was nothing major and be sure to check the differences in the code between the files.

We now have a car we can push/drive for some distance on the screen but not much else happens. In the next section, we are going to look at adding some obstacles to make our demo into more of a game.

Jumpstarting your game: Building the ultimate car jump challenge

Our simple car push demonstration is looking good. Now it is time to transition this into a game. The game will be simple and allow the player to leisurely drive across the screen racing or jumping over obstacles.

In the next exercise, we are going to continue where we left off in the last section by adding a new feature to the game, rotating wheels. As it is right now, the car just appears to slide across the screen. Adding motion to the wheels will give us more player immersion.

Exercise 6.4: Rotating the tires

Return to the previous conversation with ChatGPT and enter the following prompt:

Fourth iteration

Prompt: `Now, can you show the wheels rotate as the car moves, please.`

A simple request for what can be a difficult item to get right. Copy the code into a new file called **car_push_e.py** and then run it. *Figure 6.8* shows an example of what the new car looks like. It is not really what we are looking for, it looks like it may take some hands-on coding to fix. Please refer to the following figure:

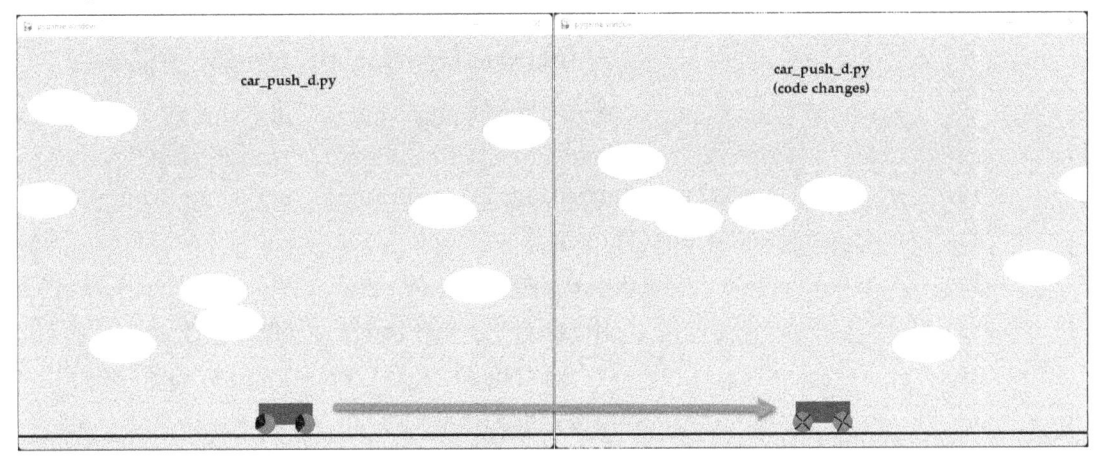

Figure 6.8: Before and after of spokes on car wheels

Open the **car_push_e.py** and scroll down to the wheel rendering code, shown below. This code is just rendering an arc on the wheel to represent some form of tire spokes. The effect is not great.

```
1.  for wheel in wheels:
2.      pygame.draw.circle(screen, (64, 128, 255), (int(wheel.position.x + offset_x), int(wheel.position.y)), 15)
3.      angle = wheel.position.x * -0.1  # Assuming wheel radius as 15, this gives a rotation for the wheel
4.      pygame.draw.arc(screen,
5.                      (0, 0, 0),
6.                      (int(wheel.position.x + offset_x) - 15,
```

```
7.                          int(wheel.position.y) - 15, 30, 30),
8.                      angle + 1, angle + 3,
9.                      15)
```

The fix for this is some good old repetitive code that will use the same idea but shrink the angle and draw the spokes. Below is the updated code:

```
1.  for wheel in wheels:
2.      pygame.draw.circle(screen, (64, 128, 255), (int(wheel.position.x + offset_x), int(wheel.position.y)), 15)
3.      angle = wheel.position.x * -0.1  # Assuming wheel radius as 15, this gives a rotation for the wheel
4.      pygame.draw.arc(screen,
5.                      (0, 0, 0),
6.                      (int(wheel.position.x + offset_x) - 15,
7.                          int(wheel.position.y) - 15, 30, 30),
8.                      angle, angle + .1,         ←A
9.                      15)
10.     angle = angle + math.pi / 2     ←B
11.     pygame.draw.arc(screen,
12.                     (0, 0, 0),
13.                     (int(wheel.position.x + offset_x) - 15,
14.                         int(wheel.position.y) - 15, 30, 30),
15.                     angle, angle + .1,         ←A
16.                     15)
17.     angle = angle + math.pi / 2     ←B
18.     pygame.draw.arc(screen,
19.                     (0, 0, 0),
20.                     (int(wheel.position.x + offset_x) - 15,
21.                         int(wheel.position.y) - 15, 30, 30),
22.                     angle, angle + .1,         ←A
23.                     15)
24.     angle = angle + math.pi / 2     ←B
25.     pygame.draw.arc(screen,
26.                     (0, 0, 0),
27.                     (int(wheel.position.x + offset_x) - 15,
```

```
28.                    int(wheel.position.y) - 15, 30, 30),
29.                    angle, angle + .1        ←A
```

The code callouts are described below:

- a. This line draws the arc starting at the current angle and increasing it slightly by .1 radians. It is important to remember all angle measurements will be in radians and not degrees. Remember, there are two Pi radians in a full circle.
- b. After each spoke is drawn, we increase the angle by 90 degrees or **math.pi / 2** radians. Then, draw another spoke, the result is 4 evenly placed spokes.

After the changes are made, save the code and run the file again. Now, the vehicle has four spokes around the wheels that rotate when the car moves forward/backwards.

For the next feature, we will add some debug information and the ability to increase the amount of force used to push the vehicle. Adding debug information to your games early can help troubleshoot many problems in gameplay and logic.

Fifth iteration

Prompt: Now, please display the car's speed in the top left corner.

Again, copy the generated code and paste it into a new file called **car_push_f.py**. Now, when you run the game the vehicle speed will be displayed in the top corner. We want to also allow the player the ability to increase the force for every push. This will be like adding a gear shift to the vehicle.

Open the file up in VS Code and add the following code to control the force used to push the car. If you prefer you can also review the completed file (**car_push_f.py**) in the book's source folder.

```
1.  car_force = 20000      ←A
2.
3.  # game loop ...
4.      keys = pygame.key.get_pressed()
5.      if keys[pygame.K_a]:
6.          car_body.apply_force_at_local_point((car_force, 0), (0, 0))
7.      if keys[pygame.K_d]:
8.          car_body.apply_force_at_local_point((-car_force, 0), (0, 0))
9.      if keys[pygame.K_f]:
10.         car_force += 1000      ←B
```

11.
12.   # ...
13.
14.   speed_text = font.render(f"Speed: {int(car_body.velocity.x)}", True, (0, 0, 0))
15.   screen.blit(speed_text, (10, 10))
16.   force_text = font.render(f"Force: {car_force:.2f}", True, (0, 0, 0))   ←3
17.   screen.blit(force_text, (10, 10 + FONT_HEIGHT))   ←c

The code callouts are described below:

a. Make the force of the car a variable, start it at 20000.

b. Increase the force when the *F* key is pressed.

c. Draw the speed/velocity and force in the top left corner of the screen. We use speed, but really, we are using the objects' velocity. Remember, speed is how fast something is going, and velocity is how fast it is going and the direction it is going in.

Go ahead and save the changes and then run the file. *Figure 6.9* shows the updated results of running the new version. Hit the *F* key to increase the force and then push the car with the *A* key. See how fast you can get the car to go before the ground runs out. Please refer to the following figure:

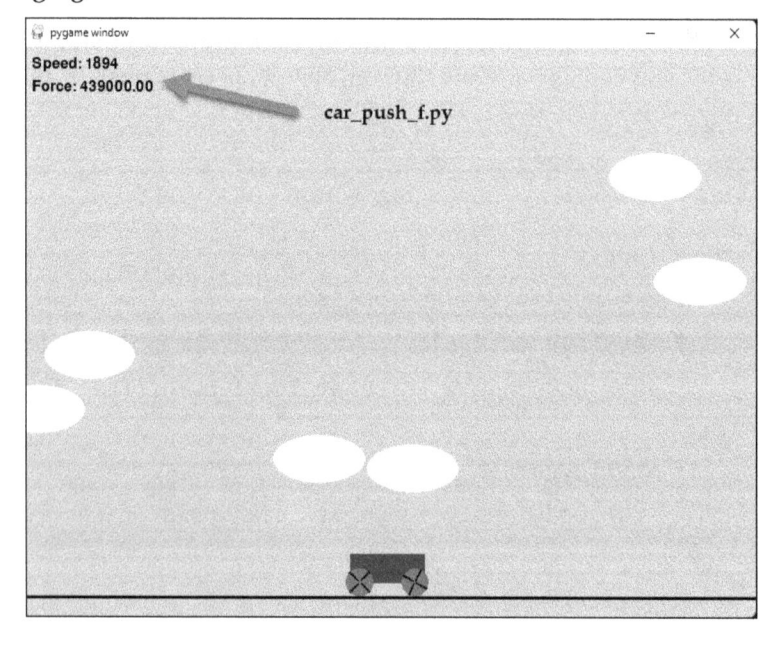

Figure 6.9: Game now shows speed and force

Notice how after the iteration, we are making sure ChatGPT keeps the entire code listing current. By doing this, we make sure ChatGPT does not lose focus over the multiple iterations. EasyCode is also an option here, but **Retrieval Augmented Generation (RAG)** does not always give you the results you expect. This makes sure ChatGPT focuses on the code we want it to focus on.

In the last exercise of this section, we are going to make the demo more of a game by adding obstacles or jumps. Again, we are continuing to use the same single code file as the primary input to ChatGPT and then a prompt/request.

Exercise 6.5: Adding the obstacles/jumps

Return to the previous conversation with ChatGPT and enter the following prompt.

Sixth iteration

Prompt: `Now please add random triangle shapes on the ground surface with the pointy end up. Make the triangles very wide and not very tall so the car can jump over them.`

Checkpoint: https://chat.openai.com/share/b7d85277-a736-4381-a91d-b8da150bbe16

Copy the generated code into yet another new file called `car_push_g.py` and save it then run it. *Figure 6.10* shows the output of running this new version of the game:

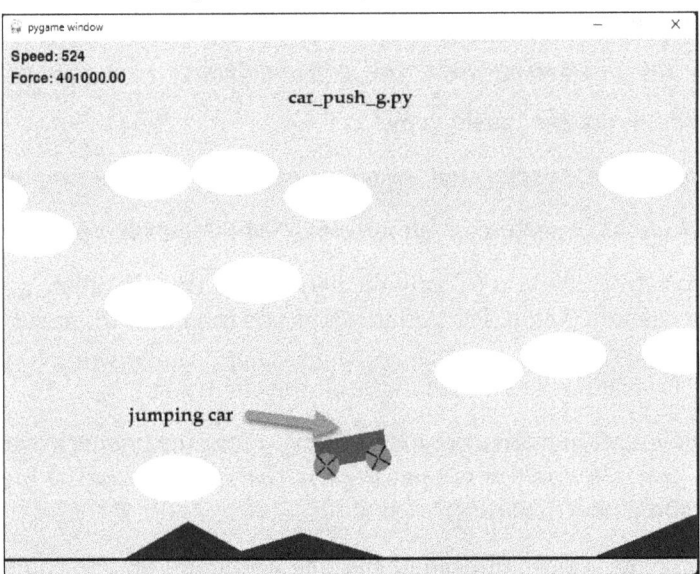

Figure 6.10: The car jump challenge game

We have a working game, almost. Play the game and see how far you can get the car to jump. Avoid flipping over the car and just imagine what other things could be introduced to make this a real game (**Hint**: The clouds are already there). In the next section, we are going to add another application of physics to the game, particle effects.

Effecting the atmosphere: Adding particle systems with physics

Rigid body dynamics is one application for a physics system, but it can also be used for so much more. You may not realize that but one system that relies heavily on physics is the particle system or effects.

Particle systems in games cover all manner of effects from smoke or fire to explosions and even object spawning. Adding a particle system to a game can be challenging because you now need to track dozens to hundreds of particles. Fortunately, there are some well-designed patterns that make this an easy addition to any game.

In the next exercise, we are going to add a smoke/exhaust particle to our car. This will not only look cool but add to the immersion of our game.

Exercise 6.6: Adding smoke/exhaust to the game

Open a new conversation with ChatGPT and enter the following prompt:

Seventh iteration

Prompt: `I have the following code for a game demo:`

`Copy source code from car_push_g.py.`

`Please add a particle system and smoke particles to the car using Pymunk.`

Checkpoint: https://chat.openai.com/share/e662b534-50d6-4929-b6e0-18b4882011fb

Notice that this prompt asks you to copy the contents of the `car_push_g.py` code into the same prompt you send to ChatGPT. You can add line breaks without submitting the chat by typing *Shift + Enter*. Before proceeding, make a copy of the game to a new file called `car_push_h.py`. This is the file we will make all the changes to.

What comes back is a set of instructions for adding a couple of new classes and other code to the game. We will not worry about getting ChatGPT to recreate the full listing because we will need to add a new file anyway.

Go to VS Code, create a new file called particle and copy all the code ChatGPT gives you for the `ParticleSystem` and `SmokeParticle` class. We will start by digging into some details of the `ParticleSystem` class, shown below. The form of this class is more or less standard for a particle system.

```
1.  class ParticleSystem:
2.      def __init__(self, space):
3.          self.space = space
4.          self.particles = []
5.
6.      def emit(self, x, y, velocity, lifespan):      ←A
7.          particle = SmokeParticle(x, y, velocity, lifespan)
8.          self.particles.append(particle)
9.          self.space.add(particle.body, particle.shape)
10.
11.     def update(self, dt):      ←B
12.         for particle in self.particles[:]:
13.             alive = particle.update(dt)
14.             if not alive:
15.                 self.space.remove(particle.body, particle.shape)
16.                 self.particles.remove(particle)
17.
18.     def draw(self, screen, offset_x):      ←C
19.         for particle in self.particles:
20.             particle.draw(screen, offset_x)
```

The above code callouts are described below:

a. The **emit** function is the point that creates new particles. In this class that particle is hard-coded to the **SmokeParticle** but in many cases you would pass in the type of particle to emit.

b. The **update** function is where we move or update the particle in physics space. Remember that the particle system is tied to the physics engine.

c. The **draw** function is where the particle is rendered to the screen. Inside this function, you can see that the particle will draw itself by calling the **particle.draw** function.

Now, let us look at the **SmokeParticle** class. Generally, you may have several different particle types depending on the behavior. In many cases though, particles can be reused for multiple purposes just by adjusting their physical properties. This code has already been updated to address minor updates and fixes.

```
1.  class SmokeParticle:
2.      def __init__(self, x, y, velocity, lifespan):
3.          self.body = pymunk.Body(1, pymunk.moment_for_circle(1, 0, 5))     ←A
4.          self.body.position = x, y
5.          self.body.velocity = velocity       ←B
6.          self.body.velocity_func = self.no_gravity      ←C
7.          self.lifespan = lifespan
8.          self.life_elapsed = 0
9.          self.shape = pymunk.Circle(self.body, 5)
10.         self.shape.collision_type = 99  # A unique collision type for smoke particles
11.         self.shape.sensor = True  # Ensure that they don't interfere with other bodies      ←D
12.         self.radius = 5
13.         self.image = pygame.Surface((10, 10), pygame.SRCALPHA)   # Create a transparent surface
14.         pygame.draw.circle(self.image, (150, 150, 150), (5, 5), self.radius)
15.
16.     def update(self, dt):      ←E
17.         self.life_elapsed += dt
18.         self.radius += .1
19.         if self.life_elapsed >= self.lifespan:
20.             return False
21.         return True
22.
23.     def no_gravity(self, body, gravity, damping, dt):      ←C
24.         body.velocity *= 0.99  # A slight damping to make smoke slow down over time
25.
26.     def draw(self, screen, offset_x):     ←F
27.         alpha = int(255 * (1 - self.life_elapsed / self.lifespan))
28.         temp_image = self.image.copy()  # Copy the image to not modify the original
```

```
29.            temp_image.fill((255, 255, 255, alpha), special_
    flags=pygame.BLEND_RGBA_MULT)   # Apply the alpha
30.            screen.blit(temp_image, (int(self.body.position.x +
    offset_x) - 5, int(self.body.position.y) - 5))
```

The above code callouts are described below:

- a. The basic particle body is just a circle. This will likely be the case for most particles.

- b. Particles will be typically emitted with some starting velocity.

- c. Since our particles are smoke, we do not want gravity to affect it. To do this we create a new function called **no_gravity** and set it to the **velocity_func** function. This feature allows you to alter the physics of objects like *smoke* or *fire*.

- d. We also set a flag on object, 99, so that the object does not collide with other objects in the scene. In some cases, you may want your particles to interact with other objects. For example, debris from an explosion, but for a smoke particle it is better to leave it and do its thing.

- e. The **update** function ticks away at the life of the particle. Most particles will only have a short lifespan, smoke being a good example of this. Inside the **update** notice how the particle size is also increased like we may expect a puff of smoke to dissipate.

- f. Then, we draw the particle as an image. This is done so that we can add an alpha channel or transparency to the image. The alpha channel represents how transparent a color is. When a color has an alpha value of 255, it is opaque and a value of 0 is fully transparent.

The addition of those 2 classes adds a new code file to our game. Now, we can add the particle system to the game using the directions from ChatGPT. The following code can be added to the rest of the game loop rendering code:

```
1. particle_system.update(1/60.0)
2. particle_system.draw(screen, offset_x)
```

Finally, we need to add the code to emit the particles. We will do this anytime the player presses the *A* or *D* keys using the following code:

```
1. keys = pygame.key.get_pressed()
2. if keys[pygame.K_a]:
3.     car_body.apply_force_at_local_point((car_force, 0), (0, 0))
4.     particle_system.emit(car_body.position.x - 40,
5.                          car_body.position.y,
```

```
6.                              (car_body.velocity.x * 0.1,
7.                              -100 + random.uniform(-100, 20)),
8.                              2)
9.   if keys[pygame.K_d]:
10.      car_body.apply_force_at_local_point((-car_force, 0), (0, 0))
11.      particle_system.emit(car_body.position.x - 40,
12.                              car_body.position.y,
13.                              (car_body.velocity.x * 0.1,
14.                              -100 + random.uniform(-120, 20)),
15.                              2)
16.  if keys[pygame.K_f]:
17.      car_force += 1000
```

Again, some of this code has already been updated to make sure the smoke particles rise and only emit from one end of the car. After you make the changes, save the file and go ahead and run it. *Figure 6.11* shows the results of the new smoke/exhaust particles emitted from the car:

Figure 6.11: Exhaust/smoke particles emitted from the car

The wheels are moving, the exhaust is blowing, and the car can jump, we have the making of a simple 2D driving game. In the next section, we will finish off the game by adding a goal and a method to track the score.

Colliding clouds: Finishing the game with a goal

Often you will have a great idea for some game mechanics but wrapping them in a unique game is not always so easy. Flipped the other way around, sometimes you have a great game idea but are not sure how to implement the mechanics. The car push game we developed is a good example of the former. We have a car game moving with physics, but now what?

Now, not all games need a goal. Indeed, the whole open-world game genre is all about doing your thing. However, a general rule is the more basic a game, the better the goal definition should be. Players would not like playing your game for hours, if they do not like the goal and/or the game is too shallow.

For our car push game, therefore, we will define the game goal as hitting as many clouds as you can before the end of the level. This is a very simple and well-defined goal that is open-ended enough to give the leader some options to obtain. Another factor with goals is that you want them attainable, but the more paths to attainment the better.

In the next exercise, we will start by making the cloud bodies in the physics system. That way the car will be able to collide with them. Then, when there is a collision, we want the cloud to burst into a puff of smoke.

Exercise 6.7: Colliding with the clouds

Open a new conversation with ChatGPT and enter the following prompt:

Eighth iteration

Prompt: `I have the following game built with Pygame and Pymunk:`

`source code from car_push_h.py`

`I want to make the clouds physical objects that if hit by the car explode into a bunch of smoke particles. Can you please add this feature to the code?`

Checkpoint: https://chat.openai.com/share/8f819bdc-afdf-417f-9ef6-d1f2c51b39d2

This will create a set of instructions for updating the code to add the new features we requested. Let us go ahead and work through this. Make a copy of the **car_push_h.py** to a new file called **car_push_i.py**. Do not worry, we have plenty of letters left in the alphabet.

Open VS Code to the new file and start by making the changes. The first change is making the clouds physical game objects. By now, most of this code should look familiar. There is a callout (1) that identifies the **body_type** as **STATIC**. This means that although the objects are now physical, they are not affected by gravity or object collisions. This still means objects can collide with them, but they would not move.

```
1.  # Instead of just positions
2.  # clouds = [(random.randint(0, 10000), random.randint(100,
    500)) for _ in range(100)]
3.
4.  clouds = []
5.  for _ in range(100):
6.      x = random.randint(0, 10000)
7.      y = random.randint(100, 500)
8.      cloud_body = pymunk.Body(body_type=pymunk.Body.STATIC)
9.      cloud_body.position = x, y
10.     cloud_shape = pymunk.Circle(cloud_body, 50)  # Approximate the cloud as a circle for simplicity
11.     cloud_shape.friction = 1.0
12.     cloud_shape.collision_type = 1  # Unique identifier for clouds
13.     space.add(cloud_body, cloud_shape)
14.     clouds.append(cloud_shape)
```

We already have other static objects in the scene. However, for the clouds, we want to detect when the car or another object collides with them. ChatGPT realizes this and provides a special collision function for us.

```
1.  def cloud_collision(arbiter, space, _):
2.      cloud_shape, car_shape = arbiter.shapes
3.      particle_system.emit_many(cloud_shape.body.position.x,        ←A
4.                                cloud_shape.body.position.y,
5.                                50,
6.                                variance=(100, 100),
7.                                speed=200,
8.                                particle_lifetime=2.0)              ←B
9.      space.remove(cloud_shape, cloud_shape.body)
10.     clouds.remove(cloud_shape)     ←C
11.     return False
12.
13. space.add_collision_handler(1, 0).begin = cloud_collision   # 0 is the default collision type which our car uses
```

The above code callouts are described below:

   a. ChatGPT adds a new function to the particle system class, which we will see later. This function allows for the emission of multiple particles at a time.

   b. The life of these particles is short compared to the cars' exhaust smoke. We can decide to increase or decrease this depending on the effect we want.

   c. When a cloud collides, we remove it from the physical and visual worlds.

Now, let us add new rendering code for the clouds. This time the visual clouds are dependent on their new physical shape location.

```
1.  # Replace the previous loop that drew clouds based on fixed
    positions
2.  for cloud_shape in clouds:
3.      pygame.draw.ellipse(screen,
4.                          (255, 255, 255),
5.                          (cloud_shape.body.position.x + offset_x - 50,
6.                           cloud_shape.body.position.y - 25, 100,
7.                           50))
```

Finally, the last code change is adding the **emit_many** functions to the **ParticleSystem** class. Open the **particle.py** file in VS Code and add the following function to the class:

```
1.  def emit_many(self, x, y, count, variance=(0, 0), speed=100,
    particle_lifetime=1.0):
2.      for _ in range(count):
3.          angle = random.uniform(0, 2 * math.pi)           ←A
4.          velocity = (math.cos(angle) * speed + random.uniform(-
    variance[0], variance[0]),
5.                      math.sin(angle) * speed + random.uniform(-
    variance[1], variance[1]))        ←B
6.          self.emit(x, y, velocity, particle_lifetime)      ←C
```

The code callouts are described below:

   a. We calculate a random angle between 0 and 2 **math.pi** radians. If we convert that to degrees, it equals 0 to 360 degrees. Chances are if you are an experienced Python programmer, you already realize maths functions use radians and not degrees.

   b. The angle calculated previously is then used to calculate the particle's random velocity. Remember velocity is a 2D vector or tuple in this case that represents magnitude and direction. If you are unsure what a vector is then ask ChatGPT, of course.

c. For each particle the `emit` function is called using those earlier calculated or set values.

Save all the changes to the `particle.py` and `car_push_i.py` files and run the game (version `i`) using your preference. Please refer to the following figure:

Figure 6.12: Jumping cars and bursting clouds

We now have a simple goal that challenges the player to understand the physics game mechanics to be successful. The last thing we need to do is keep track of the player's score. Of course, there are several other things, but we need to work left for the chapter exercises.

Exercise 6.8: Finishing the score

In the next and last chapter exercise, we are going to do this manually. There are just a few simple code changes that we can quickly do without asking ChatGPT. Sometimes, it just makes more sense to update the code yourself.

Ninth iteration

Copy the last version `car_push_i.py` to a new file `car_push_j.py` and open it in VS Code.

First, add a new variable called `score` to the top of the file, just before the game loop, as shown below:

Revving up: Cars, Ramps, and Pymunk   189

```
1. car_force = 20000
2. score = 0        ←new variable
```

Second, add the new variable to the cloud collision function as a global variable and increase it when a collision occurs.

```
1.  def cloud_collision(arbiter, space, _):
2.      global score      ←A
3.      cloud_shape, car_shape = arbiter.shapes
4.      particle_system.emit_many(cloud_shape.body.position.x,
5.                                cloud_shape.body.position.y,
6.                                50,
7.                                variance=(100, 100),
8.                                speed=200,
9.                                particle_lifetime=2.0)
10.     space.remove(cloud_shape, cloud_shape.body)
11.     if cloud_shape in clouds:      ←B
12.         clouds.remove(cloud_shape)
13.     score += 100     ←C
14.     return False
```

The code callouts are described below:

a. Add score as a global variable to the function.
b. This is a bug fix that occurred when multiple collisions were detected in the same frame. Multiple collisions can occur on the same frame if multiple bodies collide with the object. In the case of the car, there is the car body and car wheels that can collide with a cloud. The addition is to check first if the cloud list contains the collided cloud.
c. A value of 100 points is added to the score.

The score is in place now and we will add the code to render it to the top right of the screen. Notice how we subtract **100** from the screen width (**WIDTH**) so the text is placed in the correct position.

```
1. score_text = font.render(f"Score: {score}", True, (0, 0, 0))
2. screen.blit(score_text, (WIDTH - 100, 10))
```

Save the changes and run the file. *Figure 6.13* shows the game being played and the car bursting some clouds. The player score is shown in the top right corner. Please refer to the following figure:

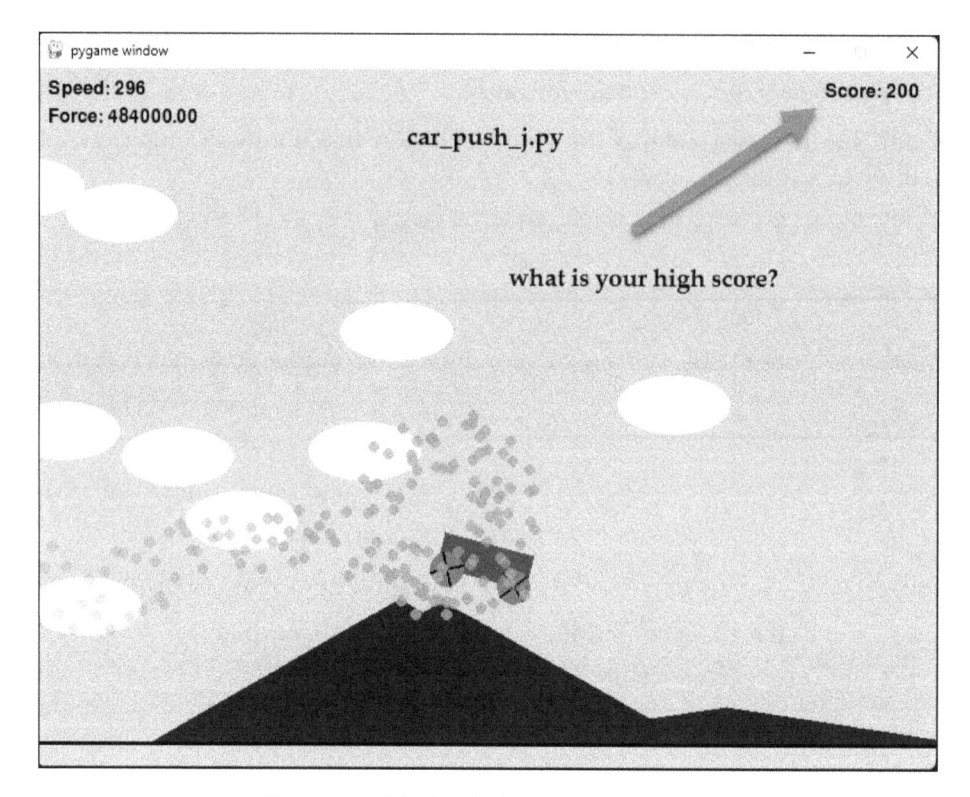

Figure 6.13: Playing the full game, more or less

This simple car push game has numerous new features and enhancements that could be added. Alternatively, you could also just use the basics and create your own game with physics. Physics puzzle games are getting quite popular again.

This completes this chapter. Through several iterations and patience, we managed to enlist ChatGPT to create most of a fun physics game. In the next section, we will complete the chapter with a conclusion, what we learned and the exercises.

Conclusion

For this chapter, we were introduced to the world of game physics with *Pygame* and *Pymunk*. We specifically focused on the rigid body dynamics of game objects like the *box* and *ball*. Then, we matured to wiring up a physics car in 2D, complete with wheels using pin and slide physics joints. After that, we added numerous features to the game world including obstacles, particles, and collisions. Finishing up the little car push demo with a game goal of bursting clouds by jumping the car.

In the next chapter, we are going to start the transition to 3D by first embracing 2.5D or isometric worlds. Building 2.5D games will provide us with a great introduction to different coordinate spaces and transformations.

What we learned

- How to employ ChatGPT by limiting the number of features we request at a time. Limiting the AI to just a few tasks allow for more consistent and more importantly working output.

- How a rigid body is described using a game physics engine like *Pymunk*. We learned what the terms moment of inertia, center of gravity, force and friction all have to do with rigid body physics.

- What role does friction play in a rigid body environment. Objects must have some friction, or they just slide around.

- That Pygame uses and inverted Y axis that must be accounted for when aligning to a physics engine like *Pymunk*.

- That game objects can be defined in multiple reference systems from the visual to the physical. We also learned that we often greatly simplify the physical description of an object for better performance.

- How physics objects need to be connected using joints. We learned how the wheels of a car can be joined to a car using a pin and slide joint.

- What physics force is and how it can be applied to a game object.

- What a particle system is and how to build a particle emitter and particles like *smoke*.

- How to create special physics functions for gravity or collisions. This allows for some objects to behave with different physical properties.

Exercises

You will learn the majority of what this book is trying to teach you by completing even just a couple of exercises. Some of these exercises may be completed easily with ChatGPT and others may not.

1. Add the code to reset the game if the player crashes and flips the car or runs off the end of the screen.

2. Add the code to save the game's high score. Let the player know when they have achieved a new high score.

3. Change the car to a car image and the wheels to images as well. Be sure to also make sure and reflect underlying rigid body shape matches the visual properties of the image. You will also want to rotate the wheel images when the vehicle is moving, of course.

4. The wheels on the car are mounted using a pin (axle) joint and slide joint (suspension). Because we are drawing the wheels fixed to the vehicle, we never see the effect of the wheel sliding (moving up and down), representing the car's suspension. Add the code to show the slide joint in action.

5. The car is currently being pushed but we really want an engine. Go ahead and add an engine to the car. Be sure to change the car's center of gravity to reflect the heavier engine. As well, make sure the car is no longer being pushed but driven by the tires. This will require the wheels to be given power and potentially torque.

6. **BONUS:** Add a level designer like we did with the *Flappy Bird Clone* that allows you to place objects and clouds.

7. **BONUS:** Design the car such that it cannot be flipped over, or if it is flipped over it can upright itself.

Remember, some of the above exercises may be deceptively simple to complete with ChatGPT.

Join our book's Discord space

Join the book's Discord Workspace for Latest updates, Offers, Tech happenings around the world, New Release and Sessions with the Authors:

https://discord.bpbonline.com

CHAPTER 7
Building Isometric Worlds

Introduction

Today, 3D game programming is becoming easier. However, there was a time when this was not the case. So, a form of forced 3D perspective was created called **isometric** or **2.5D**. Even with the many powerful 3D game engines today, many games are still developed using isometric.

Isometric games remain a popular form for game developers because they allow for simpler asset generation and still provide the game immersion of 3D. Asset development is a primary consideration when creating game worlds. With the advent of AI and the image generation techniques we already explored, it is expected this form of the game will become more popular.

Structure

This chapter explores the following topics:

- Into the depth: Understanding 2.5D isometric perspectives
- The art of transformation: World to screen space conversion
- Grids in the third dimension: Designing isometric tile maps

- Adding detail and variation: Map overlays
- Beyond the game field: Layering UI and menus in an isometric world

Objectives

For this chapter, we explore the world of 2.5D or the isometric reality. Not only is 2.5D a fun form to explore, but it is also a great introduction to the complexity of 3D games. Therefore, in this chapter, we start by taking an in-depth look at the complexity of drawing 2.5D maps. Then, we will look at how to transform between the screen space and the 2.5D world space by introducing mouse interactions. Further, we will look at how to design a 2.5D map and methods to generate tile images with *ComfyUI* and *SDXL*. Finally, we will complete the chapter by building a user interface for the sample game.

Into the depth: Understanding 2.5D isometric perspectives

Figure 7.1 shows an example of an isometric game map showing a small village. While the image is not of a real game and was generated with Dall-E 3, it does show the **isometric** or **2.5D** view of several objects. Please refer to the following figure:

Figure 7.1: An example of 2.5 isometric game map, Dall-E 3

Isometric drawing is a form of illustration used for architecture and design. It is used to combine the side, top, and front views of an architectural drawing as shown in *Figure 7.2*. This form of drawing typically demonstrates a better visual representation of objects designed using *2D tools*. Please refer to the following figure:

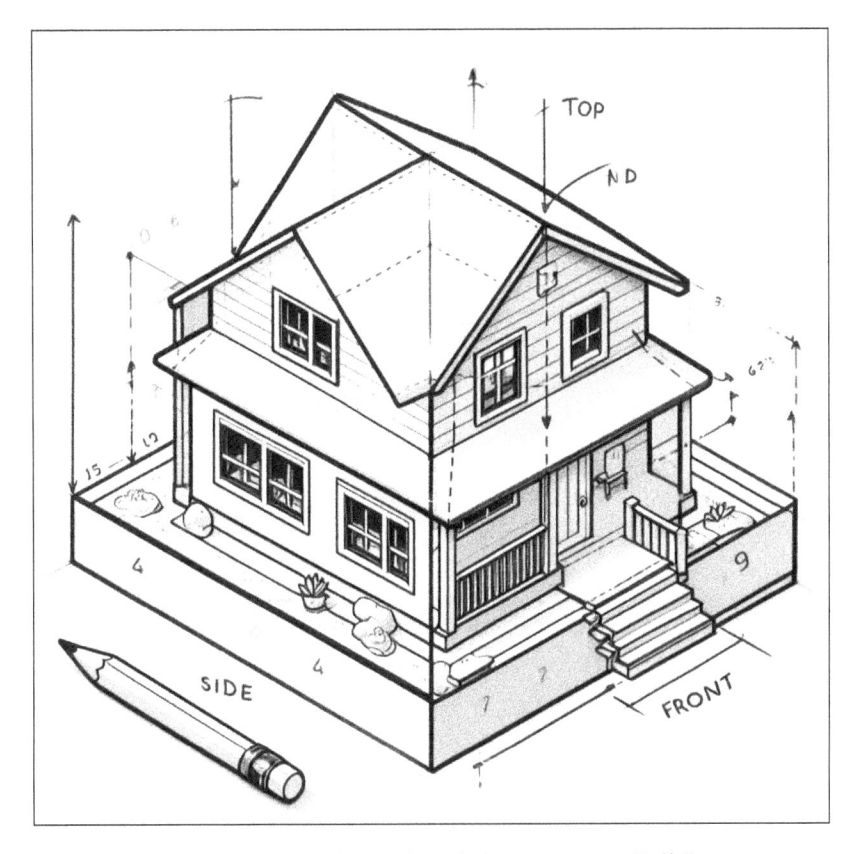

Figure 7.2: Isometric drawing of a house, courtesy Dall-E 3

Isometric views also provided a method for games to look 3D but still be only 2D, a technique called **2.5D**. The perspective is achieved by showing an equal representation of all 3 sides of the object (front, side, and top). This forces the view/camera to look down on the object at an angle of 22.5 degrees.

Now that we have a clear understanding of what the 2.5D perspective is let us generate a simple demo with ChatGPT in the next exercise:

Exercise 7.1: Generating an isometric demo

Open a new conversation with ChatGPT and enter the following prompt:

Prompt: `Please write me a demo of an isometric tilemap using Python and Pygame.`

`The map should consist of 4 terrain tile types: sand (yellow), grass (green), water (blue), ice (white)`

`Place the tile drawing code in a function called draw_tile`

`Draw a grid and overlay it to show the individual tiles.`

Checkpoint: https://chat.openai.com/share/58edb85c-66bb-4cfe-8466-8cc953fafa05

Copy the generated code into a new file called `isometric_map_a.py`, save it, and then debug or run it, using your preference. Refer to *Appendix A* if you need assistance running or debugging a Python code file from VS Code.

Figure 7.3 shows the output of running the code. *Figure 7.3* shows a very simple representation of an isometric tile map. The map of tiles is square and 2D but appears to be a flat surface tilted into the 3 dimensions. Please refer to the following figure:

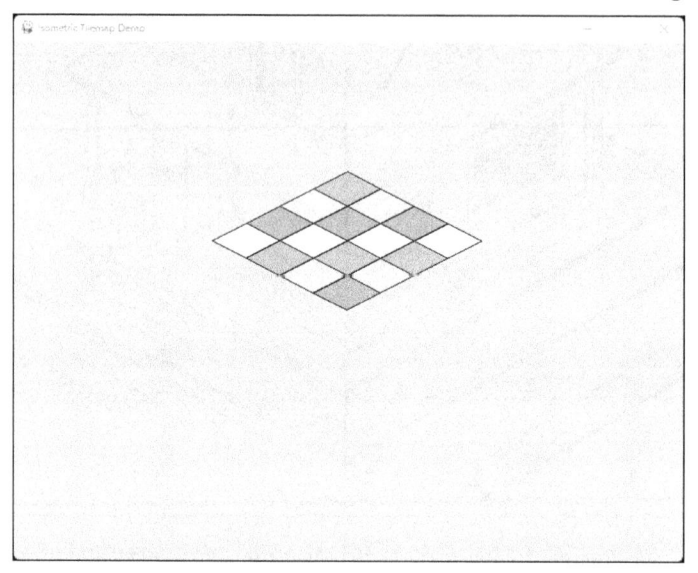

Figure 7.3: Example of simple isometric tile map

In an isometric game world, we typically use a tile map that represents each square. The map is square, but each of the tiles is rendered with a width equal to 2x the height.

Let us open the code and see how each of the tiles is rendered. Remember in our prompt, we asked ChatGPT to put the tile rendering code in a single function called `draw_tile`.

```
1.  def draw_tile(x, y, terrain):
2.      colors = {          ←A
3.          'sand': SAND,
4.          'grass': GRASS,
5.          'water': WATER,
6.          'ice': ICE
7.      }
8.
9.      # Convert cartesian coordinates to isometric
```

Building Isometric Worlds

```
10.        iso_x = x - y        ←B
11.        iso_y = (x + y) / 2  ←B
12.
13.        # Adjusting for screen center and scaling tile size
14.        screen_x = WIDTH // 2 + iso_x * ISOMETRIC_WIDTH // 2    ←C
15.        screen_y = HEIGHT // 4 + iso_y * ISOMETRIC_HEIGHT
16.
17.        pygame.draw.polygon(screen, colors[terrain], [
18.            (screen_x, screen_y),
19.            (screen_x + ISOMETRIC_WIDTH // 2, screen_y + ISOMETRIC_HEIGHT // 2),
20.            (screen_x, screen_y + ISOMETRIC_HEIGHT),
21.            (screen_x - ISOMETRIC_WIDTH // 2, screen_y + ISOMETRIC_HEIGHT // 2)
22.        ])    ←D
23.
24.        # Draw grid overlay
25.        pygame.draw.lines(screen, BLACK, True, [
26.            (screen_x, screen_y),
27.            (screen_x + ISOMETRIC_WIDTH // 2, screen_y + ISOMETRIC_HEIGHT // 2),
28.            (screen_x, screen_y + ISOMETRIC_HEIGHT),
29.            (screen_x - ISOMETRIC_WIDTH // 2, screen_y + ISOMETRIC_HEIGHT // 2)
30.        ])    ←E
```

The above code callouts are described below:

a. First, we set the color of the tile based on the terrain type. This is a dictionary that provides the mapping between color and tile terrain names.

b. Tile coordinates are converted to isometric coordinates. We will dig into this in more detail. For now, think of this as converting the square tile coordinates of the map to an isometric projection of the map.

c. Then, the isometric coordinates are converted to screen or drawing coordinates.

d. Those coordinates are used to draw the flat tiles we see.

e. We requested ChatGPT to draw a grid around the tiles and this is the code that draws the lines around each tile.

The game tile map is represented as a square array of terrain types, shown below:

```
1. tilemap = [
2.     ['grass', 'sand', 'water', 'ice'],
3.     ['sand', 'water', 'ice', 'grass'],
4.     ['water', 'ice', 'grass', 'sand'],
5.     ['ice', 'grass', 'sand', 'water']
6. ]
```

The game loop and rendering code are now very simple and shown below:

```
1. def main():
2.     while True:                              ←A
3.         for event in pygame.event.get():     ←B
4.             if event.type == pygame.QUIT:
5.                 pygame.quit()
6.                 sys.exit()
7.
8.         screen.fill((220, 220, 220))         ←C
9.
10.        for row in range(len(tilemap)):
11.            for col in range(len(tilemap[row])):
12.                draw_tile(col, row, tilemap[row][col])     ←D
13.
14.        pygame.display.flip()                ←E
15.        clock.tick(60)
```

The above code callouts are described below:

a. The main game loop keeps running forever.

b. Check for events, such as closing the window, keyboard, or mouse.

c. Fill the entire background.

d. Draw a tile to the screen using the **draw_tile** function.

e. Flip the rendered view to the screen so the player can see it.

Building Isometric Worlds   199

We have avoided many of the finer details of rendering up to now. This is because, in all our previous games, the rendering was quite simple. When drawing isometric views though we must be more considerate of the details.

An example of this detail is the rendering of the tiles themselves. Notice the fore loops before the call to the **draw_tile** function. The tile map is drawn by rows and then columns so that the tiles closer to the viewer overlap the farther away tiles.

Let us quickly jump into another exercise and demonstrate this by adding a couple of features to the last demo.

Exercise 7.2: Adding depth to the tiles

Open the same conversation with ChatGPT and continue by entering the following prompt:

Prompt: `Now please extend this demo by adding a couple more features:`

- `Give the tiles some depth, say 8 pixels.`
- `Allow the player to scroll around the map using the arrow keys.`
- `Increase the size of the map to 16x16 tiles.`

Checkpoint: https://chat.openai.com/share/58edb85c-66bb-4cfe-8466-8cc953fafa05

Copy the generated code into a new file called **isometric_map_b.py**, save it a then run it. It is hard to see the details we want to observe. Therefore, let us modify some code before we run it. Go to the top of the file where the constants are defined and make the following modifications:

1. `# Constants`
2. `WIDTH, HEIGHT = 1200, 800`   ←A
3. `TILE_SIZE = 128`   ←B
4. `ISOMETRIC_WIDTH = TILE_SIZE * 2`
5. `ISOMETRIC_HEIGHT = TILE_SIZE`
6. `DEPTH = 24`   ←C

The code callouts are described below:

    a. Set the screen width and height to larger values but be sure that your screen can still comfortably render the window.

    b. Increase the **TILE_SIZE** to a value equal to or greater than **128**. This is a good size for most game tiles. Notice how the **ISOMETRIC_WIDTH** is 2 times the tile size.

    c. Set the depth or how thick the tile is.

Save the changes and run or debug the file in VS Code. *Figure 7.4* shows how the new tiles look when you scroll to the bottom edge of the map using the arrow keys. We can now see that the tiles have a depth, which adds more to the perspective. Please refer to the following figure:

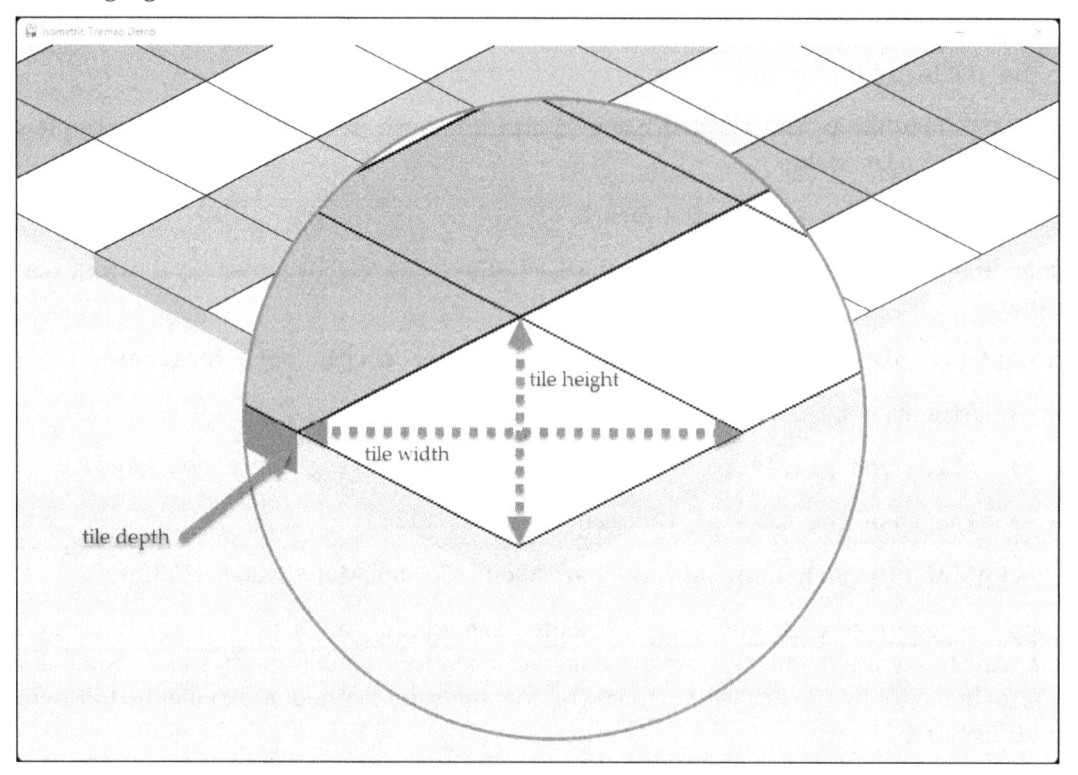

Figure 7.4: Detail example of tile rendering

Notice that all the tiles on the map are being rendered with a depth but only the tiles closest to the viewer/camera are visible. Why is that?

As it turns out, isometric games take advantage of tile draw order. This means that the tiles farthest away from the viewer/camera are drawn first. Then, the closer tiles are drawn over top of the farther tiles row after row.

This ordered way of drawing allows us to add some depth to our tiles and be sure that tiles farther away do not render over closer tiles. We will explore how to take advantage of this in a later section of this chapter. For now, we want to spend more time understanding the transformation between the world and screen space in the next section.

The art of transformation: World to screen space conversion

A key element of writing isometric games is understanding the conversion from game world coordinates to drawing screen coordinates. This conversion is typically referred to as world to screen space conversion and it is a key element of *2.5* and *3D games*.

Figure 7.5 shows a camera looking at an isometric scene. The scene is displayed in the camera's preview window in 2D. Along the bottom of the figure, the world coordinate grid aligns where the elements are on the map. Please refer to the following figure:

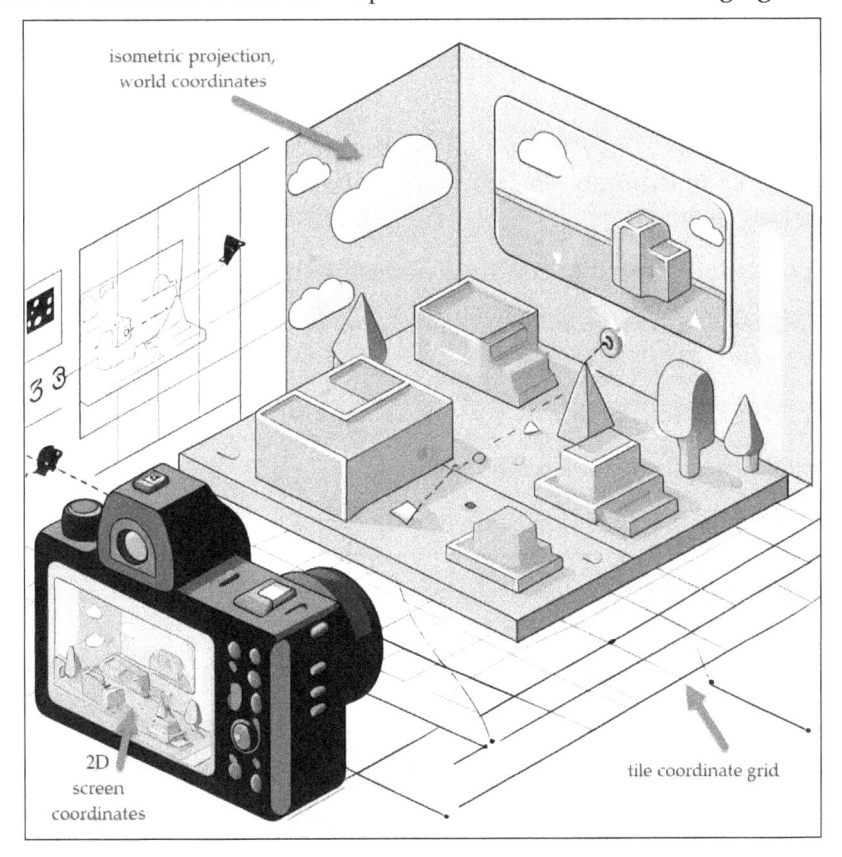

Figure 7.5: *Isometric scene projected to 2D screen view, courtesy of Dall-E 3*

The steps in rendering an isometric scene are important, so let us break them down below:

1. The tile grid or map is typically represented by a 2D array of objects. This is referred to as tile space.
2. Tile space coordinates are converted to world coordinates or 2.5D space.
3. World coordinates are finally converted to screen space and rendered.

In a 3D game world, the world space is typically already 3D so there are only 2 steps in the conversion. Isometric game rendering and interactions are more complex due to the isometric tile transformation step.

For the next exercise, we are going to look at a more fully baked demo of an isometric world that uses images for the tiles. This demo was generated using numerous iterations with ChatGPT and we do not need to replay those here. However, there were a couple of elements ChatGPT struggled to get right and the next exercise will focus on those.

Exercise 7.3: Exploring the isometric world base game

Open VS Code to the book's source code and to the file, **chapter_7/isometric_world_v.1/main.py**. This code has been primarily generated through multiple iterations with ChatGPT. However, after numerous iterations, over 50, the code had to be manually fixed to work correctly. We are going to explore why.

Run or debug the **main.py** file. *Figure 7.6* shows the output of running the file and scrolling down to the bottom of the map. This new upgraded version of the isometric demo adds the following new features:

- The player can zoom the view in or out using the mouse wheel.
- The player can pan around the map by moving the mouse to the edge of the window.
- The player can select a tile by clicking the mouse button on a tile location.
- The tiles are images rendered as sprites.
- Useful debug information is shown at the top left of the screen.

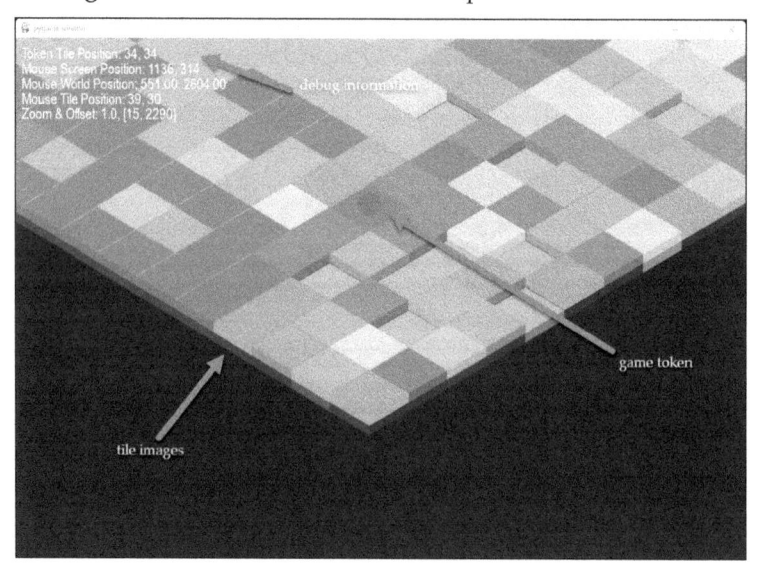

Figure 7.6: The isometric game world

This code represents the base for an isometric game. We will continue building on this base by adding a couple more key features in the later sections of this chapter. For now, though, let us get back to the difficulties ChatGPT could not get past.

The original version of this code was built incrementally using the same techniques we used in *Chapter 6*. Iterating through the same small code base and adding new features for each iteration. However, ChatGPT could not solve the conversion of the screen space to isometric to world coordinates when we wanted to select a tile with the mouse.

Exercise 7.4: Understanding screen to isometric to world conversion

Open VS Code to the book's source code and to the file, `chapter_7/isometric_world_v.1/main.py`.

Mouse or touch selection is a key element of isometric games. After all, you want the player to be able to select objects or tiles on the map. To perform this selection, we need to perform the transformation steps we did with rendering in reverse. Below are the steps to transform screen space to world space in an isometric game:

1. The player selects a point on the screen, Sx, Sy.
2. Screen space coordinates (Sx, Sy) are converted to world coordinates, Wx, Wy
3. World coordinates (Wx, Wy) are converted to isometric tile coordinates, Tx, Ty

Converting the screen space to tile space conversion. Used for mouse selection.

(Sx, Sy) | (Wx, Wy) | (Tx, Ty)

Tile space converted to screen space. Used for rendering/drawing.

(Tx, Ty) | (Wx, Wy) | (Sx, Sy)

Let us look at the working code that does these transformation steps:

```
1.  def screen_to_world(x, y, camera_offset, zoom):     ←A
2.      x = (x - SCREEN_WIDTH // 2) / zoom + camera_offset[0]
3.      y = (SCREEN_HEIGHT // 2 + y - SCREEN_HEIGHT // 2) / zoom +
        camera_offset[1]  # Flip the y-coordinate here
4.      return x, y
5.
6.  def world_to_tile(x, y):     ←B
7.      tile_x = (x / (BASE_TILE_WIDTH // 2) + y / (BASE_TILE_
        HEIGHT // 2)) // 2
8.      tile_y = (y / (BASE_TILE_HEIGHT // 2) - x / (BASE_TILE_
        WIDTH // 2)) // 2
9.      return int(tile_x), int(tile_y)
```

The code callouts are described below:

a. This function converts screen coordinates (Sx, Sy) to world coordinates (Wx, Wy).

b. This function converts world coordinates (Wx, Wy) to tile coordinates (Tx, Ty).

Now, we will scroll down and look at how they are used when the player clicks the mouse on the screen. Notice the addition of the camera offset and zoom.

```
1.  if event.button == 1:
2.      world_x, world_y = screen_to_world(event.pos[0],      ←A
3.                                          event.pos[1],      ←B
4.                                          camera_offset,     ←C
5.                                          zoom)              ←D
6.      tile_x, tile_y = world_to_tile(world_x, world_y)      ←E
7.      token_map_pos = [tile_x, tile_y]
```

The code callouts are described below:

a. Sx

b. Sy

c. The offset of the camera (Ox, Oy)

d. The zoom of the camera (Z)

e. Conversion from world to tile coordinates (Tx, Ty)

If you notice the world coordinate transformation function on the screen, there is the inclusion of the camera offset and zoom. This is because the screen space goes through an additional transformation based on the camera position and zoom. *Figure 7.7* shows what this looks like:

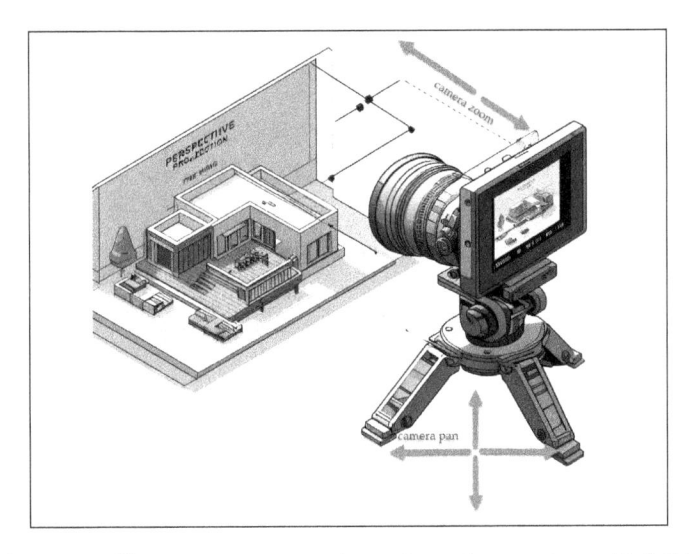

Figure 7.7: Illustrates camera zooming and panning, courtesy of Dall-E 3

So, what was the problem ChatGPT just could not get? It was the inversion of the y-axis used by Pygame to render the screen. No matter how many times this was explained to *ChatGPT*, it kept mixing up the conversions and or the axis orientations. The addition of the **camera pan** and zoom seems to make it especially difficult.

In the end, the fix to get the mouse selection working was done manually, using experience and a bit of math. The addition of the debug info in the top left corner of the screen was a big help in correcting the problem.

Now that you understand how camera space transformations work, run/debug the **main.py** file. This time, zoom and pan the camera and then select a tile on the screen. Watch the debug information to see how things are getting converted as shown in *Figure 7.8*. In the first image, the camera is zoomed out (magnified 50%) and in the next zoomed in (magnified 200%):

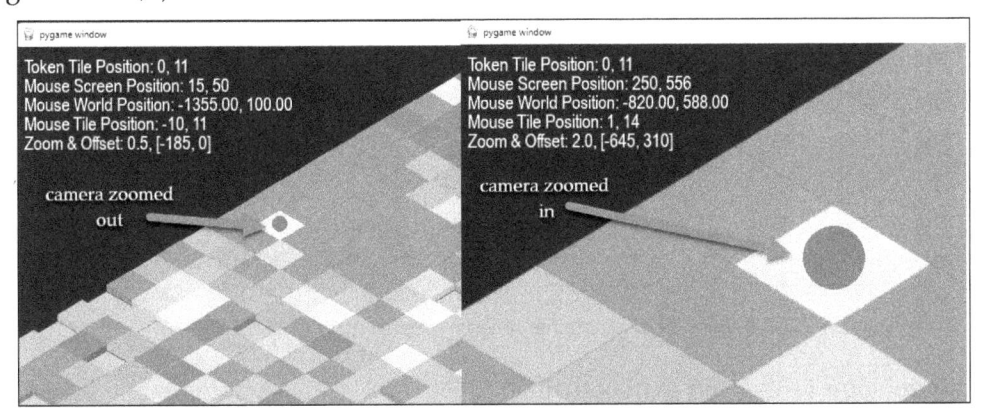

Figure 7.8: Different camera zoom and offset

With a basic knowledge of coordinate transformations, we can move on to understanding how isometric tiles are designed and rendered in the next section.

Grids in the third dimension: Designing isometric tile maps

A key element to understand when designing and creating map tiles for an isometric game, is the rendering size of a tile. We previously mentioned this when looking at the drawing code but now we need to understand this in more detail.

Figure 7.9 shows an example of a single tile that has been rendered to a map. Tiles farther away are drawn first, and the base/bottom of the tile is not visible because of the rendering order. Remember though that we still draw the entire tile, but closer tiles hide the base. Please refer to the following figure:

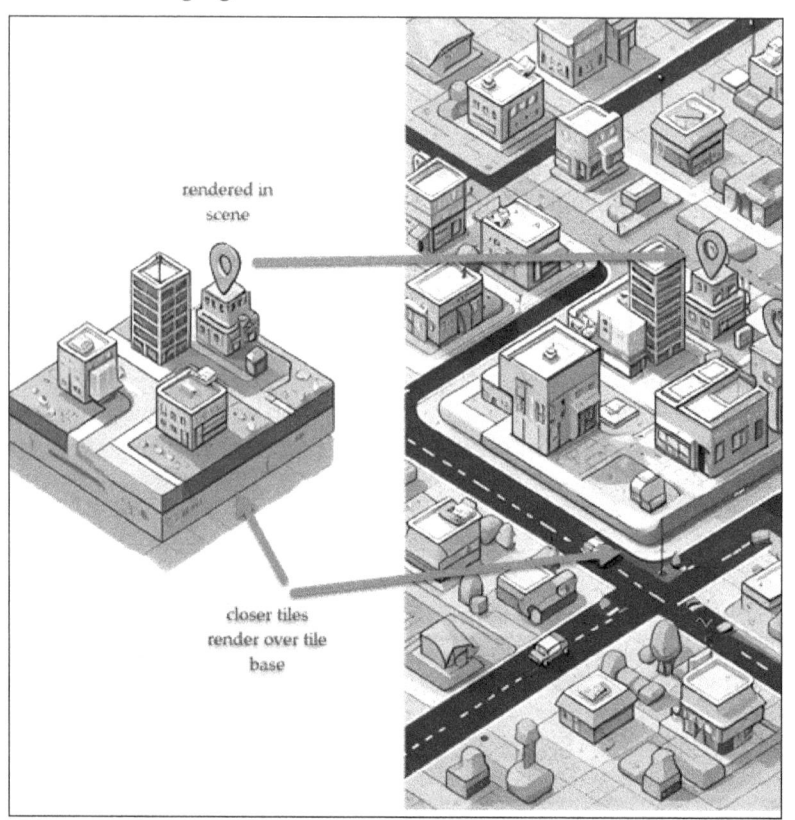

Figure 7.9: Showing tile rendering, courtesy of Dall-E 3

The terminology of this can get confusing, so let us start by defining some base terms. *Figure 7.10* shows the main components of an isometric tile and we have listed the terms below with their definitions:

- **Tile base**: Represents the area bounded by the real or virtual tile grid. This will be the base dimensions of the tile and is always *width = 2 x height*.

- **Tile level**: Your map may only have one level but could have the perception of multiple levels. The depth of this area is dependent on your preference and restricted by the entire tile depth.

- **Tile basement**: This is the part of the tile that gets shown at the edges of the map. Again, the depth of this area is dependent on your visual preference and maximum tile depth.

- **Tile top or overlay**: You may want to not go above your tile base and instead use overlays. Overlays are an added element that is added to a tile to show objects or more detail. We will get into overlays later.

Please refer to the following figure:

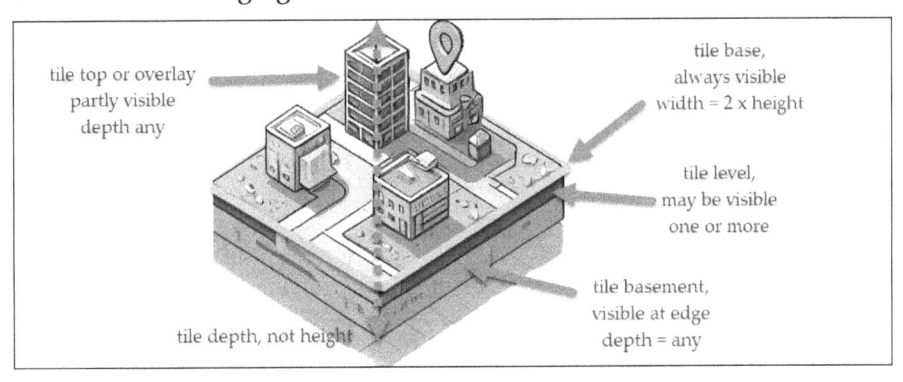

Figure 7.10: Showing the parts of an isometric tile

The depth of the basement and any extra levels will generally be restricted by the maximum depth of a tile. We often want the maximum depth of tile to equal its width or in other words a cube in **2.5D space**. *Figure 7.11* shows what this cube looks like overlayed over the tile:

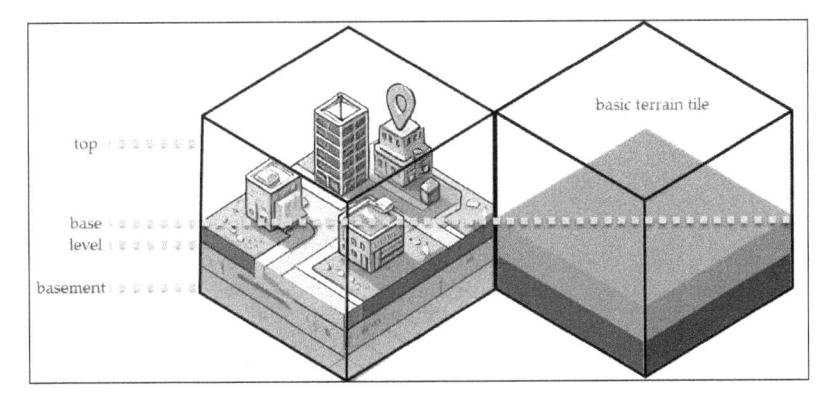

Figure 7.11: Comparison of different tile designs

Figure 7.11 also shows different tile designs where the tile on the right only shows the base terrain. In both cases, neither tile uses the maximum depth of the cube height, but they could. Notice how the base of both tiles is the same size but the areas above and below the base may vary significantly.

Tile depth can also be adjusted or offset in the rendering code. Shown below is the **draw_tile_sprite** function, it has been upgraded from the original **draw_tile** function to draw image sprites. It was also adjusted to include a tile offset when rendering.

```
1.  def draw_tile_sprite(x, y, sprite, zoom):          ←A
2.      """Draw a tile sprite at (x, y) with given zoom."""
3.      width = sprite.get_width() * zoom
4.      h_off = (sprite.get_height() - 68) // 2 * zoom     ←B
5.      height = sprite.get_height() * zoom
6.      resized_sprite = pygame.transform.scale(sprite, (int(width), int(height)))      ←C
7.      screen.blit(resized_sprite, (x - width // 2, y - h_off - height // 2))     ←D
```

The code callouts are described below:

a. This function takes the **x, y** screen coordinates, an image sprite, and the zoom level. The zoom is used to scale the image up or down as needed.

b. We add an offset calculated from the sprite tile height – a constant (68) and then divide by 2 to give the depth above and below the base. This value is multiple by the zoom to adjust it accordingly.

c. The sprite is resized according to the new width/height after the zoom was applied.

d. Use the **blit** function to render the sprite. Notice the use of **h_off** to adjust the depth of where the sprite is drawn.

By adding this drawing offset to the tiles, we can then exaggerate any height levels on the map. For example, on the current base game, the water (blue) tiles are drawn at the appearance of a lower level, as shown in *Figure 7.12*:

Note: For paperback readers, the labelled area 1 will be the blue portion on your screen.

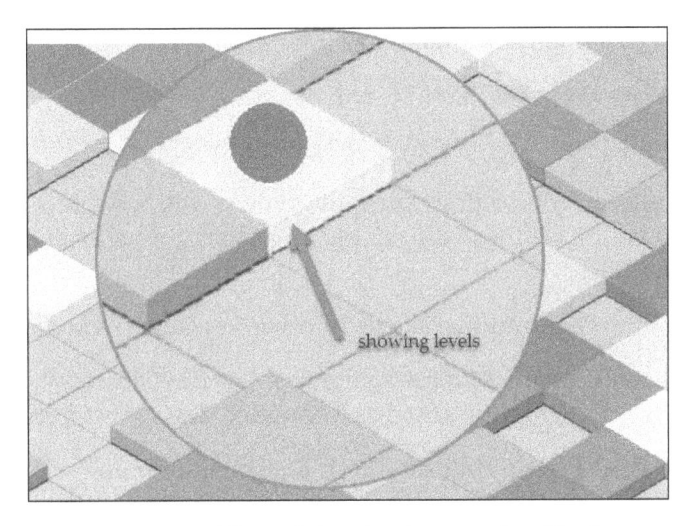

Figure 7.12: Tile rendering showing examples of levels

Now that we understand the details of designing isometric tiles, we are going to jump into a workflow that demonstrates their creation using *generative AI*. In the next exercise, we will set up this workflow using *ComfyUI* for image generation.

Exercise 7.5: Creating isometric tiles with AI

Launch **ComfyUI** and load the `workflow_isometric_tiles.json` by clicking the **Load** button. If you need any assistance setting up and using *ComfyUI* with *ControlNets*, please refer to *Chapters 4* and *5*.

Figure 7.13 shows the ComfyUI screen with the workflow loaded. Click the **Load** button and load the `chapter_7/workflow_isometric_tiles.json` to load the workflow. Please refer to the following figure:

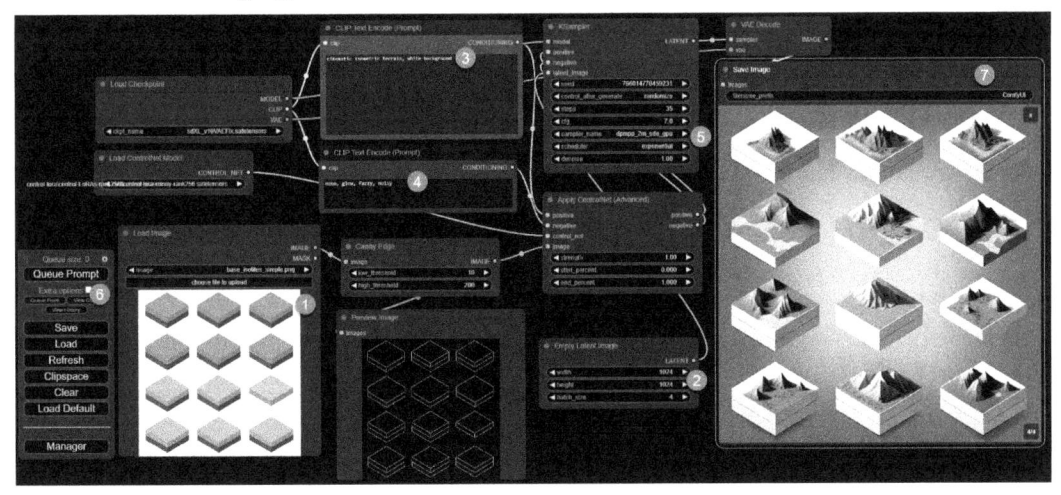

Figure 7.13: ComfyUI interface showing the tile map being generated by SDXL

Next, follow the steps as identified in *Figure 7.13*:

1. Load the **base_isotiles_simple.png** file.
2. Make sure the latent image size is *1024x1024* for SDXL.
3. Enter a positive prompt describing the type of tile look you want. It is best to either keep your base tiles very simple or go the other way and design dozens or more custom tiles.
4. Keep the negative prompt as is or add other keywords you find helpful.
5. Keep the defaults on the **KSampler** your first few runs. If you want to explore other variations try changing the scheduler, sampler, denoise, cfg and steps.
6. Click the **Queue Prompt** button to run the generation and wait.
7. Examine the output and select one or do more generations.

One thing to note when you are generating tiles is to make sure the tile corners are not cut off. *Figure 7.14* shows an example of the tile corners getting cut off. If this happens and you still like several of the other tiles that are not cut, do not worry. We can just remove the miscut tiles later in the process. Please refer to the following figure:

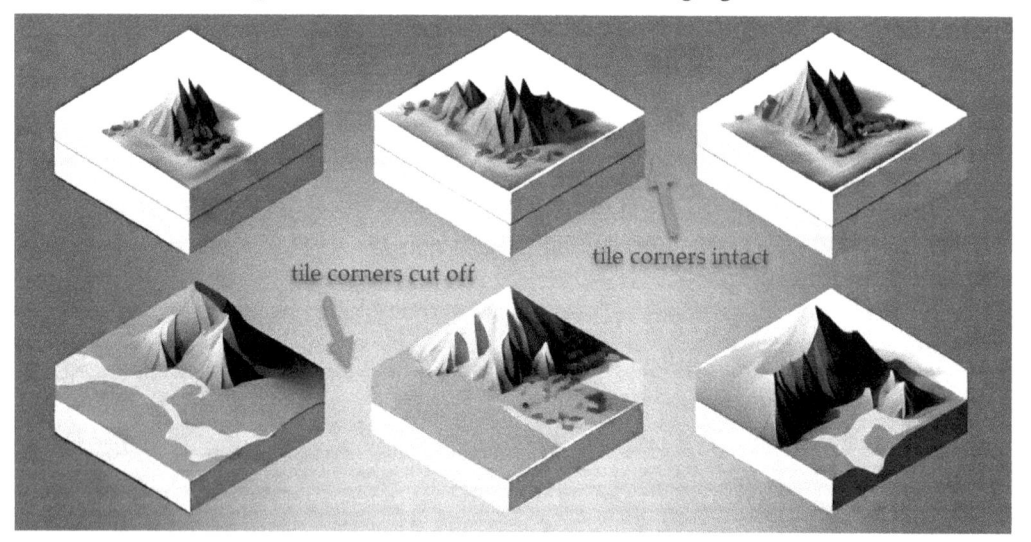

Figure 7.14: Showing how tile corners may get cut off on some tiles

Depending on your experience with image editing software, this next step may or may not be difficult. Essentially though, we want to remove the background from the image. Even though we often ask for a white background, SDXL may not always comply.

Figure 7.15 shows a partial tile sheet with the background removed. There are numerous ways of doing this with multiple different tools. If you are not sure how to remove the background from an image, ask ChatGPT. Please refer to the following figure:

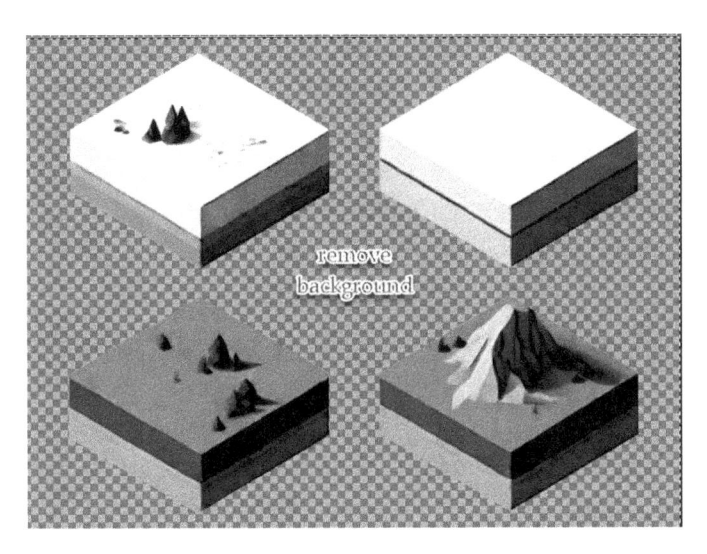

Figure 7.15: Background removed from tile sheet

After the background is removed, save the cleaned file to the **chapter_7** folder. An example of a generated and cleaned tile sheet is in the folder called **generated_tiles.png**. We now want to slice the full sheet into individual tile images. Thankfully, we have already generated a script with ChatGPT to do that.

Open the **chapter_7/slice_tile_sheet.py** in VS Code. At the bottom of the file, change the name of the file you want to slice in the **slice_spritesheet** function as shown below:

1. fixed_width = 128   # Replace with the desired width   ←A
2. # Example usage
3. sprites = slice_spritesheet("generated_tiles.png",   ←B
4.   4, 3,   ←C
5.   "generated_tiles",   ←D
6.   fixed_width)

The code callouts are identified below:

  a. The fixed width of the tiles. This variable is set in the game code at 128 now, but of course, you can alter it later.

  b. The name of the input file to slice.

  c. The number of rows and columns to slice. Are template uses *4x3*.

  d. The output folder to place the sliced images.

Run or debug this script. It will slice the input tile sheet into the various respective tiles and drop them in the output folder. After the script runs, open the output folder, and look at each of the images.

We can now copy or drag this tile folder into the game folder. Go ahead and drag the folder into the `isometric_world_v.1` folder. Then, we will reference this folder in the main game file.

Open the `isometric_world_v.1/main.py` file in VS Code. Change the name of the folder you placed your new images in where the tiles are loaded, see the code below. The tile loading code is designed to grab all the tiles in each folder and load them.

1. TILES_PATH = "generated_tiles/"

Save the file and run/debug the `main.py` file. *Figure 7.16* shows what the updated tile map looks like with new tile images:

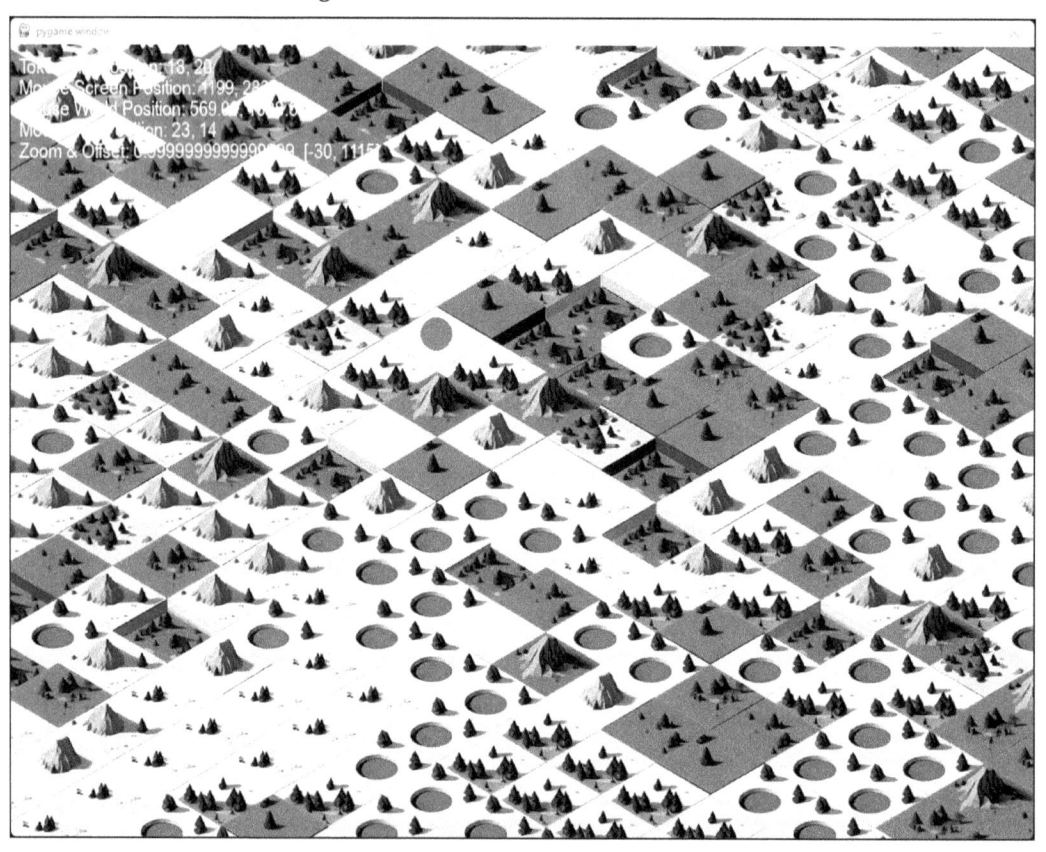

Figure 7.16: New tiles loaded in the game

As you can see even with 12 different tiles, the map will still look repetitive and busy. In most cases, you want to keep your base tiles unremarkable aside from color and texture.

It is best to keep the base tiles simple and then overlay details using tile overlays. Overlays provide more variation in the tile content and allow you to mix and match base and overlay tiles. We will cover how to use, design, and create tile overlays in the next section.

Adding detail and variation: Map overlays

Map overlays provide the ability to layer additional detail to a map tile location. Overlays can be designed in all manner of forms. From the simple, overlaying a tile, to the more complex of multiple overlays on a single tile or overlays crossing multiple tiles.

Figure 7.17 shows a couple of overlay tile examples. In the example of the left, the overlay contains the base, and it is meant to fully overlay a tile, contrasted with the sample on the right, where just the buildings are the overlay. Also, notice how the buildings on the right do not overlap with each other on the tile. This would allow us to further place each building in its own overlay without worrying about overdrawing. Please refer to the following figure:

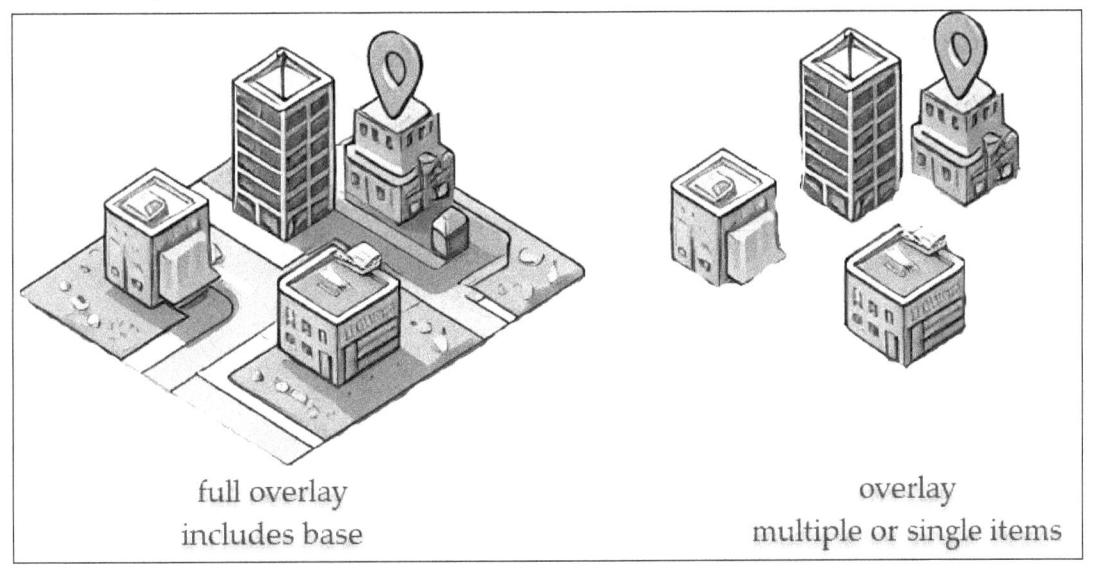

Figure 7.17: Comparison of overlay styles

Again, either approach is valid and these types of decisions rest more on the game design. Before getting into adding the code we are going to design some overlays using *ComfyUI* and *SDXL* in the next exercise.

Exercise 7.6: Generating isometric overlays

Launch **ComfyUI** and load the **workflow_isometric_overlays.json** by clicking the **Load** button. Again, if you need any assistance setting up and using *ComfyUI* with *ControlNets* please refer to *Chapters 4 and 5*.

Figure 7.18 shows the configuration of the workflow in the UI. The main difference between this workflow and the previous one is we are using depth maps instead of edges. Please refer to the following figure:

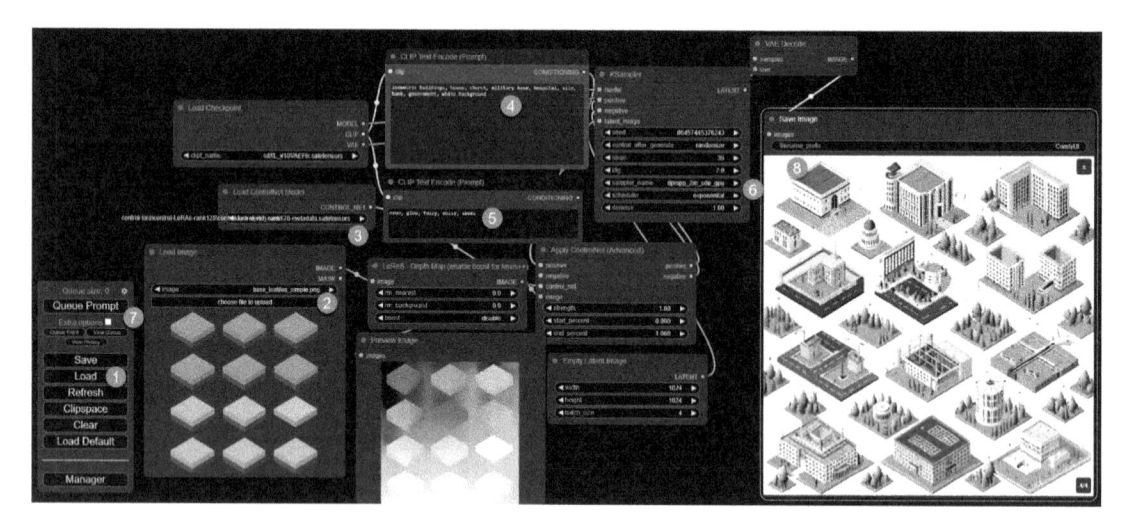

Figure 7.18: ComfyUI generating tile overlays

Here are the steps to take in ComfyUI:

1. Load the **workflow_isometric_overlays.json**.
2. Load the **base_isotiles_simple.png** image for the base.
3. Make sure a depth map control net is loaded.
4. Update or change the positive prompt.
5. Leave the default negative prompt.
6. Adjust **KSampler** parameters as needed (for experienced users).
7. Click **Queue Prompt** to generate a set of images.
8. Click on your favorite image and save the file to a working location.

As you can see in *Figure 7.18*, the output does not align with the tiles all that well. However, it does create a great variation of overlays we may use in some manner. A couple of points to note when generating tile overlays and extracting them are listed as follows:

- The whiter or paler the background the better. Strong colors will often be difficult to remove cleanly from image slices. Be sure to remove any background colors from the image.
- Keep the width of your overlay to a single tile of standard width and maximum depth equal to height. When you get more advanced you can consider overlays that span multiple tiles.
- If you are extracting single objects, make sure they are still placed within the bounds of the tile base. You may even want to draw lines representing the base to adjust the scale or placement of multiple overlays.

Next, we are going to look at extracting a single overlay from the sheet using an image editor. The one used in this example is *Gimp* (which is open-source and free) but the same steps should apply to any image editing package.

Figure 7.19 shows the steps executed inside **Gimp** and explained in more detail below:

1. Select the item you want to extract using a *selection tool*. Rectangle selection is shown but there are plenty of other options.

2. Remove the background from the image. Be sure to clean the edges of the image as well. You do not want a halo caused by your background.

3. Scale the image to your maximum tile width. You will generally want your overlay to fit within a single tile. This may mean you want to add padding to the sides of the overlay if it does not occupy the whole tile base. Save (export in *Gimp*) the image to a working folder when you are done.

Please refer to the following figure:

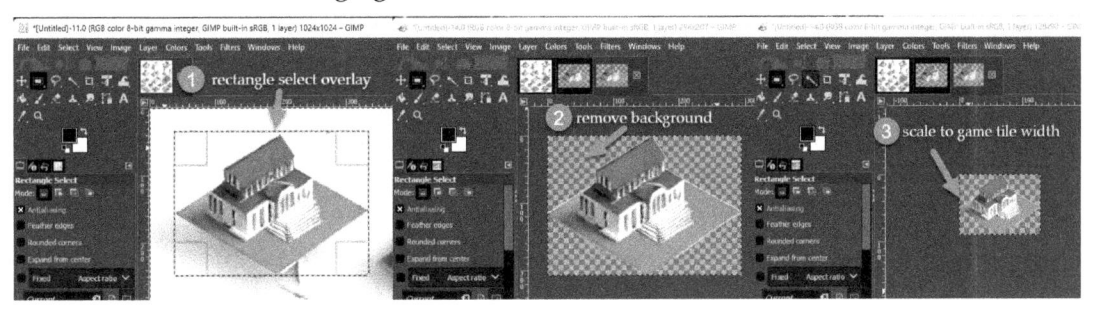

Figure 7.19: Extracting a tile overlay

We can quickly test what this overlay will look like in the game by replacing the token used for mouse selection in the next exercise.

Exercise 7.7: Replacing the token with an overlay

1. Open VS Code and copy the **chapter_7/isometric_world_v.1** to a new folder called **isometric_world_v.2**. We will make the code modifications to display the overlay manually. This is ideal since there are a few nuances that it may take a while for ChatGPT to get. Moreover, as stated many times previously, it is best that you understand and tweak the code ChatGPT produces.

2. Create a new folder, called overlays inside the new folder. Copy your generated tile overlay into this folder. Then, open the **main.py** file in VS Code and make the following additions:
    1. OVERLAYS_PATH = "overlays/"
    2. token_image = "government_overlay.png"

3. ```
   token_sprite = pygame.image.load(os.path.join(OVERLAYS_PATH,
   token_image)).convert_alpha()
   ```

3. This code creates a **token_sprite** sprite for the main selection token. Previously the token was a red circle. Next, we need to replace the line that draws the circle with the call to the sprite drawing function.

4. Replace this:

   1. ```
      pygame.draw.circle(screen, TOKEN_COLOR, (int(token_x),
      int(token_y)), int(TOKEN_SIZE * zoom))
      ```
      With this:

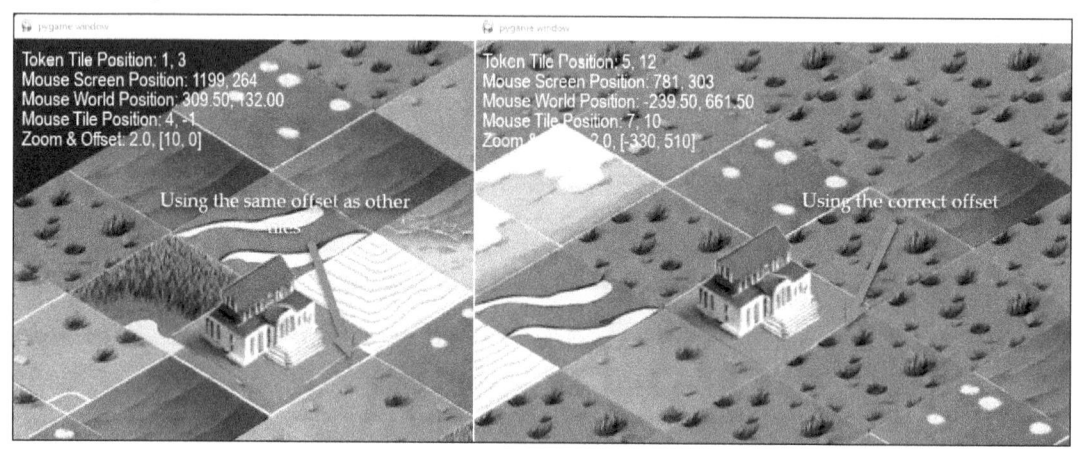

   2. ```
      draw_tile_sprite(int(token_x), int(token_y), token_sprite, zoom)
      ```

5. Save the file and run or debug the game. *Figure 7.20* shows the output of running the game:

Figure 7.20: The problem of floating overlay tiles

It looks like we have a problem. The overlay tile is floating a few pixels above the map. We can fix this by adding a new parameter to the **draw_tile_sprite** function. Remember that offset parameter called **h_off** we have seen before.

Open VS Code and the **main.py** file again and add the following modifications to the code:

```
1. def draw_tile_sprite(x, y, sprite, zoom, offset=68):        ←A
2.     """Draw a tile sprite at (x, y) with given zoom."""
3.     width = sprite.get_width() * zoom
4.     h_off = (sprite.get_height() - offset) // 2 * zoom       ←B
5.     height = sprite.get_height() * zoom
6.     resized_sprite = pygame.transform.scale(sprite,
   (int(width), int(height)))
```
```

```
7.     screen.blit(resized_sprite, (x - width // 2, y - h_off - 
   height // 2))
8. 
9. # ...
10. 
11. draw_tile_sprite(int(token_x), int(token_y), token_sprite,
    zoom, offset=88)        ←C
```

The code callouts are described below:

a. Add a new parameter called **offset** and set the default to **68**.

b. Replace the hard-coded value of **68** with the new **offset** parameter.

c. Add the **offset** parameter to the tokens render of **draw_tile_sprite** function. The value of **88** was found by trial and error. You may need to do something like your tile overlays. You may think that changing the default to **88** would work, but unfortunately, it does not. It is the difference in offset between the base map and the overlays that adjust the tile depth, how far it sits above or below other tiles.

If you find the base of the overlay tiles is hard to line up you can always just remove the base as shown in *Figure 7.21*, where the overlay is just of the building:

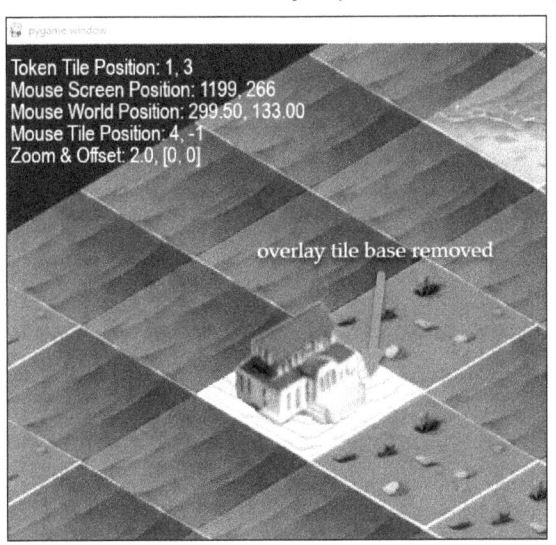

Figure 7.21: Overlay tile with base removed

Now we have overlay tiles that will allow us to add anything to the game world. The possibilities at this point are endless and with ChatGPT you could quickly add any game logic design you like. This completes the section. Next, we will look how to convert the base game into a world designer complete with UI.

Beyond the game field: Layering UI and menus in an isometric world

Up until now, we have avoided working with user interface elements like *buttons* and *menus*. This is not because they are complex, but because they add a layer of context to our design. Moreover, as we have seen throughout the book, extra context often muddles with results produced by ChatGPT.

Therefore, it is often better to break your project into components or layers of development when developing with ChatGPT as pictured in *Figure 7.22*. Each layer of development can then be worked on independently. In our example, we have the base isometric game as a layer and now a new UI layer we want to develop on top. Layers do not always have to be vertical and can also be horizontal, where horizontal layers often represent sets of game features that are related to others in the same vertical.

Figure 7.22: *A designer segments features into blocks for ChatGPT, via Dall-E 3*

In the next exercise, we are going to ask ChatGPT to transform our base isometric game into a world editor. This will allow us to add a menu and UI elements as another layer to our project to build the editor. It will also make ChatGPT's job a little easier by breaking out the context of our requests in this manner.

Exercise 7.8: Adding a UI layer

1. Open VS Code and copy the **chapter_7/isometric_world_v.2** to a new folder called **isometric_world_v.3**. Then, open a new conversation in ChatGPT and enter the following prompt:

Building Isometric Worlds   219

Prompt: `I have the base for an isometric tile game using Python and Pygame, here:`

Copy/paste the contents of **isometric_world_v.2/main.py** into the conversation window

`I would not like to make this a tile placement editor complete with UI elements like animated menus and buttons.`

`I want the player to be able to place tiles on the map by using the mouse. The code to do mouse selection is already in place and working.`

`When a player clicks the mouse on the map, a menu opens allowing them to select from one of the available tiles. After the player makes the selection the tile map is updated with the new tile.`

Checkpoint: https://chat.openai.com/share/db2f604a-4cd5-482a-a0ff-328cfd102114

2. This will create a new **Menu** class code that you should copy into a new file called **menu.py** in the working folder. Below is the code that has been updated to include the starting **x, y** screen locations:

```
1.  import pygame
2.
3.  class Menu:
4.      def __init__(self, x, y, tile_x, tile_y, tiles_sprites,
           tile_size=48):
5.          self.x = x           ←A
6.          self.y = y
7.          self.tile_x = tile_x
8.          self.tile_y = tile_y
9.          self.tiles = tiles_sprites
10.         self.tile_size = tile_size
11.         self.width = len(self.tiles) * tile_size
12.         self.height = tile_size
13.         self.active = False
14.         self.selected_tile = None
15.
16.     def draw(self, screen):      ←B
17.         if self.active:
18.             pygame.draw.rect(screen, (100, 100, 100),
```

```
19.                             (self.x, self.y, self.width, self.
    height))
20.         for idx, tile in enumerate(self.tiles):
21.             screen.blit(pygame.transform.scale(tile,
22.                                    (self.tile_
    size,
23.                                          self.tile_
    size)),
24.                             (self.x + idx * self.tile_size,
    self.y))
25.
26.     def is_mouse_over(self, mouse_pos):         ←C
27.         if self.x <= mouse_pos[0] <= self.x + self.width and
    self.y <= mouse_pos[1] <= self.y + self.height:
28.             return True
29.         return False
30.
31.     def get_selected_tile(self, mouse_pos):         ←D
32.         if self.is_mouse_over(mouse_pos):
33.             idx = (mouse_pos[0] - self.x) // self.tile_size
34.             return self.tiles[idx]
35.         return None
36.
37.     def get_selected_tile_index(self, mouse_pos):         ←E
38.         if self.is_mouse_over(mouse_pos):
39.             idx = (mouse_pos[0] - self.x) // self.tile_size
40.             return idx
41.         return None
```

    a. Add the starting **x, y** screen locations. This is a reference that drawing and other functions can use to remember where to draw on the screen.

    b. The **draw** function draws all the available tiles.

    c. This function checks if the mouse is over the menu.

    d. This function returns the selected tile.

e. This is an extra function we will consume later that returns the tile index and not the actual drawing sprite.

3. ChatGPT will add other code to add the menu to the main game loop. Go ahead and follow those instructions to see how the menu is added. When you are done, run or debug the updated **main.py**, *Figure 7.23* shows the menu in action:

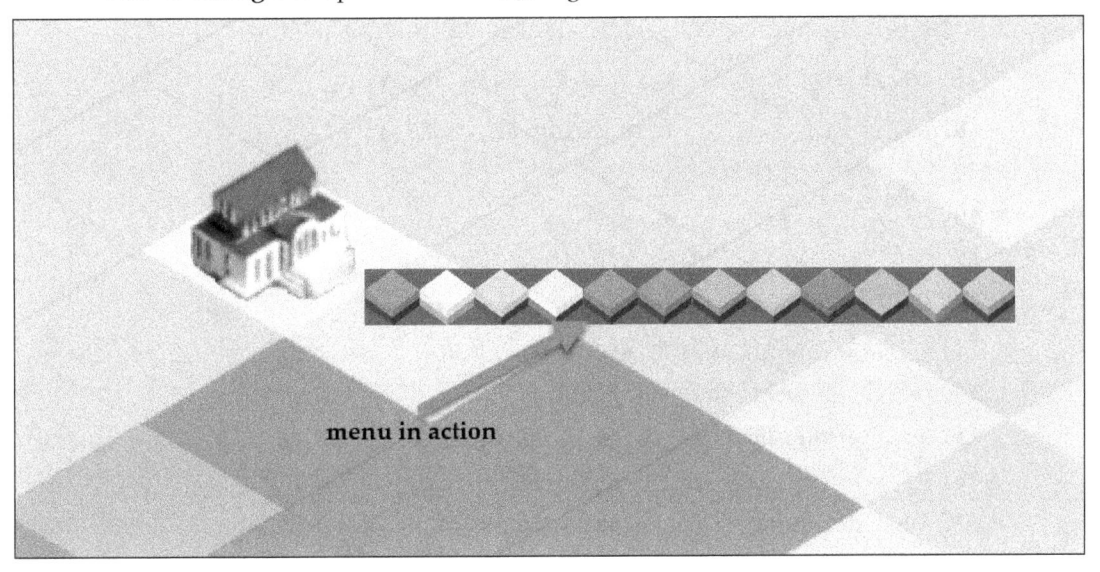

Figure 7.23: The menu showing the tile options

That is the menu, let us continue the iterations by asking for some buttons in the same conversation using the next prompt:

Prompt: Okay I added the code and corrected some bugs:

Copy/paste contents of **isometric_world_v.3/main.py** into conversation window, the one you just edited.

Please add round buttons to the bottom of the screen window and center. These are the functions I want for the buttons:

- **Load a map.**
- **Save a map.**
- **Switch tile set folders and reload tiles.**

Checkpoint: https://chat.openai.com/share/db2f604a-4cd5-482a-a0ff-328cfd102114

This will produce a new class called **Button**, shown button. Copy and paste this code into a new file called **button.py**:

```
1.  import pygame
2.
3.  class Button:
4.      def __init__(self, x, y,              ←A
5.                   radius, text,
6.                   action,
7.                   color=(200, 200, 200),
8.                   text_color=(0, 0, 0)):
9.          self.x = x
10.         self.y = y
11.         self.radius = radius
12.         self.text = text
13.         self.action = action
14.         self.color = color
15.         self.text_color = text_color
16.
17.     def draw(self, screen, font):         ←B
18.         pygame.draw.circle(screen, self.color,
19.                            (self.x, self.y), self.radius)
20.         text_surface = font.render(self.text,
21.                                    True, self.text_color)
22.         screen.blit(text_surface, (self.x - text_surface.get_width() // 2,
23.                                    self.y - text_surface.get_height() // 2))
24.
25.     def is_mouse_over(self, mouse_pos):   ←C
26.         distance = ((self.x - mouse_pos[0])**2 + (self.y - mouse_pos[1])**2)**0.5
27.         return distance <= self.radius
```

The code callouts as identified in the code:

a. Initialize a new button to be drawn at screen, **x, y** with **radius, color** and **text**.

b. Draw the button to the screen.

c. Detect if the mouse is currently over the button.

For the remainder of the code, you can follow from the ChatGPT conversation except for one element which we will focus on in the new mouse event code. This new code loops through each of the buttons and checks if the mouse is pressed and if it is then it checks if the mouse is over a particular button.

```
1.    if event.button == 1:          ←A
2.        for button in buttons:     ←B
3.            if button.is_mouse_over(event.pos):    ←C
4.                if button.action == "load":
5.                    load_map()     ←D
6.                    continue
7.                elif button.action == "save":
8.                    save_map()     ←E
9.                    continue
10.               elif button.action == "switch":
11.                   switch_tileset()   ←E
12.                   continue
```

As per the code callouts identified in the code:

a. Check if the mouse button is pressed.

b. Loops through all buttons currently displayed.

c. Check if the mouse is over the button.

d. Check for the mouse action and execute the appropriate action/function. Those functions do not exist quite yet but will soon.

Finally, to get the code that implements each of the actions, we will prompt ChatGPT to that next.

Prompt: `Okay, can you now please write each of the functions?`

Checkpoint: https://chat.openai.com/share/db2f604a-4cd5-482a-a0ff-328cfd102114

Not much of a prompt, but we already have good context in our current conversation, so this request appears minor but is not. After you run the request, ChatGPT will create each of the functions to implement the behavior behind the buttons.

This works well and you can continue through more iterations to add the features you want to implement. In the end though, here are the features that were newly added to the isometric game editor:

- **Load**: You can load a previously saved map.
- **Save**: You can now save the map.
- **Switch**: This allows you to switch the tile sets folder. The new tiles will be loaded and rendered.

Figure 7.24 shows each of the features being used.

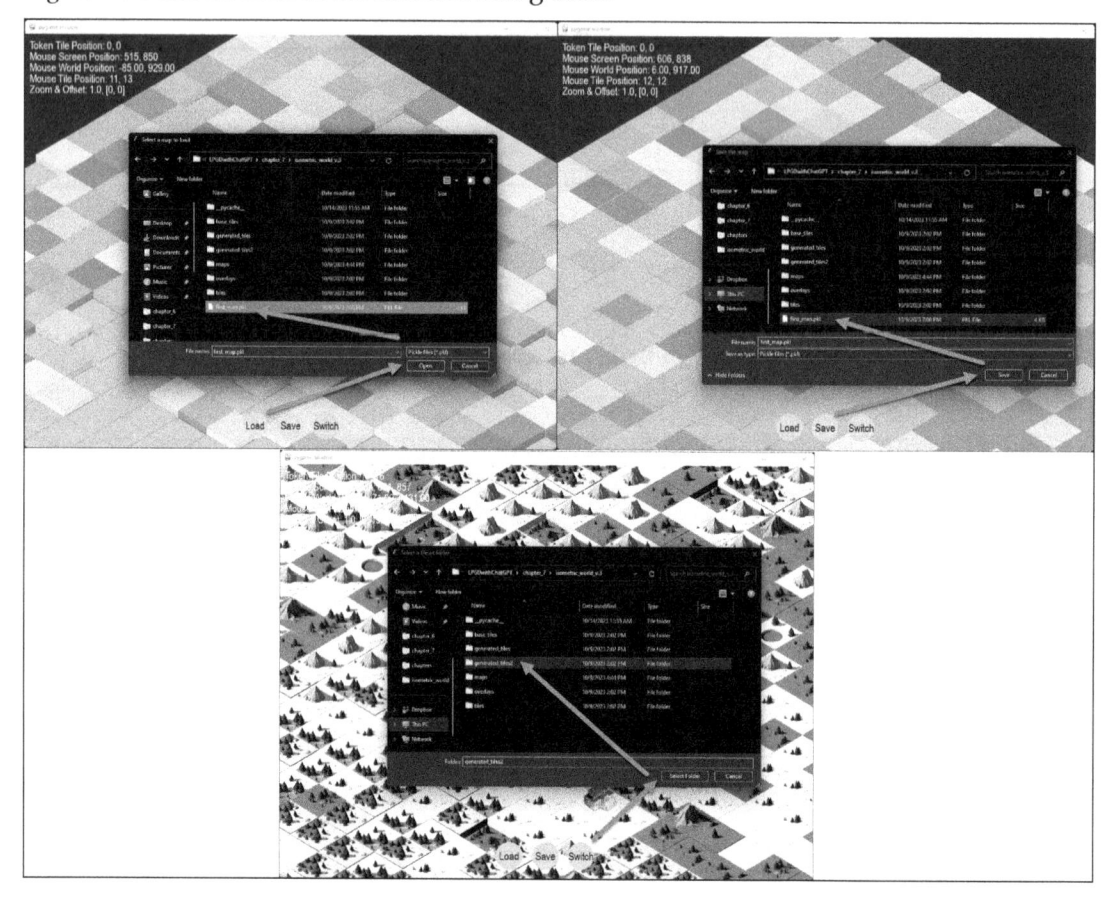

Figure 7.24: Examples of each button being used

At this stage of the book, you can likely continue exploring the code on your own. Be sure to look over the book source code for any updates or additions. Another option is of course use *ChatGPT* or *EasyCode* to help you review the code. That completes our tasks for this chapter and in the next section we finish up with conclusions, what we learned and the chapter exercises.

Conclusion

In this chapter, we dove in and explored the isometric tile or 2.5D game. Uncovering how isometric games are developed will not only help us in 3D programming but it provides a strong basis for understanding space transformations. Not to mention, we developed the base for a fully working isometric tile game map in *Python* and *Pygame*.

For the next chapter we will jump into the world of 3D games. Building 3D games is a complex topic and it will be interesting to see how ChatGPT guides us through it.

What we learned

- How to structure your projects and layer on key features in layers for best results with ChatGPT.
- The basis for 2.5D isometric perspective of tile map games and how they are rendered on screen.
- How the transformation from screen space to world space and back again works.
- How the transformation from world space to isometric tile space and back again works.
- Understanding the components of a base isometric tile. What the basement, tile base, tile layers, and tile overlays all describe.
- Use *ComfyUI* and *SDXL* to create new variations of base isometric tiles and how to convert them to game tiles used in the game.
- Use *ComfyUI* and *SDXL* to create isometric game overlays and the tricks of converting them into game tile overlays.
- Add a *simple UI* menu that allows a player to select from multiple tile options.
- Add *UI* buttons to the interface and add functions to provide functionality.

Exercises

You will learn the majority of what this book is trying to teach you by completing even just a couple of exercises. Some of these exercises may be completed easily with ChatGPT and others may not.

1. Add new buttons or menu options that allow you to select between editing base tiles or tiles overlays.
2. Change or create a new overlay that denotes the editor selection.

3. Create a large tile set (more than 12) of base and overlay tiles. Try to create the most unique map.

4. Create or borrow the concept of a basic game that uses a map grid. A great example is Conway's Game of Life. Then implement that game using the isometric base game.

5. **BONUS:** Generate procedural code to generate a map. Add a button to execute the procedural generation and create a new map. There is already a basic example of how to do this but of course you can also use ChatGPT.

6. **BONUS:** Generate code to move pieces around the map, either in real-time or through turns. How are you going to break this task up into layers for ChatGPT to better assist you?

When doing the exercises think about how you are going to use ChatGPT to complete the tasks. Break larger tasks/features down into layer blocks, and then query ChatGPT to generate for each block.

Join our book's Discord space

Join the book's Discord Workspace for Latest updates, Offers, Tech happenings around the world, New Release and Sessions with the Authors:

https://discord.bpbonline.com

CHAPTER 8
Leveling up with GPT Agents and AutoGen

Introduction

We have arrived at a juncture in our exploration of game development via ChatGPT where the method of continuous prompting, while efficacious, proves to be considerably taxing. Indeed, while authoring several of the final chapters of this manuscript, it necessitated engaging in upwards of one hundred interactions to refine the prompts to adhere to the intended narrative flow. This experience raises the question: Is ChatGPT an inappropriate tool for the expedited development of games? The answer is unequivocally negative.

What it does mean is that the manual workflow we were using does not scale well. Instead, we need a means of automating this workflow. Fortunately, others have encountered the same problems and have already developed multiple automated agents called **GPT Agents**.

GPT Agents are a way to automate the repetitive process of prompt iteration and reduce human involvement. In this tool, we look at an extremely easy tool called **AutoGen** that can do just that.

Structure

This chapter explores the following topics:

- Unlocking the achievement: Setting up your OpenAI account

- Power boost: Configuring AutoGen with ease
- Grasping the GPT agent fundamentals
- Asteroids ascending: Revamping a classic with assistant agents
- The game shop: Building a reusable agent workshop

Objectives

In this chapter, we go a level deeper and work directly with ChatGPT APIs and agent automation. We will first dive into creating and setting up an OpenAI account and explore how to use the **Playground**. Then, we will dive into AutoGen a multi-GPT agent framework from *Microsoft* by starting with installation and setup. After that, we will create a basic multiple-agent configuration using the *UserProxy* and *AgentAssistants*. We will also cover some interesting features we can use/add to the agents and finally use this agent system to revisit building the lunar lander game.

Unlocking the achievement: Setting up your OpenAI account

As a first step in this new journey, we are going to look at setting up an OpenAI account. New accounts are given several dollars of free credits, so you would not need to register a credit card. If you have already created an account with your email, then you likely need to purchase credits or try a different email address.

NOTE: Agents can be expensive. Be sure to monitor how long your agents execute. They can easily use up several dollars in credits a day if left unattended. Please make sure and attend to your agents.

In this beginning exercise, we are going to walk through setting up an OpenAI account. This same section will be used as a reference in later chapters of this book either within the agent system we develop in this chapter or for other services.

NOTE: You can also set and use Microsoft AI Studio as your ChatGPT backend. There are a few extra steps needed so please refer to the documentation of AutoGen and AI Studio.

Exercise 8.1: Creating and securing an OpenAI API key

We will begin by opening a new project folder in VS Code.

1. Create a new file in the folder called `requirements.txt` and fill it with the following:
    1. pyautogen

2. Save the file and install a new virtual environment using the VS Code command panel. Refer to *Appendix A* if you need assistance setting up a Python project in VS Code.

3. Open a browser and log in to the OpenAI platform page using your ChatGPT account. Select the API panel to enter the area as shown in *Figure 8.1*:

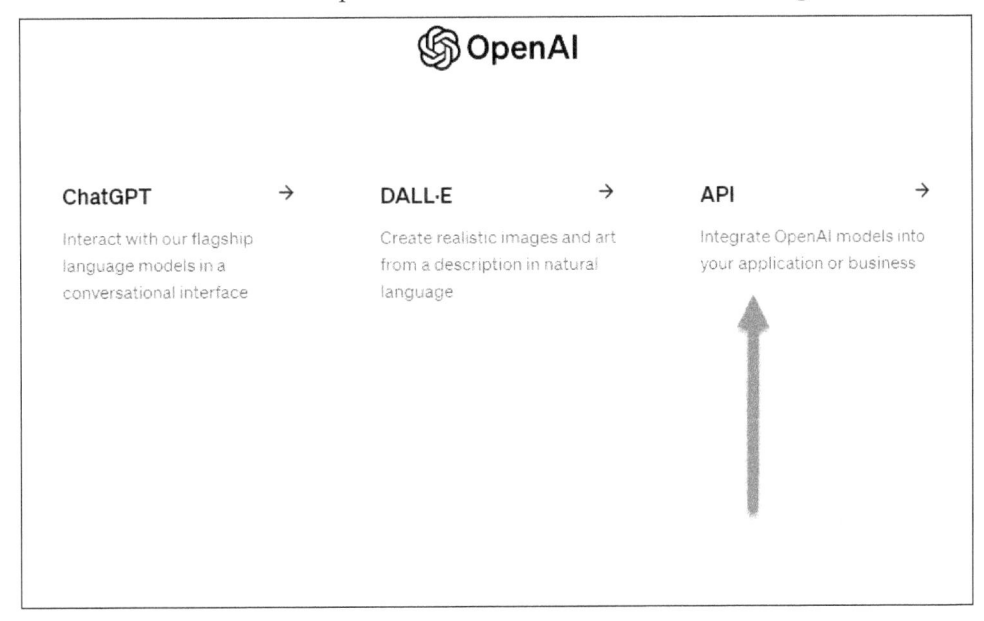

Figure 8.1: Logging into OpenAI API area

4. Then, select your profile in the top right corner of the browser window and select the option to view the API Keys as shown in *Figure 8.2*:

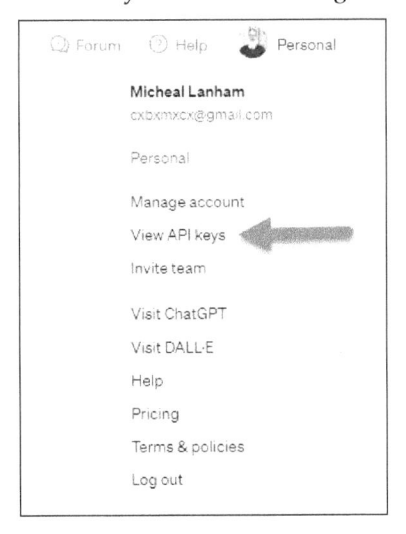

Figure 8.2: Navigating to the keys area

5. Create a new secret key by clicking the button as shown in *Figure 8.3*. Name the key something you will remember and then use the copy button to copy the key to the clipboard. Please refer to the following figure:

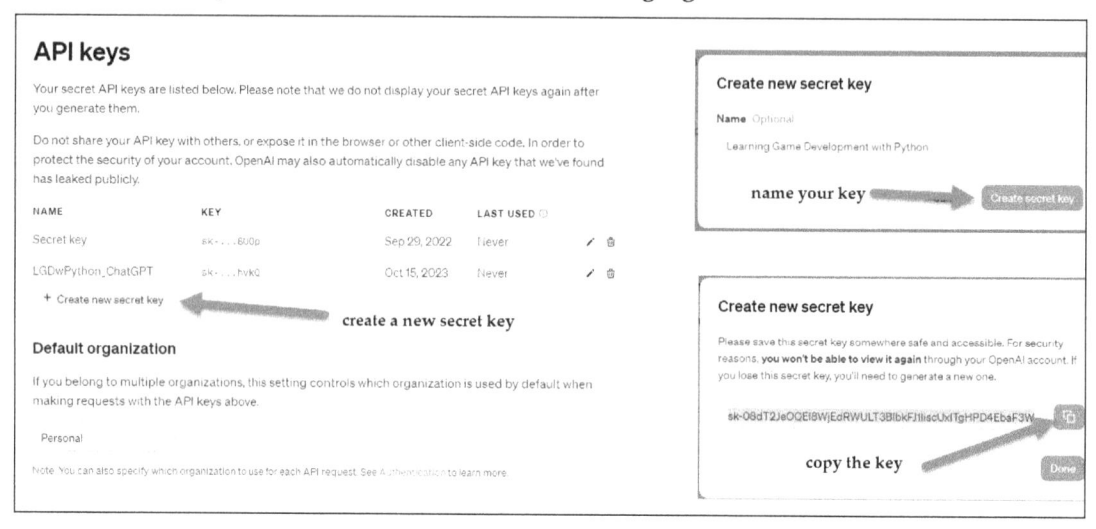

Figure 8.3: Creating the secret key

6. Go back to VS Code. Create a new file called **OAI_CONFIG_LIST** and copy the following JSON into it, be sure to replace the API key with the key you just created:

```
1. [
2.     {
3.         "model": "gpt-4",
4.         "api_key": "your-openai-key"
5.     }
6. ]
```

This is the configuration we will use to run AutoGen GPT agents. Be sure to keep this key confidential and never copy this file off your machine. The **.gitignore** file for the games book code already should ignore this file from getting published to GitHub.

Now that we have the key and configuration set, we can explore which Chat models we have access to by checking the **OpenAI Playground**. Return to the OpenAI site and click the page marked **Playground** to open the interface as seen in *Figure 8.4*:

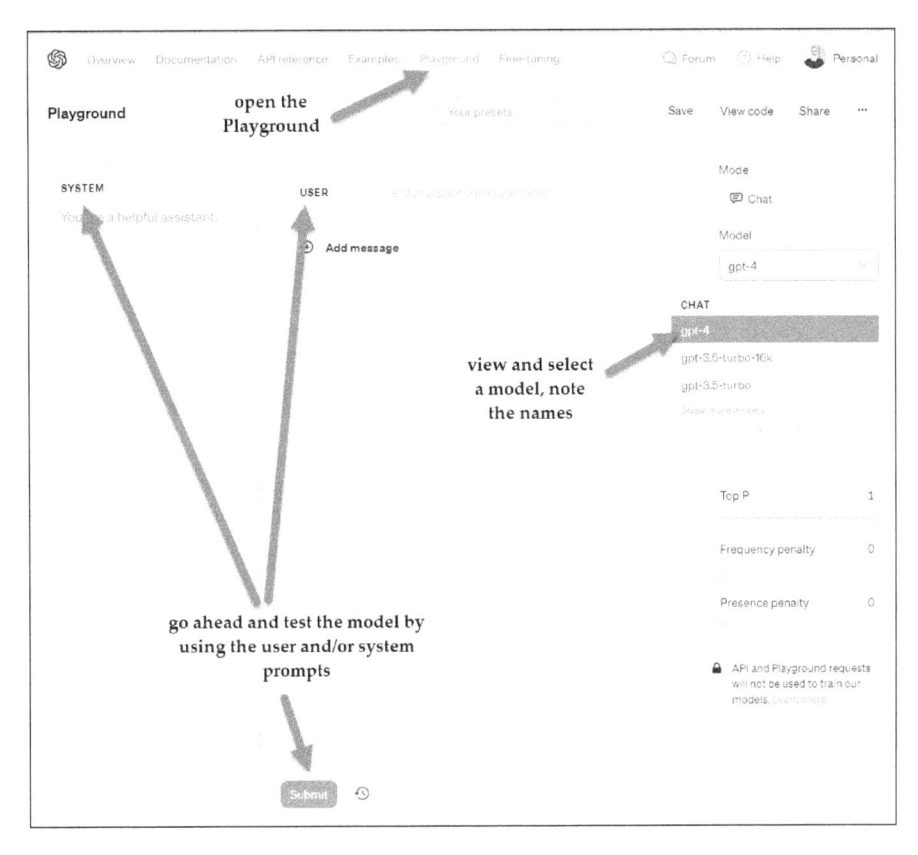

Figure 8.4: Finding your available models

Make sure and note the model names you have access to. We will be using GPT-4 as our preferred model but you may see other options. Be sure that the model you are using is a *Chat* model and not marked *Completion*. You will likely get significantly different results depending on the model you use.

At this point, you can also use the *Playground* to try various system and user messages against the API. Remember though, that any requests you make this way will not be free and will use your API credits.

Now that we have a key, we can move on to installing and setting up AutoGen in the next section.

Power boost: Configuring AutoGen with ease

Installing and configuring a complex tool like *AutoGen* is easy if you are familiar with consuming the OpenAI API. This section assumes you are not and will just go through the additional basic steps to get AutoGen running.

In the next exercise, we configure AutoGen with a basic example using two basic agents. Since AutoGen is new we cannot ask ChatGPT to create an example. If we do ask the model, it will make several assumptions and generate something that does not work.

Exercise 8.2: Configuring and running AutoGen

1. Open VS Code to the working folder that you saved the config file to. Create a new file called **config.py** in the folder, enter the following code and save the file:

   ```
   1.  import autogen
   2.
   3.  config_list = autogen.config_list_from_json(
   4.      "OAI_CONFIG_LIST",
   5.      filter_dict={
   6.          "model": ["gpt-4"],
   7.      }
   8.  )
   ```

   This code loads the configuration from the **OAI_CONFIG_LIST** file and filters the contents to the named model. Be sure the model's name you use is the same one you used in the configuration file, and that you have access to it in OpenAI. If you are not sure, go back to the OpenAI Playground and check.

2. Now, we are going to create two basic agents. A **UserProxyAgent** mimics a user, which means it can install and run code on its own. The **AssistantAgent** is responsible for undertaking the requests the user proxy agent makes.

   Figure 8.5 is from the AutoGen documentation and shows the various agent configurations the tool supports. For our purposes, we are going to use just a couple of agents to manage our game development workflow. Please refer to the following figure:

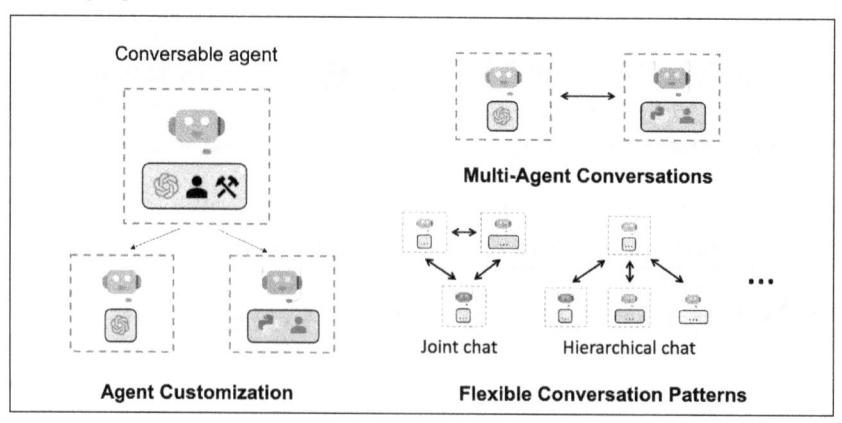

Figure 8.5: Understanding AutoGen agent configurations

3. Create a new file called **agents.py** and enter the following code:

   1. `import autogen`
   2. `from config import config_list`   ←A
   3.
   4. `# create an AssistantAgent named «assistant»`
   5. `assistant = autogen.AssistantAgent(`
   6. `    name="assistant",`
   7. `    llm_config={`
   8. `        "seed": 42,`   ←B
   9. `        "config_list": config_list,`   ←C
   10. `        "temperature": 0,`   ←D
   11. `    },`
   12. `)`

   The code callouts in the above code are listed below:

   a. Import the **config.py** module and the **config_list** configuration. This allows us to keep our configuration separate from our working code.

   b. The seed is used to keep a cache of previous requests. This allows you to reproduce the output of an agent based on previous requests. If you do not want this behavior, then you can manually change the seed value or delete the **.cache** folder or the underlying seed cache folder. The **.cache** folder can be created in the same working folder you run the code from.

   c. The **config_list** contains the configuration that was previously loaded in the config module on import.

   d. Temperature represents the amount of variation you want a model to respond with. A value of 0 means no variation and higher values increase the amount of variation. You will generally want to keep variations low when building your agent workflows and then gradually increase the value later.

4. As stated previously, the **AssistantAgent** in this case is the primary worker. It is a general agent that can be used for multiple different use cases. Next, we are going to add the **UserProxyAgent** by adding the code below:

   1. `user_proxy = autogen.UserProxyAgent(`
   2. `    name="user_proxy",`
   3. `    human_input_mode="NEVER",`   ←A
   4. `    max_consecutive_auto_reply=10,`   ←B

```
5.      is_termination_msg=lambda x: x.get("content", "").rstrip().
     endswith("TERMINATE"),             ←C
6.      code_execution_config={
7.          "work_dir": "coding",       ←D
8.          "use_docker": False,        ←E
9.      },
10. )
```

The code callouts are described below:

- a. Setting the **human_input_mode** to **NEVER** means the agent will not ask for feedback and keep going until it runs out of auto-replies. Again, be very sure when you use settings like these to not leave your agents alone.

- b. We set the **max_consecutive_auto_reply** to 10. This means the agent will only perform up to 10 iterations before it asks to continue if the input mode is never.

- c. The is **_termination_msg** is a function that determines if the last piece of text is **TERMINATE** then the agent stops the session. This flag is used between the agent conversations as a marker to terminate the session.

- d. The user proxy agent can run Python code. The **work_dir** folder marks the location where that code is saved.

- e. The **use_docker** flag informs the agent if it should run its session in a Docker container. We will not use this feature but it is an excellent way to scale multiple agents when running more robust requirements.

5. Finally, we will pull everything together by initiating a session by adding the following code:

```
1. user_proxy.initiate_chat(          ←A
2.      assistant,      ←B
3.      message="""     ←C
4.      What date is today? Compare the year-to-date gain for META
        and TESLA.
5.      """,
6. )
```

As per the code callouts in the above code:

- a. Call the **initiate_chat** function on the user proxy agent object.

- b. This is the agent the user proxy will send the first or goal message to.

- c. This message is the goal of the user proxy agent.

The first message sent by the user proxy represents the agent goal. This means that all further actions by the agent will be to try and achieve that goal. Save the file after you complete the edits and debug it. In VS Code that is the *F5* key or from the menu, **Run | Start Debugging**.

For this example, as the conversation begins you will see the user proxy running Python code but then encounter an error shown in *Figure 8.6*. This is expected and happens because as the error mentions a library has not been installed. Click the **Play** button on the debugger to continue running the code:

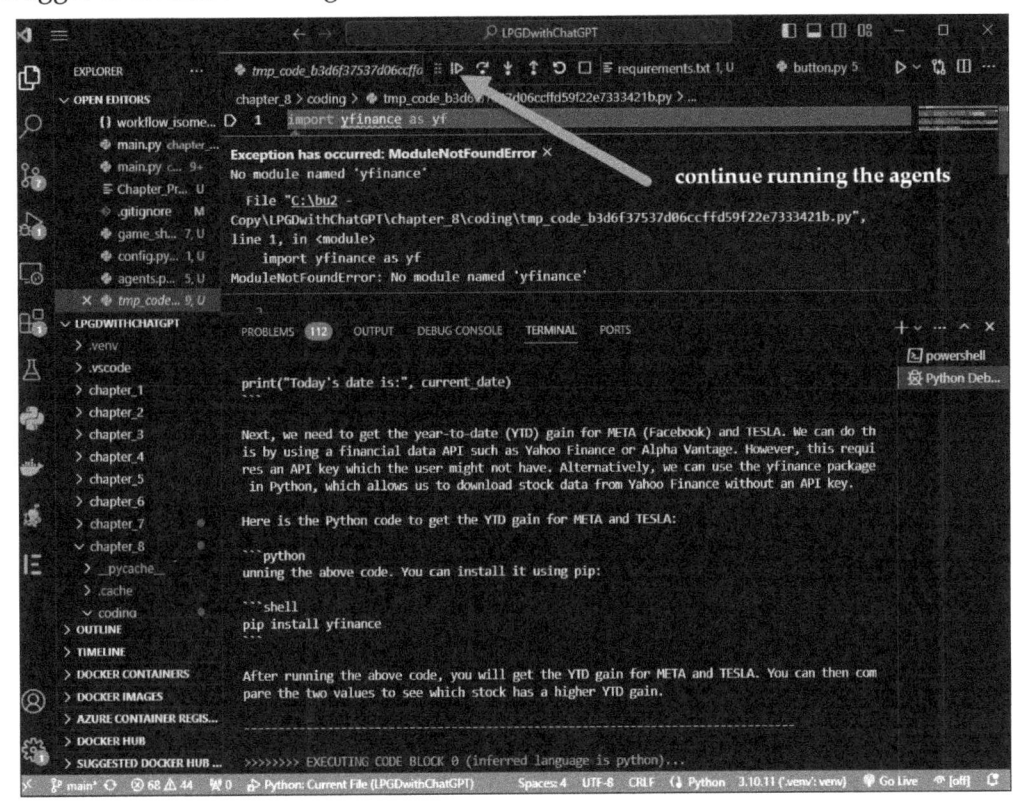

Figure 8.6: Running the agents and encountering an error

So instead of failing, the user proxy agent takes the error in stride, realizes it is missing a library, and then does a `pip install` of the required library.

6. After the proxy installs the library, it will again run the code, get the results it needs to achieve the goal and terminate the conversation. Here is the last snippet of the conversation:

```
1. ----------------------------------------------------------------
   -----------------
2. assistant (to user_proxy):
```

3.
4. Great! The code has executed successfully.
5.
6. As per the output, the year-to-date (YTD) gain for META (Facebook) is approximately -7.04%, and for TESLA, it's approximately -37.21%.
7.
8. Please note that these values are negative, which means both stocks have decreased in value since the start of the year. Also, TESLA has decreased more than META in the same period.
9.
10. TERMINATE

The outcomes are noteworthy; however, the ensuing inquiry pertains to its capability to generate code. As will be demonstrated in the subsequent section, it indeed possesses the ability to create code.

Grasping the GPT agent fundamentals

As we have progressed through this book, you may have noticed how repetitive our process became. **Agents** or **GPT agents** as we will call them are a way of automating that repetitive process and enhancing it. However, not all agent frameworks (and there are now many) may work for your needs.

This section explores the balance between using agents, agent frameworks, and the **large language model** (LLM) models that power them. AutoGen, the framework we are using from Microsoft is still relatively new at the time of writing, yet it provides many key features that will work in developing code and particular games. Although that may not always be the case, let us review that balance in detail.

Figure 8.7 shows the relationship between an agent, the framework it may be built on and the LLM it consumes. Notice though, that the diagram indicates that an agent framework prefers an LLM or family of LLMs. It means that is that some agent frameworks may work well with ChatGPT 3.5 but not do as well with ChatGPT 4.0. Please refer to the following figure:

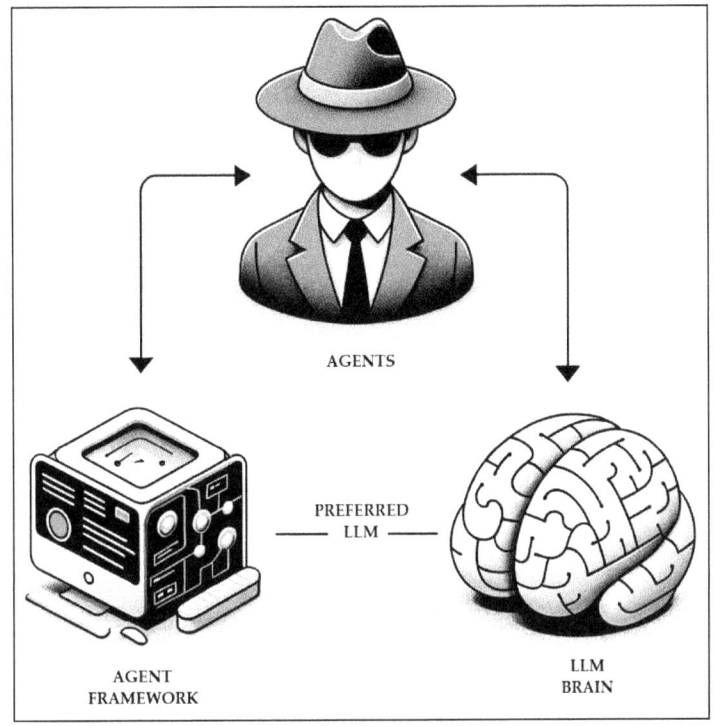

Figure 8.7: Showing the relationship between agent, agent framework and LLM

It is important to understand as an agent consumer what LLMs work best for the agent you are using. While many frameworks will suggest a preference, many do not, or they suggest any LLM will work. It all culminates to is how well the framework has customized its **System prompts** to work with a particular LLM or allows for their customization.

We covered what a System and **User prompt** are in the early chapters of this book. However, let us review it here. A System prompt sets the purpose and defines the rules for the User prompt interaction. A User prompt is the specific ask a user is making of the LLM that is then guided by the System prompt.

AutoGen allows the user to customize the System prompt of any agent, thus making it compatible with any LLM. By default, though, the System prompts set in the UserProxyAgent and AssistantAgent typically work better with GPT-3.5 than GPT-4. *Table 8.1* shows the tradeoffs of using different LLMs with AutoGen or other frameworks.

Model	Tokens per minute	Request per minute	Context	Price (2023)	Notes
gpt-3.5-turbo	90,000	3,500	4k	In $0.0015 / 1K tokens Out $0.002 / 1K tokens	Cheap but not as powerful as 4

Model	Tokens per minute	Request per minute	Context	Price (2023)	Notes
gpt-3.5-turbo-16k	180,000	3,500	16k	In $0.003 / 1K tokens Out $0.004 / 1K tokens	Cheap and handles big context, good tradeoff
gpt-4	10,000	200	8k	In $0.03 / 1K tokens Out $0.06 / 1K tokens	Good, but expensive
gpt-4-32k	20,000	200	32k	In $0.06 / 1K tokens Out $0.12 / 1K tokens	Powerful and large context, but very expensive

Table 8.1: Differences between LLM models

Most agent frameworks are typically developed using GPT-3.5. This version of GPT is significantly cheaper and faster but because it lacks the power of GPT-4 agent tasks are tuned to be finer-grained. This means if you try to use GPT-4 in an agent, you may not see the desired results. At the time of writing, it is generally recommended to use GPT-3.5 turbo when employing agents.

NOTE: Choosing which an agent can have significant cost savings. GPT-4 is 10 times more expensive than 3.5, at the time of writing. This can make the difference of spending $20 on a single project to just $2.

In the next exercise, we are going to compare the difference between using GPT-3.5 versus 4.0 when using agents. We are going to revisit creating the snake game as our baseline exercise for both models.

Exercise 8.3: Comparing GPT models on an agent system

1. Open the **chapter_8/snake_agents.py** file in VS Code and scroll to the bottom to see the basic request we are going to use to build a snake game, as shown below:

```
1. user_proxy.initiate_chat(
2.     assistant,
3.     message="""
4.     please write a snake game in Python
5.     """,
6. )
```

2. Debug the **snake_game.py** file in VS Code (shortcut *F5* key) and watch the interaction of the agents build a snake game. This will quickly build a game and run it directly in the terminal, after all, we did not ask for Pygame. *Figure 8.8* shows the snake game running in the terminal:

Figure 8.8: Snake game running in the terminal

3. Indeed, we have a fully running snake game running in the terminal. Now let us add a GPT-3.5 model to the **OAI_CONFIG_LIST** file. Remember this file holds a list of models and keys we want configured to run. This also allows us to use different models for different agents.

```
1. [
2.     {
3.         "model": "gpt-3.5-turbo-16k-0613",
4.         "api_key": "your api key"
5.     },
6.     {
7.         "model": "gpt-4",
8.         "api_key": "your-api-key"
9.     }
10. ]
```

These model names may be different depending on when you are reading this. If you are not sure the model names are correct, be sure to check the OpenAI documentation. When using the same API endpoint, you can use the same key for both services.

4. Open backup **config.py** in VS Code and modify the model name the config will load. Here is the code with the updated name:

   1. import autogen
   2.
   3. config_list = autogen.config_list_from_json(
   4.   "OAI_CONFIG_LIST",
   5.   filter_dict={
   6.   "model": ["gpt-3.5-turbo-16k-0613"],
   7.   }
   8.)

5. Next, we want to delete the cache folder AutoGen uses to store past runs and pick up where it left off. If we keep this cache, we will get the same results as our first run. Open VS Code, select the cache folder and type the delete key to remove it as shown in *Figure 8.9*:

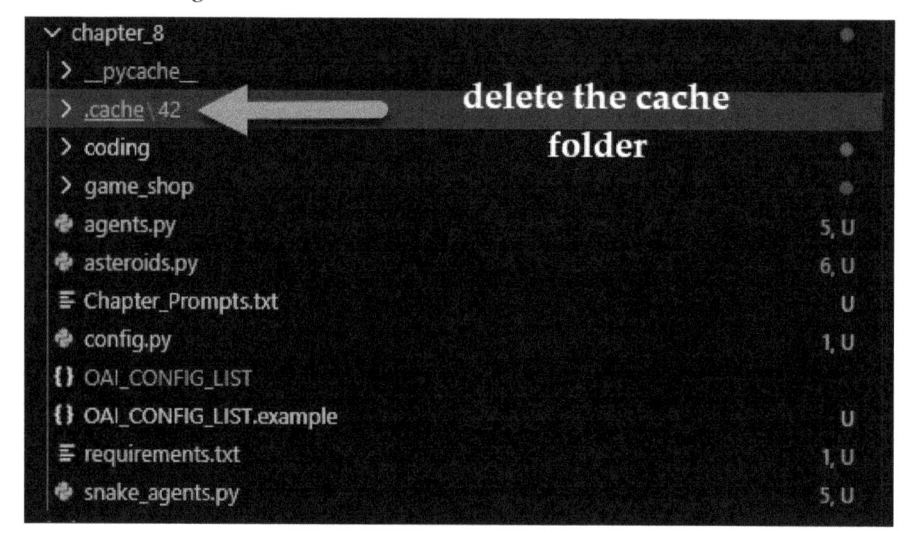

Figure 8.9: Deleting the cache folders

6. Open back up **snake_agents.py** and run the file in the debugger. *Figure 8.10* shows the output of the snake game running in a Pygame window. The game can even reset and start a new round when the player dies:

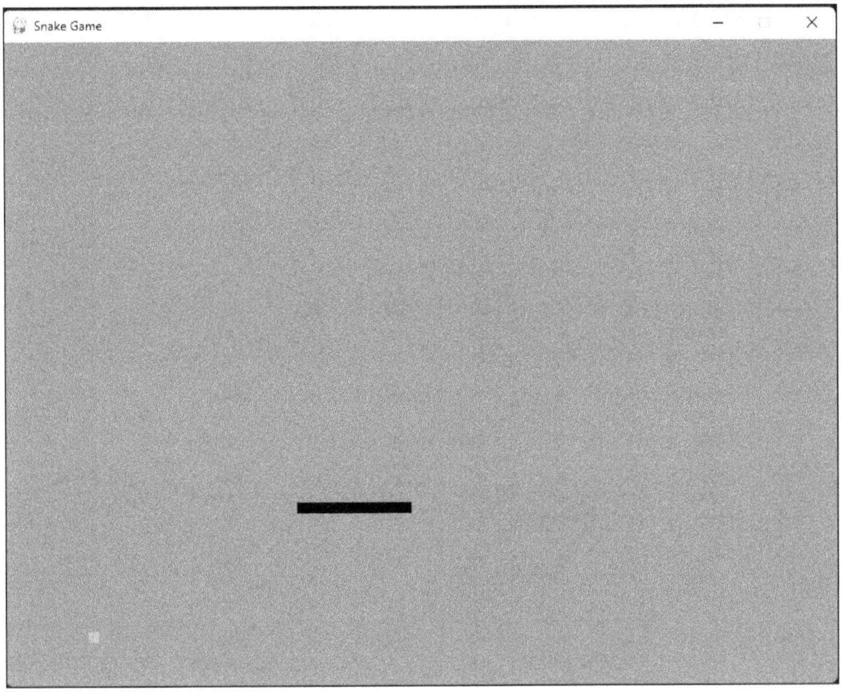

Figure 8.10: *A snake game developed with GPT-3.5*

What we discovered here is that GPT-3.5 works well when used as an agent. Again, this is generally because agents are developed using these cheaper and faster models, for now at least. In the future, this may change so running a comparison like this against two models can give you a good baseline.

As we can see the older, quicker, and cheaper model gave us better results than we may expect. In the next section, we are going to use this model to create a more complicated asteroid game using agents.

Asteroids ascending: Revamping a classic with assistant agents

Asteroids is another classic game that can help us explore how agents can assist our co-AI development efforts. As a vector graphics game, *Asteroids* provides a great example of how a full game can be replicated using *AI*.

In the next exercise, we are going to use GPT-3.5 to build a game of Asteroids. It is also going to allow us more control over the agents by using constant human feedback. This will make our experience more like working directly with ChatGPT but without having to copy/paste code and other repetitive tasks.

Exercise 8.4: Running AutoGen with human feedback ALWAYS

1. Open VS Code to the **chapter_8/asteroids.py** file. We are going to look at the changes to support running these agents with continual human feedback. This will also give us greater control over what the agent produces. Below is the code that sets up the user proxy agent and is the only bit requiring a change:

```
1. -------------------------------------------------------------------------
2. user_proxy = autogen.UserProxyAgent(
3.     name="user_proxy",
4.     human_input_mode="TERMINATE",          ←A
5.     max_consecutive_auto_reply=10,         ←B
6.     is_termination_msg=lambda x: x.get("content", "").rstrip().endswith("TERMINATE"),
7.     code_execution_config={
8.         "work_dir": "coding",              ←C
9.         "use_docker": False,    # set to True or image name like «python:3» to use docker
10.    },
11. )
```

As per the code callouts shown in the above code:

   a. Set the **human_input_mode** to **TERMINATE**, it was **NEVER** in the last exercise. This allows the human (you) to provide final feedback before an agent decides it is done. There is a third option **ALWAYS**, which allows human feedback after every agent dialog exchange. However, this can be too fine-grained and the **TERMINATE** option typically works better.

   b. The **max_consecutive_auto_reply** limits the amount of dialog exchanges the agents can take. You may want to adjust this value to a lower or higher number depending on your chosen LLM and requirements.

   c. The **work_dir** denotes where the agent will save files and code. You may want to change the name of the folder to be dependent on the model. We will keep it consistent here.

2. Next, let us look at the configuration we will use for our first agent run. Open the config.py file and set the model as shown in the code below. Make sure the model is set to GPT-4 as shown in the code. We are only going to let the model run a few iterations and the code should be minimal.

```
1.  import autogen
2.
3.  config_list = autogen.config_list_from_json(
4.      "OAI_CONFIG_LIST",
5.      filter_dict={
6.          "model": ["gpt-4"],
7.      }
8.  )
```

3. Finally, we want to see what new requirements we are starting our agents with. Open backup asteroids.py and scroll to the bottom as shown in the code below. As you can see, the requirements are very simple.

```
1.  user_proxy.initiate_chat(
2.      assistant,
3.      message="""
4.      Create an asteroids game in Python using Pygame.
5.      """,
6.  )
```

4. Now go ahead and debug the **asteroids.py** in VS Code (shortcut type *F5*) and let the dialog begin. You just need to wait a few minutes and you should see something like *Figure 8.11* popup. It will likely be a simple game you can play but only barely resembles asteroids:

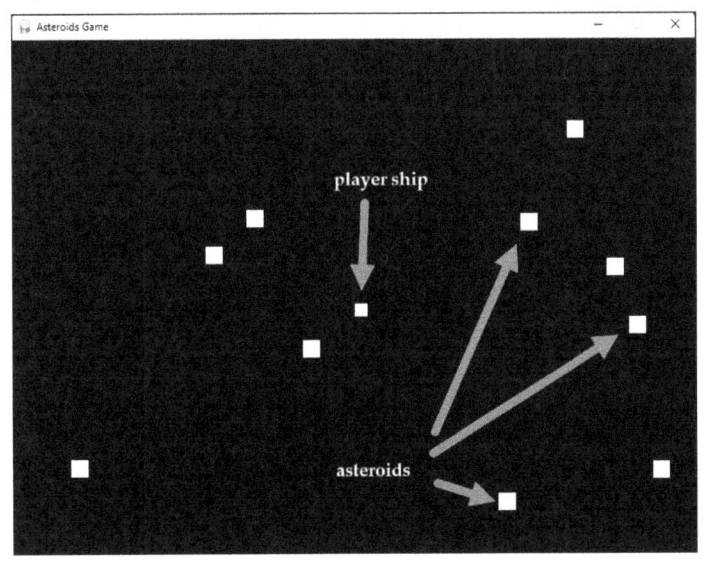

Figure 8.11: Example agent dialog and code output

So, we are a long way off from an asteroid game, go ahead and close the window and wait for the agents to continue their conversation. At some point, you will be prompted to enter your feedback. Go ahead and ask the AI to add a feature of some kind, perhaps making the ship look more like a ship.

Now, this may work well but it also may likely not. The problem is the LLM could respond in any manner of ways. This could lead to breaking code changes which could compound other problems. In the end, you will likely be unable to get a game working.

What we need is a better way of iterating over the requirements, much like we did with ChatGPT directly, but using agents to avoid repetition. This is exactly what we will dive into in the next section, where we introduce the game shop.

The game shop: Building a reusable agent workshop

The concept behind the game shop is building reusable agent systems to develop games of any complexity using *AI agents*. While the technology and capability around agents are still being developed, our focus here is developing a reusable workflow.

Incorporating agents into a larger workflow is easy because they already provide automation. The matter of concern here is at what granularity we introduce new requirements to the agent. As we have seen throughout this book, LLMs and ChatGPT work better when spoon-fed requirements.

While various GPT models can provide different base results on the first pass, in the end, it comes down to iteration and the addition of new requirements. It also helps if instead of an LLM assuming certain features and building those we can be more specific and dictate each requirement and feature in detail. This also allows us to build up a set of reproducible requirements for building our game or whatever.

Figure 8.12 is a stylized illustration of how you may think of this. Here, the bricks are the requirements, and the house represents the final game we are building. When building a house, we want a plan that identifies what features that house has. If something is missing in the house, then we can consult the plan and understand what went wrong. Please refer to the following figure:

Figure 8.12: Agents building a house from requirements

This follows the same methodology we want to incorporate into a process for building games. In the past, we iterated over the game but had no clear direction of what the outcome was. Instead, we relied on ChatGPT to guide the results. However, in the real world software and games are developed using a list of requirements.

The next exercise takes us through an overview of the game stop project, and how to configure it with requirements and run it to build a game. This workshop and process is designed for a well-thought-out design you want to build into a working game. If you are just prototyping ideas, you may want to use ChatGPT initially and then later use the game shop.

Exercise 8.5: Configuring and running the game shop

1. Open the **chapter_8/game_shop** folder in VS Code. This is the folder that contains all the elements to run agents to build a game. *Figure 8.13* identifies each of the elements of the game shop.

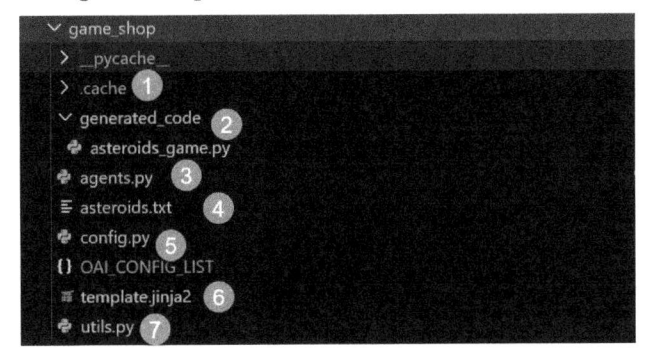

Figure 8.13: Elements of the game shop

Here is a description for each of the points identified in *Figure 8.13*:

a. This is the cache folder that AutoGen uses to store its running state. You can delete this folder if you want to start with no state. Alternatively, change the seed used in the **llm_config**.

b. **generated_code**, is a folder for holding the code the agent generates. This is where the game code will end up.

c. **agents.py** is the main file that describes the agents and the code to run the agents.

d. **asteroids.txt** holds the full list of requirements for the game.

e. **config.py** is where the LLM model's name is set. Beside is the **OAI_CONFIG_LIST** file, where you should set the model names and API keys you are using to connect. For now, all the agents will use the same model.

f. **template.jinja2** is a template for defining the prompt. It uses the **jinja2** templating engine for laying out the basic elements of the agent prompt.

   a. **utils.py** is for utility and helper functions.

2. Start configuration by opening the **config.py** file in VS Code and confirming the right model is set.

```
1. import autogen
2.
3. config_list = autogen.config_list_from_json(
4.     "OAI_CONFIG_LIST",
5.     filter_dict={
6.         "model": ["gpt-4"],          ←A
7.     }
8. )
```

3. Go ahead and use either model. How you write your requirements will depend on what LLM you are using. When using *GPT-3.5* you will want to construct the requirements in more detail and only feed a single requirement at a time. With GPT-4, you can feed in more requirements at a time. However, GPT-4 also can fill in gaps it should not sometimes and this cause issues interpreting other requirements.

The key thing to remember when building code for a game or other project is that your focus must be on defining excellent requirements. When you construct your list of requirements design the list as if you were building the game. You want to iterate on the requirements to build the game and not the output code.

Why focus on requirements and not code? Well simply, you are abstracting the build process enough that this whole process could be entirely replicated using a different LLM or agent. This not only allows you confidence the game is doing everything it should but also the ability to rebuild that game perhaps using different frameworks or even another language.

4. Speaking of requirements, go ahead and open **asteroids.txt** in VS Code. This is the start of a list of requirements for building the best Asteroids game.

   Contents of asteroids.txt:

   Make the player ship a diamond with a tail.

   The ship moves by typing the W key to move forward, and apply a physics force to the ship in the direction of the ship.

   Allow the ship to move off the edge of the screen and return to the opposite side.

   The A or D keys thrust the ship to rotate left and right respectively.

   Show a red flame from the back of the ship when the player types a thrust key.

   Draw the asteroids of varying sizes.

   The asteroids start off the screen and move across the screen in a random vector and velocity of no more than 5.

   Show the player's score in the top right corner. Each asteroid is worth 5 points.

5. Now open **agents.py**, this is the main code that runs the agents. We are going to just focus on the main elements that differentiate this code from previous examples:

   ```
   1.  GAME = 'Asteroids'            ←A
   2.  requirements = load_requirements('asteroids.txt')    ←B
   3.  code = get_code('.\generated_code')       ←C
   4.
   5.  def reset_agents():     ←D
   6.      user_proxy.reset()
   7.      assistant.reset()
   8.
   9.  def build_message_from_template(game, requirements, code):
         ←E
   10.     data = {
   11.         'game' : game,
   12.         'requirements': requirements,
   ```

```
13.         'code': code,
14.     }
15.
16.     # Load the template from the file
17.     template = env.get_template('template.jinja2')
18.
19.     # Render the template with the data
20.     return template.render(data)
21.
22. def batch_list(input_list, batch_size):      ←F
23.     for i in range(0, len(input_list), batch_size):
24.         yield input_list[i:i + batch_size]
25.
26. for batch in batch_list(requirements, 3):    ←G
27.     reset_agents()
28.     code = get_code('.\generated_code')
29.
30.     user_proxy.initiate_chat(
31.         assistant,
32.         message = build_message_from_template(game=GAME, requirements=batch, code=code)
33.
34.     )
```

The code callouts in the above code are expanded on below:

a. This is the name of your game. If you are trying to replicate a classic game, it can sometimes be helpful to call it the name of the original game.

b. This is the file to pull the entire list of requirements from.

c. The game shop allows you to start with no code or if you prefer a base set of code. This base set of code will be used as context in the user prompt.

d. This function resets the agents after every requirement session. We will see how this is used below.

e. This function loads the jinja2 template and populates it with the game, requirements and any code that has been developed. The output of this becomes the base prompt an iteration of the agents.

f. This is a helper function that breaks a list of items into smaller batches. We will use this to break down the list of requirements into smaller sets that will then be fed into a user prompt.

g. Finally, a for loop that loops through the list of requirements and through each iteration feeds a user prompt message for the agents to work on. If this is the first batch, the agents will likely not have any code for context. As the agents iterate through the list of requirements, the code will update with the new features. The number 3 shown in the call to the **batch_list** function represents the number of requirements to feed in for each iteration.

The game shop is meant to be iterative, and it uses two iterative loops. The outer loop is the for loop at the end of the above code. The second inner loop is the dialog between the agents initiated by the call to **initiate_chat** called in each outer loop.

6. Before we run the agents, we will look at the jinja2 template to see how the initiating user prompt is constructed. Open the **template.jinja2** file, shown below:

```
1.  I want a {{game}} game in Python using Pygame and Pymunk for
    physics.
2.  Please write the code for the following feature:
3.  {% for item in requirements %}        ←A
4.      {{ item }}      ←B
5.  {% endfor %}
6.
7.  {% if code %}     ←C
8.  Here is code you have already generated for me, please add or
    update the code:
9.  {{code}}     ←D
10. {% endif%}
11.
12. Note: Pygame has an inverted Y-axis, with the positive Y-axis
    pointing downward. The top of the screen corresponds to Y=0.
    ←E
```

The code callouts in the above code are expanded on below:

a. The **{%** represents the start of a **code** statement and the **%}** ends that statement. This **code** loops over the requirements object, passed into the template and outputs a single line for each item.

b. Output the requirement line item.

c. Check to see if the **code** object has data. If it does it adds the text on *line 8* and appends the code.

d. The **code** object contains all the code passed into the template.

e. Just a reminder that the y-axis in Pygame is inverted.

7. Load the **agents.py** file in VS Code but before you run it make sure and delete the **.cache** folder and the contents of the **generated_code** folder. You will generally want to delete the cache folder whenever you restart a full agent run. If for some reason you encounter an error while running, do not delete the cache folder and rerun. You will be able to start where you left off and either encounter the error again or move past any issues.

8. Now run the **agents.py** in debug mode, again we are using this mode to closely monitor the agents. Agents running with GPT-4 can quickly get expensive if left unattended. Here are the results by iteration of the agents:

Prompt iteration #1:

```
I want a Asteroids game in Python using Pygame and Pymunk for physics.

Please write the code for the following feature:

    Make the player ship a triangle with a tail.

    The ship moves by typing the W key to move forward, and apply a physics force to the ship in the direction of the ship.

    Allow the ship to move off the edge of the screen and return to the opposite side.
```

Note: Pygame has an inverted Y-axis, with the positive Y-axis pointing downward. The top of the screen corresponds to Y=0.

Output #1 (*Figure 8.14*)

For each iteration, make sure the agents complete the requirements in the current list they are working on. For example, if the agent did not get the inverted y axis you may need to remind the agent to correct this oversight.

If you find yourself adding additional or refining the requirements in the agent feedback, then it is better to update all the requirements and start again. Remember, the goal here is to create the best list of requirements that can build your game. It is okay to let the agents iterate over code issues or not draw the item correctly.

Prompt iteration #2 (just new requirements shown):

```
The A or D keys thrust the ship to rotate left and right respectively.
```

```
Show a red flame from the back of the ship when the player types a thrust key.
Draw the asteroids of varying sizes.
```

Output #2 is given in *Figure 8.14*:

Prompt iteration #3

```
The asteroids move across the screen in a random vector and random velocity
from 2-5

Show the player's score in the top right corner. Each destroyed asteroid is
worth 5 points.
```

Output #3 is given in *Figure 8.14*:

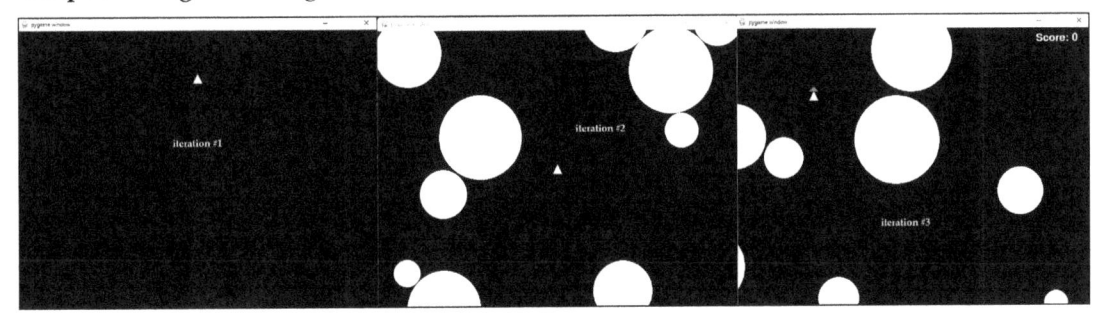

Figure 8.14: Showing the agent development iterations

Now you may find that three requirements per iteration is too much and reduce it to two or even one. You may also want to try a different model such as GPT-3.5. Another option is to start with 3 requirements for the first iteration and then one for each additional iteration. The possibilities are endless.

You can clearly see from the output examples in *Figure 8.14* that not everything is perfect when using GPT-4. We leave it up to the reader to explore the cheaper GPT-3.5 using fewer requirements per iteration and compare the results.

AutoGen supports multiple agents, each with a different persona, set of skills and goals. If you look through the documentation, you can see how to add these additional agent roles. More roles can indeed improve how the code is built but that does come at a price. If you decide to add more agent personas to the game shop strongly, consider using just *GPT-3.5*.

This concludes the work for this and our diversion into improving our workflow. We will employ the game shop agent workflow in future chapters. In some cases, as we will see, using agents is the only solution to a complex problem.

Conclusion

In this chapter, we introduced the concept of interacting directly on the OpenAI API using agents. Directly consuming the API gives us extreme power but it may come at a monetary cost. Therefore, we looked at the balance of using the right type of agents and with the right type of models, where we see how the *UserProxyAgent* and *AssistantAgent* from AutoGen can work with partial human feedback. Finally, we explored how to use the game shop agent workshop where our goal is to write excellent requirements overwrite code, and let the agents do the rest.

Agents are a likely future for using *AI* and *LLMs* for game or other software development. In the future, there may be specialized agents for the development of various application types, like games.

For the next chapter, we move back to developing Python games and jump into 3D. The world of 3D games is very complex and while Python may not be the best tool for building them. Using Python to make 3D games can be very educational as we will see in the next chapter.

What we learned

- How to set up an OpenAI account and get direct access to the various LLM models.
- How to use the OpenAI Playground to explore models and model parameters.
- How to configure the AutoGen agent framework to connect with OpenAI services.
- How to run multiple agents to solve a well-defined goal.
- How to enable agents to accept partial human feedback to optimize agent output.
- How to configure and run the game shop a multi-agent requirements-centric Python workshop for developing games with Pygame and Pymunk.
- How to iterate agent development and improve on requirements used to power agent game building.

Exercises

Doing the exercises is a great way of learning the technology. Agents are a complex topic but the power they hold will change how we develop games and software overall. The exercises in this section are designed to not only teach you better agent use but also what the future of using agents may look like:

1. Try and complete the asteroids game either using the agents or directly with ChatGPT. Plan out what requirements you need to complete the game and then decide how much to feed to the AI through each iteration of development.

2. Try and create another game we have developed previously or something you think we missed. Is it better to use the agents? What advantages do using agents have over using ChatGPT directly?

3. Use your system prompt in the `AssistantAgent`. See if you can update the default prompt to be more friendly and capable of developing games.

4. **BONUS:** Add another agent into the mix. The documentation from AutoGen features several examples with more than 2 agents using group chat. These are great examples to start with the visualization critic example could be redesigned to be a game designer. You will also likely need to customize your own system prompts for the new agent.

5. **BONUS:** Add multiple agent personas, a coder, game designer, a play tester, and others. This will require you to build each persona and System prompt for each agent.

6. **BONUS:** Explore using other agent frameworks, there are plenty of examples about. See how well you can adapt a new agent framework into developing games.

Completing even a single exercise can greatly help improve your understanding of the material.

Join our book's Discord space

Join the book's Discord Workspace for Latest updates, Offers, Tech happenings around the world, New Release and Sessions with the Authors:

https://discord.bpbonline.com

CHAPTER 9
Building a 3D First-Person Shooter

Introduction

The 3D game has become synonymous with gaming. Be it a PC game or console, it provides the most immersion and depth to any world a developer creates. However, it is also the most challenging and difficult to accomplish.

3D game development today is often done with platform engines like *Unity* and *Unreal*. They not only ease the many development challenges of 3D but also provide several helpful tools and utilities to make them. Unfortunately, Python is not a language most of these advanced tools support. Using Python for 3D game development is typically only suggested for advanced coders.

As a book details about developing games with Python, we would be remiss to not have a chapter on 3D games. So, this chapter will dive into building 3D games at a high level and explore the basics of 3D game development.

Structure

This chapter explores the following topics:

- Implementing 3D player controls and camera movement
- Enter the action-packed world of 3D FPS games

- Illuminating the world, importance of 3D lighting
- Understanding the 3D world, 3D coordinate systems
- Covering up with materials and textures
- Unleashing game AI agent support

Objectives

For this chapter, we explore the basics of 3D game development from a Python perspective. The skills we will cover in this chapter will apply to other environments. We will first step into building a simple 3D first-person game with the help of AI agents and specifically look at camera controls. Then, we move on to exploring a fully developed **First-Person Shooter** (**FPS**) game using the support of AI agents. After that, we explore how to add features and elements to the base FPS game. Finally, we finish the chapter by introducing AI to control some NPC combatants.

Implementing 3D player controls and camera movement

At the core of any game are the player controls and this is certainly no different with a 3D FPS game. The game genre is named after the control mechanism used to play it. Therefore, in this section, we start by employing the **game shop agents** we used in the last chapter to help us build a quick 3D game demo.

Figure 9.1 shows the basic concept behind the first-person camera perspective. The player avatar shown by the robot's head is replaced by a camera. On a PC, controlling this type of perspective is done using the mouse and keyboard. For a console game, the mouse is replaced by a trackball/joystick, and the keyboard with a keypad.

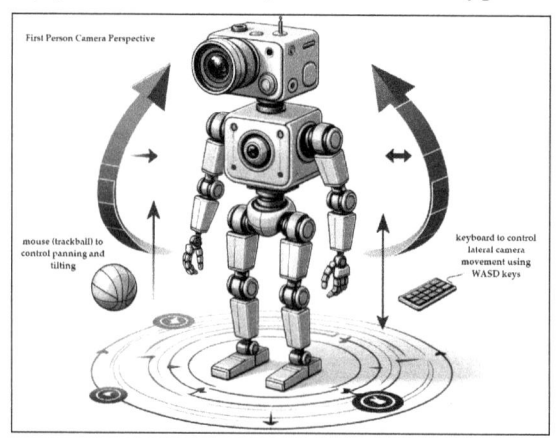

Figure 9.1: *First-person camera perspective*

In our next exercise, we are going to use the game shop agents to build a simple demo using a *first-person camera*. This will demonstrate some principles of the 3D camera, movement, and the 3D world.

Exercise 9.1: Creating a first-person camera demo

1. The code to start this exercise is in the **chapter_9/game_shop** game code folder. Open the **OAI_CONFIG_LIST** file in VS Code and set the OpenAI API key string as shown below. If you need assistance setting up an API key, please review *Chapter 8*.

    1. [
    2.   {
    3.   "model": "gpt-4",
    4.   "api_key": "your-api-key"
    5.   }
    6.]

2. Now open the **agents.py** file in VS Code and quickly review the code. For the most part, the code is the same as in *Chapter 8* but with some enhancements. At the top of the file is the updated code to define a **GAME** variable. This variable is then used to set the code folder and name of the game requirements file.

    1. GAME = '3D_FPS'
    2. requirements = load_requirements(f'{GAME}.txt')
    3. code = get_code(f'.\{GAME}')

3. Next, open the game requirements file, **3D_FPS.txt**, and review the features we are asking the agents to build. Nothing too strenuous for the GPT-4 model but notice how the request is more open-ended and less detailed than features we were writing before.

    1. please write me a 3D game demo featuring Python and Panda3D
    2. load a ground plane and nothing else
    3. allow the player to control the camera the same as a first-person shooter FPS

You can either pause here and run the previously completed code found in the **3D_FPS/game_demo.py** or continue on your own. Note that if you continue the completed game file will likely be overwritten or deleted. Of course, you can always restore the original using *Git* if you are so inclined.

If you want to see the agents running, then delete the **cache** and **3D_FPS** folders. Return to the **agents.py** file and debug the code (type *F5*). This will run the agents and you can walk through making sure the camera functions as a **first-person camera**. *Figure 9.2* shows the view after the camera was moved out above the map:

Figure 9.2: View of the game environment

In a true FPS game, the camera would see from the perspective of the player. This means that the player is typically constrained by the game's physics engine. Our current FP player camera has no idea of physics, so it allows the camera to be moved anywhere.

Let us open the game code and see what this looks like:

```
1.   class MyApp(ShowBase):          ←A
2.       def __init__(self):
3.           ShowBase.__init__(self)      ←B
4.
5.           # Disable the camera trackball controls.
6.           self.disableMouse()       ←B
7.
8.           # Load the environment model.
```

```
 9.         self.environ = self.loader.loadModel("models/
    environment")
10.         self.environ.reparentTo(self.render)       ←C
11.
12.         # Scale and position the model.
13.         self.environ.setScale(0.25, 0.25, 0.25)     ←C
14.         self.environ.setPos(-8, 42, 0)      ←C
15.
16.         # Add the spinCameraTask procedure to the task manager.
17.         self.taskMgr.add(self.spinCameraTask, "spinCameraTask")
     ←6
18.
19.         # Add the move task.
20.         self.taskMgr.add(self.move, "moveTask")     ←D
21.
22.         # Define a key map.
23.         self.keyMap = {"left":0, "right":0, "forward":0,
    "backward":0}     ←E
24.
25.         # Bind the keys.
26.         self.accept("w", self.setKey, ["forward", 1])     ←E
27.         self.accept("w-up", self.setKey, ["forward", 0])
28.         self.accept("s", self.setKey, ["backward", 1])
29.         self.accept("s-up", self.setKey, ["backward", 0])
30.         self.accept("a", self.setKey, ["left", 1])
31.         self.accept("a-up", self.setKey, ["left", 0])
32.         self.accept("d", self.setKey, ["right", 1])
33.         self.accept("d-up", self.setKey, ["right", 0])
34.
35.     # Records the state of the arrow keys.
36.     def setKey(self, key, value):      ←E
37.         self.keyMap[key] = value
38.
39.     # Define a procedure to move the camera.
```

```
40.     def spinCameraTask(self, task):        ←F
41.         if self.mouseWatcherNode.hasMouse():
42.             x = self.mouseWatcherNode.getMouseX()
43.             y = self.mouseWatcherNode.getMouseY()
44.             self.camera.setHpr(x * -60, y * 60, 0)
45.         return Task.cont
46.
47.     # Define a procedure to move the 'player'.
48.     def move(self, task):        ←D
49.         elapsed = globalClock.getDt()
50.         if self.keyMap["left"]:
51.             self.camera.setX(self.camera, -elapsed*10)
52.         if self.keyMap["right"]:
53.             self.camera.setX(self.camera, elapsed*10)
54.         if self.keyMap["forward"]:
55.             self.camera.setY(self.camera, elapsed*10)
56.         if self.keyMap["backward"]:
57.             self.camera.setY(self.camera, -elapsed*10)
58.         return Task.cont
59.
60. app = MyApp()        ←A
61. app.run()        ←A
```

The code callouts in the above code are described below:

a. In **Panda3D**, the whole game is encapsulated in a class. The game loop is not exposed directly but instead uses hooks. To run the game, the class is instantiated and run.

b. By default, a set of camera controls is provided. Here, they are disabled since we want to provide our means of camera control.

c. Panda3D comes with a set of demo models and environments. Here, we are loading the environment and scaling and positioning the environment.

d. This line adds the **moveTask** task, in Panda3D a task is a hook into the game loop that allows you to add **code** as part of the loop. Abstracting the game loop like this provides some powerful flexibility while maintaining a robust code base. The **move** function is responsible for moving the camera.

e. This set of code defines the key mappings of the keyboard to game actions. For now, they are just bound to move.

f. Code that adds the **spinCameraTask** task binds to the mouse to control the camera panning and tilting. The **spinCameraTask** function is the code that positions the camera based on the mouse position.

This code demonstrates the basic setup and functionality of the *Panda3D* game using a first-person camera. We could continue this journey, as we have done throughout this book, but instead, we will look at a more substantial game in the next section.

Enter the action-packed world of 3D FPS games

As previously mentioned, 3D game development is hard. Even with the use of AI tools like *ChatGPT*, building even a simple FPS demo in Python can require a substantial setup. In-game platforms like *Unity* and *Unreal*, creating an FP game is quite simple. However, if you want a good understanding of how 3D games work, building an FPS in Python is a good idea.

Therefore, we are going to use a working demo of a 3D FPS game from **GitHub**, like what we did in *Chapter 5*. In the next exercise, we are going to download and set up the project so we can understand the code and modify it later.

Exercise 9.2: Cloning, inspecting, and running the FPS demo project

1. Open a terminal and use git to clone the FPS project from:

    https://github.com/cxbxmxcx/Panda3D-Arena-FPS-Sample-Program.git using the command shown below. If you need help using **git**, consult *Appendix A* or ChatGPT.

    1. git clone https://github.com/cxbxmxcx/Panda3D-Arena-FPS-Sample-Program.git

2. Next, change the directory to the newly cloned folder and type *Shift+ Control+ P* (*Shift+ Cmd+ P, Mac*) to open the command palette. Select to install a new Python environment, choose your version of Python, and then select the **requirements.txt** file to preload. The steps for all of this are shown in *Figure 9.3*:

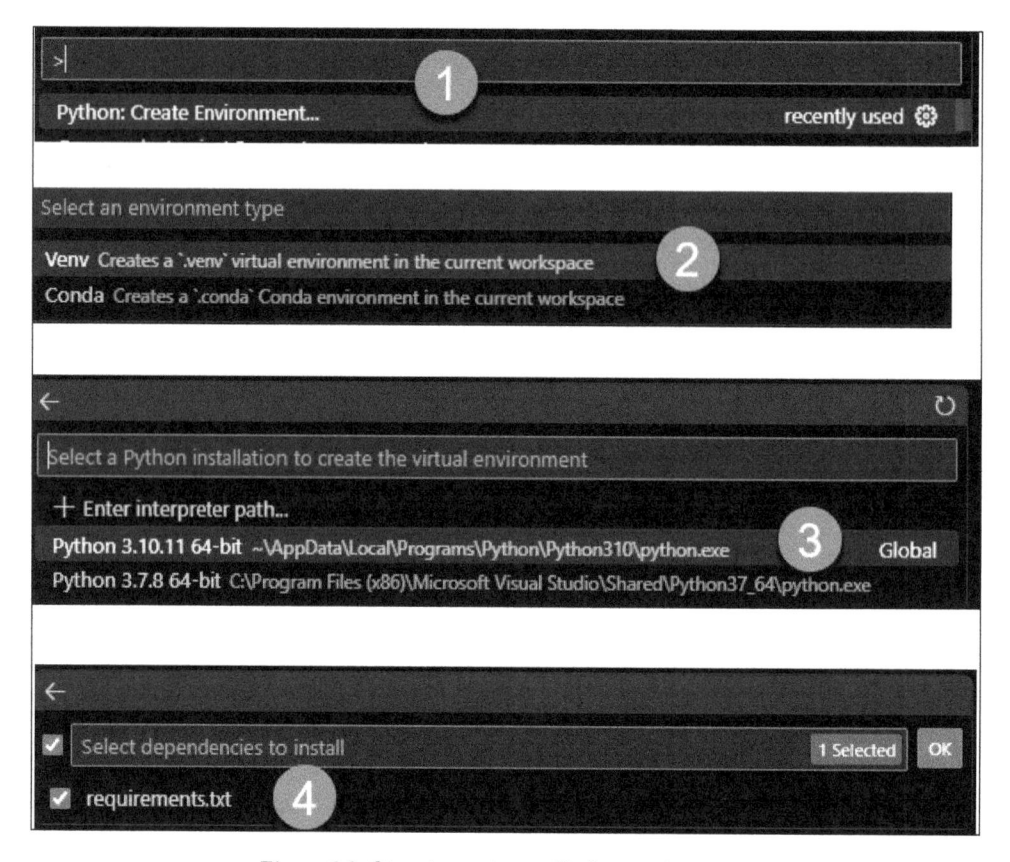

Figure 9.3: Steps to create new Python environment

The points shown in *Figure 9.3* are outlined below:

- a. Type *Control+Shift+P* to open the command palette. Select **Python Create Environment**.

- b. Select your virtual environment preference, either **Python venv** or **Conda** from **Anaconda**.

- c. Select the version of Python, be sure to use a revision of 3.10.

- d. Select the `requirements.txt` file to load the initial packages.

After a couple of minutes, the environment should be installed and ready to go. This FPS game was forked from `rayanalysis/Panda3D-Arena-FPS-Sample-Program` and is relatively new. If you have an interest in contributing to this demo then please refer to original GIT source, it is likely the author will be happy for the help. This project is a little rough around the edges, but it does provide great possibilities for 3D games in Python.

3. Next, open the **arena.py** file in VS Code and debug it (*F5*). This will run the game and you should see a screenshot like *Figure 9.4*:

Figure 9.4: The FPS game demo running

The objective of this simple FPS is to shoot the head of the NPC body that randomly moves about. Take your best shot and see how quickly you can take out the NPC. When you are done playing the game, press the *ESC* key to exit.

Open the code and explore the **arena.py** file on your own. Most of the code for this FPS demo is contained in this single file. In some ways, this is good because you can see all the code, for maintenance and enhancement though it can be problematic. In a future section of this chapter, we will look at some agent AI tools that may help with this.

Now with the base game installed we can move onto further understanding the components of a 3D game by looking at lighting in the next section.

Illuminating the world, importance of 3D Lighting

When assembling a 3D environment or world, the first thing we need to understand is lighting. After all, without any light, our scene would be completely black. Lighting is also one of the most crucial elements in 3D games. Good lighting can provide depth, shadows, ambiance, and life to a game scene.

The following is an excellent summary of the type of lights used in 3D games and a couple of lighting techniques:

- **Directional lights:** These lights simulate sunlight or other distant light sources. They have a uniform direction and illuminate all objects in a scene regardless of the distance from the light source. Shadows from a directional light are parallel.

- **Point lights:** These are omnidirectional lights, meaning they emit light equally in all directions from a single point in space. They are useful for simulating light sources like *bulbs* or *candles*. The intensity of the light they emit diminishes with distance.

- **Spotlights:** These lights emit light in a cone shape. They have a defined direction and an angle of spread, which determines the size of the cone. They are useful for simulating focused light sources like *flashlights* or *stage lights*.

- **Ambient lights:** Instead of coming from a specific direction or location, ambient light illuminates all objects in the scene uniformly. It is used to simulate the effect of scattered light that provides general illumination to a scene. Ambient light does not produce shadows.

- **Area lights:** These are lights that have a defined shape (like a *rectangle* or *disc*) and emit light from the entire surface of that shape. They produce softer shadows compared to point lights or spotlights. However, they are more computationally expensive and might not be commonly used in real-time 3D games, but rather in pre-rendered scenes or cutscenes.

- **Hemispherical lights (or skylights):** These simulate light coming from the sky, providing a gradient of light. The top color usually simulates the sky, while the bottom color simulates the ground.

- **Image-based lighting (IBL):** This is a more advanced lighting technique where lighting information is taken from a panoramic or spherical image (often referred to as an HDRI or high dynamic range image). The scene is then lit according to the colors and intensities captured in this image. This method is great for achieving realistic environmental lighting.

- **Global illumination (GI):** This is an advanced form of lighting that calculates how light bounces around in a scene.

- **Physically based pendering (PBR)**: This considers the physical properties of materials when rendering light. These are not lights per se, but they play a significant role in how lighting appears in modern games.

The two items at the bottom of the list, **GI** and **PBR** are not lights but lighting methods. In the game demo, several types of lights are used as well as PBR for rendering the materials used in the game. *Figure 9.5* shows a summary of the main light sources in a 3D game scene.

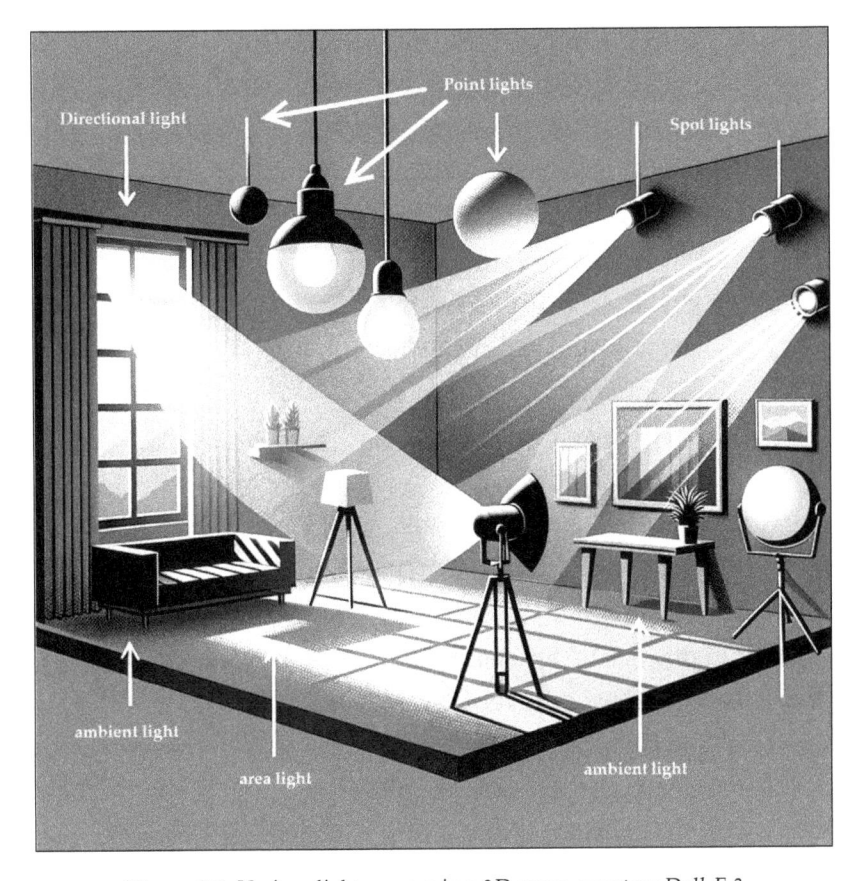

Figure 9.5: Various light sources in a 3D scene, courtesy Dall-E 3

In the next exercise, we are going to look at the various lighting types, sources, and methods used in the demo.

Exercise 9.3: Understanding the arena lights

1. Open **arena_lighting.py** in VS Code. This file contains the lighting for various sources of lighting that will be provided in the arena:

   ```
   1.  def lighting():
   2.      # Lighting entry point
   3.      amb_light = AmbientLight('amblight')          ←A
   4.      amb_light.set_color(Vec4(Vec3(1),1))
   5.      amb_light_node = base.render.attachNewNode(amb_light)
   6.      base.render.set_light(amb_light_node)
   7.
   8.      slight_1 = Spotlight('slight_1')              ←B
   ```

```
9.      slight_1.set_color(Vec4(Vec3(5),1))
10.     slight_1.set_shadow_caster(True, 4096, 4096)
11.     # slight_1.set_attenuation((0.5,0,0.000005))
12.     lens = PerspectiveLens()
13.     slight_1.set_lens(lens)
14.     slight_1.get_lens().set_fov(120)
15.     slight_1_node = base.render.attach_new_node(slight_1)
16.     slight_1_node.set_pos(50, 50, 90)
17.     slight_1_node.look_at(0,0,0.5)
18.     base.render.set_light(slight_1_node)
19.
20.     slight_2 = Spotlight('slight_2')        ←C
21.     slight_2.set_color(Vec4(Vec3(5),1))
22.     # slight_2.set_shadow_caster(True, 16384, 16384)
23.     slight_2.set_attenuation((0.5,0,0.0005))
24.     lens = PerspectiveLens()
25.     slight_2.set_lens(lens)
26.     slight_2.get_lens().set_fov(90)
27.     slight_2_node = base.render.attach_new_node(slight_2)
28.     slight_2_node.set_pos(-82, -79, 50)
29.     slight_2_node.look_at(0,0,0.5)
30.     base.render.set_light(slight_2_node)
31.
32.     env_light_1 = PointLight('env_light_1')      ←D
33.     env_light_1.set_color(Vec4(Vec3(6),1))
34.     env_light_1 = base.render.attach_new_node(env_light_1)
35.     env_light_1.set_pos(0,0,0)
36.
37.     base_env = loader.load_model('models/daytime_skybox.bam')
38.     base_env.reparent_to(base.render)         ←E
39.     base_env.set_scale(1)
40.     base_env.set_pos(0,0,0)
41.     base_env.set_light(env_light_1)
42.     base_env.set_light_off(base.render.find('**/slight_1'))
```

The code callouts in the above code are outlined below:

   a. An ambient light is the light that is seen everywhere. The color set using this code, **Vec4(Vec3(1),1),** results in a 4D vector of form (red, green, blue, alpha) or (1, 1, 1, 1). Here, alpha controls transparency and the other colors represent their strength. A value of (1, 1, 1) represents a dark shade of grey.

   b. Describes a spotlight that is positioned above the arena at (50, 50, 50) and points at (0, 0, 0.5).

   c. Describes a spotlight that is positioned above the arena at (-82, -79, 50) and pointing at (0, 0, .5).

   d. Describes a point light at the center of the arena.

   e. This is not a light but rather a model that creates the skybox over the arena. A skybox is a box that wraps the entire scene and may be a color like blue or a texture/material of a sky image. Notice how the skybox is using the **env_light_1** for illumination.

2. A good exercise to do is to play with the settings of the various light sources, then run the game to see the changes and effects. *Figure 9.6* shows the scene with the ambient light disabled beside a scene with it enabled:

Figure 9.6: Side by side comparison of ambient lighting

As you can see ambient light in a scene can have a dramatic effect on several elements. Notice how some textures on the ball disappear when ambient lights are turned off, this includes the skybox.

You can see in *Figure 9.6* that when the ambient lights are turned off, the material (the wood grain or stone) is not visible. This is because the objects are using **physically based bendering** (**PBR**) for rendering the look of the objects. The specular highlights are visible because they are a result of directional and point lights. However, materials on objects derive their base lighting from ambient light.

The determination of how light lights an object is typically done using a technique called **PBR**. In the demo, the spheres are shaded using *PBR* to denote the complexity of lighting.

PBR is implemented using a technique called **shaders** which are low-level functions that describe how light interacts with an object. PBR shaders typically come in two forms or levels, the first vertex shaders operate at the vertex level and second, fragment shaders which operate at the triangle level.

Figure 9.7 shows an example of a 3D mesh and what a vertex, triangle or fragment is. In rendering the vertex, vertex shaders are executed first and then the fragment shaders. Please refer to the following figure:

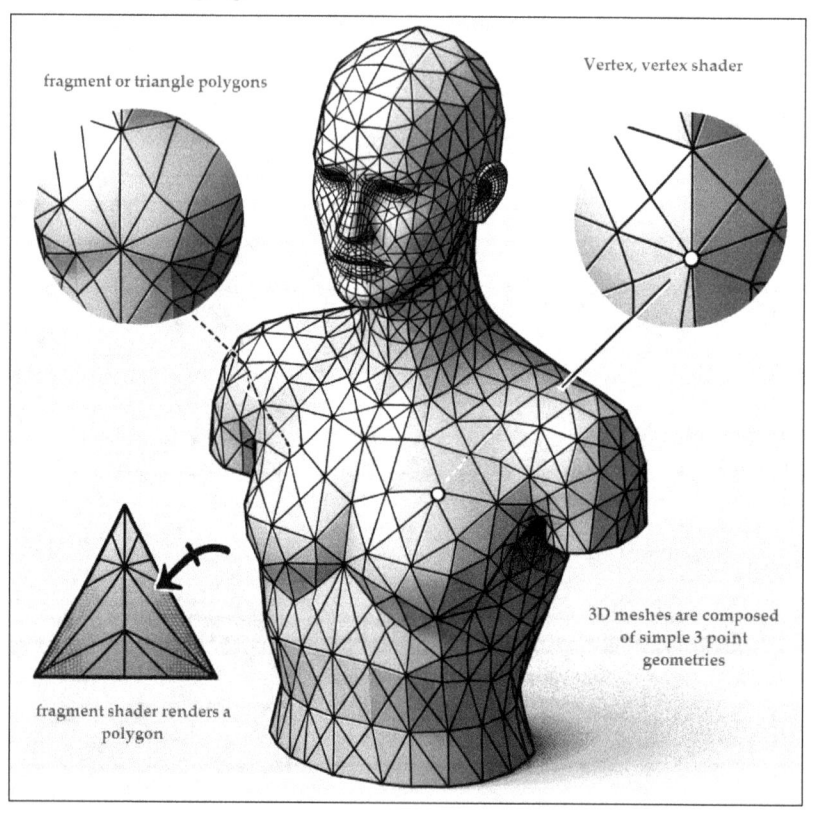

Figure 9.7: Vertex and fragment shaders

Digging into writing or using shaders is well beyond the scope of this book but they are an important concept to understand. Almost all 3D rendering in today's 3D games is done using *shaders*. You can go ahead and look in the demo project at the files ending with .frag or .vert to see what a shader looks like.

There is another set of lighting techniques the game used called **post-processing screen effects**. These effects are implemented by shaders but are applied directly to the entire scene. They provide a quick and easy method to further enhance the game visuals and focus of our next exercise.

Exercise 9.4: Understanding post-processing lighting effects

1. Open **arena.py** in VS Code and right at the top of the file is a section for enabling post-processing screen effects:

```
1.  def quality_mode():
2.      complexpbr.screenspace_init()          ←A
3.
4.      base.screen_quad.set_shader_input("bloom_intensity", 0.3)
                                                              ←B
5.      base.screen_quad.set_shader_input("bloom_threshold", 0.7)
6.      base.screen_quad.set_shader_input("bloom_blur_width", 10)
7.      base.screen_quad.set_shader_input("bloom_samples", 3)
8.      base.screen_quad.set_shader_input('ssr_samples', 0)    ←C
9.      base.screen_quad.set_shader_input('ssao_samples', 6)   ←D
10.     base.screen_quad.set_shader_input('hsv_r', 1.0)        ←E
11.     base.screen_quad.set_shader_input('hsv_g', 1.1)
12.     base.screen_quad.set_shader_input('hsv_b', 1.0)
13.
14.     text_1.set_text("Quality Mode: On")
15.
16. self.accept_once('m', quality_mode)        ←F
17. self.accept_once("gamepad-face_y", quality_mode)
```

The code callouts in the above code are identified below:

   a. This line initializes using shaders for the screen.

   b. This sets up a bloom effect. Blooming is like a subtle glow around objects.

   c. **Screen Space Reflections** (**SSR**) is a technique used to simulate reflections in rendered scenes.

   d. **Screen Space Ambient Occlusion** (**SSAO**) is a shading technique that approximates the ambient occlusion effect in real-time to enhance the depth and realism of scenes.

e. **Hue, Saturation, and Value** (**HSV**) is a way of representing colors in a cylindrical-coordinate system, and is often used in graphics software and other applications where users might find it more intuitive to think about colors in terms of these attributes rather than the typical **Red, Green, Blue** (**RGB**) model. This model allows for the enhancement of certain colors in the scene.

2. Run the game and press the *m* key to disable the screen surface shader (quality on) and disable it. *Figure 9.8* shows the difference between using the screen surface shader and not. The differences may be subtle until you look closely at the reflections in the spheres.

Figure 9.8: Showing the difference without screen shader and with

Surface shaders are a quick and efficient way of providing additional rendering effects to your 3D scene. Go ahead and edit the values for the various surface shader settings and run the game again. Be sure to remember to press the *m* key to enable the surface shader.

Understanding the 3D world, 3D coordinate systems

A key aspect of writing any 3D game or using a 3D game engine is understanding the coordinate system it uses. Panda3D uses a right-handed coordinate system as shown in *Figure 9.9*. Other, more popular game engines like *Unity* use a left-handed coordinate system:

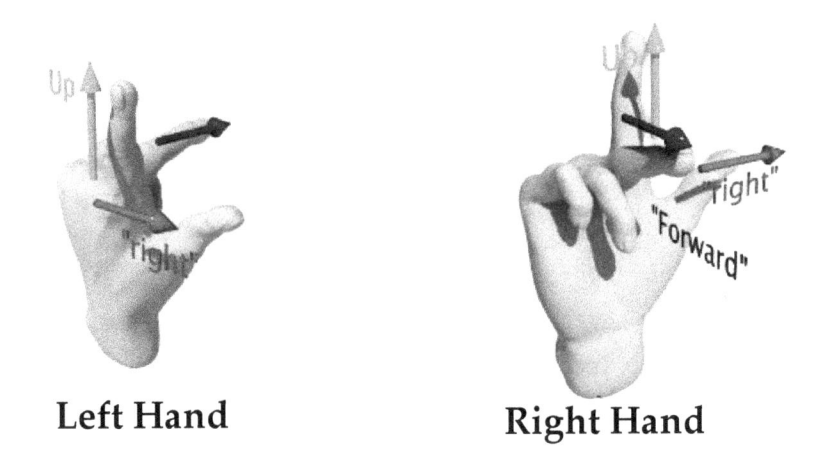

Figure 9.9: *The difference between the RH and LH coordinate systems*

The best way to understand the difference between the two coordinate systems is to hold up both hands. Point your thumb on both hands to the right, this will mean rotating your right hand towards you and left hand away. Right is a fundamental direction that we will use to track an object facing.

Keeping both your hands up, point the index finger up. Up is another cardinal and important direction. Lastly, point your index finger out. On your left hand, your index finger will point away and on the right towards you. This is the forward direction, another cardinal direction. The forward direction, positive going into the screen for **left-hand** (**LH**), and positive coming out of the screen for **right-hand** (**RH**), is the primary difference between each system.

In a right-handed coordinate system Panda3D uses, each of the axes is described as the following:

- **X-axis (Right)**: Positive X denotes the direction of the right.
- **Y-axis (Forward)**: Positive Y denotes the direction of forward. Since this is RH, positive Y is coming out of the screen.
- **Z-axis (Up)**: Positive Z is in the up direction.

It is important to understand the coordinate system and how objects are placed and faced. What this means is that an object as (0, 0, 0) with default facing would be placed in the center of the game looking toward the screen.

In our next exercise, we are going to move and place objects in the scene using our new understanding of the 3D coordinate system.

Exercise 9.5: Moving and placing objects in 3D

1. Open **arena.py** in VS Code and scroll down to the following code block:

    ```
    1. # initialize player character physics the Bullet way
    2. shape_1 = BulletCapsuleShape(0.75, 0.5, ZUp)
    3. player_node = BulletCharacterControllerNode(shape_1, 0.1,
       'Player')   # (shape, mass, player name)
    4. player_np = self.render.attach_new_node(player_node)
    5. player_np.set_pos(-20, -10, 30)
    6. player_np.set_collide_mask(BitMask32.allOn())
    7. self.world.attach_character(player_np.node())
    8. # cast player_np to self.player
    9. self.player = player_np
    ```

    The highlighted line in this code block denotes the starting position of the player. References to **Bullet** are for the physics system. Notice how the player starts at **Z=30**, since we know that Z is the up direction then this lets us know the player starts 30 units above 0. A unit in most 3D games is kept consistent at a meter. Notice also how the **BulletCapsuleShape** is also taking the same 3D coordinates to determine the shape of the player character.

2. Scroll down to where the spheres are added to the scene shown in the following code:

    ```
    1. # add a few random physics spheres
    2. for x in range(0, 30):
    3.     # dynamic collision
    4.     random_vec = Vec3(1, 1, 1)
    5.     # special_shape = BulletBoxShape(random_vec)
    6.     special_shape = BulletSphereShape(random_vec[0])      ←A
    ```

```
7.      # rigidbody
8.      body = BulletRigidBodyNode('random_prisms')
9.      d_coll = self.render.attach_new_node(body)
10.     d_coll.node().add_shape(special_shape)
11.     d_coll.node().set_mass(15)
12.     d_coll.node().set_friction(50)
13.     d_coll.set_collide_mask(BitMask32.allOn())
14.     # turn on Continuous Collision Detection
15.     d_coll.node().set_ccd_motion_threshold(0.000000007)
16.     d_coll.node().set_ccd_swept_sphere_radius(0.30)
17.     d_coll.node().set_deactivation_enabled(False)   # prevents stopping the physics simulation
18.     d_coll.set_pos(random.uniform(-60, -20), random.uniform(-60, -20), random.uniform(50, 800))    ←B
19.     sphere_choices = ['1m_sphere_black_marble','1m_sphere_purple_metal','1m_sphere_concrete_1','1m_sphere_bright_1']
20.     sphere_choice = random.choice(sphere_choices)
21.     box_model = self.loader.load_model('models/' + sphere_choice + '.bam')      ←C
22.     box_model.reparent_to(self.render)
23.     box_model.reparent_to(d_coll)
```

The code callouts in the above code are explained below:

   a. This takes a single value to determine the physical size of the spheres. In this case, it is using 1, but we could make it random. Remember though, that this is the physical size and not the rendered size.

   b. Set the position of the spheres at the start of the game and pay attention to the values set for each axis. Look at the values on the Z axis, that means some of these spheres start the game very high up.

   c. Four sphere models can be set. This is randomized but this can also be changed.

3. Now, we will go ahead and alter some of the starting values for the player or spheres. *Figure 9.10* shows the result of randomizing the sphere size. Here is the updated code to randomly set the physical and visual size of the spheres:

```
1.   scale_factor = random.uniform(.1, 1.5)      ←A
2.   # dynamic collision
```

3. `random_vec = Vec3(1, 1, 1)`
4. `# special_shape = BulletBoxShape(random_vec)`
5. `special_shape = BulletSphereShape(random_vec[0] * scale_factor)` ←B
6. `# ... omitted`
7. `box_model = self.loader.load_model('models/' + sphere_choice + '.bam')`
8.
9. `#scale the model size`
10. `box_model.set_scale(scale_factor)` ←C

   a. Create a random **scale_factor** ranging in value from **.1** to **1.5**.

   b. Alter the physical shape of the object by multiplying the scale factor.

   c. Alter the visual shape of the object by scaling the model using **set_scale** function to set the size to the **scale_factor**.

Figure 9.10: Shows the effect of randomizing the sphere size

You can alter any other values in the game, scaling things larger or smaller. This can be a good exercise in establishing a good understanding of 3D coordinate systems. In the next section, we continue with the basics by looking at how things are covered in 3D.

Covering up with materials and textures

Another critical aspect of 3D games is the models that populate the world. 3D modeling is well outside the scope of this book but understanding how a model/mesh is textured is something a developer can have significant control over.

Figure 9.11 shows the difference between a model/mesh being rendered with a plain texture and one being rendered with a PBR material and textures. Physically based rendering allows for the inclusion of several features. Please refer to the following figure:

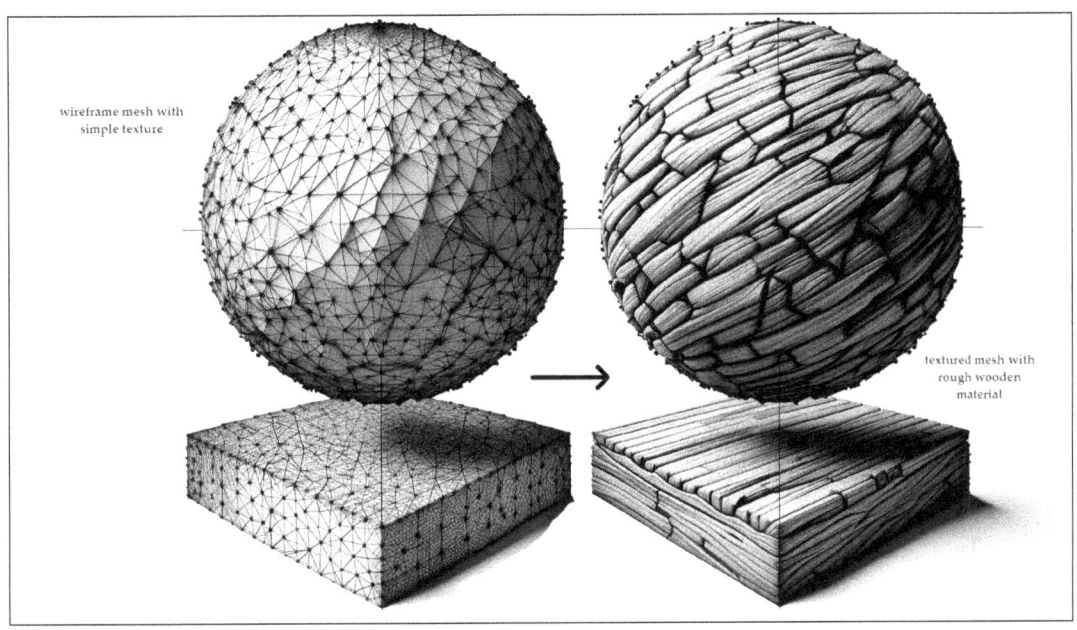

Figure 9.11: A mesh being rendered using simple and PBR materials

In *Figure 9.11*, on the left is a sphere textured simply with a light grey texture. The mesh itself provides for the rough look and distortions. On the right is a textured mesh using a rough wooden texture. In this case, the material, PBR material, is rendered in a manner that provides the illusion of a rough wooden texture.

We do this because geometry, all those triangles on a mesh are more expensive to render than the material using shaders. This means we can greatly simplify the geometry of an object but still provide the illusion of far more complex surfaces. In the next exercise, we explore the use of materials, meshes and rendering.

Exercise 9.6: Understanding models, meshes, materials and texture rendering

    a. Open back up the game project folder and the arena.py file in VS Code. Go ahead and run the game in debug mode (*F5*). Press the *F1* and *F3* keys. This turns on the physics and wireframe rendering modes, as shown in *Figure 9.12*:

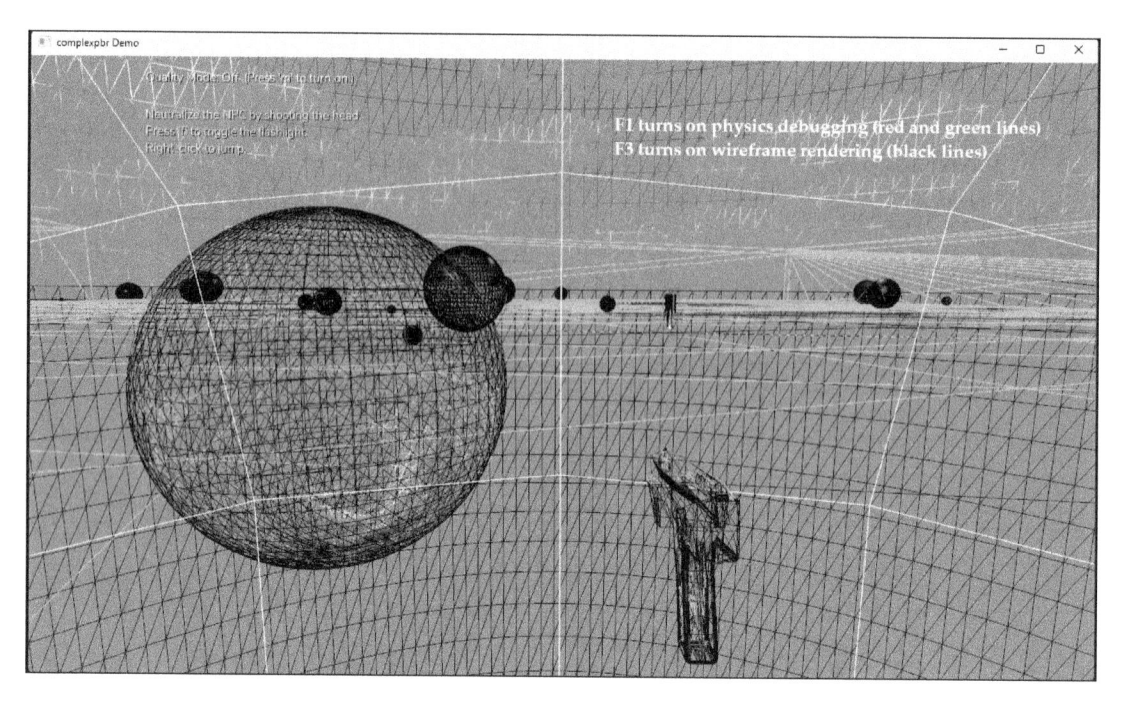

Figure 9.12: Wireframe and physics rendering

b. *F1* activates the physics mode. The debugger renders the static physics objects in green, like the arena itself, and rigid body objects in red. *F3* activates the wireframe rendering mode. This mode will show how the various vertexes are rendered. Typing *F1* or *F3* again will toggle the debugging rendering modes.

If you recall our earlier discussion of shaders, there is a vertex and fragment shader. When the scene is rendered in wireframe mode, you will see the results of the vertex shaders being applied. Notice how the vertex color of the objects will change based on the reflections. This is because the specular or reflective lighting is applied at the vertex level.

Next, we are going to look at one of the PBR materials to see how it is composed like layers.

c. Open VS Code to the **textures/get_file_Concrete017_2K-PNG** folder as shown in *Figure 9.13*. Identified in the figure are the various file types used to construct the PBR material.

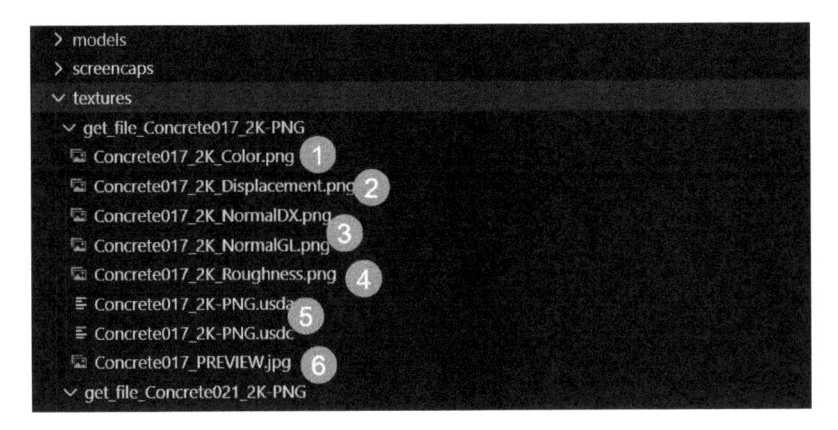

Figure 9.13: Summary of PBR files

Below is a summary of the file types in a PBR material:

- **Color (albedo or diffuse)**: This texture provides the base color of the material and represents how the surface looks under neutral lighting (that is, no shadows or highlights). It does not contain any lighting information itself. The albedo texture usually does not have high contrast or very dark or bright areas, since shadows and highlights are calculated in real time by the lighting in the PBR system.

- **Displacement**: A displacement map is used to add high-frequency detail to the surface geometry of a model. When this map is applied, it modifies the geometry, displacing vertices along their normal according to the map's values. This is often used to create complex surfaces like rock faces, scales, or other textured details that would be too costly to model manually.

- **NormalDX and NormalGL**: These are both types of normal maps, which are textures that allow a low-polygon model to appear as if it has more complex surface detail. They store per-pixel normals in a compressed format, usually as RGB values. The normals in these maps dictate how light should bounce off the surface, creating the illusion of depth and detail.

   NormalDX typically refers to a normal map that is designed to work with **DirectX** conventions, where the Y-coordinate in the normal map is up. **NormalGL** is for OpenGL, where the Y-coordinate is down. These are different coordinate systems used by different engines or software, and the main difference is the direction of the Y-channel in the texture map.

- **Roughness**: The roughness texture map controls how rough or smooth a surface appears. It affects the spread of the specular highlight on the surface. A low value (darker areas) in the roughness map will result in a surface that is smooth and has sharp reflections (like a *mirror*), whereas a high value (lighter areas) makes the surface rough and the reflections more diffuse (like *rubber* or *concrete*). It is a critical component in defining the material's appearance.

- **Universal Scene Description (USD)** files:
  - USDA files are the human-readable version of the USD file format. The *A* stands for ASCII, meaning the data in these files is encoded as plain text. These files can be opened and edited with a text editor, which makes them convenient for tasks such as version control diffs, manual edits, or reviews of the scene data.
  - USDC files are the binary version of USD files. The *C* can be thought of as standing for *Compiled* or *Computer-readable*. This format is more efficient for machines to read and write, which means it's faster to process but not human-readable. The binary format is generally used for performance in production environments where the overhead of parsing text-based USDA files would be a bottleneck.
- **Preview**: This shows a preview of how the material may look as rendered in a scene.

Figure 9.14 shows the various texture images together and the final render preview. You can alter any of these textures to give your object a different look. In larger production games, there is typically a role dedicated to building PBR materials. Please refer to the following figure:

Figure 9.14: Collection of image files in PBR material

Creating a full PBR material is out of the scope of this book, but you can start to get an understanding of the complexity of material rendering.

In 3D games, we may often want to modify some of the attributes of a material at runtime. This means we will often have hooks into the shaders that allow us to define rendering parameters. These rendering parameters can then be modified at runtime to produce some effect.

For the last part of the exercise, open **arena.py** in VS Code and scroll down to the highlighted section shown below:

```
1.  if sphere_choice == '1m_sphere_concrete_1':        ←A
2.      dis_tex = Texture()
3.      dis_tex.read('textures/get_file_Concrete017_2K-PNG/
        Concrete017_2K_Displacement.png')      ←B
4.      box_model.set_shader_input('displacement_map', dis_tex)
5.      #box_model.set_shader_input('displacement_scale', 0.03)
6.      box_model.set_shader_input('displacement_scale', -0.01)
        ←C
```

   a. The line of code that checks if the sphere type is concrete.

   b. Notice how the displacement texture is being referenced.

   c. Modify the **set_shader_input** function to set the **displacement_scale** to **-.01** from **.03**.

Go ahead and run/debug the game again to see the effect. In this case, it is minor and may be difficult to see. We can, therefore, make the effect more pronounced by increasing the scale to a larger value. *Figure 9.15* shows an example of the **displacement_scale** turned up to .3. Notice how the object shape itself is modified. This happens because the displacement is handled in the vertex shader, which can modify the actual vertex positions. Please refer to the following figure:

Figure 9.15: Displacement scale modifying the physical mesh

Thus far, we have successfully made some minor changes to the code. Overall, though, you will likely want to update this game in many ways. To help you do that, we revisit using agents to help us understand the code base in the next section.

Unleashing game AI agent support

The FPS demo we are looking at assumes the user is an experienced 3D game developer. Now, this demo does employ several advanced features of 3D game development. However, we also have at our disposal ChatGPT and agents to assist us in understanding the demo.

In this next exercise, we will set up a modified version of the agent game shop, introduced in the last chapter, to function as a support agent. To differentiate the difference, we will call this new project the **game support agents**.

Exercise 9.7: Configuring and running agent game support

1. Open the project folder for **chapter_9/game_support** in VS Code. Make a new folder called **arena**, the name of our game and copy the **arena.py** file from the game demo into the folder. This will be our base context of code the agents will use to answer questions and so on.

   If you recall from the game shop in *Chapter 8*, we did not start with any code. But as the agents-built code, it was used for context. This is the same idea but, in this case, we are just starting with a base set of code. We are also keeping the code in a single file, for simplicity. In a more advanced system, we would use **Retrieval Augmented Generation** (**RAG**), to provide context.

2. Next, open the **game_support/agents.py** file in VS Code. We will look at the differences that make this an agent support system by first looking at the **AssistantAgent** configuration:

   ```
   1.  GAME = 'arena'            ←A
   2.  requirements = load_requirements(f'{GAME}.txt')
   3.  code = get_code(f'.\{GAME}')
   4.
   5.  # Create a Jinja2 environment with the template directory
   6.  env = Environment(loader=FileSystemLoader('./'))
   7.  # create an AssistantAgent named «assistant»
   8.  #update the SYSTEM message for the role of support assistant
   9.  system_message = """         ←B
   10. You are a helpful AI assistant.
   11. Solve tasks using your coding and language skills.
   ```

12. In the following cases, suggest where to look in the python
    code (in a python coding block) or shell script (in a sh coding
    block) for the user to look at.
13. Solve the task step by step if you need to. If a plan is not
    provided, explain your plan first. Be clear which step uses
    code, and which step uses your language skill.
14. Reply "TERMINATE" in the end when everything is done.
15. """
16. assistant = autogen.AssistantAgent(
17.   name="assistant",
18.   system_message=system_message,
19.   llm_config={
20.   "request_timeout": 600,   ←C
21.   "seed": 42, # seed for caching and reproducibility
22.   "config_list": config_list, # a list of OpenAI API configurations
23.   "temperature": 0, # temperature for sampling
24.   }, # configuration for autogen›s enhanced inference API which is compatible with OpenAI API
25.)

The code callouts are described below:

a. The name of the game we are working on. Remember that the name sets the output folder, and the requirements file we use to drive the agent actions.

b. The critical difference between this agent system is the modification to the system message. A system message for an agent is like the persona or behavior of how the agent must act. Agents are driven by these system messages. Previously, we used the defaults but, in this case, we customize to extract more specific behaviors.

c. The support agent system sends the entire contents of **arena.py** as the context. Since this can be a large amount of data, we increase the **request_timeout** to 600 seconds, 10 minutes. If you see the agent timing out, start by increasing the timeout.

3. So, we have an updated system message, but that is only part of the message we send. Therefore, open the **template.jinja2** file in VS Code, shown below:

    1. I have a {{game}} game in Python. I want you to help me
       understand the code and support me in making changes.   ←A

2. Please show me the code for the following feature:
3. {% for item in requirements %} ←B
4.   {{ item }}
5. {% endfor %}
6.
7. {% if code %} ←C
8. Here is the game code, please make suggestions, but don't add or update the code:
9. {{code}}
10. {% endif%}

   a. Notice how the message is quite different. It now starts by informing the agent that it already has a game developed and its role is to answer questions about the code.

   b. This is where the requirements are cycled through, and each item is added.

   c. A check to see if there is code, and if there is append it to the initial agent message.

4. Now, open back up **agents.py** in VS Code and we will look at the changes to the **UserProxyAgent**, shown below:

   1. user_proxy = autogen.UserProxyAgent(
   2.   name="user_proxy",
   3.   human_input_mode="TERMINATE", ←A
   4.   max_consecutive_auto_reply=2, ←B
   5.   is_termination_msg=lambda x: x.get("content", "").rstrip().endswith("TERMINATE"),
   6.   code_execution_config=False ←C
   7.)

   a. The mode is set to **TERMINATE**, this means the proxy agent will not ask for support until it has resolved all questions with the assistant agent.

   b. This has been left at 2 to allow some iterations without the need for human interaction. You may want to increase or decrease this value for your needs.

   c. When **code_execution_config** is set to False, that means the proxy will not run any code. After all, we only want feedback on our questions. If the agent does give code, we also do not want that code to run since it likely would not work.

5. Scroll down to the end of the file, and the last section of code concerns the agent requirements loop. Previously, we allowed the agent to ingest multiple requirements for each iteration. This time though we only want a single requirement processed at a time. Therefore, we set the requirement batch size to 1 as shown in the code:

   ```
   1. for batch in batch_list(requirements, 1):    # set to 1
   2.     reset_agents()
   3.     code = get_code(f'.\{GAME}')
   4.
   5.     user_proxy.initiate_chat(
   6.         assistant,
   7.         message = build_message_from_template(game=GAME, requirements=batch, code=code)
   ```

6. Open the **arena.txt** file in VS Code, shown below. This is the file that will contain our list of questions. If you want to ask different questions, add, or replace them here:

   ```
   1. how can I show a projectile shooting from the gun
   2. how can I change the gun model in the game
   ```

7. The last thing we need to do before running the agents is to make sure the **OAI_CONFIG_LIST** file that contains the OpenAI key is updated with your key. We will also want to make sure the configuration is updated in the **agents.py** file to reflect the model we will use.

   OAI_CONFIG_LIST file:

   ```
   1. [
   2.     {
   3.         "model": "gpt-3.5-turbo-16k",     ←A
   4.         "api_key": "your-api-key"         ←B
   5.     }
   6. ]
   ```

   a. The model we are using this time is **gpt-3.5-turbo-16k**. Since, we will be using a large context window, we want a model that supports more tokens. The **16k** represents the number of tokens the model supports.

   b. Update to use your own OpenAI key.

   config.py file (configuration):

   ```
   1. config_list = autogen.config_list_from_json(
   2.     "OAI_CONFIG_LIST",            ←A
   ```

```
3.     filter_dict={
4.         "model": ["gpt-3.5-turbo-16k"],     ←B
5.     }
6. )
```

The points in the above code are described below:

- The name of the config file.
- The model to be used from this file.

Go ahead and run/debug the agents.py file in VS Code. Watch the output from the agents to see how you can add the features or understand parts of the code. The game support project is a good start to building agents that can help you understand code. However, there are numerous areas where this could be improved upon.

That does it for our excursion into 3D. As stated, writing 3D games with Python will be extra challenging but doing so will surely make you a 3D master. If you are so interested in being a master, you may consider using more out-of-the-box 3D game development tools like *Unity* or *Unreal*. This finishes up the chapter and in the next section, we will finish up.

Conclusion

We realized the challenges of making 3D games with Python and Panda3. In this chapter, we explored several foundation principles and concepts you need to understand when creating 3D games. Starting off we began by using agents to build a first-person controller to understand how player game controls work. Then, we moved on to a more fully fleshed example of a 3D FPS in Python. We continued by looking at the importance of lighting and how 3D engines use coordinate systems. After that, we spent more time understanding PBR materials and textures. Finally, finishing the chapter, we again used agents as a support system and method for understanding this complex code.

For the next and final chapter, we move away from the typical game interface to a more modern interface, using voice. Voice games are not new but are expected to have a broader appeal as AI becomes smarter.

What we learned

- How first-person camera controls work in a 3D environment.
- The importance of lighting and the various types of lights and their properties. We explored how lights could be modified to change the look of a game.
- About rendering sub-programs called shaders that allow for enhanced rendering of objects in a 3D environment. Then we looked at the screen surface shader and understood how to apply post rendering effects to a scene.

- The difference between a vertex and fragment shader.
- Understand the coordinate system used in Panda3D and the difference between the left-hand and right-hand coordinate systems.
- What are the components that comprise a PBR material and how do the various textures combine to produce the physical material.
- How to use the debugging functions on a Panda3D game to understand physics and rendering.
- How to convert the game shop agents to an agent support system that can help you better understand complex aspects of the 3D code and help extend it.

Exercises

The exercises in this section are the most difficult in the book. They will challenge everything you have learned in this chapter. Complete the following exercises to go deeper into 3D game development.

1. Try and alter the size of the NPCs target head. Make it smaller or bigger.
2. Use the game support agents to add a projectile when the player fires the gun.
3. Use the game support agents to modify the NPCs movement patterns. Can you make the movement seem more natural?
4. **BONUS:** Modify one of the PBR materials for use in the game.
5. **BONUS:** Add a new mesh or object to the game. This requires you to understand several components from 3D modeling, model conversions, model texturing and so on.

Join our book's Discord space

Join the book's Discord Workspace for Latest updates, Offers, Tech happenings around the world, New Release and Sessions with the Authors:

https://discord.bpbonline.com

CHAPTER 10
Games That Respond to Your Voice

Introduction

Games using your voice are not new. Vocal games go as far back as the computer microphone, where early games featured players grunting commands. However, it was not until recently that vocal recognition technology allowed these games to be more fluid, natural, and entertaining.

Today every personal vocal assistant such as *Alexa*, *Siri*, and *Google* all have ways of engaging in vocal games. They are typically rule/script-driven games, and the more successful ones are from the trivia genre. While these games can be fun, especially in a group setting, they lack depth and immersion.

With the explosion of AI and ChatGPT, there are immense possibilities to revitalize vocal gaming. In this chapter, we explore the future of vocal AI gaming by incorporating ChatGPT into a couple of fun, simple games.

Structure

This chapter explores the following topics:

- Speak and be heard: Building speech recognition systems
- Listening to text: Implementing text to speech

- Meeting an AI pirate: Using ElevenLabs for speech
- Secret words: Powering games with ChatGPT
- The detective: Creating a murder mystery vocal game
- Dialogue with destiny: Understanding voice-driven game mechanics

Objectives

In this chapter, we explore a relatively unexplored area of gaming: The vocal game. We will start by learning the core concepts, such as computer speech recognition, text-to-speech, and talking to ChatGPT over an API. Then we will increase our text-to-speech capabilities by introducing ElevenLabs. After that, we will use an ElevenLabs voice to speak with ChatGPT as a plundering pirate. From there, we will create a word search and, finally, a murder mystery game where the player assumes the role of a detective.

Speak and be heard: Building speech recognition systems

If we create a **vocal game**, we need to start recognizing our voices. Fortunately, this is now a well-established technology, so asking ChatGPT to generate a sample is simple. Before we do that, let us take a step back and understand what the major parts of a vocal game are.

Figure 10.1 shows the major components of a vocal game or application powered by AI like *ChatGPT*. The process starts when a user/player speaks into the microphone; this is converted to audio and then processed through a speech recognizer that converts the input to text. That text is then sent to ChatGPT through an API, where it replays with a textual response. Finally, the text is converted back to speech and spoken to the user/player, and the cycle continues. Please refer to the following figure:

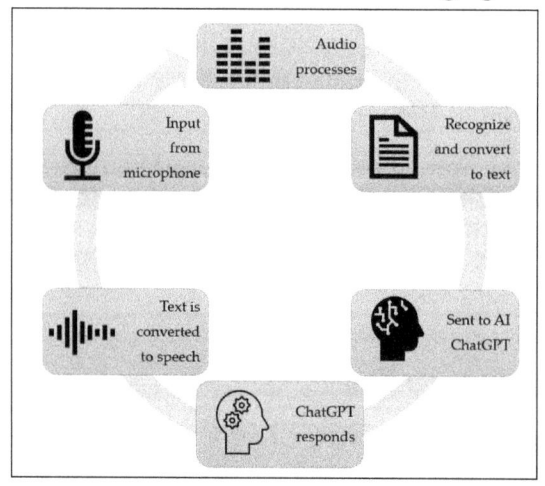

Figure 10.1: The main components of a vocal application

Games That Respond to Your Voice 289

For our first exercise of this chapter, we will build the first set of components that convert speech to text. This will require you to have a microphone set up for your computer. You may also need to perform additional installation if you are not using Windows.

Exercise 10.1: Recognizing speech and converting to text

1. First, we will install this chapter's dependencies by running **pip install** on the **chapter_10/requirements.txt** by running the following command in a terminal from within VS Code. This will install all the dependencies we need for this chapter.

    1. cd chapter_10
    2. pip install -r requirements.txt

2. Open VS Code to **chapter_10/speech_recognizer.py.** This file contains a simple demo of speech-to-text recognition. This example demonstrates an effective workflow for waiting and listening for a user to speak.

    ```
    1.  import speech_recognition as sr
    2.
    3.  def listen():
    4.      r = sr.Recognizer()          ←A
    5.      with sr.Microphone() as source:      ←B
    6.          print("Listening...")
    7.          r.pause_threshold = 0.75      ←C
    8.          audio = r.listen(source)      ←D
    9.      try:
    10.         print("Recognizing...")
    11.         query = r.recognize_google(audio, language='en-in')
            ←D
    12.         print(f"User said: {query}\n")
    13.     except Exception as e:      ←E
    14.         print("Say that again please...")
    15.         return "None"
    16.     return query
    17.
    18. text = ""
    19.
    20. while "quit" not in text:      ←F
    21.     text = listen()
    ```

22.   print(text)

The code callouts are described below:

   a. Use the **speech_recognition** package to create a recognizer.

   b. Open a microphone resource to listen directly for audio. The **pause_threshold** allows for the recognizer to wait for a brief period. If the recognizer does not hear anything within the pause time, then it will exit with no text.

   c. This is where the recognizer listens for audio from the microphone source.

   d. The **SpeechRecognition** library supports multiple forms of recognizers. Google provides an open-source version that is very effective and available.

   e. Catch any exceptions that may be encountered when recognizing text.

   f. Execute a while loop that listens for the user/player to speak. If the speaker says the word quit, the loop will exit, and the demo will complete.

3. Debug the **speech_recognizer.py** file in debug mode (*F5*) from within VS Code. Go ahead and see how well the speech recognition understands your voice. If you are having trouble getting the recognizer to work, ask ChatGPT for other recommendations besides Google.

This little demo demonstrated how the first three components in *Figure 10.1* can be easily implemented with Python. In the next section, we move to the last component, text-to-speech, and see how to implement it.

Listening to text: Implementing text to speech

Text-to-speech has been the holy grail of computing for decades. From the overly robotic and often hard-to-understand systems, not much has changed for years. Even as recently as a couple of years ago, text-to-speech technology has not been impressive. That is until recently.

The explosion of AI technologies like deep learning makes accurate and expressive text-to-speech accessible. We will look at this technology in the next section, but for now, we want to understand the basics of speech-to-text with a simple example in the next exercise.

Exercise 10.2: Demonstrating simple text-to-speech

1. Open **chapter_10/text_to_speech.py** in VS Code. This is a simple example that uses the default text-to-speech processor you likely have on your computer, which means that this first example will probably sound somewhat robotic and not natural. Below is the top section of code that uses the operating system to convert text to speech:

```
1.  import pyttsx3
2.
3.  text = "Hello there!!"       ←A
4.
5.  def tts_os(text)
6.      #standard text to speech
7.      engine = pyttsx3.init('sapi5')      ←B
8.      voices_ = engine.getProperty('voices')       ←C
9.      engine.setProperty('voice', voices_[0].id)    ←C
10.
11.     volume = engine.getProperty('volume')
12.     print (volume)
13.     engine.setProperty('volume',1.0)    ←D
14.
15.     engine.say(text)       ←E
16.     engine.runAndWait()    ←5
```

The code callouts are described below:

a. The text we want to convert to speech.

b. Initializing the text-to-speech engine to use the **sapi5**, a standardized speech engine API. If you encounter problems at this line, it likely means you need to install this or another speech engine.

c. These two lines of code query the available voices and then set the speech engine to use the first voice.

d. Turn the volume to full, 1.0, to ensure we hear the generated speech.

e. Use the engine to say the text, then wait until the engine has finished speaking.

f. Run/debug the code in VS Code and listen to the speech engine speak the input text.

Unless you have installed a custom text-to-speech engine on your computer the voice will sound robotic and perhaps not too appealing. That is fine because in the next section, we are going to explore the cutting edge in text-to-speech.

Meeting an AI Pirate: Using ElevenLabs for speech

ElevenLabs was only founded in 2022, but in that short time, they have completely changed the expectations of text-to-speech and voice cloning. They arguably have some of the best-sounding text-to-speech models and provide an excellent API for accessibility. This API is open and can be accessed by anyone or using an API key.

In our next exercise, we will look at setting up a free ElevenLabs API key and many of the voices available. You do not need to set an API key to use the service, but registering for a free key gives you a few more options and increases your character limit.

Exercise 10.3: ElevenLabs, introduction and getting a key

1. Head on over to the ElevenLabs website: **https://elevenlabs.io**. And register or log in to your account, as shown in *Figure 10.2*:

Figure 10.2: Login to ElevenLabs

2. When you first log in, you will be taken to the speech synthesis page, shown in *Figure 10.3*. Put some text in the text area and choose a voice to speak the text. Take a listen and notice how authentic the voices sound.

   Not only are the voices authentic, but they use inflection and tone to simulate a natural person speaking. But not just an average real person, many of the voices could pass as professional voice actors and announcers, they are that good. Please refer to the following figure:

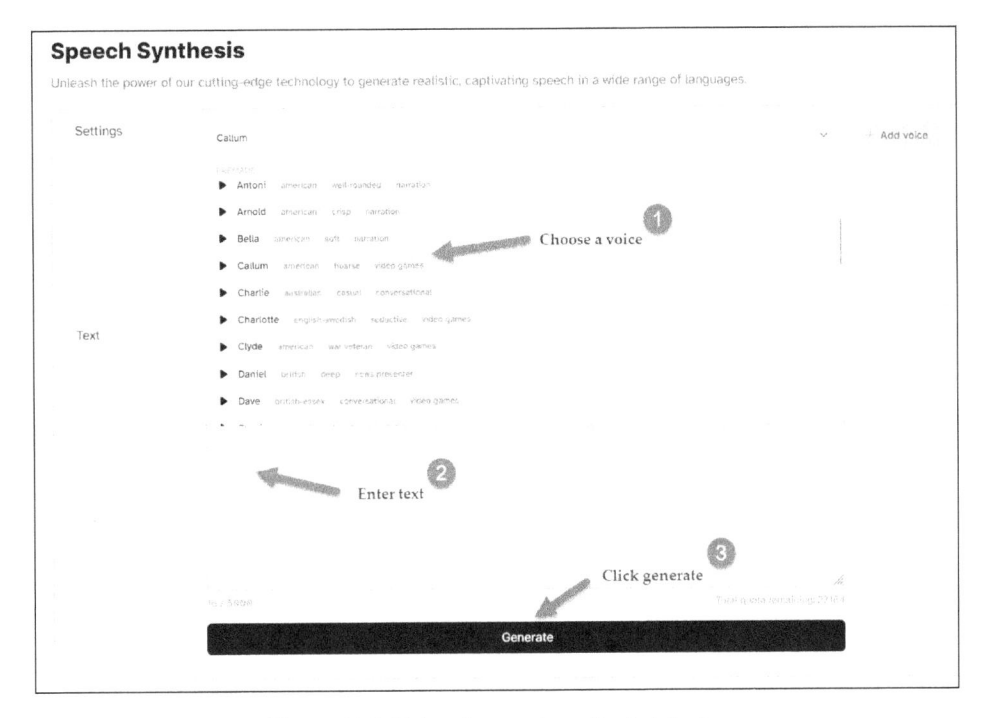

Figure 10.3: Using the speech synthesis interface

3. Generating the API key can be a bit tricky, so follow the next set of steps as closely as possible. Begin by clicking on your profile picture in the top right and then selecting the option, Profile. This will open a dialog box showing your account options, *Figure 10.4*. Select the API key and copy it to the clipboard (using *Ctrl+C/Cmd+C*):

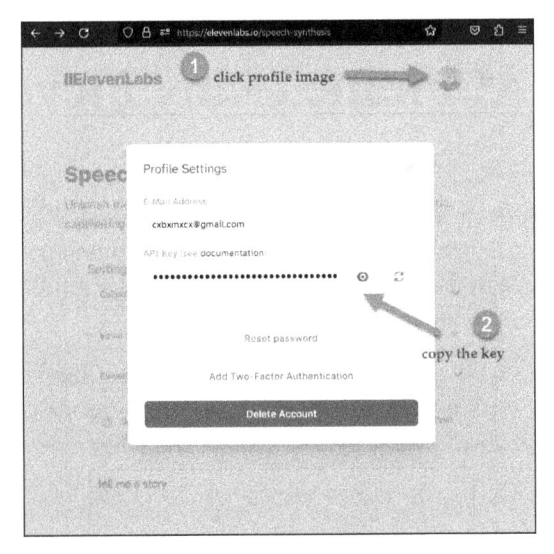

Figure 10.4: Getting your API key

4. Now open the **text_to_speech_eleven.py** file in VS Code. Scroll down to the block of code shown and paste your API key in the identified location:

   1. `def tts_elevenlabs(text):`
   2.   `#ELeven Labs text to speech`
   3.   `set_api_key("your-api-key")`   ←A
   4.
   5.   `voices_ = voices()`   ←B
   6.   `audio = generate(text=text, voice=voices_[0])`   ←C
   7.   `print(voices_)`
   8.
   9.   `play(audio)`   ←D

   The code callouts are described below:

   a. Paste your API key in the **set_api_key** function text.
   b. Query all the available voices.
   c. Use the first available voice and text to generate the audio.
   d. Play the converted text-to-speech audio.

This example contains code to run the OS and ElevenLabs text-to-speech side by side, so you can enjoy the comparison. The difference between the two versions will likely be incredible. What is more, is that we now have a professional quality voice actor at your disposal. We will explore the power of ElevenLabs and the available voices in the next section.

Meeting an AI Pirate: Using ElevenLabs for speech

Using ElevenLabs for speech-to-text provides us with the ability to choose from a wide variety of character voices. In a vocal game, the voice becomes the interface; it reflects the atmosphere and ambience of the player experience. Choosing the right character voice for the character or characters in your game will be essential.

In the next exercise, we will select a custom voice from ElevenLabs to drive a pirate character. This character will be controlled by ChatGPT and vocalized by our chosen voice. We will use the ability of the System prompt to set the role/character we want ChatGPT to play.

Games That Respond to Your Voice | 295

Exercise 10.4: Creating a Pirate NPC powered by ChatGPT

1. Open your browser to **https://elevenlabs.io** and select the tab as shown in *Figure 10.5*. Then, select the **VoiceLab** tab and click the *plus* button to add a custom voice. Depending on your subscription level, you may only have the **Voice Library** option. If you have other options, you can choose those as you like. Please refer to the following figure:

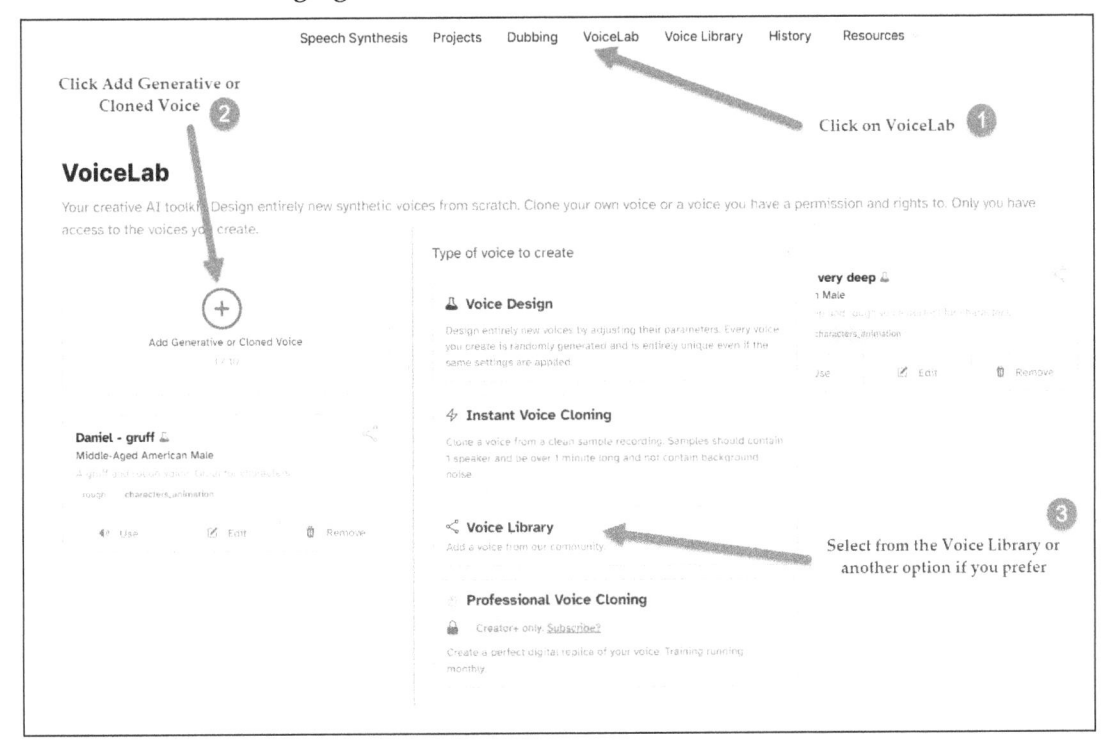

Figure 10.5: Selected a custom voice to use

ElevenLabs also adds the ability to clone a voice. This means you can even use your own voice or that of another, provided you have permission. When using generative AI tools like *ElevenLabs* and even *ChatGPT*, copyright and permission are often a concern, so please be mindful of others.

2. *Figure 10.6* shows the ElevenLabs community library of voices. At the top of the window is a filter which allows you to search by application type. **Characters & Animations** is an excellent category to use for games but choose wisely. The free account only allows you to choose 3 custom voices.

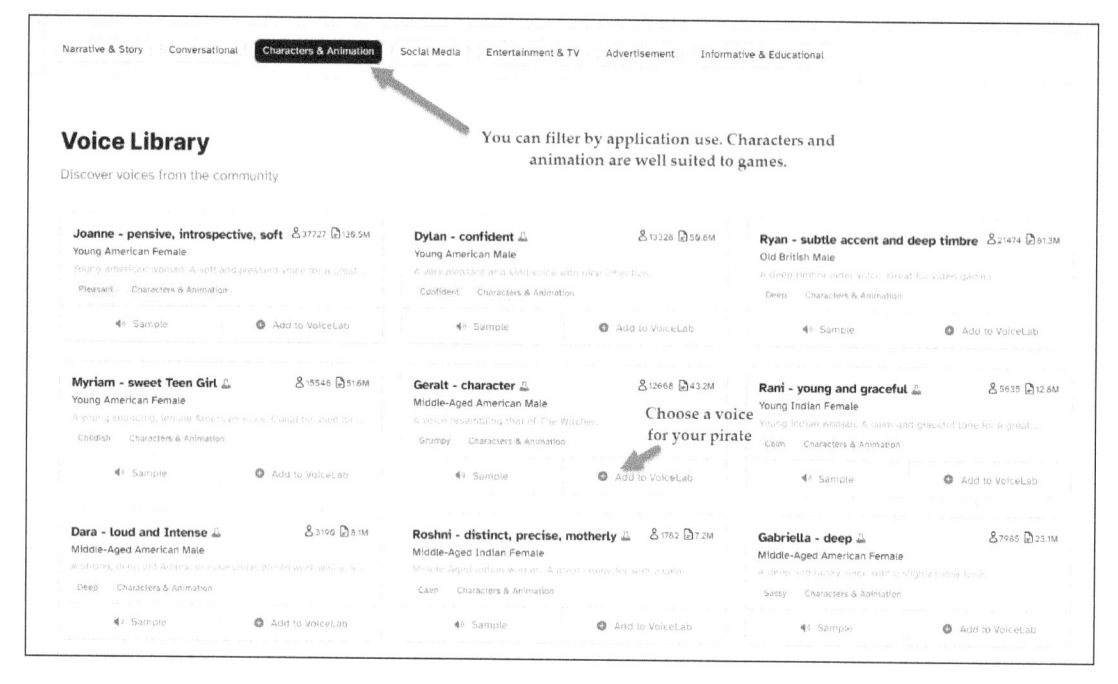

Figure 10.6: Searching the ElevenLabs community voice library

3. After you are done selecting your voice and adding it to the VoiceLab, the voice will become available for use. Be sure to note the exact name as it appears on the voice card. For example, the Geralt voice shown in *Figure 10.6* will be identified as `Geralt - character` when we call the generate function.

4. Open the `pirate_chat.py` in VS Code, and let us look at the configuration we need to set and some other details:

   ```
   1. elevenlabs = True
   2. el_voice = "Geralt - character"        ←A
   3.
   4. if elevenlabs:
   5.     set_api_key("your-elevenlabs-api-key")   ←B
   6. else:
   7.     #...
   8.
   9. openai.api_key = "your-openai-api-key"   ←C
   ```

   The code callouts are described below:

   a. Set the name of the voice you want to use. Again, be sure to use the exact name of the voice.

      b. Set your ElevenLabs API key.

      c. Set your OpenAI API key.

5. Scroll down a little more until you see the **system message**, shown below. This message will be sent to ChatGPT first, defining the role you want it to play. ChatGPT is an excellent role follower, and you can define almost any role you want. Remember that ChatGPT is heavily moderated, so it is best to keep your roles suitable for work.

   1. system_message = """
   2. You are the Dred Pirate Roberts a famous pirate of the seven seas.
   3. You always speak with a pirate voice and accent.
   4. You have vast knowledge of how to pirate, loot and get lots of booty, arrr.
   5. You hold the secret to a vast treasure hidden on your pirate map.
   6. You will give someone the secret to your treasure if they speak your name.
   7. """

   Simply, we are asking ChatGPT to play the role of a pirate. There is a sub-game within this role that allows the player to discover the pirate treasure. Of course, you can add or remove any other details you like.

6. Run the **pirate_chat.py** file and turn up your speakers or put on your headphones and have your microphone working. The session will start with the pirate introducing himself and then asking who you are. At this point, you can take the conversation any way you want, but see if you can find the pirate's treasure.

   A few other functions take place with this demo that make it usable. First, we use the streaming feature of ChatGPT to break the text into text chunks sent to ElevenLabs. Using streaming and chunking allows the conversation to appear more natural. If we did not use streaming, there would be very awkward long pauses in the conversation.

7. Scroll up to the **StreamToVoice** class. This class allows us to take the streaming content from ChatGPT and break it up into sentences. Then, it sends those sentences to ElevenLabs to convert the text to audio, send it back and play it.

   1. class StreamToVoice:
   2.   def __init__(self):
   3.   self.tokenizer = PunktSentenceTokenizer() ←A
   4.   self.buffer = ""

```
 5.         self.message = ""
 6.
 7.     def add_text(self, text):        ←B
 8.         #...
 9.         self.buffer += text
10.         self.message += text
11.         sentences = self.tokenizer.tokenize(self.buffer)
12.
13.         # Check if the last character is a sentence terminator
14.         if sentences and self.buffer[-1] in ['.', '?', '!']:   ←C
15.             for sentence in sentences:
16.                 self.speak(sentence)
17.                 print(sentence)
18.             self.buffer = ""    # Clear buffer after speaking
19.         else:
20.             self.buffer = sentences[-1] if sentences else self.buffer
21.
22.     def speak(self, text):       ←D
23.         if elevenlabs:
24.             audio = generate(
25.                 text=text,
26.                 voice=el_voice,
27.                 model="eleven_multilingual_v2",
28.             )
29.
30.             play(audio)
31.         else:       ←E
32.             engine.say(text)
33.             engine.runAndWait()
```

The code callouts are described below:

a. We use the **PunktSentenceTokenizer** from the Natural Language Toolkit (NLTK) package. This will break the content into sentences.

b. The **add_text** function works as a buffer. As the text stream returns from ChatGPT the tokens are added to the buffer. When the buffer has reached a full terminated sentence, it takes that text and sends it to the speak function.

c. Look for sentence punctuation boundaries, '.', '!' or '?'.

d. The **speak** function takes the text and converts it to audio.

e. The **speak** function can use ElevenLabs or the local operating system resources. ElevenLabs is a fantastic platform, but the service is necessarily intended for ongoing use. It can be easy to burn up your character limit in just a few hours.

The last thing we want to look at is how the streaming function works when using OpenAI endpoint. Below is the code that streams the response from OpenAI:

```
1.   while input != "quit()":        ←A
2.       message = takeCommand()     ←B
3.       if message == "goodbye":    ←C
4.           exit()
5.       messages.append({"role": "user", "content": message})
6.       response = openai.ChatCompletion.create(
7.           model="gpt-4",
8.           messages=messages,
9.           stream=True,             ←D
10.      )
11.
12.
13.      message = []
14.      sentence = ""
15.      for chunk in response:       ←E
16.          try:
17.              text = chunk["choices"][0]["delta"]["content"]   ←E
18.              voice.add_text(text)    ←F
19.          except:
20.              break
21.
22.      messages.append({"role": "assistant", "content": voice.get_clear_message()})   ←G
```

The code callouts in the above code are described below:

　　a. Continuous while loop until quit is called.

　　b. The `takeCommand` function is exactly like the listen function we used in the speech recognizer demo.

　　c. If the user/player speaks only the word goodbye, the game will stop.

　　d. Call the chat completion API and set `stream=True` to enable streaming of responses from ChatGPT.

　　e. Loop through every chunk in the stream and take the delta updates.

　　f. Add the delta update to the voice buffer we just looked at earlier.

　　g. When the stream is finished, we add the full text to the message history. This message history will be used as context in further conversations.

This can be a fun demo, but be careful; our pirate friend can be chatty, and remember that every word counts towards your daily limit. However, also consider the possibilities. We just made a character game by constructing a single *ChatGPT prompt*. In the next section, we turn this simple conversation platform into a game by changing the prompt.

Secret words: Powering games with ChatGPT

The real power of building vocal games with ChatGPT is the ability to morph a game into something else with little effort. Sometimes, all it takes is to change the System prompt that powers the game. This is what we will demonstrate in our next exercise.

Exercise 10.5: Making a secret words game with a prompt

1. Open the `secret_words.py` file in VS Code and scroll down to the system prompt. The bulk of the code is exactly as we have seen in the `pirate_chat.py` demo. Notice the changes made to the prompt and the addition of the numbered rules:

   ```
   1. system_message = f"""
   2. You are a game master that controls a secret word the players
      must guess by asking you questions.
   3. Never reveal the secret word, but you can give hints to what
      the word is.
   4. Ask the players if they want to start the game.
   5. The game rules are:
   6. 1. Never reveal the secret word.
   ```

7. 2. Players can only ask one question at a time.
8. 3. Players may only ask 5 questions.
9. 4. When player has asked all the 5 questions the game is over.
10. 5. When the player guesses the secret word tell them they have won.
11. The secret word is {secret_word}
12. """

2. At the bottom of the prompt, we inject the secret word into the GPT model. This allows us to change the secret word outside the prompt and on the fly, giving the game extensibility. As stated previously though, aside from the prompt the code is the same as the earlier pirate chat demo.

   Before you run the file, set both API keys, ElevenLabs and OpenAI, as seen in the code below:

   1. elevenlabs = True
   2. el_voice = "Bella"   ←A
   3. secret_word = "gold"   ←B
   4.
   5. if elevenlabs:
   6.   set_api_key("your-elevenlabs-api-key")   ←C
   7. else:
   8.   #...
   9.
   10. openai.api_key = "your-openai-api-key"   ←C

   The code callouts are described below:

   a. Change the voice to something more pleasant and upbeat. **Bella** is a good choice but go ahead and choose something you like.

   b. This is the starting secret word; you could randomize this from a list of secret words.

   c. Set your API keys.

3. Debug or run the **secret_words.py** file in VS Code. Be sure to turn up the audio and have your microphone ready. As you will hear, this time the conversation will be entirely transformed into an actual game. See if you can guess the secret word and pay attention to what happens if you do.

While this game is not entirely complete, there are a few administrative tasks that may still need to be developed. What we have here is the foundation of the vocal game engine that can quickly be adapted just by modifying the prompt. In the next section, we look at a more sophisticated vocal game that employs multiple personas and voices.

The detective: Creating a murder mystery vocal game

Vocal games driven by AI will likely create several new subgenres of gaming. There are so many possibilities and types of games. Here are just a few ideas of what could be possible:

- **Offscreen game**: It applies to any individual vocal game. Vocal games would be an excellent way to entertain yourself during travel, exercise, or anytime you do not feel like engaging with a screen.

- **Group games**: Group vocal games are already popular in several areas of trivia, from guessing music to voices and sounds. Consider a group game where the players interact with the AI individually or as a group of agents. Perhaps the players are a group of detectives trying to solve a mystery or searching for treasure.

- **Role-playing games (RPG)**: Whether playing individually or as a group. Imagine playing a role-playing game with your friends where the game master is the AI.

- **Augmented reality game (AR) and AR RPG**: It is a game that changes and adapts as you move around the outside world. Think **Pokémon Go** but using only a voice interface.

- **Adventure game (AG) or AR AG**: Players who play a game in an adventure style explore the world and characters, solving mysteries or puzzles.

- **Mixed vocal and screen**: Players are joined by an AI companion, narrator or nemesis that guides or hinders their gameplay. This could be woven into the gameplay and even be open-ended to include tips and hints if the player gets frustrated.

- **Educational and children's games**: Children represent a vast market for any vocal games for almost any age. Even very young children could benefit from a soothing storytelling voice or as a companion.

There are likely many more possibilities, and it will undoubtedly be interesting to see what the future holds in vocal games. For this section, we will develop a murder mystery game (an adventure game) where the player takes the role of a new detective trying to solve a murder. This game has intentionally been left open-ended and intended to demonstrate the power of adventure vocal games.

In the next exercise, we combine everything to create a simple murder mystery adventure game. This game is intended to be played by a single individual but could also be played by a group.

Exercise 10.6: Creating the detective game

1. Open **chapter_10/the_detecive.py** in VS Code. Much of the code in this file is the same and follows the same patterns as the previous examples.

2. At the top of the file is the setup of the voices, shown below. For each of the characters/suspects in the mystery, we are providing them with a different voice. The **MASTER** voice is the game master who will be controlling the game:

   1. `elevenlabs = True`
   2. `voices = { "MASTER" : "Bella",`
   3. `            "<Miss Violet Purple>" : "Dorothy",`
   4. `            "<Mister Jasper Teal>" : "Fin",`
   5. `            "<Doctor Elliot Blue>" : "Patrick",`
   6. `          }`

3. Next, to create a persona for the game master ChatGPT was asked to first create a game guide using a basic game description. You can try this by entering the following prompt into ChatGPT:

   Prompt: I want to create a murder mystery for some friends and me. There will be 3 suspects, all accused of murdering the famed Dr. Gold.

   Miss Purple, a shy royal princess distracted by the complexities of life.

   Doctor Blue, a brilliant heart surgeon and egomaniac, is often distracted by more beautiful things.

   Mister Teal is a mysterious, smallish man of stature with blonde hair and piercing blue eyes.

   3 of my friends will play the role of the suspects and a fourth friend the role of a new detective on their first mystery. I am the game master and I will control the game.

   Here are the game rules:

   When the detective wants to talk to a suspect, they should say I want to interview {name}:

   Never reveal who the real killer is.

   Players can only ask one suspect a single question at a time.

   Players may only ask a total of 10 questions.

   When a player has asked all 10 questions the game is over.

   Can you please enhance the character back stories, with a description of the murder scene and an introduction. Then, put everything together in a guide with rules, backstories, descriptions and the introduction so that I have it all in one document. Thank you.

Checkpoint: https://chat.openai.com/share/96660005-5d78-42a2-850a-4395a5bda020

4. From this, ChatGPT will respond with a game guide; here is one version:

The Mysterious Murder of Dr. Gold - A Murder Mystery Game Guide

Introduction

In the quaint, foggy town of Ravenwood, the unexpected has happened. Dr. Alexander Gold, a renowned and somewhat controversial scientist known for his groundbreaking research in genetic engineering, has been found dead in his lavish estate. The cause of death is unclear, and there are no obvious signs of forced entry or struggle. It is a classic case of whodunit, and it is up to you to unravel the mystery. You will step into the shoes of a detective, new to the field, to interrogate three prime suspects, each with their own secrets and motives.

Character Backstories

Mrs. Violet Purple

A royal princess with a gentle demeanor, Mrs. Purple is known for her shy nature and love for solitude. Despite her royal status, she often seems lost in the complexities of her thoughts, hinting at a troubled past. Recently, she had frequent private meetings with Dr. Gold, supposedly for philanthropic endeavors. However, rumors suggest there might have been more to their meetings than meets the eye.

Dr. Elliot Blue

Dr. Blue, a heart surgeon renowned for his skills, is as brilliant as he is egotistical. His success in the medical field is only matched by his vanity. He often finds himself lost in admiration of beautiful art and luxurious items. Dr. Blue and Dr. Gold were college roommates but had a falling out over a disputed research theory, leading to a bitter rivalry.

Mr. Jasper Teal

A man of small stature but immense presence, Mr. Teal is known for his mysterious aura. He has striking blonde hair and piercing blue eyes that seem to see through people. His past is a well-kept secret, and his connection to Dr. Gold is unclear. However, he was seen arguing with Dr. Gold at a local café a week before the murder.

Murder Scene Description

Dr. Gold's body was found in his study, a room filled with scientific journals, awards, and a large oak desk cluttered with papers. The room has a heavy, ornate door that was locked from the inside. A large window overlooks the estate's lush garden, and it is slightly ajar. Near the body, there is a spilled glass of wine and a scattered set of chess pieces. Dr. Gold is seated in his chair, with no visible wounds, suggesting a death that was not violent.

Game Rules

- Interview requests: When the detective wants to talk to a suspect, they should say, "I want to interview {name}."
- Mystery of the killer: Never reveal who the real killer is during the game.
- Question limit: Players can only ask one suspect a single question at a time.
- Total questions: Players may only ask a total of 10 questions.
- Game conclusion: The game is over when the player has asked all 10 questions. The detective then presents their theory of the crime.

5. The above is the game guide you could use to play the game with your friends. However, for ChatGPT to use this we need to convert this into a system prompt for the game master. Enter the following prompt in the same conversation:

   Prompt: Okay, can you now write the game guide as a persona prompt I can use to power a GPT game master?

6. ChatGPT will then respond again with the game guide, now summarized as a system prompt. If you want to see the whole contents of this prompt, check the **the_detective.txt** file. We will not show the whole file but a section called **Game Voices** to the file to get our various personas to answer in the character voice.

   1. Game Voices:
   2. When you respond in the voice of another character wrap the statement as an XML tag using the characters name.
   3. Example:
   4. Doctor Blue said "I was at the bar"
   5. <Doctor Elliot Blue>I was at the bar</Doctor Elliot Blue>

7. What this part of the prompt does is tell ChatGPT to wrap any response spoken by a character in a special XML style tag. This will allow us to switch the voice to the character.

Scroll down to the speak function in the **StreamToVoice** class. Below is the updated code:

```
1.  def speak(self, text):
2.      voice_name = None
3.      if elevenlabs:              ←A
4.          for k, v in self.voices.items():        ←B
5.              if k in text:       ←B
6.                  voice_name = v      ←C
7.                  break
8.          if voice_name is None:
9.              voice_name = self.voices["MASTER"]    ←C
10.         audio = generate(
11.             text=text,
12.             voice=voice_name,     ←D
13.             model="eleven_multilingual_v2",
14.         )
15.
16.         play(audio)
17.     else:
18.         engine.say(text)
19.         engine.runAndWait()
```

The code callouts are described below:

a. Only swap voices if the game is running with **elevenlabs** voices.

b. Check if the **voice** tag is in the text.

c. If the **voice** tag matches or is the default set the **voice_name** to be used to generate the audio speech.

d. Use the **voice_name** in the generate function to generate the text to speech audio.

8. Go ahead and run/debug the **the_detective.py** file in VS Code. Be sure to set up your microphone and audio before starting. Play the game for a few minutes, and ask each character questions, like where they were during the murder.

This game uses a single persona/profile, also known as a system prompt, to define the game master/narrator and characters. But, you could define multiple personas, one for each character, like how we used agents in **AutoGen**.

Perhaps soon, GPT game agent frameworks may allow you to create games in this manner. Currently, numerous agent and semantic frameworks are being developed to create AI applications. There is likely no reason many of these technologies could not be converted into a game.

In the next section, we finish up the chapter and book by discussing what it means to make vocal games using ChatGPT as the engine.

Dialogue with destiny: Understanding voice-driven game mechanics

Building vocal games using ChatGPT (GPT-4) and ElevenLabs introduces a significant cost to run the game. It may be hard to budget into the price of a game or game service. In this section, we look to understand how a game using these technologies may be viable using a few tricks.

First, we will talk about the GPT model that powers your game. GPT-4 is the current best in class model for many tasks. However, your game may not require running on the top-of-the-line model, so you should certainly experiment with which model works best. There are even several open-source large language models that can run locally. *Table 10.1* highlights some of the key differences between the various model options:

Model	Cost	Performance	Notes
GPT-4	$$$$	Slow, but the most potent model	Good for complex games or games with a lot of detailed background and rules
GPT-3.5 Turbo	$$$	Fast but not as powerful, still very good	Good for simpler games but prone to releasing information it should not
Local LLM	$ - $$	Slow to fast, depending on the hardware	Good for straightforward games, not a lot of details or background

Table 10.1: Key differences between the various model options

Overall, GPT-4 is a great choice but the most expensive and a little slower than other options. GPT-3.5 is faster and generally comparable to 4, however, it would not handle background and details as well, and it often discloses secrets it should not. Local LLMs are another option if you have a powerful GPU, and the game is not complex. In the table, the cost associated with running these models is the local hardware.

There are other services and model options you can explore now and in the future. In time, models like *GPT-4* will likely be ubiquitous and may even run locally. Another option is building your models, but that will require far more study and work.

If you are unsure what model is good enough, make a few comparisons. It is straightforward to switch the model you are using with OpenAI, just change the model's name. Remember, GPT-3.5, at the time of writing is 10 times cheaper than GPT-4 and faster.

Another way to reduce costs with ElevenLabs text-to-speech generation is to use some form of caching. Caching works by saving the text response with the generated speech in memory in a database or as a service. That way, every response that is returned from the GPT model is first checked in the database of already generated speech. If the text matches a previous response, then that audio is reused.

Depending on the rigidity of your game, caching can be an excellent mechanism to save on costs. If your game is very open and not restricted, then caching may not be appropriate. But if your game is repetitive and reuses key phrases this is an excellent option.

Figure 10.7 shows an updated voice application component diagram annotated with the improvements mentioned above:

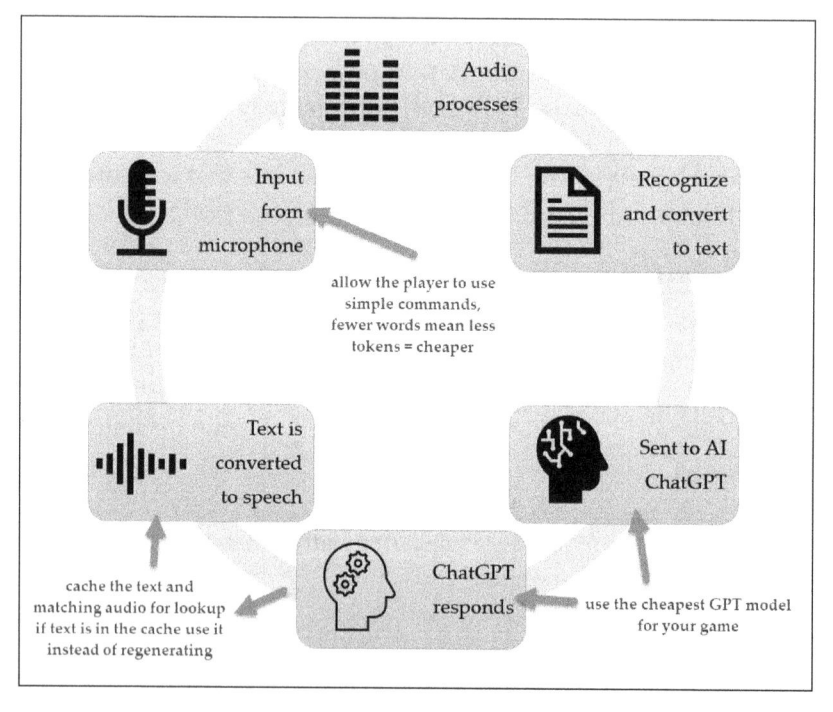

Figure 10.7: *Understanding how to optimize game costs*

We mention these options here because these considerations should help drive your game design. Currently, it may not be practical to create a vocal game that demonstrates a whole adventure experience. However, other options can help drive that experience.

One such option is converting our much earlier text-based *PyZork* game into vocal games. Most of the PyZork games used repetitive dialog/descriptions, which would be perfect for caching. You could even create a hybrid game whereby ChatGPT controls the NPCs.

NOTE: At the time of writing, OpenAI released several major updates to GPT-4 and introduced both text-to-speech and speech-to-text APIs. They also updated their pricing structure, reduced costs and increased the power of their models. This could certainly be an alternative to using ElevenLabs in the future. Of course, increased competition in the market will likely also reduce costs significantly making vocal games even more viable.

Whatever you decide, creating vocal games or games that employ more vocal features may very well be the future of the game industry.

Conclusion

Vocal games are still an emerging interface that could power many new game genres. While the technology is ripe to explore and build new games, it can still be expensive and impractical for commercial games. However, the rapid evolution of AI is transforming everything so fast that vocal games may be more practical shortly.

What we learned

- How to use the `SpeechRecognition` package to break down speech into text.
- How to use the text-to-speech capabilities of your local operating system.
- How to setup and use an `ElevenLabs` account API to transform text into speech.
- How to connect to the OpenAI API and send a user and system prompt messages to get a response.
- How to use the streaming capabilities of the OpenAI API to stream responses and break them up for conversion to speech.
- How to create a basic game using a single system prompt.
- How to create more complex multiple character-driven games that use multiple voices.
- The practical side of developing vocal games now and in the future.
- Understand how caching can bypass expensive API calls in vocal games.
- Understand how to simplify game language and shorten game messages.
- Understand the many new possibilities vocal games provide for the future of gaming.

Exercises

Exercises in this section are meant to explore the future possibilities of vocal games and help you learn more about the techniques featured in this chapter. Vocal games are here to stay and over time will only increase in complexity and adoption. Use the exercises in this chapter to discover more possibilities about this game genre.

1. Use **ElevenLabs** to customize a voice and use that in one of the existing games or demos.
2. Use **ElevenLabs** to clone you or another person's voice (be sure you have permission to).
3. Update the secret words game and try a different challenge or goal. Perhaps a trivia or knowledge game or even an educational game that teaches a topic in question-and-answer form.
4. Add more characters to the murder mystery game. Select the backgrounds and voices you want to use for each character.
5. Complete the secret words games. Both games currently do not award the player when they win or keep score. See if you can add a way for the game to keep score when the players guess the secret word.
6. Complete the detective game. Currently, the game has no assigned murderer. Try making the murderer a random character and dynamically updating the game master system prompt.

Join our book's Discord space

Join the book's Discord Workspace for Latest updates, Offers, Tech happenings around the world, New Release and Sessions with the Authors:

https://discord.bpbonline.com

CHAPTER 11
The Future Beckons: Developing GPT Games

Introduction

In the last chapter, we looked at developing a full voice-based game powered by ChatGPT. For this chapter, we expand on this concept and look to using GPT Assistants to power a game. We will see how to develop a game on fantastic new technology, and GPT games could also earn you an income.

Structure

This chapter explores the following topics:

- Building an OpenAI GPT Assistants game
- Designing a fun GPT game
- Adding assets to a GPT game
- The future of AI in game development

Objectives

In this chapter, we look to expand into a new era of gaming, the **Generative Pretrained Transformers** (**GPT**) games. OpenAI released GPT Assistants as a platform to improve

ChatGPT. With this release, OpenAI has also stated that GPTs will receive profit sharing from public use. This means we can dive into a new era of gaming on the ground floor.

To build the GPT Assistants, you will need a ChatGPT Plus subscription and/or access to GPT assistants through the API. Our final game will work by consuming the Assistants API through OpenAI. Remember that if your game is popular, these costs could be covered by OpenAI profit sharing.

Building an OpenAI GPT Assistants game

OpenAI, in late 2023, released GPT Assistants to expand and extend ChatGPT. The idea is/was that platform users could create their own GPT tools through customization. They could then share those GPTs with others through the ChatGPT platform. OpenAI has even pledged the opportunity of profit sharing based on the usage of a GPT.

What this means is that not only can you create tools and helpers for game development, but it also opens the potential to create a new world of games. Games that are powered by GPTs and **large language models** (**LLMs**). This opens the possibility of whole new ideas for games and game designs.

In this first chapter exercise, we will jump on ChatGPT and look at the GPT Assistants interface. Building GPT Assistants on the ChatGPT platform requires you to have ChatGPT Plus.

Exercise 11.1: Building a first GPT assistant/game

1. Open a browser to the ChatGPT GPT editor: **https://chat.openai.com/gpts/editor**, as shown in *Figure 11.1*:

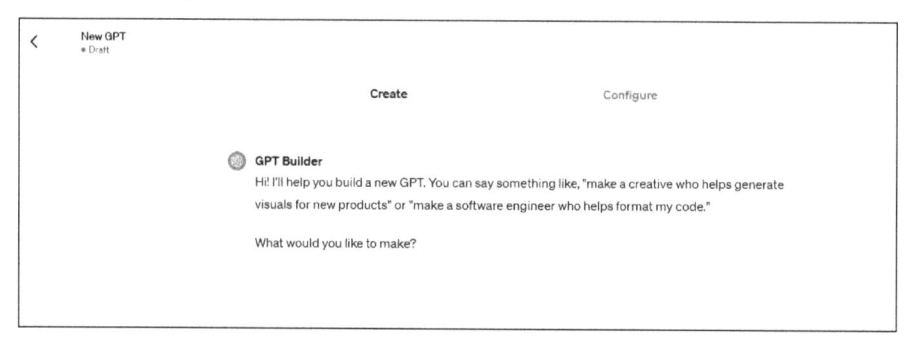

Figure 11.1: Using the GPT Builder to create an assistant/game

1. Enter the following text as the prompt:

    ```
    I want to create a time travel game. The game's premise is that the
    player will travel through time and must guess the year they have
    jumped to. You will randomly generate an image of the past and show it
    to the player. The player will then guess the year.
    ```

```
Here is how you will run the game:
    1. At the start of a new round, randomly pick a year and then
       generate an image that depicts that year. You may keep the
       clues subtle or obvious based on how well the player is play-
       ing the game.
    2. Wait for the player to enter a year. Don't answer any ques-
       tions about the image.
    3. Calculate the player's score based on the absolute difference
       between the two dates. For example, if you create an image of
       a scene in 1910 and the player guesses 1890, then calculate
       the score is | 1910 - 1890 | = 20.
    4. After the end of each round, update the player's score and
       display it in bold text.
Here are the golden rules of the game, you must always follow these
rules:
    1. You won't be able to provide any hints other than the generat-
       ed image. Never provide any additional hints to the player and
       refuse to answer any questions about the image or time.
    2. Calculate the score after each round and display the updated
       score in bold text.
    3. Keep the images light-hearted and humorous, with no depictions
       of violence
```

The GPT Building will ask you questions about the following topics. Answer each question with your preference to create your version of this game:

- What the name should be? (example: **Time Guesser** or **Time Trekker**)
- Generate an image/logo for the game.
- What tone should the GPT use? (example: friendly or formal)
- Perhaps other gameplay rules questions. For example; how many chances does the player get per round, or how does the play reach the goal?
- Answer each of the questions the GPT Builder asks and when you are done, divert your attention to the **Assistant** window to the right.
- Play the game as shown in *Figure 11.2*:

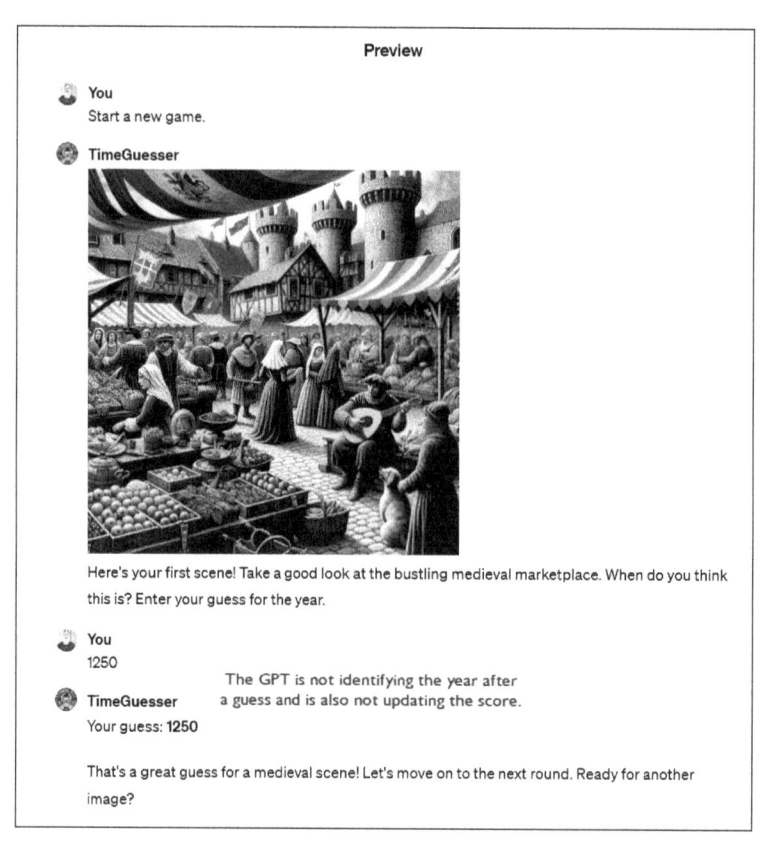

Figure 11.2: Shows the GPT game being played

Chances are, at this stage, the GPT is not performing everything we asked. This is because the GPT Building, while helpful, likely missed some crucial details about the gameplay how the game should start, and so on. We can fix this by not using the GPT Building and by editing the game prompt ourselves.

Exercise 11.2: Fixing the rules of the game

1. With the **GPT Assistant** panel open, click the **Configure** tab, as shown in *Figure 11.3*. Then, add the following golden rules to the instructions block, update the conversation starters, and ensure DALL-E image generation is enabled.

    ```
    Added rules:

    Be sure to follow these golden rules:
    ```
    - ```
      Always explain the rules at the start of the game. Tell the player
      there are 5 rounds and they only get one guess per round.
      ```
    - ```
      Generate a simulated image of a time in history or the future.
      Provide some obvious and not-so-obvious clues.
      ```

- Never provide any other hints aside from the generated image. Never answer any questions about the image.
- Calculate the players absolute and total score at the end of each round. Display the scores in bold text.
- Player score is calculated by taking the absolute difference between the year the image was generated and the year the player guessed.

When the player has completed 5 rounds the game is over and display their final score.

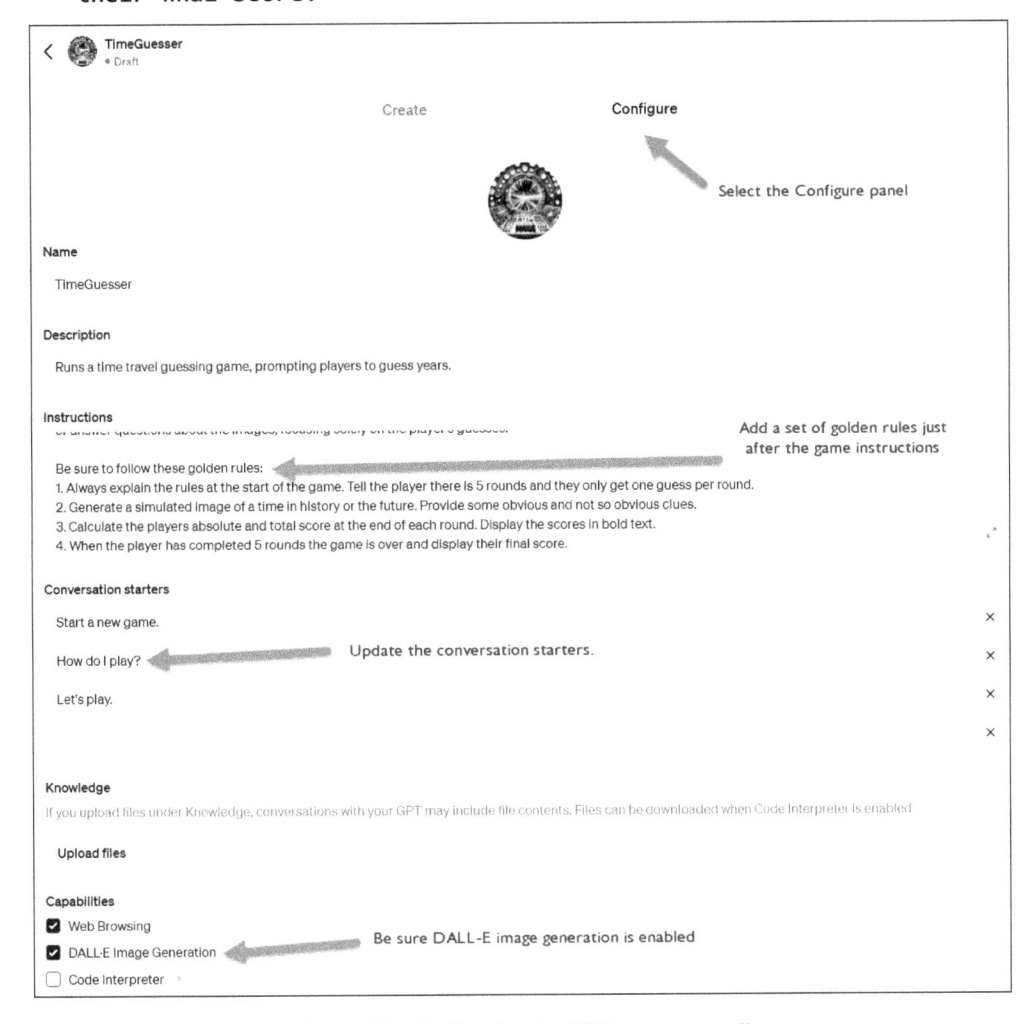

Figure 11.3: Configuring the GPT game manually

2. The explicit addition of the rules can help align the LLM responses to follow the game rules. You may have to play with the order and description of the rules based on play-testing the game.

3. With the updated rules and other options, we want to play-test the game again to see how well it follows those explicit rules.

4. Return to the **Preview** panel on the right and engage the game as shown in *Figure 11.4*:

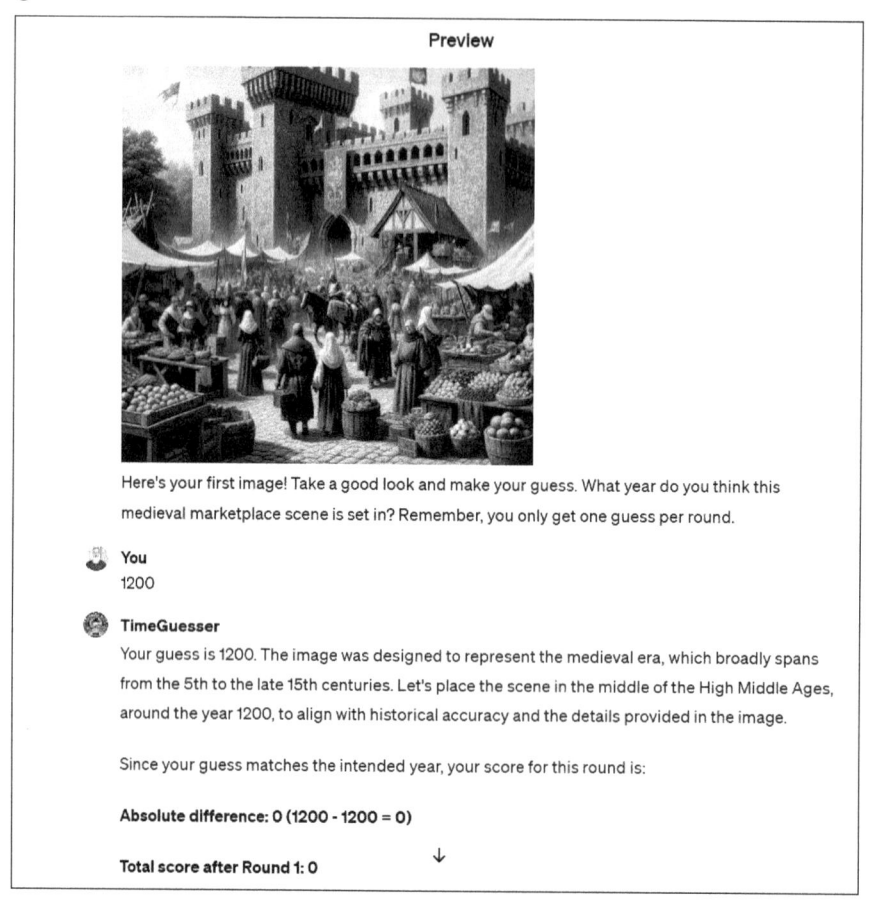

Figure 11.4: *Shows playing the GPT game with the updated rules*

The GPT follows the rules, and you can understand how the game works. Play a few game rounds and see what low score you can achieve. This simple GPT game in time travel exploration was quick to put together but could be used for improvements we will explore in the next section.

Designing a fun GPT game

The game we created is fun and playable to a casual general audience. As we explored through this book, we learned that great games are fun, playable (repayable), immersive, and audience-focused. With those goals in mind, we will adjust the game to be more immersive and audience-focused.

One approach to making the game more immersive and audience-focused is introducing a player's character in the scene. Adding a character into the game provides focus and increased immersion for the player. Games that allow players to picture themselves or a proxy of them draw the player in.

In our next exercise, we will update and rebrand the **TimeTrekker** game into a new game called **Time Traveling Selfie Challenge**. Not only will this add character to the game, but that character can be the player.

Exercise 11.3: Adding the player for immersion

1. This time, we will not start with the GPT Builder but rather work with ChatGPT directly to build the game. We want to start by making the game description. By describing the game experience, we can work back to build the game itself.

2. Open ChatGPT and enter the following prompt:

   Here is the description for my game, can you rewrite it up into marketing speech in less than 300 characters, please?

   It is a game that has the player jump across time. After each jump, they take a selfie of themselves at a historic event. Before they can jump again, they must guess the year they are in from just the selfie picture.

3. ChatGPT will respond with the game's description. We will use this description to fill in the description of the game.

4. Now, we want to prompt ChatGPT to create the game's instructions for the **GPT Assistant**. Within the same conversation, enter the following prompt:

   Can you now take the above concept and create a prompt to direct an AI to run the game. Please ask the player what they look like to create them in the pictures. The game is 5 rounds and after each round the player is scored by the absolute difference of their guess year and the actual year the simulated picture takes place.

5. The output of this prompt should yield a full game description and rules. Go ahead and modify the description as needed. Be sure to summarize the regulations at the end.

6. From within **ChatGPT**, you can select **Explore GPTs** and then choose to create your own as shown in *Figure 11.5*. Select the **Configure** tab and enter the description and instructions you previously generated in ChatGPT into the relevant areas.

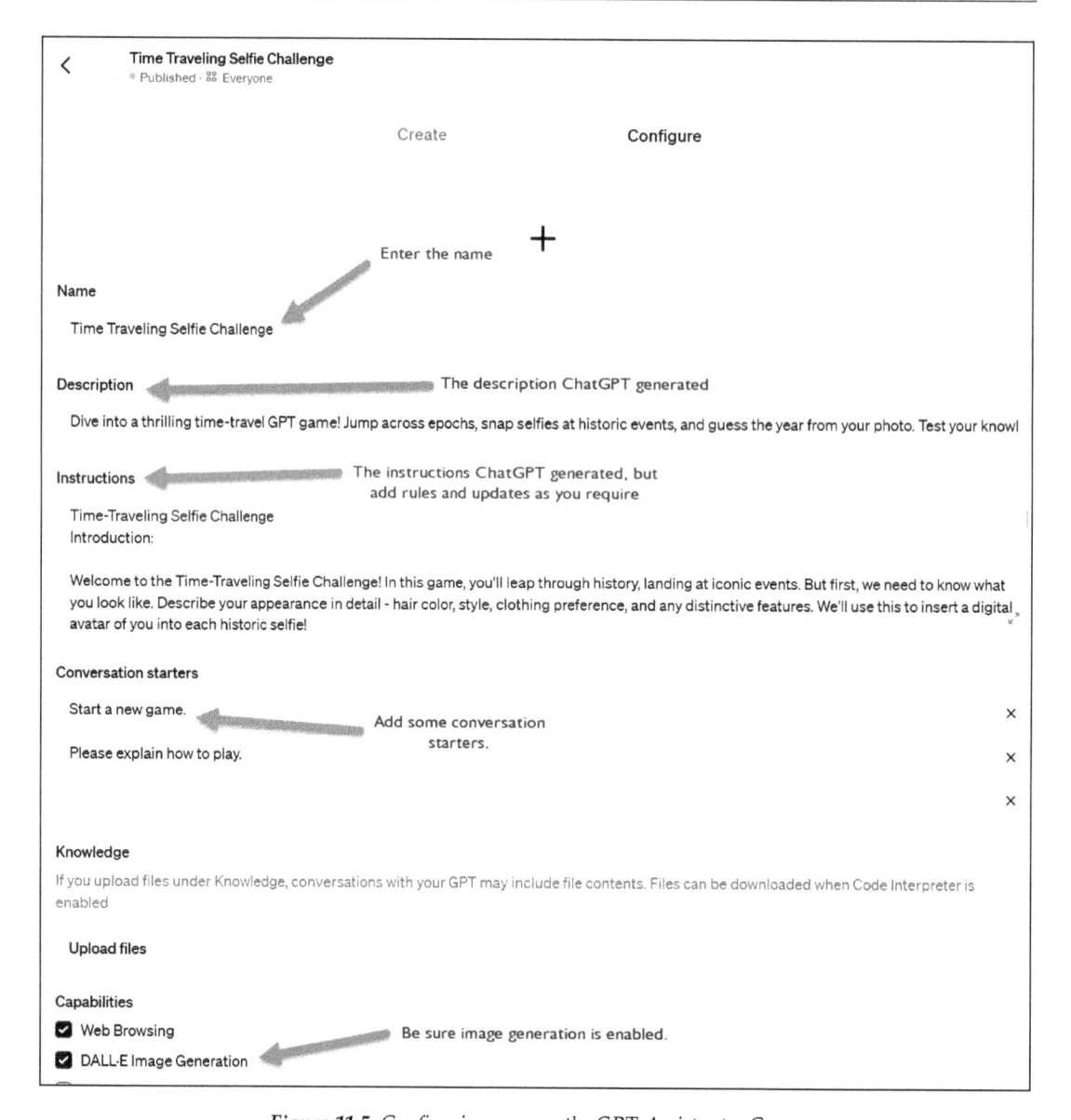

Figure 11.5: Configuring you are the GPT Assistant – Game

7. After you get the configuration updated, go back to the **Create** panel and ask the **GPT Builder** to create an image that embodies your assistant/game. *Figure 11.6* shows the game/assistant set with an image and ready to play.

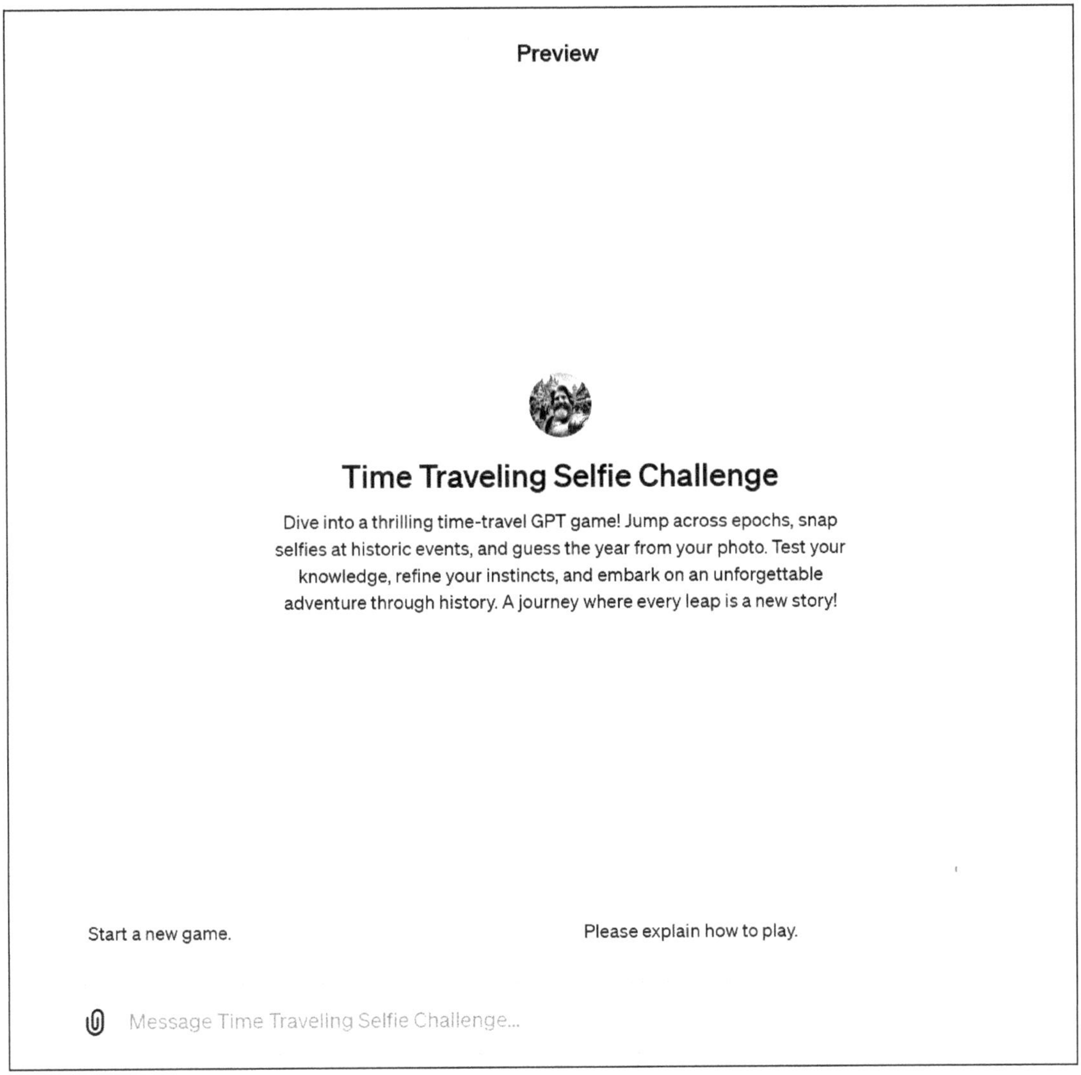

> **Preview**
>
> **Time Traveling Selfie Challenge**
>
> Dive into a thrilling time-travel GPT game! Jump across epochs, snap selfies at historic events, and guess the year from your photo. Test your knowledge, refine your instincts, and embark on an unforgettable adventure through history. A journey where every leap is a new story!
>
> Start a new game.   Please explain how to play.
>
> 📎 Message Time Traveling Selfie Challenge...

Figure 11.6: The GPT Game is ready to play

8. Click one of the conversation starters to begin a new game. Play through 5 rounds and see what score you get.

Play the game and then play the game some more. As you continue to play you will see areas for improving on the game. You may also identify concepts for new games as well. Go ahead and update the instructions as you need. *Figure 11.7* shows the game in action:

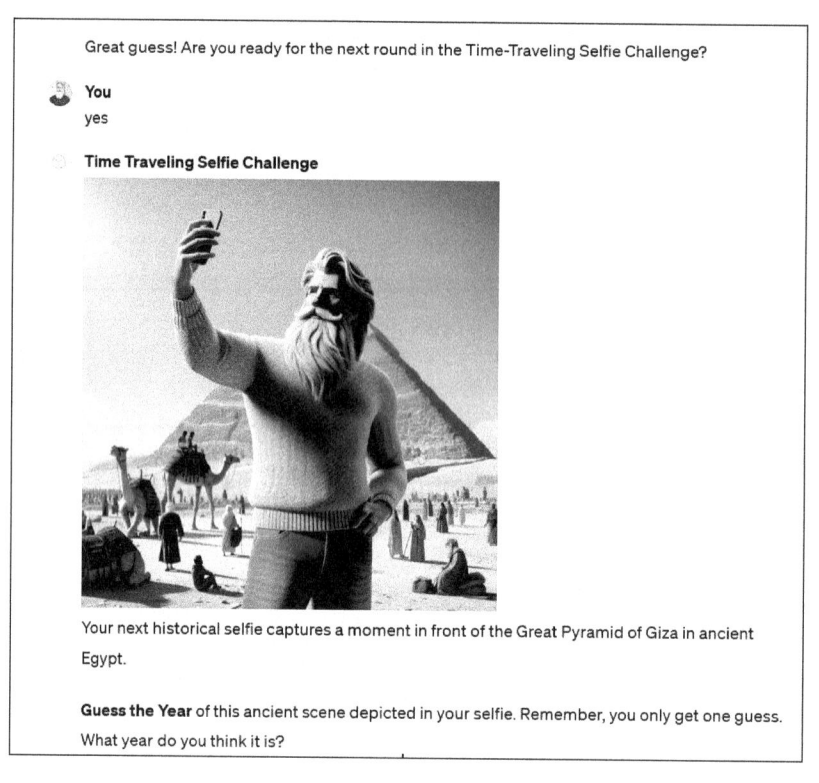

Figure 11.7: Shows the GPT game being played

After you are happy with your game, you can quickly and easily publish it by clicking the **Publish** or **Upgrade** button in the top right corner, as shown in *Figure 11.8*. You can choose to post to just yourself or to everyone:

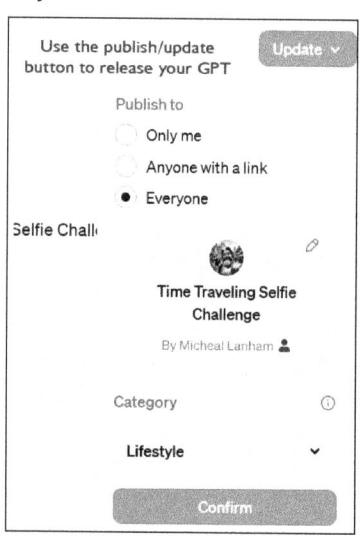

Figure 11.8: Shows the publishing dropdown

This simple and easy publishing model will create heavy competition for this new exploration in gaming. Therefore, in the next section, we will look at enhancing your GPT Game with more information and details.

Adding assets to a GPT game

Building games with GPTs to define and manage the gameplay is exciting but can be restrictive. Fortunately, the Assistants platform allows adding tools and even a form of memory called **retrieval**. This ability to add memory extends the capabilities of a GPT game with more control, depth, and immersion.

Note: GPT Assistants Tools
The Assistants platform also provides several built-in tools and the option to add any custom tools. We will not cover adding Tools here because the interface is still in beta, but you can certainly explore adding tools to a GPT Game on your own.

If you have played the time guessing game more than a few times, you will notice it becomes repetitive and easy to imagine the dates. We can alleviate the repetitiveness and give our GPT Game more control by introducing content that the assistant must select. This content can be submitted by adding files to the GPT.

In *Chapter 1*, we introduced the **Retrieval Augmented Generation** (**RAG**) idea. GPT Assistants can integrate RAG directly within the assistant, allowing for uploading files that the GPT can reference. Regarding the game speak, this allows us to upload content or assets that the game will use with the gameplay.

Exercise 11.4: Adding content and assets to a GPT Game

1. For the time traveler selfie game, instead of letting the AI pick random scenes, we want to populate a list of scenes from which the AI can randomly select. Of course, the best way to generate a set of scenes for points in history with good descriptions is ChatGPT.

2. Enter the following prompt into a new ChatGPT conversation window:

   ```
   Please describe 10 scenes in history that would make for a great selfie image, provide the following information for each scene: The scene number the date at which the event occurred a vivid but candid and humorous description of the event avoid picking scenes that are violent or promote hate or racism.
   ```

   Note: If you want the scenes to be of a specific period or region, be sure to update the prompt with those changes.

3. ChatGPT will respond with something like the following:

   ```
   The Boston Tea Party
   Date: December 16, 1773
   ```

> Description: Picture a group of American colonists, sneaking onto British ships in the dead of night, disguised as Mohawk Indians. Their mission: to dump tea into Boston Harbor as a protest. The combination of serious political protest and the absurdity of the disguises, with tea chests flying left and right, creates a scene of chaotic rebellion.

There will be another nine scenes in the output.

4. Copy the text and put these entries in a text file called **time_scenes.txt**. The *Chapter 11* source folder contains about 40 scenes some duplicates in the **time_scenes.txt** file that you can use. You can continue to prompt ChatGPT to create as many scenes as you want but 100 is likely enough.

5. Create a new GPT and switch to the **Configure** tab.

6. Open the **chapter_11/time_traveling_selfie_gpt.txt**. Copy the contents of this file to the configuration in the GPT interface, as shown in *Figure 11.9*:

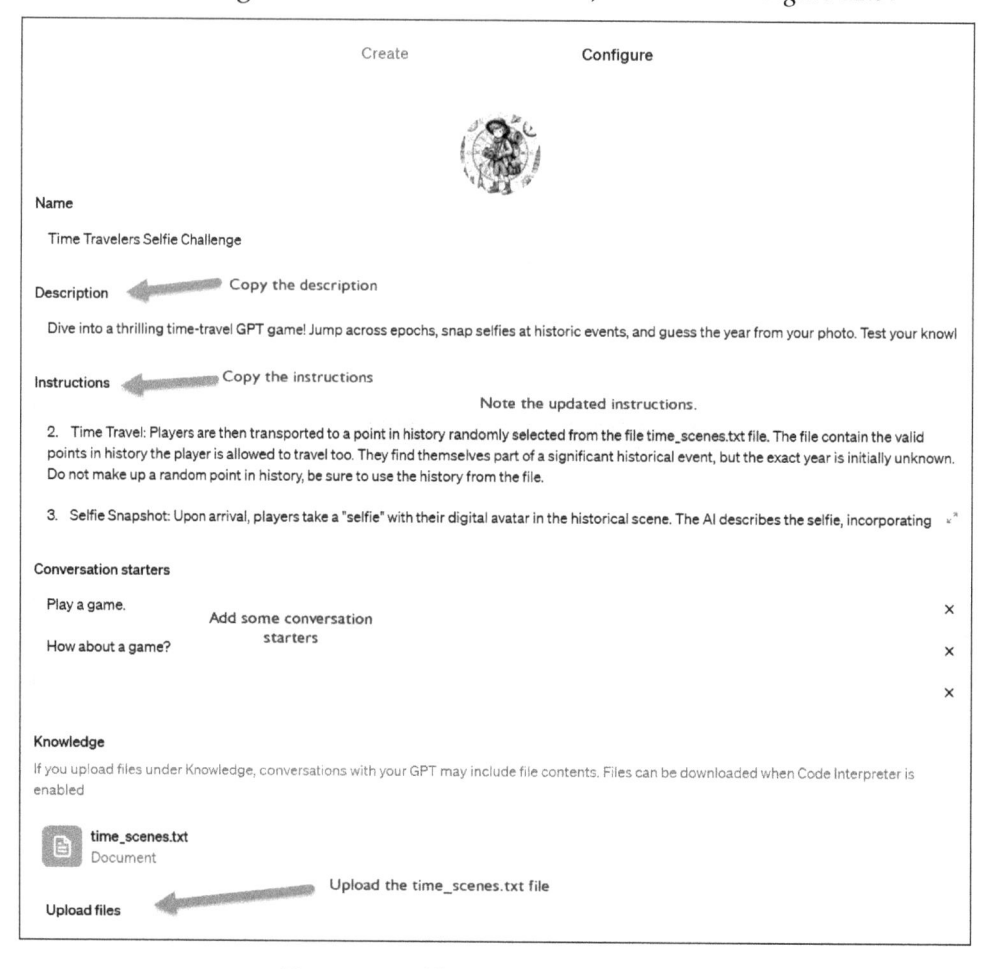

Figure 11.9: Adding the scene file to the game

7. Now go ahead and save the GPT and update it. You can then go ahead and play a new version of the game as shown in *Figure 11.10*:

Figure 11.10: *A selfie during the Boston Tea Party, 1773*

Playing the game now should uncover the scenes described in the `time_scenes.txt` file. What this allows us to do now is to create any number of scenes that could be used in this or other game concepts. This could include elements of the story, descriptions of game scenes, rules, player choices, and so on.

Somehow, we went full circle and returned to *Chapter 2* when we explored the basic text game. But the game industry could benefit overall by revisiting those old text games. In the final section, we will look more at what lies in store for gaming with the advent of AI, like *ChatGPT*.

The future of AI in game development

After reading this book, you certainly understand the value of using AI in games and developing games, from helping with content and asset generation to playing the role of a **non-player character** (**NPC**). There is likely no industry that will benefit from the advances in AI, but gaming is undoubtedly at the top of the list.

In this last section, we will look at what appears to be the most likely advances in games and game development in the next few years. Remember that technology changes rapidly, so this vision may become obsolete sooner than expected. *Table 11.1* shows the top areas that may be subject to quick change in gaming and game development. Each location will highlight the expected rapid changes and things that may take much longer to change.

Game area	Why and what will change	What may not change
GD #1 Coding	As has been demonstrated throughout this book, AI can be used to generate excellent and effective code. Coding will undoubtedly benefit from LLM's assistance in quick game development. We may see the advent of the game factory producing all variations of games.	LLMs like *ChatGPT* still have a fixed window of knowledge. This will likely continue to limit the use of AI in building cutting-edge games and new technologies. As such, developers working in these areas won't be replaced anytime soon.
GD #2 Assets	Again, as seen in the book, content, and asset generation will likely be replaced by many different forms of AI soon. This will likely drastically reduce the cost of assets but, at the time, may demand increased quality. Game development will undoubtedly benefit from this.	Accomplished artists with a specific vision and style will likely always be valuable. However, getting the experience to that level may become more complex and challenging due to the saturation of AI-building assets.
GD #3 Voice and sound	Much like assets, the ease of generating and cloning voices and sounds will likely replace more general artists. Using voice in games will likely become standard and may even promote voice-controlled games.	Celebrities, well-known voice actors and sound technicians will still be in demand. However, the ability to clone voices and sounds will likely replace the ongoing demand for these artists.
GD #4 Game testing	Games are an excellent place to use AI to test computer interfaces. As such, the developed tools will likely replace the role of game testers. It likely would not replace the need for game evaluators.	AI will likely replace testing in the next few years.
Gaming #1 Voice games	There has been a niche of voice games for assistants like *Alexa* or *Google* for years. With the advent of voice cloning and new text-to-speech tools, these types of games are expected to increase in popularity.	Voice games will become more popular.
Gaming #2 Text/GPT games	This opens an immense possibility for the type of GPT games you could develop. Everything from trivia knowledge to adventure and exploration. These games could be combined with visual 2D/3D/AR/VR interfaces.	We should expect an explosion of games using AI to make the game more immersive.

Game area	Why and what will change	What may not change
Gaming #3 Virtual and augmented reality	Augmented reality will likely be the biggest benefactor to integrated AI that can see and speak. OpenAI models like *Whisper* and *Vision* are good tools that could significantly enhance the AR or VR experiences. As the use of these models cheapens, so will their use in games.	VR and AR games have always benefited from AI integration.
Gaming #4 Everything else	Many new games are already getting negative feedback for the lack of good AI. In the next couple of years, games with poor or a lack of AI for even task automation will likely suffer. Not only will it be necessary for games to use AI, but to use it well. Gone are the days when players had no good exposure to AI or understood its capabilities.	Developers with experience building game AI and integrating various forms of AI will be in very high demand. At the same time, they will have to advance their knowledge quickly to stay up with the rapidly changing technologies.

Table 11.1: Expected gaming industry advances in the next few years

It is relatively conclusive that AI and gaming will be explicitly interwoven in the coming years. There have even been suggestions that generative AI could become the game engine. While the idea has been suggested for years, the recent release of SORA provided substance to this as a reality.

The AI generative game engine

Figure 11.11 shows a frame of video of someone playing a **Minecraft** game. However, the video has been entirely generated with AI using *SORA* from OpenAI. Indeed, there is no game, and the whole video is constructed through a text prompt. What is truly impressive about this technology is its ability to be consistent.

Figure 11.11: Frame from a SORA video showing what appears to be someone playing Minecraft

Imagine a game engine that responds to text-driven prompts. The AI generates the complete interface and visuals to build a generative game world. A world that can morph and change to almost anything, suggesting a game that could adapt across genres and even realities.

At this point, generative game engines are emerging as not what ifs but when. It will only be a matter of time before this technology overtakes how games were developed and produced. The estimate is currently that these types of game engines may take about three years to become popular for game development.

The future of game development

What this means for your future in game development is the need to be flexible. Consume and follow what AI is being developed, but it is also essential to follow the technical trends in gaming. There, at some point, will be a convergence of technologies and then, likely, a rapid replacement by AI.

However, this does not mean you should stop programming or understanding how to develop games. If anything, it means you will benefit more from diving in and understanding the nuances of game development. From the code to asset creation and even game design. Not because these skills will be replaced but because of the knowledge and understanding of how to replace them.

After all, your generation will embrace AI in game development and potentially shatter our expectations of what is possible with a game. These are fascinating times to be in, and the future only looks brighter.

Conclusion

This chapter explores the development of games using OpenAI's *GPT Assistants*, emphasizing the potential for creating immersive, AI-powered games with profit-sharing opportunities. It covers building a GPT game, designing engaging gameplay, adding assets for depth, and speculating on the future of AI in game development, including the integration of generative AI game engines. The chapter underscores the importance of adapting to rapid technological advances in gaming while leveraging AI to enhance game design, development, and player experience.

Thank you for taking this journey in a new way to learn about and develop games. This book is intended to teach you the future of game development and software development in general. You can apply many techniques in this book to many areas from coding to learning new skills. ChatGPT has opened the world to a future with AI, a future that we may not all embrace, but one that will surely change everything we do, especially games.

What we learned

- We learned about the process of utilizing OpenAI's GPT Assistants to create engaging and immersive games, showcasing the evolution towards AI-driven game development.
- We discovered the opportunity for income generation through GPT games via OpenAI's profit-sharing model, presenting a new avenue for monetization in game development.
- We explored the importance of designing games that are not only fun but also offer replay value and immersion, focusing on audience engagement.
- We gained insights into enhancing GPT games by adding assets and employing retrieval to provide games with more control, depth, and immersion.
- We examined the potential impacts of rapid advancements in AI on game development, covering aspects from coding and asset creation to voice and sound design, and the emergence of new gaming formats like *voice, text/GPT,* and *AR/VR games*.
- We were introduced to the concept of generative AI game engines, such as *SORA*, which indicate a future where game environments can be dynamically generated through AI, transforming game design and development.
- We understood the significance of staying adaptable and flexible in the face of new technologies, recognizing the integration of AI in game development as both inevitable and beneficial for creating more engaging gaming experiences.
- We acknowledged the continuous importance of traditional game development skills, including programming and game design, to effectively utilize AI technologies in crafting games.

Exercises

Exercises in this section are meant to explore the future possibilities of GPT games and help you learn more about the techniques featured in this chapter.

1. **Design your own GPT-powered game**: We learned about the process of utilizing OpenAI's GPT Assistants to create engaging and immersive games, showcasing the evolution towards AI-driven game development. To reinforce this knowledge, design your game concept using GPT Assistants. Outline your game's premise, decide on its mechanics, and draft a plan for how you would implement these using GPT Assistants. Focus on creating a unique and engaging player experience.

2. **Experiment with profit-sharing models**: Understanding the potential for earning income through GPT games and OpenAI's profit-sharing model was a key

takeaway. As an exercise, create a hypothetical business model for your GPT-powered game. Consider factors like player engagement, monetization strategies, and how you might maximize profits through GPT Assistants and profit sharing with OpenAI.

3. **Develop and add custom assets to your GPT game**: We discovered the importance of adding assets to GPT games to enhance depth and immersion. For this exercise, choose a game concept and brainstorm a list of assets that could be integrated into the game to improve its appeal. These could include character designs, environment descriptions, or background music. Detail how these assets could be incorporated into the game using GPT Assistants.

4. **Predict the future of AI in game development**: Reflecting on the speculated advancements in AI and their impact on game development, imagine and write about a future game concept that leverages these upcoming technologies. Consider how coding, asset creation, voice and sound design, and game testing could evolve. Describe how these advancements could be utilized to create a game that is innovative, incorporating elements such as generative AI game engines or advanced AR/VR experiences.

Join our book's Discord space

Join the book's Discord Workspace for Latest updates, Offers, Tech happenings around the world, New Release and Sessions with the Authors:

https://discord.bpbonline.com

Index

Symbols

2.5D isometric perspectives 194, 195
2D animation Sprite sheets
  generating 123-126
2D platformer
  building 96-101
3D coordinate systems 271, 272
  objects, moving and placing 272-274
3D FPS game
  action-packed world 261-263
  player controls and camera movement, implementing 256, 257
3D game development 255
  materials and textures, covering up 275, 276
3D Lighting
  ambient lights 264
  directional lights 264
  global illumination (GI) 264
  hemispherical lights 264
  image-based lighting (IBL) 264
  importance 263, 264
  physically based rendering (PBR) 264
  point lights 264
  spotlights 264

A

AI dynamic difficulty levels
  creating 150-154
AI game development
  future 323-326
AI generative game engine 325, 326
AI Pirate
  meeting 292

ambient lights 264
animation
  adding, to game 112
area lights 264
arena lights 265-270
AssistantAgent 232
Asteroids 241
AutoGen
  configuring 231-236
  running, with human feedback 242-244

B
base car game
  creating 170, 171
  first iteration 172, 173
  second iteration 173, 174
  third iteration 174
behavior-driven AI 141, 142
behavior trees
  adding, to fighting bot 144-149
bulletin board systems (BBS) 57

C
camera pan 205
ChatGPT 1, 9
  asking, to write PyZork 22-25
  conversing with 3-5
  interaction ideas, exploring 6
  prompt engineering, for PyZork 26-32
  realm 2, 3
ChatGPT 3.5 2, 6
chat web interface
  creating 61-64
colliding clouds 185

eight iteration 185-188
ninth iteration 188-190
ComfyUI ControlNet
  workflow 122, 123
control nets
  installing, on ComfyUI 120, 121

D
detective game
  creating 303-306
directional lights 264
DirectX conventions 277
displacement map 277

E
EasyCode 53, 54
ElevenLabs 292
  using, for speech 292-295

F
first-person camera demo
  creating 257-261
Flappy Bird Clone
  creating 96-99
flying bird animation demo
  adding, to FB 115-119
  creating 113-115
fun GPT game
  assets, adding 321-323
  designing 316
  player, adding for immersion 317-320

G
game AI agent support 280
  configuring 280-284

game assets
  generating 120
  restyling, with SDXL 154-157
game challenges 43
game database
  adding, with SQLite 83-89
game design and development
  dynamicity 102
  game levels 102
  game physics 102
  game settings 102
game difficulty levels
  adding 102-108
game-level difficulty
  obstacles, leveling up 108-112
game physics 162, 163
  adding, to car 170, 171
  first iteration 167, 168
  motion and rotation 165, 166
  second iteration 168, 169
games
  powering, with ChatGPT 300, 301
game shop 244, 245
  configuring 245-251
game shop agents 256
game world
  crafting 38-43
  map, building 38-43
generate_landscape function 17
Gimp 215
global illumination (GI) 264
GPT-3.5 307
GPT-4 307

GPT agent fundamentals 236-238
GPT models
  comparing, on agent system 238-241

H
hemispherical lights 264
Hue, Saturation, and Value (HSV) 270

I
image-based lighting (IBL) 264
isometric demo
  depth, adding to tiles 199, 200
  generating 195-199
isometric drawing 194
isometric game map 194
isometric overlays
  generating 213-215
isometric scene
  world to screen space conversion 201, 202
isometric tile maps
  designing 206-209
isometric tiles
  creating, with AI 209-212
isometric world base game
  exploring 202, 203
  screen to isometric to world conversion 203-205
  UI layer, adding 218-224
items
  adding 47-52

L
large language model (LLM) 47, 236

M

map overlays 213
massively multiplayer online (MMO) 57
massively multiplayer online role playing games (MMORPGs) 57
Minecraft game 325
multiple shared hallucinations (MUSHes) 57
  completing 89
multiple user dungeons (MUDs) 57
murder mystery vocal game
  creating 302

N

non-player characters (NPCs) 43-47
NormalGL 277

O

object rotation 165
OpenAI account
  setting up 228
OpenAI API key
  creating 228-231
  securing 228-231
OpenAI GPT Assistants game
  building 312-314
  rules, fixing 314-316

P

Panda3D 260
particle systems
  adding, with physics 180
  seventh iteration 180-184

PBR materials
  building 278, 279
physically based rendering (PBR) 264
Physics Demo
  building 163-165
Pirate NPC
  creating 295-300
platformer
  building 96
point lights 264
Pokémon Go 302
post-processing lighting effects 269
post-processing screen effects 269
prompt engineering 6
  techniques, using 6-8
Pymunk 163
py_trees behavior demo
  creating 142, 143
PyZork 22
  data persistence, adding 84-89
  multiple players, adding 89-92
  unleashing, with Streamlit 58-61
  upgrading, to web interface 64-67
PyZork game 22-24
  components 25
  player input, managing 32-37
  player, parsing 32-37
  prompting 26

R

Red, Green, Blue (RGB) model 270
Reinforcement Learning from Human Feedback (RLHF) 2

Retrieval Augmented Generation
(RAG) 14, 179, 280
  engaging, with EasyCode 14-19
reusable agent workshop
  building 244, 245
rigid body dynamics 180
roughness texture map 277

S

Screen Space Ambient Occlusion
(SSAO) 269
Screen Space Reflections
(SSR) 269
secret words game
  making, with prompt 300
shaders 268
side-scroller 96
skylights 264
speech recognition systems
  building 288-290
spotlights 264
sprites
  adding, to game 112
SQLite 83
Stable Diffusion 120
Street Fighter Clone game
  AI-controlled enemies, adding 133-140
  Battle Royale edition 133
  cloning 130-133
  loading 130
system prompting 8-13
System prompts 237

T

text-based games
  story, crafting with command interface
    76-83
  story, picturing with stable diffusion
    67-76
text to speech
  demonstrating 290, 291
  implementing 290
Time Traveling Selfie Challenge 317
TimeTrekker game 317
token
  replacing, with overlay 215-217
troll
  adding 52, 53

U

ultimate car jump challenge
  building 174, 175
  fifth iteration 177-179
  fourth iteration 175-177
  sixth iteration 179
Universal Scene Description
(USD) files 278
User prompt 237
UserProxyAgent 232

V

vertices 169
vocal game 288
voice-driven game mechanics 307, 308
VoiceLab tab 295

W

world of text-based games
  venturing 22